MOVIES of the SIXTIES

MOVIES of the SIXTIES

EDITED BY ANN LLOYD
CONSULTANT EDITOR
DAVID ROBINSON

ORBIS · LONDON

Many of the illustrations come from stills issued to publicize films made or distributed by the following companies: ABC, Action Films, Allied Artists, Alpha, Andrea Films, Kenneth Anger, Anglo Amalgamated, Anouchka Films, Artists Associés, Avco Embassy, BBS Studio Barrandov, Georges de Beauregard, British Lion, Les Films du Carosse, Československý Film, Champion, Cinema Center, Cineriz, Citel, Cocinor, Compton-Cameo, Constantin Film, Copacabana, Daiei, Dear Films, Dino De Laurentiis, Stanley Donen, Drew Associates, Stephen Dwoskin, EMI, EON, Euro International, FR3, Factory Films, Famous Artists, Filmways, Filmverlag der Autoren, First Artists, Gaumont, Felix Greene/SF Chronicle, Greenwich Films, Robert and Raymond Hakim, Hammer, ICAIC, IPC Films, Kairos Film, Kindai, Stanley Kramer, Leacock-Pennebaker, Lira Film, Lux, MCA, MGM, Mafilm, Maran Film, Marianne, Mirisch, Mosfilm, Vicomte de Noailles, PAA, PAX, Palomar, Paramount, Parc Films, Pathé, Films de la Pléiade, Film Polski, Carlo Ponti, Produzione Europée Associates, RKO, Rank, Rastar, Republic, Rome-Paris Films, Sedif, Seven Arts, Shamley, Silver Films, Solar, Robert Stigwood, Svensk Filmindustri, Tango Films, Titanus, 20th Century-Fox, Unifrance, United Artists, Universal, Vic Films, Vides, Viva International, Hal B. Wallis, Warner Brothers, Wolper Films, Woodfall, World Film Services, Richard Zanuck.

Acknowledgments: Lindsay Anderson, Martyn Auty, Leo Castelli Gallery New York (Collection of Mr and Mrs Burton), Cinegate Ltd, Ciné-Images, Frank Conner, Contemporary Films, Stephen Dwoskin, Greg Edwards Archive, Ed Emshwiller, Joel Finler Collection, Peter Gidal, Ronald Grant Archive, David Hine, Archivio IGDA, Derek Jarman, Ian Knight, Kobal Collection, Museum of Modern Art Film Stills Archive, National Film Archive, National Film Board of Canada, Other Cinema, D.A. Pennebaker, Popperfoto, David Robinson Collection, Steve Roe, Stiftung Deutsche Kinemathek, Talisman Books, Paul Taylor, Bob Willoughby.

Although every effort is being made to trace the present copyright holders, we apologize in advance for any unintentional omission or neglect and will be pleased to insert the appropriate acknowledgment to companies or individuals in any subsequent edition of this publication.

Facing title-page: David Hemmings with fashion model Verushka in *Blow-Up* (1966) in which he accidentally photographs a murder but the evidence mysteriously disappears

Abbreviations used in text

add: additional; **adv:** advertising; **anim:** animation; **art dir:** art direction; **ass:** assistant; **assoc:** associate; **chor:** choreography; **col:** colour process; **comm:** commentary; **cont:** continuity; **co-ord:** co-ordination; **cost:** costume; **dec:** decoration; **des:** design; **dial:** dialogue; **dial dir:** dialogue direction; **dir:** direction; **doc:** documentary; **ed:** film editing; **eng:** engineer; **ep:** episode; **exec:** executive; **loc:** location; **lyr:** lyrics; **man:** management; **mus:** music; **narr:** narration; **photo:** photography; **prod:** production; **prod co:** production company; **prod sup:** production supervision; **rec:** recording; **rel:** released; **r/t:** running time; **sc:** scenario/screenplay/script; **sd:** sound; **sp eff:** special effects; **sup:** supervision; **sync:** synchronization; **sys:** system. Standard abbreviations for countries are used. Most are self-evident but note: A = Austria; AUS = Australia; GER = Germany and West Germany after 1945; E.GER = East Germany.

Editor
Ann Lloyd
Consultant Editor
David Robinson
Editorial Director
Brian Innes

Senior Editor
Graham Fuller
Senior Sub Editor
Dan Millar
Chief Sub Editor
Jane Henderson
Sub Editors
Lindsay Lowe, David Roper
Editorial Assistant
Susan Leonard

Research Consultant
Arnold Desser
Picture Researchers
Dave Kent, Sue Scott-Moncrieff, Sandy Graham
Research
Kingsley Canham, Paul Taylor, Sally Hibbin, Julian Petley

Designers
Ray Kirkpatrick, John Heritage

© 1983 Orbis Publishing Limited, London
First published in hardcovers by Orbis Publishing Limited, London 1983
Reprinted 1985
First published in paperback 1984
Reprinted 1985

Printed in Italy by Eurograph S.p.A., Milano

ISBN: 0-85613-522-4 (hardback)
ISBN: 0-85613-663-8 (paperback)

CONTENTS

INTRODUCTION

In 1960 the film achieved its 65th anniversary. The decade which followed was to witness the greatest revolution produced in world cinema in three-quarters of a century, excluding perhaps the upheaval produced by the introduction of sound in the late Twenties. External historical events were to some extent responsible. World War II had in many countries produced the same effect, artificially prolonging the careers of those artists who had already been active for many years before it and interrupting or delaying the beginnings of younger artists. In consequence, at the end of the War there was a distinct watershed, a change-over of generations; and by and large the new generation was ready and mature by the start of the Sixties.

In America the era of the McCarthy witch-hunts had also profoundly shaken up the film industry, and only in the Sixties came the rehabilitation and recovery of the careers of many fine artists who had been banished from Hollywood. There had been other incitements to revolution: the old Hollywood structures and studios had been broken up, the new rivalry of television had changed the structure of the audience and forced new technical developments upon the film industry. In turn, the technical innovations affected aesthetic approaches. The new, huge, wide screens were inimical to the classic use of montage that had prevailed since the time of D.W. Griffith.

The Sixties, too, brought new opportunities for cultural cross-fertilization with the proliferation of international film festivals and ciné-clubs, and by the new contacts and experiences brought to American film-makers who were often forced to work in foreign countries in order to employ blocked currency. Film art and technique became international in a way that had not been so since the babel of sound had come to stay.

At the Cannes Film Festival of 1959 most of the major prizes were swept up by new French directors, and the journalists coined the phrase *nouvelle vague*. Many of these young French film-makers, including François Truffaut, Jean-Luc Godard and Claude Chabrol, had begun their careers as critics and in their films they put into practice ideas they had painstakingly promoted in their influential magazine *Cahiers du Cinéma*. The early films of the *nouvelle vague* enjoyed great commercial success worldwide and made it possible for upwards of sixty new directors to make their first films in the next couple of years. Many fell by the wayside but a new generation was consolidated.

In Britain the revolution actually preceded the French New Wave and, again, most of its major figures and its impetus came from a magazine, *Sequence* (1946–52), even though by this time it was defunct. The editors of *Sequence* included Lindsay Anderson and Karel Reisz. Fighting for a new British cinema which would reflect the realities of national life, of the working class and regional England, Anderson, Reisz and Tony Richardson presented a series of programmes of short films under the general title of 'Free Cinema'. Their chance to make feature films came with the period of general cultural upheaval in the late Fifties, and the first films of the new British school, Jack Clayton's *Room at the Top*, Richardson's *Look Back in Anger*, Reisz's *Saturday Night and Sunday Morning* and Anderson's *This Sporting Life* were all from works by the writers of Britain's literary revolution. Renaissances in the British cinema tend to be short-lived; but this one left a permanent effect on the style, content and confidence of British films.

For Italy, too, the early Sixties were years of miracles. Michelangelo Antonioni and Federico Fellini were already established names, but it was *L'Avventura* and *La Dolce Vita*, both made in 1960, that launched their international fame. The year 1961 brought the debuts of Pier Paolo Pasolini with *Accatone* and Bernardo Bertolucci with *La Commare Secca* (1962), as well as the first major successes

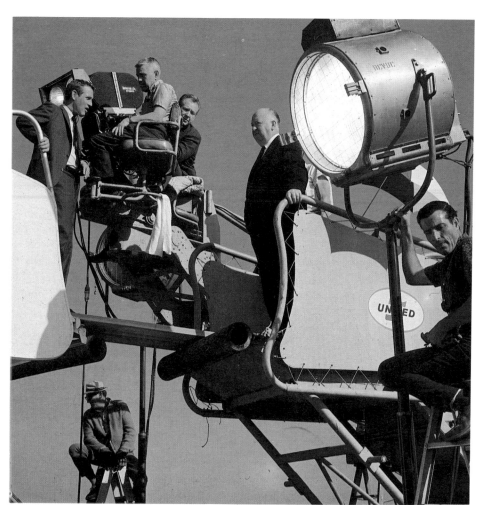

*Hitchcock faces his star Paul Newman
the set of* Torn Curtain *(1966), the s[
thriller film in which sexual motivatio[
murder is replaced by political expedien[*

of Ermanno Olmi (*Il Posto*) and Francesco
Rosi (*Salvatore Giuliano*).

Every country discovered its cinematic
identity. The reform of the Swedish film
industry brought out a whole new generation of directors where before Ingmar
Bergman had stood in solitude. In Germany the Sixties saw a revived pride in
film culture and the debuts (albeit not
always glorious) of Alexander Kluge,
Jean-Marie Straub, Werner Herzog,
Rainer Werner Fassbinder. In Holland,
Belgium and Denmark, young people who
might at another time have written
novels, turned to the cinema as the
medium of the time.

In the socialist East, too, there were
good years. The death and disavowal of
Stalin had brought a new period of relaxation, openly acknowledged in Grigori
Chukhrai's *Clear Skies* (1961). Soviet films
began to treat both history and the present day in human rather than heroic
terms. Old directors like Grigori Kozintsev,
Josif Heifitz and Mikhail Romm were
newly invigorated and a new generation
which included Andrei Tarkovsky, Andrei
Konchalovsky and Sergei Paradzhanov
came to the fore.

In Hungary a reorganization of the film
industry gave their chance to a brilliant
new group of film-makers headed by the
innovatory Miklós Jancsó. Poland's new
enfants terribles, Jerzy Skolimowski and
Roman Polanski, were both soon to emig-
rate; so was the Yugoslav Dušan Makaveyev. Czechoslovakia's brilliant New
Wave, headed by Miloš Forman, was to be
abruptly dispersed by the political events
of 1968.

The revolution, as the pages that follow
amply show, was worldwide, spreading
from the Far East to Latin America where
the Brazilian *Cinema Novo* made itself a
political force, and the revolutionary
cinema of Cuba revived something of the
mood and thrill of the great days of Russia
in the Twenties. Towards the end of the
decade, when real-life revolution was in
the air, film-makers everywhere felt themselves a part of it.

Even if it was less apparent, there was
revolution, too, in the great monolith of
Hollywood. New directors like John
Cassavetes, Arthur Penn, Roger Corman,
Sam Peckinpah and Mike Nichols were to
give a new character to American films.
After the Sixties the movies were never
quite the same again.

DAVID ROBINSON

8

THE FRENCH NOUVELLE VAGUE

After knocking for years, young French directors finally broke down the door and entered film production with an unprecedented energy and enthusiasm

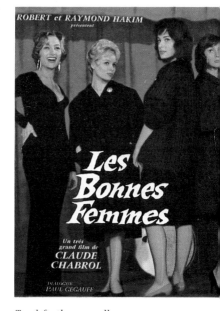

The talking-point of 1959 in the film world was the sudden emergence of the French *nouvelle vague* ('new wave'). It was an astonishing burst of creative activity which saw forty young directors given the opportunity to make their first films over the next year. It seemed to herald new approaches and techniques that would revolutionize the industry.

It was all, of course, a misunderstanding – or, at least, an exaggeration. A famous publicity photograph purports to show the '*nouvelle vague*' at the Cannes Film Festival of 1959. This was the year in which François Truffaut, banned from attending as a critic because he had savagely derided the standard of the French entries in his magazine column, returned as a film-maker to take the Best Direction prize with *Les Quatre Cents Coups* (1959, *The 400 Blows*). Since the 'young Turks' of criticism had proved their point by making successful films – so the industry's reasoning ran – let them have their heads and hope that some of them will bring in the money.

The photograph shows, sitting on the steps of the *Palais du Festival* at Cannes, a group of young filmmakers, namely: François Truffaut, Raymond Vogel, Louis Félix, Edmond Séchan, Edouard Molinaro, Jacques Baratier, Jean Valère, François Reichenbach, Robert Hossein, Jean-Daniel Pollet, Roger Vadim, Marcel Camus, Claude Chabrol, Jacques Doniol-Valcroze, Jean-Luc Godard and Jacques Rozier.

If many of these are not exactly household names today – well, that was the way the *nouvelle vague* went. Some of these directors were not noticeably talented. Some, like Vadim and Molinaro, were even then making films indistinguishable from the commercial norm, except that the directors came from a younger generation. Even this last categorization did not always apply. Marcel Camus won the Festival's *Grand Prix* with *Orfeu Negro* (1958, *Black Orpheus*), a slice of picturesque exoticism that could have been made at any time during the past ten

years but which earned him the accolade of '*nouvelle vague*'. He was 47 at the time.

Nevertheless, there *was* a *nouvelle vague*, given a tenuous identity and unity only because the sudden influx of new directors was the result of inexorably critical pressure that had been brought to bear on the French film industry over a number of years; and because when the dam of tradition and box-office caution finally gave way, the most talented newcomers – Godard, Truffaut, Chabrol, Jacques Rivette and Eric Rohmer – also happened to be critics collaborating on *Cahiers du Cinéma*, the magazine which had articulated and applied most of that pressure.

The first rumblings of discontent were given influential expression in 1948 by Alexandre Astruc in an article called 'The Birth of a New Avant-Garde: *Le Caméra Stylo*', which fulminated against the assembly-line method of producing films which the French industry had inherited from Hollywood, and where front-office interference ensured that maverick films were tailored to fit tried-and-trusted formulas:

'Our sensibilities have been in danger of getting blunted by those everyday films which, year in year out, show their tired and conventional faces to the world.'

The great film-makers, Astruc argued, directors such as Renoir, Welles and Bresson, were using the camera much as a writer uses a pen (*stylo*), to make a personal statement or to describe a personal vision. When Astruc came to illustrate his arguments by making films such as *Le Rideau Cramoisi* (1953, *The Crimson Curtain*), *Les Mauvaises Rencontres* (1955, Bad Encounters) and *Une Vie* (1958, *One Life*) the results were stiff and glacially correct, intelligent but fatally tinged with the aura of artiness that invariably used to infect Hollywood Movies on the rare occasions when they aimed for 'art'.

But the seed had been sown. In the early Fifties *Cahiers du Cinéma* took Astruc's argument a stage further in a series of close critical analyses of the

Top left: the nouvelle vague *directors at Cannes, 1959; from front left, the rows consist of (first) Truffaut, Vogel, Félix, Séchan; (second) Molinaro, Baratier, Valère; (third) Reichenbach, Hossein, Pollet, Vadim, Camus; (fourth) Chabrol, Doniol-Valcroze, Godard, Rozier. Top right: a carnival scene in Rio de Janeiro from* Orfeu Negro *Above: four shop girls are disappointed in their dreams of a better life; left to right: Ginette (Stéphane Audran), Rita (Lucile Saint-Simon), Jane (Bernadette Lafont) and Jacqueline (Clotilde Joano)*

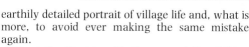

Above: André Bazin, who died in 1958 at 40, helped to found Cahiers du Cinéma *and encouraged the younger critics who were to become the principal film-makers of the* nouvelle vague

Above: Jack Nicholson plays an introspective night-time disc jockey in Bob Rafelson's The King of Marvin Gardens. *His outgoing, ambitious brother lives in a fantasy world on the fringes of crime and is finally shot dead by one of the women he lives with. The unusual Atlantic City locations and the feeling of an unpredictably off-beat genre movie recall the sense of discovery in the early* nouvelle vague *films. The title comes from the game of* Monopoly *(American version)*

work of outstanding film-makers such as Hitchcock and Hawks who had worked exclusively within the major studio system, mostly in Hollywood itself. Similar articles and reviews drew attention to Samuel Fuller, Robert Aldrich, Don Siegel and Jacques Tourneur who had higherto been neglected as mere studio journeymen. All these critiques amounted to a demonstration of how a creative personality could surface even if the script was uncongenial to the director or had to be shaped to fit box-office preconceptions.

These ideas were formulated as what later came to be known as the '*auteur* theory', after a cautionary article by the critic André Bazin, '*La Politique des Auteurs*', published in 1957. *Cahiers du Cinéma*'s concepts were unique in the history of the cinema's avant-garde movements in that they accepted the realities of the film industry and the need to keep an eye on the box-office. Even so, the argument ran, a true film-maker could shape characters, situations and attitudes in order to impose a distinctive personal style. He should infiltrate his personal preoccupations and, if necessary, transform alien material into his own.

The early films of the *Cahiers du Cinéma* critics are not immediately recognizable as 'Art' – in the sense that a Henry James novel, as opposed to a pulp thriller by David Goodis or Cornell Woolrich, is considered to be 'Art'. Truffaut started his career in feature films with a down-to-earth tale of a delinquent boy, *The 400 Blows*, and then moved into gangster territory with *Tirez sur le Pianiste* (1960, *Shoot the Pianist*) based on a David Goodis thriller. Godard began with *A Bout de Souffle* (1960, *Breathless*), a casually joky gangster story, continued with *Le Petit Soldat* (1960, The Little Soldier), an exploration of political conscience so pragmatic that it was banned as unacceptable to either Right or Left, and then proceeded in *Une Femme Est une Femme* (1961, *A Woman Is a Woman*) to dismantle the mystique of the Hollywood musical with a destructive curiosity that left the pieces lying around like a disembowelled clock. Chabrol might have been guilty of headily abstract theological speculations in his first feature, *Le Beau Serge* (1958, *Handsome Serge*), but he was careful to anchor them in an

earthily detailed portrait of village life and, what is more, to avoid ever making the same mistake again.

Shoot the Pianist, with its mercurially shifting moods and ambiguity as to whether it means to make the audience laugh or cry, is of course far from Hollywood's gangster conventions. It is as much part of Truffaut's personal world as *Breathless* is idiosyncratically Godard's. At first glance, Godard seems to be playing the genre game with absolute fidelity. His hero Michel Poiccard (Jean-Paul Belmondo) pays a small-time thug's tribute of imitation to Humphrey Bogart; there is raw and

---

Pretending to make genre movies, young directors ditched the over-literary 'tradition of quality'

---

contrasty photography, with casual bursts of violent action – all dedicated 'to Monogram Pictures', Hollywood's Poverty Row home of the cheap action flick.

At second glance, the unorthodox three-part structure of the film dominates. Sandwiched between the swift, staccato beginning and ending, the elaborately sinuous sequence of Michel Poiccard's lengthy bedroom conversations with his girl (Jean Seberg), who will eventually betray him to the police, suggests that this man, apparently living only for the moment, *may* perhaps be shyly envisaging a future for himself. Even in this film which delivers the pleasures of action to its audience,

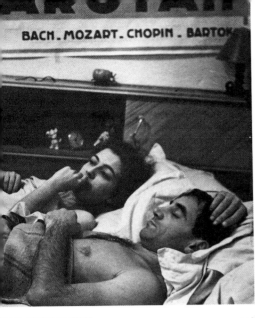

Godard has managed to subvert the genre conventions by inserting a time of reflection, a long moment when thought is more to the fore than violence.

In the early days of the *nouvelle vague*, each new film was a major event, eagerly awaited by anyone who cared about cinema, and excitedly scanned for conceptual innovations and technical audacities. But these were all too quickly transformed into the newly current clichés of film-making when industry hacks gratefully adopted them as ready-made sales packaging for conventional films.

Now the dust has settled and audiences barely notice – to cite the most obvious example – the jump-cuts once hailed with critical jubilation as the most radical new departure offered by *Breathless*. As a number of older film-makers somewhat tetchily pointed out at the time, there was nothing new about jump-cutting: the technique had been familiar in Hollywood for years, and little or no critical excitement had been noticeable when, six years before Godard and *Breathless*, Kurosawa used it every bit as systematically in *Shichinin No Samurai* (1954, *Seven Samurai*).

But where Kurosawa used the jump-cut in its traditional role as a purely technical means towards an end – speeding up the action, keeping things constantly on the move – Godard lent it an additional, metaphorical dimension. In *Breathless* the jump-cutting does indeed keep the film racing along in amiable pastiche of the Monogram B movies; but, acquiring an undertone of insolence through being identified with Belmondo's raffishly but ineffectually Bogartian Michel Poiccard, the technique *also* implies a parody-appraisal of the

Hollywood thriller genre as a whole.

Looking back, it is apparent now that the *nouvelle vague* films – Godard's in particular – generated so much electricity because they comprised a critique of both the cinema's past and its present, rejecting what was worthless in film history, sifting out what remained valid, raising signposts for future exploration. As Godard remarked in an interview in 1962:

'Criticism taught us to admire both Rouch and Eisenstein. From it we learned not to deny one aspect of the cinema in favour of another. From it we also learned to make films from a certain perspective, and to know that if something has already been done there is no point in doing it again. A young author writing today knows that Molière and Shakespeare exist. We were the first directors to know that Griffith exists. Even Carné, Delluc and René Clair, when they made their first films, had no real critical or historical background. Even Renoir had very little; but then of course *he* had genius.'

Today, Godard is marking time on the sidelines; Truffaut is mired in self-congratulatory stagnation; Rivette is obsessively burrowing into what may well turn out to be a blind alley; Chabrol and Rohmer are fruitfully harvesting their own limited idiosyncratic fields. It has been left to American film-makers to seize the initiative. Such films as *The King of Marvin Gardens* (1972), *Badlands*, *Mean Streets*, *Pat Garrett and Billy the Kid* (all 1973), *The Conversation* (1974), *Night Moves*, *The Wind and the Lion* (both 1975), rather than recent French films, have been examining film history and attitudes to cinema in order to initiate new departures.

TOM MILNE

Top left: in bed with Léna (Marie Dubois), a waitress from the bar where he plays piano, Charlie (Charles Aznavour) recalls his earlier life as a concert pianist, Edouard Saroyan, a career cut short by his wife's suicide, in Shoot the Pianist. *Top right: Truffaut's first feature led to a whole series of autobiographical films about Antoine Doinel (Jean-Pierre Léaud). Above far left: Truffaut also wrote the original story for* Breathless *as an early draft for the same series, to be about the boy grown up after reform school and the army. But Godard's Michel (Jean-Paul Belmondo) and Patricia (Jean Seberg) are his own characters though he followed Truffaut's plot-line quite closely. Above left: shooting a scene near Geneva for* Le Petit Soldat; *in the car, Bruno Forestier (Michel Subor) is making a first, unsuccessful attempt to assassinate a Swiss radio commentator sympathetic to the cause of Algerian independence. Above: stalemate between lovers Emile (Jean-Claude Brialy) and Angéla (Anna Karina) in* Une Femme Est une Femme; *in which she wants a baby, but he doesn't*

Directed by François Truffaut, 1962

Prod co: Les Films du Carrosse/SEDIF. **prod man:** Marcel Berbert. **sc:** François Truffaut, Jean Gruault, from the novel by Henri-Pierre Roché. **photo** (Franscope): Raoul Coutard. **ed:** Claudine Bouché. **cost:** Fred Capel. **mus:** Georges Delerue. **song:** Boris Bassiak. **ass dir:** Georges Pellegrin, Robert Bober. **narr:** Michel Subor. **r/t:** 105 minutes. Paris premiere, 27 January 1962. Released in USA and GB as *Jules and Jim*.
Cast: Jeanne Moreau (*Catherine*), Oskar Werner (*Jules*), Henri Serre (*Jim*), Vanna Urbino (*Gilberte*), Boris Bassiak (*Albert*), Sabine Haudepin (*Sabine*), Marie Dubois (*Thérèse*), Jean-Louis Richard (*first customer in the café*), Michel Varesano (*second customer in the café*), Pierre Fabre (*drunkard in café*), Danielle Bassiak (*Albert's friend*), Bernard Largemains (*Merlin*), Elen Bober (*Mathilde*), Kate Noëlle (*Birgitta*), Anny Nielsen (*Lucy*), Christiane Wagner (*Helga*).

Based on a little-known autobiographical novel written by Henry-Pierre Roché when in his seventies, *Jules et Jim* was François Truffaut's third film and is still the one by which he is most affectionately known. Endlessly inventive and unquenchably high-spirited, it is one of those rare films which, after no more than a single viewing, inspire virtually total recall. Even its soundtrack continues to possess a naggingly memorable life of its own, thanks to Jeanne Moreau's breathy giggle, Oskar Werner's softly accented French and, not least, Georges Delerue's haunting theme music, which over the years has become almost the signature tune of the *nouvelle vague*.

Most astonishing of all, however, is the masterly ease with which, in this tale of an intermittently felicitous *ménage à trois*, Truffaut modulates between comedy (or rather, gaiety), drama and, ultimately, tradegy, while deploying a battery of perilously modish devices – jump cuts, freeze frames, nostalgic iris shots. His numerous imitators have managed only to hitch these techniques to the kind of broad comic romp of which Tony Richardson's *Tom Jones* (1963) might be the prototype. Though the triangle formed by Jules, Jim and the flighty, elusive Catherine is, in its restlessly shifting sympathies, anything but eternal and too often overcast to be considered unreservedly idyllic, none of the film's more sombre elements ever succeeds in snuffing out its youthful exuberance. For an example of how subtly it functions, one need look no further than Catherine herself, in Jeanne Moreau's enchanting and somehow 'definitive' performance. Rarely has the cinema invested one of its classic *femmes fatales* with such generous helpings of humour, charm and tenderness. Yet *fatale* she unquestionably is: figuratively, by the cavalier treatment which she metes out to her pair of suitors, capriciously switching her amorous attentions from one to the other and back again, even ditching both of them for the more immediately gratifying stimulation of an affair with a casual pick-up; and literally, at the end, when she nonchalantly drives Jim and herself headlong into the Seine. It is, above all, Catherine's mercurial femininity which has allowed the film to wear so much better than those sweatily explicit dramas of uncensored passion made during the same period (for instance, Jack Clayton's *Room at the Top*, 1959). Sex here is fun, at least on occasion. If the three protagonists fail to arrive at a workable 'design for living' no moral condemnation is implied by Truffaut: less unconventional relationships prove equally doomed.

Prior to their relationship with Catherine, the two Bohemian young men are so bewitched by the placidly mysterious features of a Greek goddess on a lantern slide that they promptly set off for the Adriatic to catch a glimpse of the original sculpture. Catherine, too, is an 'ideal' woman (the most perfectly realized, perhaps, in Truffaut's extensive gallery of portraits), all things to both men, separately or together – and the tragedy of the final suicide is not only her own and Jim's death, but the inconsolable solitude of Jules.

The balance between tragedy and comedy, so miraculously maintained throughout, derives also from the fact that, as the characters never physically age (though at the end Moreau sports granny glasses, the face behind them is just as radiantly, mischievously beautiful), it is from outside that the passage of time comes abruptly and cruelly to impinge on their intimate universe.

World War I, evoked in newsreel footage that is startlingly stretched out to the full dimensions of the CinemaScope screen, causes the two friends to fear that one might kill the other (his name notwithstanding, Jules is German).

Then, suddenly, it is already 1933, as in a cinema the trio watch more newsreel footage of book-burning in Nazi Germany. And the advancing years are more benignly telegraphed by the ubiquitous Picasso paintings, passing through several stages of the artist's evolution. From the very beginning, however, the film has ominously hinted at the impermanence of their happiness: Catherine's first whimsical leap into the Seine; her ritualized burning of letters from past lovers ('old flames'), which almost results in her self-immolation; and the spectre of jealousy in a Rhineland chalet, a striking crane shot encapsulating both a nervously pacing Jim downstairs and Catherine and Jules romping ecstatically in the upstairs bedroom.

Of all the *nouvelle vague* directors, it is Truffaut alone who has carried on the tradition of French lyricism out of Vigo and Renoir despite once being its most vitriolic critic: in *Jules et Jim* his feeling for the countryside, sensuously captured by Raoul Coutard's ravishing black-and-white photography, is worthy – as is the whole film – of Renoir's *Une Partie de Campagne* (1936, A Day in the Country). And if Godard was without question the more revolutionary figure, it is surprisingly hard to imagine the course of contemporary cinema bereft of Truffaut's inimitable (though often imitated) delicacy and charm.   GILBERT ADAIR

Below: Truffaut discusses a point with Jeanne Moreau who gives a moving performance as the capricious Catherine

In pre-World War I Paris, two young men, the German Jules and Frenchman Jim, form an indestructible friendship (1). The situation changes however when Catherine, a beautiful but volatile young woman, enters their lives (2) and begins an affair with the diffident Jules (3).

They marry and, with their small daughter (4), settle in Germany; when war breaks out soon after, the once inseparable friends find themselves conscripted on opposite sides. After the war Jim, now a successful journalist in Paris, pays the couple a visit, during which he is deceived into believing that they are idyllically happy (5). But Jules sadly confesses in a letter that he is unable to hold on to Catherine and even encourages his friend, in a desperate attempt to keep his wife, to sleep with her (6).

Jim, no less defeated by her capricious moods and casual infidelity, soon returns to Paris and the passively loyal girlfriend, Gilberte, whom he had left behind. Several years pass. Jules and Catherine settle in Paris and the friends seem, on the surface, to have resumed their earlier relationship (7). But Jim, having recovered his independence, refuses to see it swallowed up once more in what he knows to be an unworkable situation. Whereupon the ever-inscrutable Catherine invites him into her car and drives them both into the Seine. Jules is left alone (8).

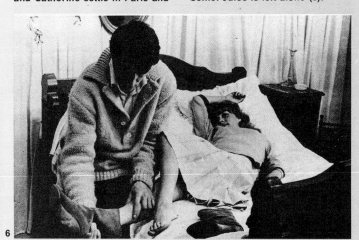

In François Truffaut's opinion the qualities required by a director in order to make worthwhile films are 'Sensitivity, intuition, good taste and intelligence . . . A little of one of these will yield very little, but a great deal of any one of them will make an appealing film, and a lot of all four will make a masterpiece.' Over the years Truffaut's films have exhibited all these attributes in varying degrees and combinations, and he is still one of the most fascinating of contemporary directors

A keyword in gaining access to the inner world of François Truffaut, and thus to his life and films, is fear.

It may not be the only way in but it is a good start. Take, for example, his longstanding admiration for Hitchcock and the master's manipulation of audience response by playing on deep-rooted psychoses and fears; then look at Truffaut's own portraits of timid male characters from Charlie (Charles Aznavour) in *Tirez sur le Pianiste* (1960, *Shoot the Pianist*) through variations on the distinctly non-macho character of Antoine, played by Jean-Pierre Léaud in a series of films, to Pierre Lachenay (Jean Desailly) in *La Peau Douce* (1964, *Silken Skin*) and so on; the list is endless.

Then consider Truffaut's own extreme timidity during interviews, presentations, film festivals and, indeed, on all public occasions. His instinctive fear of self-revelation, an apparent contradiction in one whose films contain more transparently autobiographical elements than those of almost any other film-maker, leads him – maddeningly – to veer

away from an intimate exploration of the heights and depths of joy and sorrow just when he seems about to plunge right in.

The reason may be partly this personal fear of revealing his private emotions, and partly his professional need to reverse the normal progression of life towards degradation and death by at least an open, if never a riotously happy, ending to his films. *L'Histoire d'Adèle H.* (1975, *The Story of Adèle H.*) and more recently *La Chambre Verte* (1978, *The Green Room*) do run somewhat counter to this tendency, though the forest of flaming candles at the end of *The Green Room* does provide a visual uplift to counter the pessimism of the rest of the film. In general it is probably true to say that if the heights and depths of the human condition are rarely plumbed by Truffaut, the huge shifting grey area in between comes in for a fair bit of attention.

The facts behind the fiction

François Truffaut was born in Paris on February 6, 1932. He was an only child and was

Top: Truffaut (behind camera) as the director of the film within his film Day for Night. *Above left: Cyril Cusak and Oskar Werner as the firemen whose job it is to burn books in the futuristic* Fahrenheit 451 *(1966). Above: Antoine (Jean-Pierre Léaud) is found out in* The 400 Blows *when his mother appears after he has used her 'death' as an excuse to play truant from school*

brought up by his grandmother until the age eight when his mother and adoptive fath rather reluctantly took over. They are reflecte in many of Truffaut's films from *Les Quat Cents Coups* (1959, *The 400 Blows*), the story a little boy misunderstood and mistreated his parents, teachers and the police, *L'Homme Qui Aimait les Femmes* (1977, *T Man Who Loved Women*), the portrait of a ma completely obsessed by women.

Truffaut stated in a recent interview wit this writer that he never knew who his re father was and is not even sure of havir French nationality. His adolescence was

14

François Truffaut

Above: Truffaut directing Jacqueline Bisset on the set of Day for Night. Below left: the story of an ill-fated affair. Below: Louis Mahe (Jean-Paul Belmondo) and the wife (Catherine Deneuve) who is slowly poisoning him in Mississippi Mermaid

The man who loves movies

articularly difficult period, punctuated by ruancy from school, frequent clandestine trips o the cinema, at least one unrequited love-ffair – which later appeared in *Antoine et 'olette*, an episode from *L'Amour à Vingt Ans* 1962, *Love at Twenty*) – and the founding of his wn ciné-club at the age of 15.

At this point he encountered the film critic nd editor of *Cahiers du Cinéma*, André Bazin; a rucial encounter which was to lead to the tart of his career as a film critic with the eriodical after his dishonourable discharge rom army service in 1953. He also wrote for a umber of other journals including *Arts*, *inémonde*, *Elle* and *Le Temps de Paris*, and in 956 he worked as assistant to Roberto Rossellini on three scripts but none were ever lmed.

rom criticism to creativity

As a critic, Truffaut was one of the key figures esponsible for the establishment of the '*auteur* heory', expounded most clearly in his 1958 nanifesto: studios were to be abandoned in avour of location shooting; dialogue was not o be based on literary adaptation but on

conversational speech verging on improvisation; stars were not vital and the only qualification that was needed in order to direct a film was the desire to make a personal statement with the camera as directly as a writer does with the pen.

Truffaut was as vigorous and vicious in denouncing the establishment figures of French cinema of the Forties and Fifties – most of whom he dismissed as merely skilled adaptors – as he was passionate in defending film 'authors' such as Howard Hawks and John Ford, many of whom were first accorded such status by Truffaut and his fellow critics on the journal *Cahiers du Cinéma*. He became known as the *enfant terrible* of French film criticism, but most importantly he became *known*.

The song remains the same

In 1959, at the age of 27, Truffaut made his first feature film (rivalling *Jules et Jim* in popularity) – *The 400 Blows*. He was not young in comparison with the Hollywood pioneers of the silent era and the early days of sound, nor even with the American movie-brats of the Seventies, but he *was* young in relation to the

norm in France during the Fifties. He has since directed some twenty films but by the time *Shoot the Pianist* and *Jules et Jim* (1962) were completed, all his key statements had been made, thereby proving his own theory that a film-maker expresses himself most fully in his first three films and afterwards merely reworks these themes *ad infinitum*.

Similarly, many elements from Truffaut's first three features can likewise be traced back to his short *Les Mistons* (1957, *The Mischief Makers*), about the first sexual stirrings of a gang of boys and the girl who becomes the object of their desires. For instance the impossibility of prolonged happiness, the role of fate, the bitter-sweet tone, the importance of women and the intoxication with cinema – all these themes appear for the first time in 1957 and are still prominent almost a quarter of a century later.

The concept of the short-lived nature of happiness runs through the whole of Truffaut's cinema rather like the novelist Thomas Hardy's view of happiness as being 'but the occasional episode in a general drama of pain'. The idea occurs intensely in an idyllic

JEAN DESAILLY · FRANÇOISE DORLEAC
starring in
A FILM BY
FRANÇOIS TRUFFAUT
SILKEN SKIN
(la peau douce)

scene at the lakeside chalet in *Les Deux Anglaises et le Continent* (1971, *Anne and Muriel*). fleetingly in *Jules et Jim*, and on isolated occasions like the fairground outing or when Antoine's parents take him to the cinema in *The 400 Blows*. Happiness for Truffaut's characters may be enjoyed briefly before it degenerates into the boredom of marriage as in *Domicile Conjugal* (1970, *Bed and Board*), or is terminated by death as in *Shoot the Pianist, Jules et Jim, La Mariée Etait en Noir* (1968, *The Bride Wore Black*) and *The Green Room*.

The man who distrusted women
Women feature strongly in Truffaut's films and fall into three major categories – dream goddesses, mother figures or whores. The last group usually provide consolation when the first two have failed as in *Baisers Volés* (1968, *Stolen Kisses*) and *Bed and Board*. The jokey idea that 'All women are whores except my mother and my sister' provides an interesting clue to

the male attitudes prevalent in Truffaut's films. The man is vulnerable, liable to rejection (as Truffaut's own mother rejected him) and therefore prone either to despise or to idealize women which leads to an inability to involve himself in the fluctuations and imperfections of a long-term relationship.

Bernadette (Bernadette Lafont) is an idealized sex-object in *The Mischief Makers*, inaccessible and therefore desirable; Catherine (Jeanne Moreau) is initially merely an enigmatic smile in *Jules et Jim*, in the pursuit of which a close male friendship is destroyed and two deaths ensue; Julie (Jeanne Moreau) is literally a man-killer in *The Bride Wore Black* as is Julie/Marion (Catherine Deneuve) in *La Sirène du Mississippi* (1969, *Mississippi Mermaid*).

However, in *The Man Who Loved Women*, the hero's compulsive need to sleep with women is possibly a reaction to his mother's treatment of him as a boy, and to her string of lovers. All of this inexorably leads back to *The Mischief Makers* and the portrayal of the female praying mantis devouring the male in copulation.

Surfacing from solitude?
There is clearly a great deal of solitariness in Truffaut's universe, despite his attempts to people it with substitute families, a gallery of warm stock-characters, and despite the recollection by Madame Tabard (Delphine Seyrig), in *Stolen Kisses*, that her father's final verdict on life had been 'People are fantastic'. Yet at crucial moments in their lives most of the characters are alone or else return to solitude.

Even so grounds for hope seem to exist. There is the simple existence of children and their presence in most of Truffaut's films. From survival in *The 400 Blows* to civilization in

Left: Julie (Jeanne Moreau), a widow out for revenge, with Bliss (Claude Rich) who is soon to be one of her victims in The Bride Wore Black. *Above left: Christine (Claude Jade) and Antoine (Jean-Pierre Léaud) find that wedded bliss is not up to expectations in* Bed and Board. *Above: Charles Denner, as The Man Who Loved Women, keeps a 'friend' waiting while talking to another on the phone. Below left: Isabelle Adjani in the title role of this true love story*

L'Enfant Sauvage (1970, *The Wild Child*) and the indulgent celebration of childhood in *L'Argent de Poche* (1976, *Small Change*), Truffaut seems to protect and defend the innocence and purity of childhood and adolescence on the screen almost as a form of compensation for the neglect and unhappiness he himself experienced.

Another compensatory factor in Truffaut's world is the very existence of the cinema – 'The cinema reigns supreme', as he says in *La Nuit Américaine* (1973, *Day for Night*). His philosophy is that films reflect life, films are life and in watching, making and talking films one is never alone. The actors and crew make up an ideal family, writing, shooting and editing being part of the conception and gestation process. The film is born and the next one begins. Just like life, or better than life, for films never die.

Gradually, as fresh pieces slot into place, Truffaut reveals more fragments of himself film by film. It is a foregone conclusion that there will never be any dramatic full-frontal revelations, but fleeting perceptions of the private parts of Truffaut's mental and emotional universe are building into an increasingly fascinating picture.   DON ALLEN

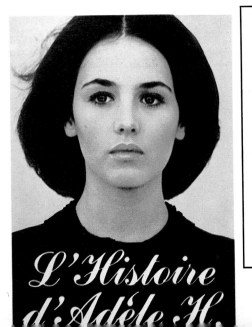

Filmography
1955 Une Visite (short) (+sc, +co-ed). **'56** Le Coup du Berger (short) (actor only). **'57** Les Mistons (short) (+sc) (GB/USA: The Mischief Makers). **'58** Une Histoire d'Eau (short) (co-dir). **'59** Les Quatre Cents Coups (act +co-sc) (GB/USA: The 400 Blows). **'60** A Bout de Souffle (co-sc only) (GB/USA: Breathless); Tirez sur le Pianiste (+co-sc) (GB: Shoot the Pianist; USA: Shoot the Piano Player). **'61** Tire au Flanc (co-prod. sup. co-sc only) (GB: Sad Sack; USA: The Army Game). **'62** Jules et Jim (+co-sc) (GB/USA: Jules and Jim); L'Amour à Vingt Ans *ep* Antoine et Colette (+sc) (FR-IT-JAP-GER-POL) (GB/USA: Love at Twenty). **'64** La Peau Douce (+co-sc) (GB: Silken Skin; USA: The Soft Skin). **'65** Mata Hari, Agent H-21 (co-sc only) (FR-IT). **'66** Fahrenheit 451 (+co-sc) (GB). **'68** La Mariée Etait en Noir (+co-sc) (FR-IT) (GB/USA: The Bride Wore Black); Baisers Volés (+co-sc) (GB/USA: Stolen Kisses). **'69** La Sirène du Mississippi (+sc) (FR-IT)

(GB/USA: Mississippi Mermaid). **'70** L'Enfant Sauvage (+co-sc, act) (GB/USA: The Wild Child); Domicile Conjugal (+co-sc) (FR-IT) (GB/USA: Bed and Board). **'71** Les Deux Anglaises et le Continent (+ co-sc, narr) (GB: Anne and Muriel; USA: Two English Girls). **'72** Une Belle Fille Comme Moi (+co-sc) (GB: A Gorgeous Bird Like Me; USA: Such a Gorgeous Kid Like Me). **'73** La Nuit Américaine (+co-sc, act) (FR-IT) (GB/USA: Day for Night). **'75** L'Histoire d'Adèle H. (+co-sc, act) (GB/USA: The Story of Adèle H.). **'76** L'Argent de Poche (+co-sc) (GB/USA: Small Change). **'77** L'Homme Qui Aimait les Femmes (+co-sc) (GB: The Man Who Loved Women; USA: The Man Who Loved Love); Close Encounters of the Third Kind (act. only) (USA). **'78** La Chambre Verte (+co-sc, act) (GB/USA: The Green Room). **'79** L'Amour en Fuite (+co-sc) (GB: Love on the Run). **'80** Le Dernier Métro (+co-sc).

The Dark Humours of Claude Chabrol

Chabrol is generally considered a satirical chronicler of contemporary France, but this view does not do justice to his humour, his originality or his recurrent obsessions

Born in Paris on June 24, 1930, Claude Chabrol was to spend more time in the Cinémathèque and the art-movie houses than at the University. A critic for *Cahiers du Cinéma*, he was known less for his aggressiveness than for the humour and diversity of his cinematic tastes. He declared, in discussing American crime movies, that there are no 'big' or 'small' subjects for films; but on the whole he wrote few theoretical texts. His book on Hitchcock (in collaboration with Eric Rohmer) published in 1957, was a subtle cocktail of the serious and the ironic.

Shortly before that he came into a little inheritance and made his cinema debut as producer and co-scenarist of a short film by Jacques Rivette, *Le Coup du Berger* (1956, Fool's Checkmate). He was also to be technical adviser on Godard's *A Bout de Souffle* (1960, Breathless). Thus he had an early familiarity with the financial problems of film-making. To create his first movie he needed money. So he had the idea of making another very low-budget film put together so as to obtain a *prime à la qualité* (an official grant awarded to certain 'intellectual' films). With the money from the bursary he was able to make the other film on which he had set his heart.

But that film, *Les Cousins* (1959, The Cousins), was a commercial failure, as were the films that followed it. Chabrol has been accused of black gloominess, of misogyny, even of fascism. It must be appreciated that the characters in his early films are for the most part stupid, feeble or even repugnant. But through them Chabrol conveys both a deep-seated pessimism, only alleviated much later in his career, and a fascination with stupidity – a fascination that does not preclude pity.

The lack of success of these ambivalent films forced him for a few years to direct any commercial assignment he could get, notably a series of spy-films shot as parodies of the James Bond films – for example, *Marie-Chantal Contre le Dr Khâ* (1965, Marie-Chantal Against Dr Khâ). On his return to serious subjects, particularly with *Les Biches* (1968, *The Does*), public taste had altered. The outrages of the *nouvelle vague* had become acceptable, and Chabrol's qualities could be seen in their true light; he is actually a humorist with a touch of tenderness. The cruelty of some of his portrayals is the product of a clear-sighted and lively intelligence.

Food for thought

His chosen subjects have a realistic surface, somewhat in the tradition of Jean Renoir or Julien Duvivier: couples threatened by adultery, impulsive passions leading to crimes committed by respectable members of the lower middle class – more often than not set in the provinces. What is more, the 'moral' of these stories is eminently rational: *La Femme Infidèle* (1968, The Unfaithful Wife), for example, is a homage to fidelity. Onto the satirical truth of his depiction he grafts a personal feature which quickly becomes something noteworthy: for instance, in each of his films he plays a minor comic role; and gastronomy, that 'typically French' weakness or perhaps merit, occupies an ever more important place. Three meals divide the dramatic development of *Que la Bête Meure* (1969, Killer!) into acts like a classical tragedy. Conflicts are knotted up and unravelled around the family dinner table in *Le Scandale/The Champagne Murders* (1967), in *La Femme Infidèle*, in *Juste Avant la Nuit* (1971, Just Before Nightfall). It is at table, too, that decisions are taken in *Les Biches*, and in *La Muette* (The Mute Woman – also the name of a Paris district), a nightmare

Above left: Chabrol plays a practical joke for the benefit of TV's Omnibus cameras. Below left: Anthony Perkins and Stéphane Audran in The Champagne Murders. *Below: Jean-Paul Belmondo, Madeleine Robinson and Jean-Louis Trintignant in* Web of Passion

Above: Frédérique (Stéphane Audran) and Why (Jacqueline Sassard) form the Lesbian side of a love-triangle in Les Biches, *Chabrol's return to critical success. Above right: Anna Douking as a masochistic woman killed by her lover in* Just Before Nightfall

comic sketch from *Paris Vu Par . . .* (1965, Paris Seen by . . .) in which Chabrol plays the role of a pharmacist. A wedding banquet is the opening scene for *Le Boucher* (1970, The Butcher). The food that is or is not shared with the inhabitants of another place – that ancient theme of folk tales – returns in *Alice ou la Dernière Fugue* (1976, *Alice, or the Last Escapade*). As if to highlight the importance of this motif, the film-maker has stated that he shoots only in locations where he can be sure of finding good food.

So Chabrol presents a seemingly comforting portrait of contemporary France. Of course he depicts it in a corrosive, even vicious, fashion: silliness, meanness, pettiness abound. But this picture corresponds in the eyes of the average spectator to a well-established literary tradition of realistic studies of Parisian and provincial life as in classic authors. Moreover the satirical aspects of his work are balanced out by the true sympathy in his representations of women or children.

A family resemblance

Looked at more closely, certain aspects of his work become less straightforward. Chabrol is not merely an entertainer doubling as a psychologist and 'prodigiously gifted', as one critic wrote in 1967, though certainly from film to film he has acquired a faultless craftsmanship. He has built up around himself a fairly permanent team of technicians, including the cameraman Jean Rabier and the composer Pierre Janssen. He uses the same actors as often as he can, in particular his wife. Stéphane Audran. The result is that his later films have a 'family look', and consequently a common style over and above their common themes.

Chabrol appears to take different starting points and work from very diverse subject matter: American detective novels transposed to France; original scripts based on sensationalist newspaper reports; or alternatively a fantasy basis, as in *Alice*. Almost all his films share an atmosphere which cannot be reduced to the realism already mentioned, nor to the evident moralism of the director. The climate that reigns in his films, the element remembered about them, is more deeply obsessional.

Stupidity and madness

If Chabrol is fascinated by stupidity, it is not simply because 'there are no limits to it', as he himself has pointed out, but also 'because it is dangerous'. More often than not his characters avoid stupidity only to fall prey to another danger – madness. This is something more fascinating, less mediocre than stupidity. Often it is the fruit of a frustrated passion or of a totally unreasonable demand. Even when it is caused by a neurotic trauma, the sufferer (in Chabrol's eyes no madman can be happy) is an object worthy of our compassion.

Possibly Chabrol's most successful film from this point of view is *Le Boucher*. It is essentially a drama with only two important characters, whom it brings face to face: a schoolteacher, Hélène, and a butcher, Paul, both equally possessed of passionate desires despite all appearances to the contrary. Paul conceals a terrible neurosis which periodically leads him to murder young girls. Hélène, at the opening of the film, is a potential 'old maid', scared of love and practising yoga – something the director defines as 'a gymnastico-mental religion leading nowhere'. Gradually Hélène ceases repressing her true nature and blossoms as she falls in love. Simultaneously her intelligence develops but it leads her to suspect that the object of her love is a 'monster'. And since this monster is neither retarded nor unsympathetic, and since he in turn realizes that he is suspected by the woman he loves, his suicide in

Above: Michel Piccoli and Orson Welles with statue of Zeus in Ten Days' Wonder. *Below and below right: poster and similar still from* Red Wedding, *a drama of provincial adultery and murder, almost banned for political indiscretions. Right: Stéphane Audran, Isabelle Huppert and Jean Carmet form a family group in* Violette Nozière, *based on a real-life murder case. Below far right: Bruce Dern in* The Twist *(1976), with Stéphane Audran as his unfaithful wife*

er presence becomes an act of love.

Similar flashes of insanity recur in many of ae films, indicating their true dimension, hich is not so much realistic as metaphysical, ncerned with absolute values. In *A Double ur* (1959, *Web of Passion*) a father hopes to ear the eyes out' of an unknown murderer, ho is eventually discovered to be his own son. husband who has gone violently mad is the arting point for *La Rupture* (1970, The Break- >); the behaviour of the normal characters, ho then put the blame on the heroine, his ife, also looks as if it stems from some mental stability. In *Les Innocents aux Mains Sales* 975, *Innocents With Dirty Hands*) the heroine the end of the film sinks into a kind of remeditated insanity as the only means to again her integrity. The examples could be ultiplied to include even those films where habrol seems to be more concerned with ocial environments and the problems of mar- ed couples.

nity and diversity

is this sort of obsession that ensures the unity 'Chabrol's work, since it is found as often in ae films with a strict dramatic structure as in aose which are less carefully worked out or en botched. What is curious is that those ms that deal most obviously with madness or bsurdity contain realistic and convincing etails, whereas the works of social analysis, ach as *La Femme Infidèle*, *Les Noces Rouges*

(1973, *Red Wedding*) or *Just Before Nightfall*, include traces of wildness or terror.

From time to time Chabrol has been beset by a kind of academicism, pursuing falsely bright ideas: *Landru* (1963, *Bluebeard*) falters after a masterly opening; *Violette Nozière* (1978) fol- lows historical accuracy too closely to be enthralling. Occasionally he has tried to de- scribe worlds he scarcely knows – for instance, the revolutionary milieu in *Nada* (1973) – and failed in the attempt. His constant mixing of styles is disconcerting for the viewer, but allows the essential to come through, whether the plot is linear, as in *La Femme Infidèle*, or contorted, as in *Killer!*, by being absorbed in the *mise-en-scène*.

Chabrol's personal style allows him to be seen apart from both traditional French rea- lism and his *nouvelle vague* colleagues. It was overtly inspired by Murnau, by Hitchcock and sometimes by Fritz Lang. He enjoys multiply- ing the points of resemblance between one of his films and another. For example, the heroine is called Hélène in *La Femme Infidèle*, in *Killer!*, in *Le Boucher*; and she is called Léda (Helen's mother in Greek mythology) in *A Double Tour*. Chabrol has also been influenced by Orson Welles; and in *La Décade Prodigieuse* (1971, *Ten Days' Wonder*) he took great pleasure in casting Welles in the role of Théo ('god' in Greek) in a film which is about the violation of the Ten Commandments and in which 'God' is presented as a jealous criminal.

Chabrol conclusively proves his artistic in- dependence by wilfully ending his films with a shot that evokes his own withdrawal from the story he has been telling. Thus the camera pulls back from the reconstructed family group in *La Femme Infidèle*, as it does from the car accident in *Alice*. The sense of decor, the growing concern with colour, excellent direct- ing of actors – all these ultimately convey, despite the mixed look of Chabrol's film, a precise coherence underlying his entire work.
GERARD LEGRAND

The Stars of the New Wave

The *nouvelle vague* in France introduced not only a number of directors whose new or recycled ideas were found to be urgently needed, but a new wave of equally welcome new faces

The French stars of the Fifties were to a great extent the French stars of the Thirties and Forties – Jean Gabin, Fernandel, Edwige Feuillère, Gérard Philipe and company were still big box-office names at the art houses in New York or London.

Bardot

Their popularity was eclipsed – especially in America – by the advent of Brigitte Bardot (b. 1934) in *Et Dieu Créa La Femme* (1956, . . . *And God Created Woman*). She played to capacity in cinemas which had never before featured a foreign-language film – even if, because of her success, these were likely to turn up dubbed. For a time, she and her director and mentor, Roger Vadim, seemed to be part of the *nouvelle vague* ('new wave'). That wave was still breaking – and she was refusing all Hollywood blandishments to go and film there – when its beginnings were examined in the winter of 1960 at London's National Film Theatre, whose patrons were therefore seeing Mlle Bardot as a portent of the new movement.

Well, so she was, if only in the freer treatment of sex.

Certainly in those far-off days French movies meant spice to the less serious art-house patrons. Undoubtedly lovers went to bed together in French films, as they seldom did in British and American ones. There was desperation in the couplings of the tragic romances, an *ooh la la!* naughtiness in the comedies, and melodrama in the red-light tales which played the more dubious houses.

Bardot herself was far from such qualities, being young, fresh, free and frank in her enjoyment of her body. The first image of her in Vadim's film – sunbathing naked, lying on her stomach – is unforgettable. Melodrama certainly was not absent from the film, and no matter that it was Vadim's intention to exploit her potential as a sex-symbol, she is always cheering – except when she does not get her own way, which is inclined to make her sulky. It is entirely understandable that she and the bridegroom (Jean-Louis Trintignant) miss the wedding feast because they have a more

pressing matter to attend to, and why, for th[e] same reason, she and her brother-in-law rom[p] in the surf instead of seeking the privacy of th[e] bushes a few yards away.

Jeanne Moreau

Sex not only played a part in *Les Amants* (1958[,] *The Lovers*) – one of the first *nouvelle vague* film[s] – but was its whole *raison d'etre*, to the exten[t] that there was much speculation as to whethe[r] it could be shown outside France. It was th[e] second film made by Louis Malle with his the[n] mistress Jeanne Moreau (b. 1928). The first ha[d] been *Ascenseur Pour l'Echafaud* (1958, *Lift to th[e] Scaffold*) in which she had gloomed abou[t] Paris waiting for her lover. Moreau had bee[n] in films ten years, but it was Malle wh[o] transformed her from a bright *ingénue* to [a] woman of the world: sensual, intense an[d] seemingly complex in her thoughts. In *Lift t[o] the Scaffold* two peripheral characters – [a] young crook and his girlfriend – bed down in [a] motel in the casual manner which was t[o] become symptomatic of the *nouvelle vague.*

Meanwhile, except in subject matter, *L[es] Amants* was a rather old-fashioned film[.] Jeanne Tournier (Jeanne Moreau) finds he[r] husband odious and her lover ridiculous, an[d] seems not to have given a passing thought t[o]

Opposite: Jeanne Moreau and Brigitte Bardot together in Viva Maria! *Above: Before Winter Comes (1969) Anna Karina as a young woman who shares her love with the Russian deserter (Topol). Above right: Anouk Aimée as the enigmatic* Justine

the stranger Bertrand (Jean-Marc Bory), a friend of friends who is staying the night . . . until, unable to sleep, she wanders into the garden to find him there, apparently equally restless. At first irritated, she lets him approach, and after bedding and bathing together, she leaves with him in the morning. Partly because his approach to sex is so uncomplicated, Bertrand is likeable. And Bory was certainly one of the new breed – unhistrionic and not particularly handsome. He thereafter played mainly supporting roles, while Moreau went on to become an international star.

Since she and Bardot represented – at opposite ends of the scale – the new sexuality, they were eventually teamed in Malle's *Viva Maria!* (1965) but, over-publicized during production, and underwritten, it was rather a damp squib. By that time Moreau had made a number of films in English, including *The Victors* (1963) and *The Yellow Rolls Royce* (1964), proving herself relatively less interesting in that language – despite having learned it from her Lancashire-born mother. Her range was demonstrated in her films with the *nouvelle vague* directors – as the blonde Riviera gambler in Jacques Demy's *La Baie des Anges* (1963, *Bay of Angels*), as a frustrated school-teacher in Philippe de Broca's *Chère Louise* (1972, *Louise*) and in François Truffaut's *Jules et*

Jim (1962), as the beloved of those two playmates. She also worked with Truffaut on the forgettable *La Mariée Etait en Noir* (1968, *The Bride Wore Black*), and played herself – unbilled and very briefly – in both his *Les Quatre Cents Coups* (1959, *The 400 Blows*) and Jean-Luc Godard's *Une Femme Est une Femme* (1961, *A Woman Is a Woman*) – proving that there was mutual admiration among these players and directors. Their off-screen friendship testified that they were *copains*.

Anna Karina

Une Femme Est une Femme was a virtual homage to Anna Karina (b. 1940), a Danish model whom Godard had met and liked, and who starred in the then banned *Le Petit Soldat* (1960, *The Little Soldier*). He was also married to her from 1961 to 1967, and – particularly in *Une Femme Est une Femme* and *Vivre Sa Vie* (1962, *It's My Life*) – she was seldom off the screen, watched lovingly by the camera as she was, in turn, coquettish, spirited and generally adorable.

Anouk Aimée

One reason for the lack of traditional stars in the films of the *nouvelle vague* was that their makers could not afford the fees, but certainly Anouk Aimée (b. 1932) had been a leading actress for more than ten years when Demy devised *Lola* (1961) with her in mind – and as with Karina in Godard's films, she was to be seen in all her moods. Both she and the film are enchanting, though she had a much bigger international success in *Un Homme et une Femme* (1966, *A Man and a Woman*) directed by

Claude Lelouch, and in Fellini's *La Dolce Vita* (1959, *The Sweet Life*) Hollywood decided that only she could play the title-role in the film of Lawrence Durrell's novel *Justine* (dir. George Cukor, 1969). She has never really been interested in acting, however, and for a time she turned her back on film-making during her marriage to Albert Finney. Recently her career looks like moving forward again, if her appearance in Bellochio's *Salta nel Vuoto* (1980, *Leap into the Void*) is any indication.

Catherine Deneuve

Of the other actresses thrown up by the *nouvelle vague*, perhaps the most successful has been Catherine Deneuve – discovered by Vadim, and at her best in Jacques Demy's musical *Les Parapluies de Cherbourg* (1964, *The Umbrellas of Cherbourg*). Demy made a follow-up, *Les Demoiselles de Rochefort* (1967, *The Young Girls of Rochefort*) as bad as the other is good – which is a pity, for it was the only time Deneuve co-starred with her warmer and more radiant sister, Françoise Dorléac (b. 1942). Dorléac was indeed a *nouvelle vague* star, having worked for many of the new young directors of the Sixties before her death in a car crash in 1967. Deneuve's career was also then at its peak – in films such as Polanski's *Repulsion* (1965) and Buñuel's *Belle du Jour* (1967).

Below left: Mississippi Mermaid *was the only Truffaut film in which either Catherine Deneuve or Jean-Paul Belmondo acted. Below: Deneuve's sister Françoise Dorléac (publicity shot), whose career was brought to a tragic and untimely end in an automobile accident*

Above left: Stéphane Audran and Oliver Reed in La Dame dans l'Auto Avec des Lunettes et un Fusil *(1970). Above: Audran with former husband Jean-Louis Trintignant in* Les Biches. *Left:* Hiroshima, Mon Amour – *Emmanuelle Riva's most memorable screen performance. Bottom left: Annie Girardot in* La Bonne Soupe *(1963). Bottom right: arch-rivals Delon and Belmondo in* Borsalino

actress (b. 1927) whose film debut was in one of their first movies – *Hiroshima, Mon Amour* (1959, Hiroshima, My Love), in which she falls in love on a visit to Japan, and reminisces about her experiences in the war. She also appeared notably in Franju's *Thérèse Desqueyroux* (1962, *Therese*), as a modern Madame Bovary, and in *Léon Morin, Prêtre* (1961, *Leon Morin, Priest*), as the lonely widow unwillingly drawn to the village priest (Jean-Paul Belmondo), despite her being Jewish, communist and atheist, and possibly lesbian as well. Too little has since been seen of the delicate talents of this non-starry actress.

Annie Girardot

As much might be said, at least in Britain and the United States, of the equally gifted Annie Girardot (b. 1931), whose career spans the *nouvelle vague* with ease, but who must be listed with these players of her generation since she continues to be by far France's most popular female star. Equally adept at comedy and drama, at playing shy spinsters or extrovert housewives, she was especially fine in De Broca's *Tendre Poulet* (1977, *Dear Inspector*) as a lady detective felicitously teamed with Philippe Noiret as a professor. However, she only appeared in one truly *nouvelle vague* film – *La Proie Pour L'Ombre* (1961, *Shadow of Adultery*) – directed by Alexandre Astruc, one of the independent young directors to whom the rising film-makers looked for inspiration.

Belmondo le fou

Before bounding to fame in Godard's *A Bout de Souffle* (1960, *Breathless*), Jean-Paul Belmondo (b. 1933) had appeared in *Charlotte et Son Jules* (1958, Charlotte and Her Guy) – a short by Godard – and in Chabrol's *A Double Tour* (1959, *Web of Passion*). His leading roles were in unimportant films, among which could be included Claude Sautet's *Classe Tous Risques* (1960, *The Big Risk*) since it was completely overlooked in the rush to praise *Breathless*. Belmondo himself was surprised since he had had little faith in Godard's haphazard shooting methods and his vague little tale, much preferring Sautet's film, in which he played the last staunch friend of an ageing gangster (Lino

Stéphane Audran

Stéphane Audran (b. 1933) is, with Karina, the other *nouvelle vague* wife, having married Claude Chabrol in 1964, after an earlier marriage to Jean-Louis Trintignant, who sourly speaks of her as the one who wanted him to be a prominent actor – which is reflected in the commanding and sometimes conniving wives she often plays. She first acted for Chabrol in *Les Cousins* (1959, The Cousins) and has appeared in most of his films, following him into the commercial subjects he did when his career dipped. Not too interesting in the early film, she was magnificent in the one which revived his reputation – *Les Biches* (1968, *The Does*) – as a particularly sophisticated, and lesbian, Parisienne. Seemingly indispensable in his tales of murder and marital infidelity – and particularly as the schoolmistress in his best film *Le Boucher* (1970, The Butcher) – she has been singularly unlucky in more recent English-language films, which include *The Black Bird* (1975) opposite George Segal, and *Eagle's Wing* (1979).

Emmanuelle Riva

Another actress favoured by the *nouvelle vague* directors was Emmanuelle Riva, a stage

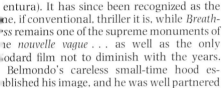

entura). It has since been recognized as the [fi]ne, if conventional, thriller it is, while *Breath[le]ss* remains one of the supreme monuments of [th]e *nouvelle vague* . . . as well as the only [G]odard film not to diminish with the years.

Belmondo's careless small-time hood es[ta]blished his image, and he was well partnered [b]y actress Jean Seberg (b. 1933), an American ['n]ame' whom Godard had got for a song. The [s]uccess of the film brought her more offers in [F]rance, but apart from De Broca's *L'Amant de [C]inq Jours* (1961, *Infidelity*) she seemed hap[p]iest in commercial movies, returning tem[p]orarily to Hollywood at the end of the decade [f]or *Paint Your Wagon* (1969), among others. A [fa]ltering career and depression contributed to [h]er suicide in 1979.

Belmondo showed himself to be an actor of [a]stonishing virtuosity – playing roles ranging [fr]om factory worker to student to loutish [c]ountry boy to withdrawn priest. In *Cartouche* [(1]962, *Swords of Blood*) he played a French [R]obin Hood for De Broca, and had an even [b]igger success with that director's marvellous [o]d adventure tale *L'Homme de Rio* (1964, *That [M]an From Rio*). He dislikes chichi or 'minority' [fi]lms, but said that he owed it to the directors [h]e started with to appear in their films – and [th]us made Godard's *Pierrot le Fou* (1965, *[P]ierrot the Fool*), Malle's *Le Voleur* (1967, *The [Th]ief*), Truffaut's *La Sirène du Mississippi* (1969, *[M]ississippi Mermaid*), Chabrol's *Docteur Popaul* [(1]972, *Scoundrel in White*) and Resnais' *Stav[s]ky . . .* (1974). He certainly believed in the [l]ast-named, because he invested his own [m]oney in it, but like all these films it did [d]isastrously less business than his unabash[e]dly commercial movies. Thus now he sticks [t]o these usually light-hearted thrillers, relent[l]essly playing himself. His annual film is in[v]ariably the year's biggest box-office product [i]n France, perhaps because audiences know [th]at as his own producer he refuses to sell his [fi]lms to television.

[A]lain Delon
[B]elmondo's popularity was challenged at the [st]art – and still is – by Alain Delon (b. 1935) [w]ho was in fact 'made' by two directors who [w]ere the antithesis of the *nouvelle vague* – René

Clément and Luchino Visconti. It could not be said that since his debut Delon has flowered as an actor, but he has developed a harsh manner which can be effective in tough roles, such as Melville's *Le Samourai* (1967, *The Samurai*) and Jacques Deray's *Borsalino* (1970), which Delon produced, cannily pitting himself against the more easy-going Belmondo.

Three men on a wave
After Belmondo, the central male player of the *nouvelle vague* must be Jean-Pierre Léaud (b. 1944) who was still in his early teens when he played in Truffaut's autobiographical *Les Quatre Cents Coups*, and he has subsequently played the same character – Antoine Doinel – in the rest of the series. As an adult actor he is mild and mousy, but he worked consistently throughout the Sixties, including making several films for Godard.

Also associated with the first *nouvelle vague* films are Jean-Claude Brialy (b. 1933) and Gérard Blain (b. 1930) – both unknown when Chabrol featured them in his first film, *Le Beau Serge* (1958, *Handsome Serge*). It did little to help them get better known, but they and Chabrol became famous a few months later with *Les Cousins*, which established their screen personae – Blain as the reserved, un[c]ertain country lad, and Brialy as the cynical and supercilious Parisian. Since that of Brialy was the stronger, he became the bigger star, only recently moving from romantic leads into supporting roles. And indeed, Brialy waxed as

Top left: Jean Seberg in Saint Joan *(1957) – the Preminger movie which launched her career. Top: in* Le Beau Serge *Serge (Gérard Blain) and François (Jean-Claude Brialy) try to rediscover the friendship they had known as children. Above: both Jean-Pierre Léaud and François Truffaut play actor and film-maker in* La Nuit Américaine *(1973,* Day for Night*) – characters strongly resembling themselves*

Blain waned. Both actors have also written and directed; Blain has appeared in one American film – *Hatari!* (1962), but Brialy, like Belmondo, seems to have turned down all transatlantic offers.

Jean-Pierre Cassel
Jean-Pierre Cassel (b. 1932) would so much like to be an international star *and* a song-and-dance man – for which there are few opportunities in France – that he took over one of the leading roles in *A Chorus Line* at the Theatre Royal, Drury Lane, London. He has also appeared in some British films, including *Those Magnificent Men in Their Flying Machines* (1965) and *Murder on the Orient Express* (1974). However, best remembered is his nimble charm in De Broca's early films, a series of fresh and funny comedies – *Les Jeux de l'Amour* (1960, *Playing at Love*), *Le Farceur* (1960, *The Joker*) and *L'Amant de Cinq Jours* – as well as in the title-role of Renoir's *Le Caporal Epinglé* (1962, *The Vanishing Corporal*).

DAVID SHIPMAN

TIME ZONES

The cinema is an art of time and space; past, present and future time can be manipulated and permutated to give fascinating new perspectives on human experience

Until the beginning of the Sixties, the concept of time in the movies appeared to have altered little from the earliest narrative films. Following models laid down in drama and the novel, the action of the classic story film took place within a central time span. In addition it had a pre-history, either in the form of preliminary scenes or a rolling printed legend, or implied in subsequent action or dialogue; and something of what happened 'after' The End was suggested, if only at the cliché level of riding off into the sunset, a familiar equivalent to literature's 'they lived happily ever after'.

In order to appreciate fully the challenge posed by a handful of French and Italian films to the conventional way that time is shown in film, it is necessary to go back to the narrative methods of the silent cinema. The opening to a Western, for example, might consist of a landscape shot with a title superimposed: '1885, the grasslands of Wyoming'; and in that shot would be established the time and space of the story about to unfold.

Such a film might then develop its story through consecutive action, relying on a combination of natural time indications (daylight succeeded by dusk and night) and stylistic devices such as the slow dissolve, the fade-in or fade-out, and intertitles in the style of 'Came the dawn'. Whatever techniques film-makers evolved to convey the passing of time, it was clear that 'space' – the sense of where the action is happening – was an essential part of the equation. As the moment of the film changed from shot to shot, so invariably did its space, since a shot basically depicted what was happening, and when, and where.

In the progression from one shot to the next – the result of splicing two shots together – lay a simultaneous development in space and time that permitted action to follow an acceptable logic. When the action shifted (or, more correctly, when the director and the editor cut) to another locale, the logic of the scene was held together by the notion of continuity whereby soundtrack, image, lighting, costume, props and characters' behaviour were made to follow on from the preceding shot.

The insistence of film-makers on continuity was fundamental to the practice of both making and viewing movies. They believed that to break the 'rules' which temporal and spatial continuity demanded would confuse, disorientate and even offend the audience. But that was precisely what had begun to happen in the films of Godard, Resnais and Antonioni in the early Sixties; and it was almost certainly because these film-makers were so familiar with the classically composed narrative films of John Ford and Howard Hawks that they were able to break the 'rules' and get away with it. Yet there is some anticipation of the European 'New Wave' dislocation of the space-time continuum to be found in the American *films noirs*.

Films noirs make frequent use of the flashback structure. A precursor of the genre, *Citizen Kane* (1940) is an admirable example of the narrative film whose chronology is turned inside out so that the

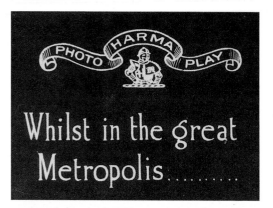

Left: in silent films intertitles were used freely both for dialogue and to give information or make transitions from one scene to the next. Below: Fred MacMurray as a fatally wounded life insurance salesman who records his confession to the murder of a client for the love of a bad woman the client's blonde wife, in Double Indemnity. *Bottom: Jane Greer as a fascinating* femme fatale *about to murder the treacherous partner of her lover, a private detective, in* Out of the Past

flashbacks become the main action – as, for example, in the memorable scene of the young Charlie Kane playing outside in the snow while indoors his future is decided. Another striking case where flashback exceeds its explanatory role, displaces the 'present tense' and dominates the narrative occurs in Robert Siodmak's *The Killers* (1946) in which an investigator digs into the past and the story returns only sporadically to the present.

Fred MacMurray speaking his confession as the framing device of Wilder's *Double Indemnity* (1944) or the long, elliptical flashback and tortuous plot twists of Jacques Tourneur's *Out of the Past* (1947) provide further illustrations of how time in the *film noir* is used fatalistically, to create a mood of an irretrievable past and of a pre-determined future from which there is no escape. The principle is demonstrated most vividly in Rudolph Maté's *D.O.A.* (1949), crime thriller that hinges on a murder victim's finding his killer in the few hours before the radioactive poison takes effect.

Just how the 'rules' of temporal and spatial

Top: in D.O.A. *Edmond O'Brien plays a man dying of radioactive poison who manages to find and kill his murderer before his own death. Top right: multiple images of Delphine Seyrig in* Last Year in Marienbad; *the feather-trimmed dress was designed by Bernard Evein. Above: Claude Rich as the time-traveller and Olga Georges-Picot as his girlfriend, who dies mysteriously in Glasgow, in* Je T'Aime, Je T'Aime

continuity were broken in innovatory French and Italian films of the early Sixties has been the subject of thorough analyses by such theorists as Noël Burch, and Peter Wollen.

In his book *Praxis du Cinéma* (Paris, 1969; English translation, *Theory of Film Practice*), Burch proposes five categories within which film time operates. The first is that of absolutely continuous action from one shot to the next, the most obvious way that time is seen to pass in film; the second is where the action is abbreviated or truncated, in the interest of economy of expression, by cutting, for example, from the beginning of an action to its conclusion without slavishly depicting each step on the screen. It is this thoroughly familiar narrative technique that Godard pushes to extremes in *A Bout de Souffle* (1960, *Breathless*), as Resnais had less notoriously done in *Hiroshima, Mon Amour* (1959, Hiroshima, My Love). The result is a sensation of action 'quoted' rather than properly represented.

Burch's third category concerns films where some period of time has been omitted from the story-telling process and the viewer must find clues in a clock, a line of dialogue, a change of dress and so on in order to determine where in time the movie is. Such ellipses of time are common in the work of Resnais but particularly played upon in *L'Année Dernière à Marienbad* (1961, *Last Year in Marienbad*).

Finally Burch lists two categories of time reversal in film: the first, which is fairly rare, involves the repetition of a small part of a film's action by means of an overlapping cut to gain a deliberate effect, as in the scene of the bridge being raised in Sergei Eisenstein's *October* (1927). The other category is the infinitely more common reversal called the flashback. Unless, however, the dates of the flash-back are clearly designated, the viewer is unlikely to be able to measure the time spanned by the flashback or even to be certain whether it is not a flash-forward. This complex juggling of different tenses – movements *elsewhere* in time rather than specifically backwards or forwards – is what makes *Last Year in Marienbad*, for instance, such a remarkable and influential film.

Resnais' previous film, *Hiroshima, Mon Amour,* deals with a fusion of public and private senses of time. When the film cuts from the bodies of the French girl and the Japanese man making love to the radiated bodies of the atom-bomb victims, it is making a simultaneous shift in time and space that questions whether private and public memories can lie side by side. Indeed the tragedy of the film is the inability of the hero and heroine to reconcile these conflicting memories; and their isolation from each other is emphasized spatially in the scene in the Japanese café where they are sitting separately but looking intently at each other. Towards the end of the film Resnais demonstrates how inextricably the past is bound up with the present: in flashback the girl is seen cycling out of the French town of Nevers at night, but the music on the soundtrack is Japanese and its source of origin is the café in Japan where she is relating the scene to her lover.

If memory is not to be trusted, runs the argument of *Hiroshima, Mon Amour* and *Last Year in Marienbad*, then perhaps the past is a tissue of illusions; and since the past largely determines the present, how 'real' can the present be? Certainly, *Last Year in Marienbad* offers no answers; its purpose is to raise the questions, suggesting that memory, if not a lie, is at best only a partial truth. The fascination of this film resides almost entirely in its form and structure; that is why it is a key work of modernist cinema where formal and structural concerns are at least as important as aesthetic and thematic ones.

Time can be slowed down, speeded up or reversed in film to show previously unrevealed facets of life

The setting of *Last Year in Marienbad* is a metaphor for the structure of memory. With its corridors, rooms, mirrors and formal gardens, it translates into spatial terms the action or possibly inaction of memory. Guests at the hotel are sometimes shown motionless, as if fixed in time; yet there is also a formal dance sequence and there are scenes of an erotic passion that might be, or might have been (the tense remains uncertain). Resnais mobilizes all the facilities of the film medium to create visual analogies for the operation of memory – over-exposure of certain scenes, rapid editing and so on – but *Last Year in Marienbad* is not simply an exploration of memory; it is ultimately and inevitably as much a film about spatial relationships as it is a film on the nature of time.

The collective force of these two early Resnais features extended beyond the work of Resnais himself and eventually played its part in reshaping the narrative conventions of American cinema in films such as Sidney Lumet's *The Pawnbroker*

Top left: in Providence *a dying writer (John Gielgud) makes up fantasies about his legitimate son (Dirk Bogarde), the son's wife (Ellen Burstyn) and his illegitimate son (David Warner) before enjoying his seventy-eighth birthday celebration with them. Top right: Anouk Aimée and Jean-Louis Trintignant in one of the colour-tinted scenes from* A Man and a Woman. *Above: in* Red Desert *Monica Vitti plays an anguished housewife whose neurotic behaviour is enacted in the industrial setting of the Ravenna region of Italy's eastern seaboard*

(1965), where bold use is made of the unexplained shock flashback as memory. Closer to home, Claude Lelouch's popular love story *Un Homme et une Femme* (1966, *A Man and a Woman*) added a fashionable gloss to a time-fractured tale that would have been unthinkable before Resnais and Godard.

Of all the later Resnais films, it is in *Je T'Aime, Je T'Aime* (1968, I Love You, I Love You) that the idea of recurrence, implicit in the title, is most intriguingly developed. It tells the story of a man trapped between past and present and 'jumping' everywhere in time as the events of his life accumulate. In Resnais' continuing struggle to come to terms with the processes of time, it was inevitable that he should eventually draw upon the conventions of science-fiction cinema.

Since movement through time and space is an axiom of science fiction, Resnais' interest in the genre was hardly surprising even if he did not turn out a conventional science-fiction movie. An unlikely list of directors also made forays into the genre. Jean-Luc Godard blended it with his favourite thriller genre in *Alphaville* (1965); but Chris Marker, Resnais' former editor, made a brilliant short film *La Jetée* (1962, The Pier) which reiterated the importance of memory in its tale of a World War III survivor who is sent back in time. François Truffaut's solitary excursion into science fiction – unless his acting performance in Spielberg's *Close Encounters of the Third Kind* (1977) is included – was a less successful because more conventional literary adaptation, *Fahrenheit 451* (1966).

In Hollywood, however, the most notable science-fiction movies were those such as Frankenheimer's *The Manchurian Candidate* (1962) that pursued the theme of time and memory in a story of brainwashing, and the same director's *Seconds* (1966) where an ageing businessman attempts to cheat mortality through bionic surgery but ends up caught in the inexorable progression of time.

What is significant about science-fiction movies of the Sixties, the decade of space-travel and moon-walking, is that most of the films are set in the near future. In *Dr Strangelove, or How I Learned to Stop Worrying and Love the Bomb* and *Seven Days in May* (both 1964), the future is so ominously close that it is arguable whether they count as science fiction at all. Yet Stanley Kubrick's *2001: A Space Odyssey* (1968) implies by its title a future which is just around the corner, where technology governs and almost takes over the life of twenty-first-century man. The paradox is that although the trend appeared to bring the time of science fiction closer to

our own day, the setting of such films was more often out in space, as compared with the science-fiction dramas of the Fifties that usually brought the bug, pod or saucer down to our familiar earth.

Returning to the present tense, the work of Michelangelo Antonioni is most memorable for its painterly qualities, its interplay of figures in a landscape, but his primary concern is with movement, which is by definition an action in or through space and time. The originality of Antonioni lies in the way he utilizes movement inside his images, within the shot, to give a sense of the duration of time. As distinct from Resnais, Antonioni makes little use of memory, preferring to penetrate his characters 'by following them with the camera to discover their most hidden thoughts'. Thus character is revealed not in the instant but in the duration of a shot, sequence or film.

As with Resnais or Godard, the absence or, at best, arbitrary nature of plot means that character becomes more elusive and must be revealed in the give-away details of small gestures – a look, a turn of the head, smoking a cigarette – rather than in any kind of plot-motivated performance. This helps to explain why Antonioni shoots in long takes, since it allows more time for such character traits to be revealed.

Between *Il Grido* (1957, *The Cry*) and *L'Avventura* (1960, *The Adventure*), the style has clearly undergone some tightening up through the insistence on more rapid cutting. *L'Avventura* is, after all, a loose kind of detective story concerning the search for a missing girl, Anna, but the adventure is really what goes on between the characters *around* the search and derives its extraordinary tension from the camera's close observation of movements and actions.

An overview of Antonioni's work from the period immediately after neo-realism when he made *Le Amiche* (1955, The Girl Friends) through *Il Grido* to *Deserto Rosso* (1964, *Red Desert*) reveals that the more interested he becomes in the inner progress of time, the more the physical spaces of his films become open – as in the vast bare landscapes of the Po Valley in *Il Grido* and the ever-present sea and sky of *L'Avventura*. With *La Notte* (1961, *The Night*) the affair which is the central dramatic action of the film occurs almost in one night and against a backdrop of an inhospitable urban landscape which was to be seen more prominently in the later *Red Desert*. Marooned in time and cut off from any chain of causality that might explain how they have come to their present situation, Antonioni's characters have by the time of *L'Eclisse* (1962, *The Eclipse*) and *Red Desert* arrived at a kind of stasis.

MARTYN AUTY

Alain Resnais

Le cinéma, mon amour

Alain Resnais has regularly worked with varied and highly individual writers; yet his recurrent interest in time and memory and his personal style have given unity to his small but distinguished output

There are few masters of modern cinema whose work is more strongly marked by paradox than that of Alain Resnais. He is the creator of a distinctive filmic universe who nevertheless refuses to follow the predominant tendency of contemporary film-making practice – particularly in the 'art cinema' sector – and to present himself as the complete author of his films. Even to talk of 'the films of Alain Resnais' is to risk over-simplification, since each work bears the mark of different collaborators: writers (often with distinctive literary worlds of their own), composers and, of course, varying teams of actors, usually including

three or so leads. Thus, though Resnais' name is indissolubly linked to the avant-garde area of film-making and he is widely seen as an aloof, intellectual film-maker, his approach in many ways approximates far more to that of the great Hollywood directors, John Ford, say, or George Cukor, and his elaborate working methods cry out for the resources of a major Hollywood studio. Similar contradictions run throughout his life and work.

A remarkable generation

Alain Resnais was born at Vannes, Brittany, in 1922 and so belongs to a generation of remarkable film-makers who strongly shaped European cinema in the Sixties and Seventies, including the Italians Pier Paolo Pasolini and Francesco Rosi, the French writer-directors Chris Marker and Alain Robbe-Grillet, Miklós Jancsó from Hungary and the Polish-born Walerian Borowczyk. It is in relation to the work of such film-makers, and not that of the purely French *nouvelle vague* directors, that his career should be judged. Though he made his breakthrough to feature film-making at the

same time as Jean-Luc Godard, François Truffaut and Claude Chabrol, Resnais was ten years older and the shaping forces on his life and work were quite different.

The only child of a provincial pharmacist, Resnais was troubled during childhood by delicate health and much of his early reading was of authors to whom a lonely, intelligent asthmatic was likely to be drawn: Marcel Proust, Aldous Huxley, Katherine Mansfield. From his mother, who educated him at home, he also derived an abiding love of serious music which is very apparent from his choice of scores for his films. But at the same time he developed his life-long passion for comics, especially Mandrake and Dick Tracy (his collection is said to be one of the best in France), and for popular writing of a sub-literary kind, typified by the serials chronicling the adventures of Fantômas.

Resnais studied acting, began a course in film-making at the *Institut des Hautes Etudes Cinématographiques* (IDHEC), the French film school and worked professionally as a film editor. While thus hesitating about the line his career should take, he continued as a passionate amateur film-maker. He had begun with 8mm while still in his teens and later went on to make at least two films of feature length in 16mm. All this early work is lost but, from the accounts by Resnais and his friends and collaborators, it seems that these early films had a personal and often improvisatory quality absent from his subsequent 'official' work.

It was out of a series of studies of painters undertaken in 16mm that Resnais' career as a professional director grew. In 1948 he was commissioned to remake in 35mm a study of *Van Gogh* (1948) initially shot in 1947. He followed this with *Gauguin* and a masterly account of Picasso's *Guernica* (both 1950). In these first documentaries he is concerned to clarify his approach to his subject, confronting it without critical or stylistic preconceptions. Already at this period he had plans and projects for feature films, but in fact the next

Top left: Resnais at work on Muriel, *made on location in Boulogne; he is seen here with Delphine Seyrig. Below left: the French National Library in* Toute la Mémoire du Monde. *Below: concentration-camp scene from Auschwitz in* Night and Fog

Above left: Emmanuelle Riva and Japanese lady in Hiroshima, Mon Amour, *a prize winner at Cannes. Above: Delphine Seyrig and Giorgio Albertazzi in* Last Year in Marienbad. *Left: Yves Montand and Ingrid Thulin in* La Guerre Est Finie, *Resnais' most romantic film. Bottom left: Jean-Paul Belmondo stars with Anny Duperey in* Stavisky . . ., *a period story about a swindler*

eight years were to be spent in documentary work. Together with Georges Franju, he became a dominant figure in French documentary at a time when it far surpassed French feature film-making in its commitment, intelligence and originality.

The five short films completed by Resnais between 1950 and 1958 were on totally divergent subjects: colonization and native art in *Les Statues Meurent Aussi* (1953, Statues Also Die); the Nazi concentration camps in *Nuit et Brouillard* (1955, *Night and Fog*); the French National Library in *Toute la Mémoire du Monde* (1957, The Whole Memory of the World); industrial safety in *Le Mystère de l'Atelier 15* (1957, The Mystery of Workshop 15); and the manufacture of polystyrene in *Le Chant du Styrène* (1958, Styrene Song). Aside from the obvious intelligence and commitment apparent in such a film as the masterly *Night and Fog*, the most remarkable aspect of this series of works is its freedom from any Griersonian concept of documentary as 'the creative interpretation of actuality'. Far from concealing his own directorial presence and attempting to let 'reality' speak for itself, Resnais uses his subjects as pretexts for stylistic experiment. In these short films he develops the particular approaches that will characterize all his early feature-film work – a separation and re-fusion of the elements of image, music and text – and perfects a working method which involves collaboration on equal terms with a writer of real literary quality, such as Paul Eluard for *Guernica* and Raymond Queneau for *Le Chant du Styrène*.

Time and memory
Alain Resnais' debut as a feature film-maker came with *Hiroshima, Mon Amour* (1959, Hiroshima, My Love), which was scripted by the novelist Marguerite Duras. Four further features followed in the Sixties, and in each of them he collaborated with a novelist who had little or no previous experience of feature-film scriptwriting: with Alain Robbe-Grillet on *L'Année Dernière à Marienbad* (1961, *Last Year in Marienbad*); with Jean Cayrol on *Muriel, ou le*

Temps d'un Retour (1963, *Muriel*); with Jorge Semprun on *La Guerre Est Finie* (1966, *The War Is Over*); and with Jacques Sternberg on *Je T'Aime, Je T'Aime* (1968, I Love You, I Love You). It is a measure of Resnais' influence that his first four collaborators all went on to direct feature films of their own.

Though all are highly original, these five films have a considerable stylistic homogeneity. There is a constant return to the problems of time and memory. In *Hiroshima, Mon Amour* past and present come together as two love affairs, 14 years apart, are fused in a woman's mind. By contrast, *Last Year in Marienbad* refuses all chronology. The attempt to separate real and imaginary, this year and last year, is merely one of the many traps set by the writer, Alain Robbe-Grillet; like Duras, he was a pioneer of the *nouveau roman* ('New Novel') and, also like her, went on to become a leading French film-maker of the Sixties and Seventies. In *Muriel* (the writer of which, Jean Cayrol, had previously scripted *Night and Fog*), the focus is again different. Here the strangeness of the film stems from a strict adherence to chronology – even when two simultaneous actions are described – and an openness to the chance occurrences and hazards of shooting. It is one of those rare films that keep strictly to the geography of the real-life setting, the port of Boulogne.

La Guerre Est Finie, a look at the life of a Spanish Communist activist in exile, makes extensive use of what can only be called the 'flash-forward' shots that anticipate events that may or may not unfold in the way the hero, Diego, expects. Perhaps the most original of the films in this respect is *Je T'Aime, Je T'Aime*, a pseudo-science-fiction story in which logic and chronology are almost totally abandoned in favour of an apparently random interweaving of levels of time and reality, actually reflecting an emotional logic that leads inevitably to the hero's death.

All five works reflect those aspects of time which Alain Robbe-Grillet defines in his critical writings as the prime characteristic of modern fiction – a present tense:

'. . . which is continually inventing itself . . . which repeats itself . . . modifies itself, contradicts itself, without even accumulating enough bulk to constitute a past.'

Into the Seventies

Je T'Aime, Je T'Aime was a commercial failure. Its release coincided with the political upheavals of May 1968 when a new kind of commitment was expected of film-makers. Six years elapsed before another Resnais film was released. His two films of the Seventies, *Stavisky . . .* (1974), from another script by Jorge Semprun, and *Providence* (1977), an English-language production from a script by the British dramatist David Mercer, are works which display to the full Resnais' meticulous control of every aspect of film-making. There is, however, a certain loss of force. Immaculately shot where the earlier films had been radically inventive, they seem cold and unapproachable, and are marred by a certain shallowness of conception.

No such reservations are needed about *Mon Oncle d'Amérique* (1980, *My American Uncle*), scripted by Jean Gruault, which is Resnais' freest film since *Je T'Aime, Je T'Aime*. Though the project dates back many years, the authors have succeeded in maintaining a light and ironic tone. The film interweaves the story of three disparate characters – two men and a woman who has contacts with both – with an exposition by the French biologist Henri Laborit of his theories about human and animal

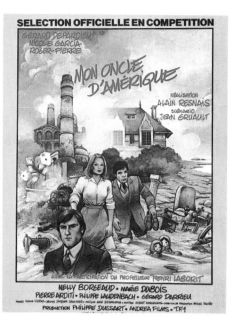

Above: a Cannes Film Festival poster for My American Uncle, *Resnais' first big commercial success. Bottom left: Ellen Burstyn and David Warner in* Providence

action and aggression, and with crucial reference points from Forties films starring Jean Gabin, Jean Marais and Danielle Darrieux. With its counterpointing of documentary and fiction, personal memory and didacticism, film recollections and contemporary engagement, *My American Uncle* forms a perfect summing-up of Resnais' career.   ROY ARMES

Filmography

1935 Fantômas (8mm short) (unfinished); L'Aventure de Guy (8mm short) (+photo+ed). '45 Le Sommeil d' Albertine (short) (photo+ed only); Schéma d'une Identification (short). '46 Ouvert pour Cause d'Inventaire. '47 Visite à Lucien Coutaud (short); Visite à Félix Labisse (short); Portrait de Henri Goetz (short); Visite à Hans Hartung (short); Visite à Max Ernst/Journée Naturelle (short); Visite à Oscar Dominguez (short); Le Bâton (short) (ass ed only); Visite à César Doméla; La Bague (short); L'Alcoöl Tue (short) (dir under pseudonym). '48 Malfray (short) (co-dir); Châteaux de France (short); Van Gogh (short) (+ed). '49 Tournée Boussac en Afrique Noire (ed only); Paris 1900 (ass dir + ass ed only); Versailes et ses Fantômes (sp. eff. only). '50 Gauguin (short) (+ed); Guernica (short) (co-dir+ed). '51 La Chanson du Mal-Aimé (ass ed only). '52 Compromitas (ed only); Saint-Tropez, Devoir de Vacances (short) (ed only). '53 Les Statues Meurent Aussi (short) (co-dir+ed). '54 Aux Frontières de l'Homme (short) (ed only). '55 La Pointe Courte (co-ed only); Nuit et Brouillard (short) (USA/GB: Night and Fog). '57 Toute la Mémoire du Monde (short) (+ed); Le Mystère de l'Atelier 15 (short) (co-dir); L'Oeil du Maître (short) (ed only); Broadway by Light (short) (ed only). '58 Le Chant du Styrène (short) (+ed); Paris à l'Automne (short) (ed only). '59 Hiroshima, Mon Amour (FR-JAP). '61 L'Année Dernière à Marienbad (FR-IT) (USA/GB: Last Year in Marienbad). '63 Muriel, ou le Temps d'un Retour (FR-IT) (USA/GB: Muriel). '66 La Guerre Est Finie (FR-SWED) (USA/GB: The War Is Over). '67 Loin du Vietnam (co-dir) (USA/GB: Far From Vietnam). '68 Je T'Aime, Je T'Aime (+co-sc). '72 L'An 01 (short) (co-dir uncred). '74 Stavisky . . . (FR-IT). '77 Providence (FR-SWITZ). '80 Mon Oncle d'Amérique (GB: My American Uncle).

Pierre-Courau et Raymond Froment présentent

L'ANNÉE DERNIÈRE A MARIENBAD

avec Giorgio Albertazzi — Delphine Seyrig — Sacha Pitoëff

Scénario et Dialogue Alain Robbe-Grillet — Réalisation Alain Resnais

1

4

LAST YEAR IN MARIENBAD

What really happened 'last year in Marienbad'? Rarely has critical speculation over a film's content been so active. It was reported that not even the director, Alain Resnais, and the writer, Alain Robbe-Grillet, were in complete agreement. Resnais claimed that an encounter had occurred the previous year while Robbe-Grillet declared that one sometimes had the impression that the whole episode was a figment of the narrator's imagination. But perhaps this much-publicized divergence of views was a calculated ploy, a hint to the spectator as to how the film should be approached – that is, with no preconceived idea. One eminent French critic, Jacques Brunius, declared unequivocally after several viewings that it was the greatest film ever made; others dismissed it as a pretentious art-movie spoof. One thing is certain: a true appreciation of the film calls for the audience's complete surrender to its unique form and mood.

The first voice to be heard is that of the narrator, faintly and then more clearly, as the camera examines the furnishings of a vast, baroque hotel with its endless, empty corridors, numbered rooms, ornate ceilings and glittering mirrors. The voice intones: 'Once again I walk, once again, along these corridors, across these salons, these galleries, in this edifice from another century . . .' In one of the great salons an audience sits motionless, watching a play. 'And now,' says the on-stage actress, 'I am yours'. The curtain falls. The play's conclusion prefigures the final surrender of the film's heroine.

Gradually, through snatches of overheard conversations, shots of curiously posed single figures or static groups, the film establishes its disturbing world, which might be dream or stylized reality. The three central characters start to reveal their identities: the melancholy woman who is staying in the hotel with a gaunt-faced man who may, or may not, be her husband and an insinuating stranger, the narrator, who claims that the woman agreed a year ago to meet him again now.

She denies all knowledge of him or previous acquaintanceship but the stranger relentlessly pursues his detailed tactic of persuasion. Does she not recall the time when, while walking through the garden, she slipped and broke off the heel of her shoe? Later on, when they are walking together, she stumbles and grabs his arm for support. This is seen in long-shot and it is uncertain whether she actually breaks the heel. Is this the scene that, according to his claim, happened in the past, or a re-enactment, or history repeating itself? In this delicate fusion between past and present

nothing can ever be quite certain.

Several questions suggest themselves. Is this strange château, set in its formal gardens, an exclusive nursing home and is the stranger perhaps the woman's psychoanalyst, striving to make her recall a past emotional experience which she has unconsciously blocked from her memory? And her clothes, quintessential expression of outré Parisian chic by Chanel . . . do they provide a clue? It seems that in general a white dress is worn for scenes in the past and black for the present – but not quite consistently. What about the

7

3

6

shadowy figure of the man who 'may be her husband' . . . husband? lover? brother? He is frequently seen playing a pre-ordained match-stick game which he invariably wins. Usually it is the stranger whom he defeats.

At one point, when the stranger seems almost on the verge of forcing the woman to admit the reality of the past events he describes and has left the couple alone, she turns to her 'husband' and begs him, with a hint of desperation, not to leave her. His reply is reasoned and cool: 'But it is you who are leaving me – you know that!' When his prediction proves true, she departs with no sense of joy or fulfilment; she seems rather to have left her haven for an unknown destination. In this contest of wills and persuasion she appears to be the victim of an inexorable fate, possibly leading to her death or some kind of oblivion.

The eternal fascination of *Last Year in Marienbad* is that each time the spectator feels sure of having grasped the key to its sphinx-like riddle, it presents another aspect to disprove his theory. Though not completely convincing, the theory of the recurrent dream is worth considering. The obsessive nature of such dreams still allows for some

measure of improvisation of the events to suit the dreamer's fancy; they can incorporate acceptance and rejection of particular elements – even adjusted replays.

When, for example, the woman asks the stranger to leave her alone, he leans against a balustrade which crumbles under the pressure. There is a quick cut-away. This must surely be a moment of fantasy and when the balustrade is next seen it ought to be intact. But it is still broken! Does this reflect the dreamer's unshakeable conviction that the event actually occurred? Is it not more likely to be the woman's wish-fulfilment, a persistent longing to rid herself of the importunate stranger. On reflection, the second explanation is more plausible. But with everything in this enigmatic film it is a matter of 'I think so'; never 'I know for sure'.

On further inspection, *Last Year in Marienbad*, with its subtle clues, its intricate juggling with past and present, its depiction of a reality that might be dream or of a dream with a hallucinatory hint of reality, takes on the aspect of a masterly detective story. The figures – for they are figures rather than personages – are moved through their

exquisitely controlled paces by a director who demonstrates the precision of a master chess player. Its enclosed world has the mesmeric

quality of a superior fairy-tale with, like many of the most haunting fairy-tales, a touch of veiled menace.   DEREK PROUSE

Directed by Alain Resnais, 1961
Prod co: Terra-Film/Société Nouvelle des Films Cormoran/Précitel/Como-Films/Les Films Tamara/Cinetel/Silver Films (Paris)/Cineriz (Rome). **prod:** Pierre Courau (Précitel), Raymond Froment (Terra-Film). **sc:** Alain Robbe-Grillet. **photo:** Sacha Vierny (Dyaliscope). **ed:** Henri Colpi, Jasmine Chasney. **art dir:** Jacques Saulnier. **mus:** Francis Seyrig. **cost:** Chanel, Bernard Evein. **sd:** Guy Villette. **r/t:** 94 minutes. World premiere: Venice Film Festival, 29 August 1961. Released in the USA and GB as *Last Year in Marienbad*.
Cast: Delphine Seyrig (*A*), Giorgio Albertazzi (*X*), Sacha Pitoëff (*M*), Françoise Bertin, Luce Garcia-Ville, Héléna Kornel, Françoise Spira, Karin Toeche-Mittler, Pierre Barbaud, Wilhelm Von Deek, Jean Lanier, Gérard Lorin, Davide Montemuri, Gilles Quéant, Gabriel Werner.

A vast, grandiose hotel, set in formal grounds, is sparsely peopled with guests standing around in statuesque poses (1) or static conversation groups, watching an obscure drama (2) or playing an apparently simple game (3). The hotel provides the setting for a strange encounter: a beautiful woman, A, staying there with M, who is possibly her husband (4), is approached by a man, X (5). He claims that they had had a close relationship here the previous year, when they had

arranged to meet again a year thence with the intention of going away together (6). She denies all knowledge of this (7). But he assails her with such persuasive detail (8) of their shared experience that her resistance crumbles and he prevails upon her to leave with him. She sits rigidly in her bedroom awaiting the stroke of midnight before joining him at the appointed rendezvous outside, from which she can see the hotel she is leaving forever (9).

9

Poet of Malaise

Michelangelo Antonioni

Antonioni once named modesty as his greatest fault, but there are some who might laugh and call it obscurity instead. MGM, for instance, After the *coup* of *Blow-Up* (1966), they invited Antonioni to America and hired him to make what was supposed to be a prestigious blockbuster about student revolt – significant, violent, sexy and profitable. It proved to be a study of space and colour, with the incidental anger of the age dissolving into the ochre desert and the reverie of a perpetual explosion. No one got its point, or realized that the film was a rhapsody.

But, for Michelangelo Antonioni, the ending of *Zabriskie Point* (1970) was a heartfelt statement about the eclipse of love and human values. He had made the film he wanted, no matter how little he seemed to grasp the American language and movie idioms. *Zabriskie Point* is about a land marred by garish constructions and development plans. But its harsh and enigmatic purity is restored at the end by an act of cinematic will: the slow-motion disruption of all the ingredients of an advertiser's dream domestic interior. The disintegration of things attains a lyrical anguish in which the song subdues the pain without drifting into travesty. This world has already given up its soul, and so objects, space and the creep of time are all that remain.

Deserted spaces

Antonioni's career seems to show a drastic alteration in the middle Sixties. He had worked in Italy on a series of pained, psychological stories of love-affairs in which the dread of failure became more universal and somehow less circumstantial. Then he left his native country and began to travel – to England, to America, to China and to the several countries that comprise the existential scene shifts of *Professione: Reporter* (1975, *The Passenger*).

But the change was less than it seemed. His movies have always been about the gaps between people and the relations between exterior and interior. *Blow-Up* has an odd insight into the real 'swinging' London, but it is much more fascinated by the way a photographer believes that his pictures have found truth at the far end of a magical park. Similarly, *The Passenger* is about the possibility of entering and leaving buildings – virtually the entire action can be expressed in those terms. Vagaries of place and time fade away as it

Above left and centre: The Passenger – *the glorious hotel standing alone in space, and Antonioni shooting part of the same film. Above right: in* Blow-Up *a promiscuous London fashion photographer, Thomas (David Hemmings, seen above with model Verushka), accidentally photographs a murder . . . but the evidence mysteriously disappears*

Below left: Cronaca di un Amore – *Paola and Guido (Lucia Bose and Massimo Girotti) have an adulterous affair, which the husband Enrico tries to have investigated. Enrico's death in a car-crash causes the lovers to panic, and Paola is left abandoned. Below:* La Notte – *a crisis in the marriage of Lidia (Jeanne Moreau) and Giovanni (Marcello Mastroianni as a novelist*

No other director seems as shy as Michelangelo Antonioni. He is unconvinced by society; his lovers look away from each other towards empty space. The director himself is so withdrawn, hesitant or difficult that he has released only one picture in the last ten years

works towards the sublime resolution in which the camera transcends one lethal room, wanders across a courtyard and then turns to look back at where it has been – like a spirit risen from the grave.

Passing strange

The Passenger is a spiritual film, and it reminds us of how in a 1957 interview, when asked what was the problem closest to his heart, Antonioni replied 'Can there exist a saint without God?' Religious authority never has a foothold in his films. Social institutions are regarded as prisons. But with his camera, Antonioni has tried to detect holiness, and

gradually he has taught audiences his own reverence for desolation.

His characters are wistful dreamers, torn between the search for satisfaction and encroaching decline, and sometimes unable to look at one another because of the pain attendant upon seeing and being seen. In the early Sixties, especially, he was treated as the studiously forlorn poet of pessimism and dismay, dissecting the wan and nervously restricted romanticism of actress Monica Vitti, who features in five of his works.

But that overlooks the real significance of detachment in Antonioni's films, and the way it has grown into something more like mystical

exhilaration. *The Passenger*, for instance, is his most resigned, calm and delighted film. It has found the world of space which people have done so much to confuse, and it has discovered beauty there. No other film-maker can invest place with such mystery and resonance, or make characters seem like pilgrims on a metaphysical threshold.

Profession: film-maker

Born in Ferrara, in 1912, Antonioni recalled it as 'a marvellous little city on the Paduan plain, antique and silent.' Already he had an intuition of the décor of his films; reality becoming an evocative model, like the deserted city in *L'Avventura* (1960, *The Adventure*).

The film's dilemma – the puzzle of a missing girl – begins to seem insoluble, but can be felt . . . like the scarred surface of the wall in *La Notte* (1961, *The Night*), when Lidia (Jeanne Moreau) pulls away a flake of rust, suggesting that the history of human time is being handled.

As a child, Antonioni played games that seem relevant to his films. He had a fascination for buildings, and he would draw plans, make façades and even construct three-dimensional models. He would add human figures to these ideal buildings, and begin to make up stories about what they were doing there. Thus the emblematic significance of an environment or

running out of ideas) leads them both to try to have affairs, but nothing comes of either dalliance. Below: in L'Eclisse Vittoria (Monica Vitti) ends a relationship with Ricardo and begins another with a young stockbroker Piero (Alain Delon), yet is unwilling to make it permanent. The film finishes with both of them failing to turn up at a pre-arranged rendez-vous.

Below right: Red Desert – Giuliana (Monica Vitti, in black) is a neurotic wife obsessed with her young son . . . until the arrival of Corrado, a visiting engineer. She tries to seduce him at a frustrated orgy (seen here), but only succeeds later when close to nervous breakdown after her son has pretended to be paralyzed as a kind of joke

33

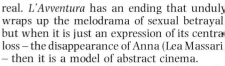

Above: in Zabriskie Point *Mark, a dissatisfied Californian student, steals a private plane; he meets Daria who also becomes a committed revolutionary. She vividly imagines blowing up an expensive villa in Death Valley. A desert love-in (here) symbolizes their attitude to bourgeois morality. Below:* The Passenger – *a famous TV documentary reporter (Jack Nicholson, here with Maria Schneider) assumes the identity of the dead man in his hotel room . . . which leads to trouble . . .*

a space: the lift-shaft in his first feature, *Cronaca di un Amore* (1950, Chronicle of a Love); the sense of fraud that hangs over the film-set in *La Signora Senza Camelie* (1953, Woman Without Camellias); the frontier of the beach in *Le Amiche* (1955, The Girl Friends); the grey wasteland of *Il Grido* (1957, The Cry) . . . and so on, to the tumult of the stock exchange in *L'Eclisse* (1962, The Eclipse), the cramped orgy room with boats looming up in the mist outside in *Deserto Rosso* (1964, Red Desert), the photographer's studio in *Blow-Up*. Finally, the African hotel, the London house, the Gaudi buildings and the impassive but glowingly

sentient Hotel de la Gloria in *The Passenger*, a film in which Jack Nicholson learns that he can be still and let himself be carried along by the sweet flow of change, time and fiction.

Just as he was intensely fashionable in the late Fifties and early Sixties, so today Antonioni is not too far from neglect. The early films are not easy to see, and thus no one could easily appreciate the Renoir-like fluency of camera movement and spatial link in *Cronaca di un Amore, La Signora Senza Camelie* and *Le Amiche*. Perhaps love has wings so that it may fly away, but in *The Passenger* the images of flight suggest escape and transcendence more than loss, and in *Zabriskie Point* the stolen aircraft is like a mythological bird.

Reality eclipsed

The series of films that began with *L'Avventura* are sometimes perilously close to self-pity and intellectual pretension. *Red Desert* is a failure of nearly unbearable and uncommunicated distress, despite the first bold use of colour and the story of the island – the first imaginary location in an Antonioni film, and the clearest sign that none of the places has been merely

real. *L'Avventura* has an ending that unduly wraps up the melodrama of sexual betrayal, but when it is just an expression of its central loss – the disappearance of Anna (Lea Massari) – then it is a model of abstract cinema.

L'Eclisse goes much further, and it is the most seriously overlooked of his films to date. Its long coda – of city sights and moments, the site of an appointment not kept, and of a street light coming on as an eclipse occurs – is a wondrous departure from the cold passion that existed briefly between Piero (Alain Delon) and Vittoria (Monica Vitti). It is as if a film-maker had managed to escape plot and character without denying humanism – and that is not far from Antonioni's total achievement.

Blow-Up never loses its beauty or its humour, never slackens its sense of the noble folly of preoccupation. More than most of Antonioni's pictures, it owes something to its source: the story by Julio Cortazar. Its people are photographs only, bewildered and hurt that they have no more substance. Nevertheless, the darkroom scenes and the reconstruction of the 'event' through pictures is a nostalgic tribute to narrative and suspense, just as Vanessa Redgrave gives an uncanny rendering of presence without explanation.

A time will come when *Zabriskie Point* and *The Passenger* will be reclaimed from indifference. It may then become apparent that no one has ever used the wide-screen better or more hopefully than Antonioni in *Zabriskie Point*, a history of the universe that makes the desert the centre of civilization. As for *The Passenger*, it is a grave and lovely bow to Romanticism, purpose and social significance – all too aware that the movement of the camera and the passage of time are more profound.

DAVID THOMSON

Filmography
1942 I Due Foscari (co-sc; +ass. dir. only); Un Pilota Ritorna (co-sc. only); Les Visiteurs du Soir (ass. dir. only) (FR) (USA: The Devil's Envoys). **'47** Caccia Tragica (co-sc. only) (GB: Tragic Pursuit); Gente del Po (doc. short) (+sc). **'48** N.U./Nettezza Urbana (doc. short) (+sc); Roma – Montevideo (doc. short) (+sc); Oltre l'Oblio (doc. short) (+sc). **'49** Bomarzo (doc. short) (+sc); L'Amorosa Menzogna (doc. short) (+sc); Superstizione (doc. short) (+sc); Ragazze in Bianco (doc. short) (+sc). **'50** Sette Canne, Un Vestito (doc. short) (+sc); La Villa dei Mostri (doc. short) (+sc); La Funivia del Faloria (doc. short) (+sc); Cronaca di un Amore (+co-sc;+ed). **'52** Lo Sceicco Bianco (co-sc. only) (USA/GB: The White Sheik). **'53** I Vinti (+co-sc) (IT-FR); La Signora Senza Camelie (+co-sc;+ed) (USA: Woman Without Camellias); Amore in Città *ep* Tentato Suicidio (+co-sc). **'55** Uomini in Più (doc) (prod. only); Le Amiche (+co-sc) (GB: The Girl Friends). **'57** Il Grido (+co-sc) (IT-USA) (GB: The Cry). **'58** La Tempesta (2nd unit dir. only, uncredited) (IT-YUG-FR) (GB: The Tempest). **'59** Nel Segno di Roma (co-dir. under pseudonym) (IT-FR-GER) (GB: Sign of the Gladiator). **'60** L'Avventura (+co-sc) (IT-FR) (USA/GB: The Adventure). **'61** La Notte (+co-sc) (IT-FR) (GB: The Night). **'62** L'Eclisse (+co-sc) (FR-IT) (USA/GB: The Eclipse). **'64** Deserto Rosso (+co-sc) (IT-FR) (USA/GB: Red Desert). **'65** I Tre Volti *ep* Il Provino; Michelangelo Antonioni (doc) (appearance as himself only). **'66** Blow-Up (+co-sc) (GB). **'70** Zabriskie Point (+co-sc) (USA). **'73** Chung Kuo/La Cina/China (doc) (+sc). **'75** Professione: Reporter (+co-sc) (IT-FR-SP) (USA/GB: The Passenger). **'80** Il Mistero di Oberwald (+co-sc;+co-ed).

BLEAK HOUSE

During the Sixties, harsh winds of economic reality blew through Hollywood and spending more money was an uncertain solution; new ideas appealed more to the youthful audiences

The Sixties began with the inspiration of John F. Kennedy's inaugural speech which claimed that America would 'bear any burden, pay any price' to keep the world as strong and pure as the United States; with the defeat of Eisenhower 'the torch has been passed to a new generation of Americans'. So it was Kennedy who first permitted the build-up of American troops in Vietnam; and under Lyndon Johnson the country was nearly torn apart by race riots and internal dissension. The decade drew to an end ironically with the presidency passing in 1969 to Richard M. Nixon, who had been Kennedy's losing opponent in the 1960 election. The nation was on the path to Watergate. Not even Hollywood could completely ignore such momentous events.

It was a decade of immense change for the American cinema as it was for American society as a whole. After the marking-time of the Fifties, when the widespread post-war prosperity combined with fear of the blacklist to produce a period of relative artistic stagnation, the Sixties was a time of revolution in Hollywood. Only in the Twenties, with the transition from silent movies to sound and all the problems consequent upon that change, was there havoc comparable to that wreaked in Hollywood during the Sixties.

Television's rising importance had led Hollywood to experiment with various forms of wide-screen projection in order to combat the domestic competition but the nature of the movies had not significantly altered. In the early Sixties Doris Day was America's Sweetheart, riding high on the crest of a wave of films such as *Pillow Talk* (1959), *Lover Come Back* (1961) and *That Touch of Mink* (1962). By the end of the decade Day's star was firmly eclipsed by the new style of movies represented by *Easy Rider* and *The Wild Bunch* (both 1969).

One element that hastened the inevitable change in movieland was the death or retirement of so many key figures from the golden years of the American film industry. Two of the Marx Brothers, Chico and Harpo, died. So did Clark Gable, Marilyn Monroe, Charles Laughton, Judy Holliday, Buster Keaton and Judy Garland. From behind the camera Michael Curtiz, Jerry Wald, David O. Selznick, Robert Rossen, Leo McCarey and Josef von Sternberg went on to the Great Cutting Room in the sky. Louis B. Mayer had died back in 1957. Jack L. Warner made only a few productions after buying the stage success *My Fair Lady* for screen adaptation. Darryl F. Zanuck achieved an important success with *The Longest Day* (1962) and then took over 20th Century-Fox again, running it with his son Richard until increasing losses at the end of the decade forced Richard's resignation in 1970 and Zanuck's own in 1971.

Sam Goldwyn no longer made films; and MGM, under the guidance of Kirk Kerkorian, appeared markedly less successful in the late sixties; Universal headed for television and the tourist industry, while Paramount sought refuge in the arms of the conglomerate Gulf and Western; Warner Brothers was absorbed into the Kinney

group. United Artists, which started life as an attempt by four independent film-makers (Mary Pickford, Douglas Fairbanks Sr, Charles Chaplin and D. W. Griffith) to free themselves from the shackles of studio interference, ironically found new salvation under the corporate umbrella of Transamerica Corporation. The jailers had relieved the inmates of control of the asylum.

If any one film made in the Sixties symbolized the end of the old Hollywood, it was *Cleopatra* (1963), the costs of which finally escalated to $40 million; 20th Century-Fox had originally wanted its producer, Walter Wanger, simply to remake the 1917 silent film of the same title starring Theda Bara. In 1962, the year of the film's production, the studio lost $39.8 million after taxes – and also, in consequence, the services of its president, Spyros Skouras.

Cleopatra was a glorious swan-song for the old Hollywood, just as its star, Elizabeth Taylor, was one of the last stars who had been successfully manufactured by the studios. By 1967 Hollywood

Top: shooting a scene in the studio for My Fair Lady; *the massive technology required for a major-budget movie is apparent in this production still. Above: Raf Vallone plays an Italian-American longshoreman about to come to a sticky end for betraying illegal immigrants to the authorities; Arthur Miller originally drafted* A View From the Bridge *in verse to heighten the intensity of the melodramatic story but changed to prose for the Broadway production. His friend Norman Rosten wrote the screenplay*

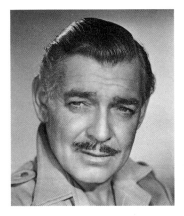

Above, from top: among the established Hollywood stars who died in the Sixties were: Clark Gable (1960); Chico Marx (1961) and Harpo Marx (1964); Judy Holliday (1965); and Boris Karloff (1969)

was regarding the phenomenal box-office returns of *Bonnie and Clyde* and *The Graduate* (both 1967) with the sort of adulation that confirmed the birth of a new era.

Both *Bonnie and Clyde* and *The Graduate* were the work of stars and directors who trained in the New York theatre rather than on Hollywood sound stages. Arthur Penn had directed two long-running William Gibson plays before his first Hollywood success, *The Miracle Worker* (1962), his second film. But it was *Bonnie and Clyde* that established him and his stars, Warren Beatty and Faye Dunaway, in the new Hollywood Establishment. Similarly Mike Nichols' *The Graduate* elevated Dustin Hoffman from minor Broadway actor to top movie star.

Another Easterner, Sidney Lumet, who made his films mostly in New York or Europe, was responsible for a change in the old order that was perhaps still more significant. In the Fifties Lumet had directed some of the best plays networked on live television from New York. A similar style can be seen in his early features, *Vu du Pont* (1961, *A View From the Bridge*) and *Long Day's Journey Into Night* (1962), both originally Broadway plays, by Arthur Miller and Eugene O'Neill respectively. In *The Pawnbroker* (1965) – in which he elicits from Rod Steiger one of the most disciplined performances of this erratic actor's career – the pawnshop owner suffers the torture of his memories of the Nazi concentration camp which he survived. When a young black prostitute (Thelma Oliver) offers her body to the pawnbroker as a bribe, the baring of her breasts serves only to remind the man of his wife's sexual humiliation in a Nazi officers' brothel. Such explicit display of nudity ran contrary to the censorship rules still current in Hollywood at that time, and the film was refused a Seal of Approval. When the film was released anyway by its intrepid distributors, the Ely Landau Organization, it was received with acclaim by critics and public alike, to the amazement of the Production Code Authority, which believed that the exposure of two such unashamed nipples to the eyes of persons who might be young or unmarried would undoubtedly cause the entire moral universe to explode. They may well have been right, of course. *Deep Throat* (1972) was only seven years away.

In the Sixties, television graduates replaced Broadway or studio-trained talent as the major new fund of writers and directors for Hollywood. Television, particularly in the halcyon pioneering days of the Fifties, was now the medium that offered excitement to creative youngsters rather than the traditional New York stage or a film industry that was feeling the cold frost caused by declining box-office figures and rising costs.

Franklin J. Schaffner and John Frankenheimer both produced films of political edge early in their careers – a chance that might well have been denied them if their early training had been in Hollywood pap rather than the best of network-television drama. Frankenheimer's *Seven Days in May* (1964) showed the former television director at his best; he conjured an immaculate performance from Fredric March as the weak American president who is about to be deposed by an ambitious general (Burt Lancaster). Schaffner cut his teeth on a feature based on author Gore Vidal's acid view of the American presidency, *The Best Man* (1964), before achieving true Hollywood fame with his Oscar for *Patton* (1970).

Two further examples of the successful television transplant were provided by Norman Jewison and William Friedkin. Jewison started earlier with such unmemorable features as *40 Pounds of Trouble* (1962) and *The Thrill of It All* (1963) before producing the goods with Steve McQueen as star in *The Cincinnati Kid* (1965) though total approval by the Hollywood establishment was denied until 1967 when *In the Heat of the Night*, which he produced and directed, won due recognition at the Academy Awards. Thereafter he teamed up with McQueen again to make the visually dazzling but ultimately empty *The Thomas Crown Affair* (1968); and his Sixties career finished with the damp squib of *Gaily, Gaily* (1969), an uninspired adaptation of Ben Hecht's autobiographical short stories.

Friedkin, on the other hand, began in much more interesting fashion with the film version of Harold Pinter's *The Birthday Party* and the riotous *The Night They Raided Minsky's* (both 1968). Again he became a truly famous director only when his flair was matched by commercial success with *The French Connection* (1971) and then, of course, *The Exorcist* (1973); but his debut in the world of features had been most auspicious.

Far left: the Allies make an unsuccessful parachute raid on a Normandy village, a tragic episode in The Longest Day, *which concerns the D-Day landings; it was one of the last blockbusters to be made in black and white. Left: Sidney Lumet directs* The Group *(1965) on location in New York; he is seen here with Candice Bergen during a wedding scene. The film, based on Mary McCarthy's novel, tells the story of a group of graduates from a girls' college during the Thirties*

Top left: Jason Robards and Norman Wisdom perform a comedy routine at a burlesque theatre in The Night They Raided Minsky's. *Top right: Sidney Poitier as a visiting policeman from the big city and Rod Steiger as a small-town Southern cop shake hands in mutual respect at the end of* In the Heat of the Night. *Above: a huge open-air set of New York was built on the 20th Century-Fox lot for* Hello, Dolly!

This is not to suggest that studio-fostered Californian talent evaporated in the Sixties. But little of it was new. Richard Fleischer, John Sturges, Stanley Kramer and Richard Brooks had all begun their careers in the Forties. Roger Corman, who started in the Fifties, was relatively new, but he operated outside traditional studio boundaries. None of them could match the originality of such television graduates as Mel Brooks, who made the now-classic *The Producers* in 1967, or his TV co-writer on *Get Smart*, Buck Henry, whose adaptation of Charles Webb's novel, *The Graduate*, devastated the film industry that same year.

One of the saddest losses of the Sixties was the virtual disappearances of the original screen musical in the tradition of *Top Hat* (1935), *Cover Girl* (1944) and *Singin' in the Rain* (1952). The few big musicals that were made had usually been Broadway successes first – which persuaded studios to invest heavily in the hope of achieving sure-fire success. *West Side Story* (1961), which translated well to the screen, was garnished with 11 Oscars; and Jack L. Warner made a considerable profit from *My Fair Lady* (1964), though he had invested a fortune in buying the rights to Lerner and Loewe's stage show.

The awesome success of *The Sound of Music* (1965) only confirmed the trend to stage adaptations, which did not diminish when screen originals failed at the box-office. For instance, actress Julie Andrews and director Robert Wise flopped in *Star!* (1968) and Rex Harrison embarrassed everyone including himself as *Dr Dolittle* (1967). The apotheosis of the Sixties musical was reached when Barbra Streisand, fresh from the excellent *Funny Girl* (1968), and Gene Kelly, who was the greatest exponent of the musical as an art-form, combined as star and director to perpetrate the dreadful screen version of *Hello, Dolly!* (1969) at a cost which 20th Century-Fox executives could barely bring themselves to admit.

Perhaps the key screen figure of the decade was James Bond. The costs of the Bond movies escalated, though they were made in English studios for economy; they increasingly rejected the Ian Fleming novels, retaining mainly the titles and some of the characters, and they had progressively more implausible plots; they were obsessed with mechanical gimmickry. Inevitably there was a trail of imitations such as the Matt Helm films starring Dean Martin, and several television series, beginning with *The Man From UNCLE* (1964–68). Though Martin Ritt's *The Spy Who Came in From the Cold* (1965), based on John Le Carré's novel, made a brief stir, the success of the Bond films meant that the spy genre placed a greater emphasis on escapism than on naturalism.

By the end of the Sixties it was obvious that the films which hit the jackpot were the ones that appealed to young people aged between 18 and 24. They now formed the bulk of the cinemas' audiences. Though some youth movies were failures – for example, *Beach Blanket Bingo* and *How to Stuff a Wild Bikini* (both 1965) – no movie after *The Graduate* and *Bonnie and Clyde* was likely to be successful unless the kids went to see it and liked what they saw.

The year 1969 saw the appearance of a number of movies that bore witness to this trend. *Easy Rider*, which cost a paltry $800,000 to make, netted Peter Fonda and Dennis Hopper a fortune as the kids 'dropped out' and tuned in to the best of the bike movies while Jack Nicholson rose to stardom on the handlebars of its fame. *The Wild Bunch* suggested that violence artfully displayed was a commercial proposition and *Butch Cassidy and the Sundance Kid* (1969) confirmed the suspicion that, though the kids might despise the old myths, they needed the new ones just as badly. Hollywood had grown up and grown fat on feeding the dreams of the millions. Whatever the superficial changes, the movie city knew that it would survive for many more years if it could discover what these new dreams were.

COLIN SHINDLER

When *The Graduate* was released in 1967, it became something of a cult film with the 18–25 age group. It represented a breakthrough for Hollywood with these young people – students and others went to see it again and again. Its popularity far outstripped the original expectations of its makers. There was even a 26-page article, assessing its merits, in the *New York Times*.

The year 1968 was to be a time of unrest around the world, particularly among students and other youth. In America that unrest eventually crystallized into opposition to the Vietnam War, but in 1967 the issue was not yet clearly focused – there was only a general dissatisfaction with the *status quo*. The anarchic mood of *The Graduate* perfectly matched the feelings of the time. It combined humour with satire on social and sexual customs, complemented by the music of Simon and Garfunkel.

Benjamin, the slightly unprepossessing hero of the film, is fresh out of college and uncertain whether to go on to graduate school. An innocent in a sophisticated society, he is seen by his elders as a means to fulfil their own ambitions, while he himself is trying to search out an honest and sincere way to live his life. Only Elaine Robinson, the daughter of his father's business partner and apparently the only other young person in his environment, is able to communicate with him. Benjamin has difficulty in relating to the world of his parents, from which he feels cut off by invisible barriers – as the words of Paul Simon's opening song, 'The Sound of Silence', suggest.

Benjamin belongs to a wealthy family in Los Angeles, affluent members of the world's richest society – financial insecurity is no longer a problem as it had been in earlier films about the difficulties of youthful characters. At his homecoming party after graduation, a family friend whispers one word of advice in his ear: 'Plastics'. Benjamin retires to his room, realizing that he is estranged from a world in which financial success is the only measure of value.

Benjamin's alienation from his culture throughout the film is symbolized by shots through glass, cutting him off from direct participation in others' experience. At the party, the guests are seen in wide-angle distortion through the eye-mask of Benjamin's new diving suit. Mrs Robinson's first approach to him is shown through a fish tank – she will be the predator in their relationship. Several times Benjamin's individual and nonconformist viewpoint is emphasized in subjective shots through the lenses of his sunglasses. When he finally runs off with Elaine, the audience sees the couple through the windows of the bus, creating a final barrier through which even their ultimate silence is unheard.

Although *The Graduate* brought the 30-year-old Dustin Hoffman to fame as a hero of youth culture, it did not establish him as a rebel in the Dean or Brando mould of the

Fifties. Benjamin graduated with honours and was the debating champion.

He is, above all, a nice guy who lives by his own standards of truth. He never really challenges the way things are; he just tries to remain personally genuine in a fundamentally hypocritical society. His uncertainty touches many chords in the audience: his difficulty in getting served at the bar, his fear of public embarrassment, his hesitancy and lack of social grace – problems every young adult has faced.

His naivety is at its height in his relationship with Mrs Robinson, Elaine's mother, who is magnificently portrayed as an alcoholic but infinitely seductive bitch by Anne Bancroft. He not unnaturally assumes that physical sex and emotional intimacy should go together. He therefore cannot understand Mrs Robinson's refusal to talk about herself and her interests even after they have made love. But Benjamin remains uncorrupted; he continues to call his mistress 'Mrs

Directed by Mike Nichols, 1967
Prod co: Avco Embassy. **prod:** Lawrence Turman. **sc:** Calder Willingham, Buck Henry, from a novel by Charles Webb. **photo** (Panavision, Technicolor): Robert Surtees. **ed:** Sam O'Steen. **art dir:** Richard Sylbert. **mus:** Dave Grusin. **songs:** Paul Simon (sung by Simon and Garfunkel). **cost:** Patricia Zipprodt. **sd:** Jack Solomon. **r/t:** 105 minutes. World premiere: Lincoln Art and Coronet Theatres, New York, 21 December 1967.
Cast: Anne Bancroft (*Mrs Robinson*), Dustin Hoffman (*Benjamin Braddock*), Katharine Ross (*Elaine Robinson*), Murray Hamilton (*Mr Robinson*), William Daniels (*Mr Braddock*), Elizabeth Wilson (*Mrs Braddock*), Buck Henry (*room clerk*), Brian Avery (*Carl Smith*), Walter Brooke (*Mr Maguire*), Norman Fell (*Mr McCleery*), Alice Ghostley (*Mrs Singleman*), Marion Lorne (*Miss de Witt*).

Robinson', implicity recognizing the distance between them in age, experience and outlook. He even explains to Mr Robinson, who is contemplating a divorce, that the affair meant no more to either of them than a gesture like shaking hands.

At the end of the film, Benjamin and Elaine remain the only two innocents. When he drags her off from the church, despite her just having married another man (whom she does not love), they get on a bus going . . . nowhere. The

aims of the rebellion have not yet been defined. But Benjamin has made his protest felt.

Mike Nichols, the film's director has said:

'If there is anything I like in *The Graduate* it is the last three minutes of it – sitting on the bus, stunned and very well aware that it's not the end of anything. They don't know what the hell to say to each other . . . Many things are possible – it's not an end. Benjamin has many choices open to him.'

SALLY HIBBIN

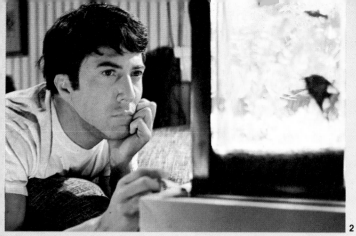

Benjamin returns home to Los Angeles after graduating from college in the east (1). At a cocktail party thrown by his parents to celebrate his home-coming, he is persuaded to show off his new diving suit. The guests all make a fuss of him but he rejects their unwanted advice and retires to his room. Mrs Robinson, the wife of his father's business partner, approaches him and talks him into driving her home (2).

When they reach her home, Mrs Robinson tries to seduce Benjamin but is prevented by the arrival of Mr Robinson (3). Their affair actually, if hesitatingly, gets started at a luxury hotel (4, 5). Benjamin is unable to communicate with his parents about his problems (6). When Mrs Robinson's daughter, Elaine, returns from college, Benjamin and Elaine are thrown together though Mrs Robinson warns him to stay away. On a date, he tries to put Elaine off by taking her to a strip joint. She runs out, crying in disgust and shame; Benjamin apologizes, realizing that she is actually the only person he can talk to.

Mrs Robinson tries to break off the blossoming romance between them by telling Elaine that Benjamin tried to rape her. Disillusioned, Elaine returns to college in Berkeley but Benjamin follows her. Elaine believes Benjamin's account (7), realizing that her mother was lying, but it is too late. Mr Robinson arrives to take her off to her wedding with a wealthy student, Carl Smith. Benjamin pursues the couple and arrives at the church as the marriage service is concluding. He runs away with the bride, using the church cross as a weapon and barrier to prevent her parents from following (8). Elaine, still in her bridal gown, and Benjamin board a bus and ride away without speaking (9).

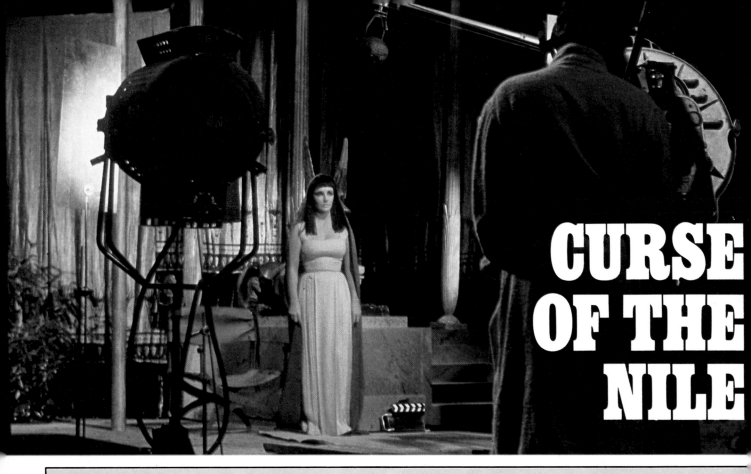

CURSE OF THE NILE

Darryl F. Zanuck

'Don't say yes until I finish talking'

Darryl F. Zanuck gained a reputation as one of Hollywood's most autocratic moguls. For over twenty years he single-handedly ran 20th Century-Fox . . . and when *Cleopatra* threatened disaster, he quickly took hold of the reins once again

The very model of a creative producer, Darryl F. Zanuck was a major force in Hollywood for over forty years – from the late Twenties at Warners until 1971 when he resigned the presidency of 20th Century-Fox. He was among that group of dynamic young producers who first made their mark during the Twenties. Of his contemporaries – Irving Thalberg, David O. Selznick, Walter Wanger – Zanuck was the only one to become head of a major studio, and he outlasted all the others.

Born in Yahoo, Nebraska in 1902, he was still in his teens when America entered the war. Although under age, he enlisted and even saw some action in France. With the war over he headed west to California and managed to break into the picture business as a gag writer, then scenarist, gradually working his way up at Warners to fully-fledged producer and finally head of production. An ambitious, hard-working man who was totally involved in film-making, he familiarized himself with every facet of the filming process and proved an expert editor, a skill that was to serve him well over the years. He was respected by those directors who worked under him, and even those who disagreed with his decisions recognized him as a true professional.

During the Twenties Zanuck played an important role in transforming Warner Brothers from a small, struggling company into one of the leading studios. He initiated the cycle of gangster movies and the Busby Berkeley musicals during the early Thirties, and set the Warners style for the decade before leaving in 1933.

Supremely self-confident ('There was only one boss I believed in and that was me.'), he immediately established his own independent production company – Twentieth Century Pictures – releasing through United Artists. And although no masterpieces or big hits were produced, virtually all the pictures made a profit – no mean feat during a period when most of the studios were fighting to recover from the Depression. Zanuck's early interest in historical romance and bio-pics is reflected in some of the titles: *The House of Rothschild*, *The Mighty Barnum* (both 1934), *Clive of India*, *Folies Bergère*, *Les Misérables*, and *Call of the Wild* (all 1935) which was given a romantic sub-plot far removed from Jack London's

Above: Zanuck filming on location. He clearly saw himself as the epitome of the Hollywood movie producer – but his business acumen was beyond question

original bleak adventure story.

Twentieth Century Pictures was the main supplier of films for United Artists around 1933–35, but Zanuck was refused any say in the policies of that organization. At that time the Fox Company was in trouble and badly in need of an imaginative production chief, while Twentieth Century

Cleopatra took years to make
. . and when it was finished . . .
everyone wondered whether it
had all really been worth it . . .

By the end of *Cleopatra* (1963) the screen was a
pile of corpses, and a star and a great studio
had nearly perished. But the most significant
demise on that prolonged, helplessly costly
epic was the public's fondness for Hollywood.
It was all too much, and no-one needed the
gossip-column wisdom that drew the links
between the decadence of modern film-making
and the passionate self-destruction of an Egyptian queen. All over the world, *Cleopatra* was
regarded as an emblem of how stupid, self-
indulgent and archaic Hollywood had become.

Out of time

After all, nothing in the mood of the early
sixties accorded with the bloated venture.
John F. Kennedy was asking Americans to
wonder what they could do for their country.
Berlin preoccupied a nervous Europe, and then
suddenly Cuba became the announced site for
the next world war. In France, the directors of
the *nouvelle vague* were making pictures that

*Left: Elizabeth Taylor prepares for a screen
test as* Cleopatra – *a role that proved the
most trying of her whole career*

seemed aware of those realities, and which
knew idioms and styles that young people used
as weapons against the stultified attitudes of
older generations. In 1960, in Hollywood,
there was an actors' strike, with the Screen
Actors' Guild crying hardship. And all the
while there was Elizabeth Taylor – over thirty
by the time the film was released! – commanding the headlines with one gorgeous but
grotesque scandal after another, and getting
$1 million up-front for the whole thing.

Out of place

Cleopatra marked the end of a certain kind of
movie imperialism, and it is important to
remember that the man originally behind it
was Walter Wanger. An odd mixture of the Ivy
League and old Hollywood, he was 65 when
the picture was initiated. Wanger had always
been ambitious for honour and admiring of
pomp: he may have been the truest Roman in
the movie. In 1951 he had shot Jennings Lang,
agent to his wife Joan Bennett, when he
thought that the two were having an affair.
Wanger had been assistant to Jesse Lasky after
World War I, and a successful independent
producer for three decades with credits for
Queen Christina (1933), *You Only Live Once*
(1937), *Stagecoach* (1939), *The Reckless Moment*
(1949), *Riot in Cell Block 11* (1954) and *Invasion
of the Body Snatchers* (1956).

It was he who dreamed of *Cleopatra* with the
determination that drove David O. Selznick

Top: the studio sets for Cleopatra *were as
impressive as those built for D. W. Griffith's*
Intolerance *(1916). Above (left to right):
Andrew Marton, director of the second unit;
Joseph L. Mankiewicz, director (brought in
to replace Rouben Mamoulian); Darryl F.
Zanuck, president of 20th Century-Fox*

could benefit from Fox's extensive sound
stages and excellent distribution. Thus a
merger was arranged, and for the next
twenty-one years Darryl Zanuck *was* 20th
Century-Fox. In his biography of Zanuck
entitled *Don't Say Yes Until I Finish Talking*
Mel Gussow quotes him as saying:

'Every creative decision was either autho-
rized, or okayed, or created by me. Every
script! There was no individual, no executive between me and the back lot. I was The
Executive. I decided whether we made
something or didn't make it. I was a One-
Man Show.'

*Below: one of Zanuck's more bizarre
pastimes was the manly sport of rhinoceros
hunting – a life-style that could easily have
been lifted straight from one of his films.
Right: the announcement of Zanuck's return
to the seat of power in 1962*

He combined a genuine feel for popular
entertainment with an earnest, if at times
pretentious, aspiration toward dealing with
serious subjects on the screen. He prided
himself on his ability to determine new
trends:

'The producer of motion pictures, like
every other person engaged in large-scale
creative enterprise, should have, above all,
the faculty of foretelling public taste . . .
Box-office returns tell the world at once
whether he has touched the public with a
success or missed it with a failure.'

Darryl Zanuck was a dynamic and

colourful character, an avid sportsman and
good family man until he suddenly turned
his back on Hollywood in 1956 and headed
for Paris alone. If his film-making and
personal life were not too happy for a time,
nevertheless his return to power at 20th
Century-Fox in the Sixties saw the old
Zanuck back in the saddle once again. And
when he finally retired in 1971, he could
look back on a record unequalled by any
other Hollywood mogul. He was truly 'the
last tycoon', and on his death in December
1979 an era came to an end.
JOEL FINLER

to make *Gone With the Wind* (1939). But
he was nearly twice Selznick's age, and he
already had a bad heart. Still, Wanger got a
script, arrived at the eventual casting and
decreed that ancient Egypt should be built at
Pinewood Studios in England. He also hired
Rouben Mamoulian as director – a man who
had made only two films in the previous fifteen
years.

Wanger got his finance and his distribution
deal from 20th Century-Fox. From 1935 to
1956 that studio had been dominated by
Darryl Zanuck, a scriptwriter turned tycoon
who loved every detail of picture-making and
had the energy to deal with it all. But in the
mid Fifties he resigned and went to Europe to
be an independent producer and to have affairs
with such women as Juliette Greco.

The studio passed under the control of
Spyros Skouras – a former theatre-owner –
who had never made a picture in his life.
Skouras was the man who bought the rights to

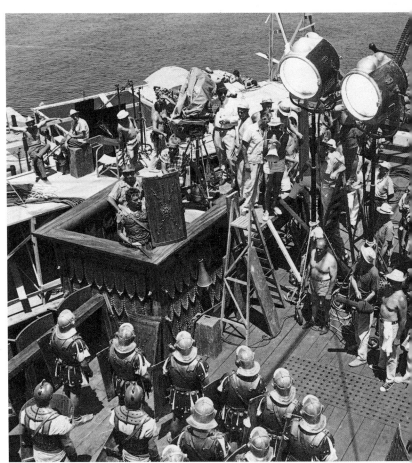

Above: Eddie Fisher, Taylor, Walter Wanger. Above right: on location at the Italian island of Ischia, Richard Burton rehearses the scene during the Battle of Actium where Mark Antony is defeated by Octavian

CinemaScope, but he was an uncertain director of operations who allowed *Cleopatra* to get out of hand, and who bought the notion that it could be filmed in England.

Out of the race

Alexandria on the Thames was withered by frost and beaten down by rains. Then, in February 1961, Elizabeth Taylor fell seriously ill with pneumonia, complications, a coma . . . and the international press corps waiting outside the clinic. The star survived, though perhaps at lasting cost to her health. The picture was put on hold and then drastically reappraised. There was very little good footage from the English shooting, and no prospect of success at Pinewood. Mamoulian was fired and replaced with Joseph Mankiewicz, who had licence to re-write the script and make the psychology of history's giants more modern. Most important, it would be shot in Rome.

So it was . . . eventually. But a fitter Taylor was now the victim of romantic assault. Under the lights, in front of the cameras, she began to fall in love with her Antony, Richard Burton. But that necessitated the end of her marriage to Eddie Fisher . . . and of Burton's to his wife Sybil. The Italian press hounded the couples, and further delayed the film.

Out at last

By 1962 20th Century-Fox was in bad shape. It had post-tax losses of nearly $40 million. Two-thirds of the studio-lot was sold off to a development company (and became Century City). The budget on *Cleopatra* was itself approaching $40 million – a sum that would need at least doubling to match today's costs. In Europe, Zanuck was making *The Longest Day* (1962) with all the care and economy of an Eisenhower. He feared for his studio stock, and was worried that *The Longest Day* might be distributed badly. So he came back to America and claimed the presidency of the ailing studio.

Thus it was Zanuck who supervised the la[st] shooting – in Egypt itself. It was he who fir[ed] Wanger (but allowed him to keep a credi[t]) subjugated Mankiewicz and ignored the sta[r]. He took *Cleopatra* to the cutting-room a[nd] with the experience of editor Elmo Williams, [he] brought it down to under four hours, until [in] the summer of 1963 the monster could at la[st] be released and sent on its way.

DAVID THOMS[ON]

CAN'T STOP THE MUSICAL

When the musical seemed to be out on its feet, it was only gathering strength for a vigorous new burst of singing and dancing and all that jazz

There was a distinct break between the musicals of the Fifties and those of the Sixties. By the end of the Fifties, the producer Arthur Freed's unit at MGM, which had been a conveyor belt of classic musical dream-worlds, was breaking up fast. Stanley Donen and Gene Kelly had left, and were soon involved in mainly non-musical projects, for which there was more demand in a Hollywood with a growing sense of social awareness. In 1960, Vincente Minnelli made his last MGM musical *Bells Are Ringing*, which also represented the final demise of Freed's group.

While these signs may not have meant the death of the genre, they certainly provided evidence of a shift in sensibility, an adjustment to a more complex world. Paeans in praise of show business, for example, were being rendered somewhat anachronistic by such scorching visions of the world of entertainment as the depictions of Hollywood itself in *Sunset Boulevard* (1950), *The Bad and the Beautiful* (1952) and *The Big Knife* (1955). With Hollywood's broadening outlook, it was becoming harder to make a musical suffused with a sense of fantasy, of the dreamer triumphant over recalcitrant circumstances, and to render it convincing.

Even so, quite a few musicals of the 'hip' Sixties were made by old survivors from MGM, notably Vincente Minnelli, Charles Walters, George Sidney and Gene Kelly. Out of these, Walters, with *Jumbo* (1962) and *The Unsinkable Molly Brown* (1964), and Kelly, with *Hello, Dolly!* (1969), remained the most traditional, with nonetheless pleasing results. Sidney met the challenge of youthful material with a typical brash energy in *Bye, Bye Birdie* (1963) and *Viva Las Vegas* (1964), although his less 'swinging' *Half a Sixpence* (1967) was ultimately more inventive. It was Minnelli, though, who showed a real ability to adapt – the formal innovations of *On a Clear Day You Can See Forever* (1970) still seem fresh today.

If these directors were representative of a specialized approach to the genre, the Sixties and Seventies musical is really notable for its lack of emphasis on the need for specifically musical talent, in both directors and performers. This was owing partly to a drying-up of reserve musical talent from Broadway, which Hollywood had always relied upon, and partly to a new stress in the genre on such elements as characterization and narrative. Directors and stars were often strongly associated with more apparently realistic genres.

With regard to directors, the results were on the whole surprisingly satisfying. William Wyler, known mainly for prestigious dramas, showed great skill with *Funny Girl* (1968). To prove how easily two already adaptable directors picked up a feel for music, Francis Ford Coppola's *Finian's Rainbow* (1967) was particularly stylish, and Norman Jewison's *Fiddler on the Roof* (1971) was imaginatively conceived for the screen. More recently, Martin Scorsese, that Italian-American poet of New York street life, made the marvellous *New York, New York* (1977). Perhaps the most noteworthy in this strain of cross-over directors was

Robert Wise. Identified more with astringent thrillers, he left his mark upon the Sixties musical with such varied but ultimately satisfactory films as *West Side Story* (1961), *The Sound of Music* (1965) and *Star!* (1968). But on the debit side must be set the inept musical sense of Carol Reed in *Oliver!* (1968) and, still worse, of Richard Fleischer in the hamfisted *Dr Dolittle* (1967).

The pattern is the same for performers. In the theatre or on screen, directors and producers have become accustomed to casting dramatic stars in musicals. When the actor Jack Klugman complained to the lyric-writer Stephen Sondheim of his own poor vocal abilities for the Broadway show *Gypsy*, Sondheim simply replied: 'I don't want a musical star. I want a person I can believe in.'

Of course, there are stars of the two decades who have been connected specifically with film musicals. Julie Andrews is the most obvious. Petula Clark was delightful and underrated in *Finian's Rainbow* and *Goodbye Mr Chips* (1969). Liza Minnelli and Barbra Streisand are both outstanding talents. Nevertheless, Sondheim's 'believable' person is manifest on the screen in such offhand, casual

Below: the Irish leprechaun Og (Tommy Steele) tries to help Sharon McLonergan (Petula Clark) to dress up in Finian's Rainbow; *Sharon's father, Finian, has stolen a magic crock of gold and Og has followed him to America in search of the leprechauns' treasure*

Above: from left to right: Marian Paroo (Shirley Jones) is a music teacher and librarian in River City, Iowa in The Music Man, based on Meredith Willson's stage show; Liza Minnelli made a dynamic Sally Bowles in Cabaret, derived from Christopher Isherwood's stories of decadent, Nazi-dominated pre-war Berlin, and gaining a period style from Bob Fosse's garish choreography; Liza Minnelli starred again in New York, New York as Francine Evans, a singer who becomes a film star, but is by then estranged from her husband Jimmy Doyle (Robert De Niro); Paul Williams is Swan, a villainous rock-music impresario and owner of the Paradise Club, while William Finley plays the disfigured Phantom of the Paradise. Below: Catherine Deneuve and Françoise Dorléac as the singing sisters in Les Demoiselles de Rochefort

musical performances as those of Rex Harrison in *My Fair Lady* (1964) or Clint Eastwood in *Paint Your Wagon* (1969). It is the approachability of this kind of star's musical manner (especially the sung-spoken style of the numbers, whether or not dubbed) that constitutes their attraction. The effect of the non-musical star depends upon the image brought over from roles in more realistic types of film. The musical has thus harnessed the iconographic significance of such stars as Natalie Wood in *West Side Story* and *Gypsy* (1962), Christopher Plummer in *The Sound of Music*, Richard Harris and Vanessa Redgrave in *Camelot* (1967), Peter O'Toole in *Goodbye Mr Chips*, Lee Marvin and Clint Eastwood in *Paint Your Wagon*, Cybill Shepherd and Burt Reynolds in *At Long Last Love* and James Caan in *Funny Lady* (both 1975).

Such stars and directors indicated a new emphasis upon the purely dramatic elements of the genre, a need to place the number in a more 'believable' world. Another manifestation of this spirit lay in the genre's growing self-consciousness and a broader social outlook. There was a tendency to deal more with everyday life and real problems, coming to the fore in the depiction of gang warfare and racial tension in *West Side Story*, office life in *How to Succeed in Business Without Really Trying* (1967), thinly-disguised prostitution in *Sweet Charity* (1969), the repression of the Jews in *Fiddler on the Roof*, the rise of Nazism in *Cabaret* (1972) and the harsh treatment of South African blacks in *Lost in the Stars* (1974). As if to clinch the point, the easy resolution, the genre's traditional concluding assertion of 'togetherness', was often eschewed in favour of such distinctly sombre endings as those of *Camelot*, *Goodbye Mr Chips*, *Sweet Charity*, *Paint Your Wagon*, *On a Clear Day You Can See Forever*, *Funny Lady* and *New York, New York*.

Similarly, there was a mocking, self-conscious tone. It is instantly recognizable in the acidic films of Bob Fosse – *Sweet Charity*, *Cabaret* and *All That Jazz* (1979) – where the numbers are explorations of various film-musical stylistic modes. It can be seen, too, in a whole variety of movies that play on the conventions of the genre: the iconography of the pop world and the media is examined in *A Hard Day's Night* (1964), *Phantom of the Paradise* (1974) and *Tommy* (1975); homage is paid to the tradition of the musical in *Let's Make Love* (1960), *At Long Last Love*, *Bugsy Malone* (1976) and *New York, New York*. There is even the unsophisticated camp nostalgia of *Grease* (1978), *Can't Stop the Music* and *Xanadu* (both 1980).

More than ever during the Sixties and Seventies musicals have been based upon Broadway hit shows. During the same period, musicals were also generally becoming super-productions, of the type represented by *West Side Story*, *The Sound of Music* and *Funny Girl*. The reason was simple: the rivalry of television. The cinema's tactic was to present audio-visual spectacles unlike anything possible on the small screen, and often to recruit proven successes from the Broadway stage. It did not always work, of course; and when it failed, the financial repercussions could be as crippling as the slow paralysis caused by television. For instance *Sweet Charity* made no profit for Universal, despite its fresh approach to previously successful material.

What is often complained of, regarding Broadway adaptations, is that the original is treated with too much reverence. But by the late Fifties, Hollywood was dealing with the type of musical drama originally pioneered by Rodgers and Hammerstein which was too integrated to allow the free adaptations once made of original stage works. Further, while these films do follow the stage shows quite closely, the results need not be as slavish and uncinematic as they were in, for example, *Man of La Mancha* (1972) and *Mame* (1973). The long list of more memorable films includes *West Side Story*, *The Music Man* (1962), *My Fair Lady*, *The Sound of Music*, *Camelot*, *Finian's Rainbow*, *Sweet Charity*, *On a Clear Day You Can See Forever* and *Cabaret*.

Of original screen musicals, outstanding by any standards was the Gallic charm of Jacques Demy's romantic evocations of French provincial life in *Les Parapluies de Cherbourg* (1964, *The Umbrellas of Cherbourg*) and *Les Demoiselles de Rochefort* (1967, *The Young Girls of Rochefort*). Scorsese's *New York, New York* was an original film musical that explored the form with all the daring and inventiveness once shown by such Betty Comden and Adolph Green scripts as those for *Singin' in the Rain* (1952) and *The Band Wagon* (1953). It centred on the off-beat

romance and failed marriage of a jazz saxophonist and a dance-band vocalist. Then there were such pleasant diversions as Marilyn Monroe's penultimate movie *Let's Make Love*, *Robin and the Seven Hoods* (1964), *Thoroughly Modern Millie* (1967) and *Goodbye Mr Chips*. Yet, on the whole, the two decades have not matched the standard of the stream of screen originals once associated, in particular, with MGM.

One of the major developments in the genre during the period was its attempt to come to terms with youth and with post-Beatles popular music. In this the musical has generally taken a patronizing attitude to the energy and subversion of both youth themes and rock music.

Rock musicals themselves usually developed over-simplified youth themes, accompanied by middle-of-the-road music more appropriate to middle-aged audiences. *Godspell* and *Jesus Christ Superstar* (both 1973), for example, merely restated conventional religious values. *Hair* had initiated the Broadway youth-musical vogue in 1968; even then, its nude dancing could only ever have offended a truly Victorian sensibility. When the screen version finally appeared, a safe 11 years later in 1979, it was nothing but a pleasant reminder of an era long since gone, the hippie heyday. Only two screen originals, *Phantom of the Paradise*, a version of the Phantom-of-the-Opera story, and *Tommy*, based on The Who's very successful LP about a deaf, dumb and blind pinball player, came near to creating the anarchy, energy and imagination missing each week from *Top of the Pops* on British television.

Then, in 1977, came *Saturday Night Fever*. All at once, the dance musical was reinvented. The disco craze spread across Europe and the United States; and this film was followed by *Black Joy* (1977), *Thank God It's Friday* (1978), *The Music Machine* (1979), *Can't Stop the Music*, *Xanadu* and *Fame* (1980). All of them pushed the new dance style as the foremost element of the genre – no-one even sings in *Saturday Night Fever*. It was only in *Thank God It's Friday* and *Fame*, though, that the dancing reflected the true energy and invention of the actual disco floor. The exhilarating bursts of movement in these films made the mannered shuffling of *Saturday Night Fever* and the skate-bound plodding of *Xanadu* seem flat-footed.

The classic musical had never fully acknowledged the black origins of such elements as tap-dancing. At least the disco musical made a stab at identifying the cultural context of its subject. The excellent *Black Joy*, concerning immigrant life in London's Brixton, and *Thank God It's Friday*, an evening in the life of a Hollywood disco club, linked the music with black artists, while the sheer skill and subversive eroticism of the solo dancing in *Fame* were inextricable from its black exponent, Gene Anthony Ray. The considerable gay influence upon disco was only limply noticed in the awful *Can't Stop the Music*, in which a pop group, the Village People, were 'normalized' by the presence of the central heterosexual couple.

Both *Saturday Night Fever* and *Xanadu* did identify disco as levelling out social inequalities. *Saturday Night Fever* splendidly utilized the dance floor as a place for stamping out problems, permitting control at least of this environment through skills that anyone could develop. *Xanadu* gave a sense of cultural harmony in its closing vision of disco as a meeting ground free from bias and prejudice.

Disco was seen by the film industry as a convenient and safe way of representing youth music and culture, and it accounted for the bulk of musicals in the late Seventies and early Eighties. But the British *Breaking Glass* (1980) explored, though only tentatively, the area of rock music's 'New Wave'.

In terms of directors, only Bob Fosse really specialized in the genre. Of the rest, both John Badham, who made *Saturday Night Fever*, and Alan Parker, of *Fame*, showed great potential, with a good feel for music, though a limited ability to provide convincing narrative contexts. All of Martin Scorsese's films were alive with music and movement; *New York, New York* explored the language of the film musical with all the cunning insight of Fosse but without the ego-flexing of the semi-autobiographical *All That Jazz*. *New York, New York* deserves recognition as one of the most entertaining and challenging musicals to appear since Freed's unit at MGM shuddered to a halt back in 1960.

MARTIN SUTTON

Above: young people travel to Israel to re-enact the last days in the life of Jesus as a rock opera in Jesus Christ Superstar. *Below: the all-singing, all-dancing finale of* Grease *features, from left to right, Jeff Conaway as Kenickie, Olivia Newton-John as Sandy Olsson, John Travolta as her boyfriend Danny Zucco and Stockard Channing as Betty Rizzo, who decides to marry Kenickie*

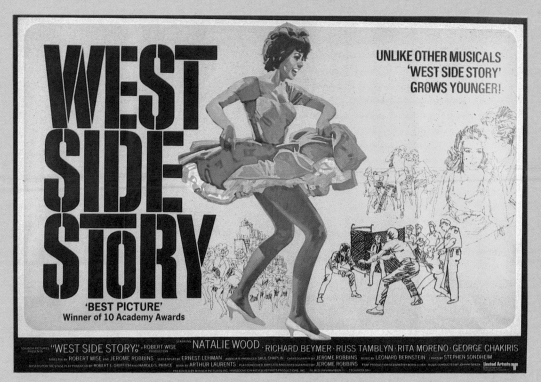

WEST SIDE STORY

UNLIKE OTHER MUSICALS 'WEST SIDE STORY' GROWS YOUNGER!

'BEST PICTURE'
Winner of 10 Academy Awards

"WEST SIDE STORY" · ROBERT WISE PRODUCTION · starring NATALIE WOOD · RICHARD BEYMER · RUSS TAMBLYN · RITA MORENO · GEORGE CHAKIRIS

direct his biggest success, another big-budget musical – *The Sound of Music* (1965). It needed other directors to see that there was a valuable exuberance and youthfulness that could be exploited to provide the material for even more exuberant and youth-orientated rock musicals of the next decade.

SALLY HIBBIN

On New York's West Side two gangs control the streets – the Jets (white teenagers) (1) and the

Directed by Robert Wise, Jerome Robbins, 1961

Prod co: Mirisch/Seven Arts. **prod:** Robert Wise. **assoc prod:** Saul Chaplin. **sc:** Ernest Lehman, based on the stage production by Robert E. Griffith, Harold S. Prince, from the book by Arthur Laurents. **photo** (Technicolor, Panavision 70): Daniel L. Fapp. **sp eff:** Linwood Dunn. **ed:** Thomas Stanford, Marshall M. Borden. **art dir:** Boris Leven, M. Zuberano. **titles:** Saul Bass. **cost:** Irene Sharaff. **mus:** Leonard Bernstein. **mus dir:** Johnny Green. **mus arr:** Sid Ramin. **mus ed:** Richard Carruth. **lyr:** Stephen Sondheim. **chor:** Jerome Robbins. **sd:** Gilbert D. Marchant. **sd rec:** Murray Spivack, Fred Lau, Vinton Vernon. **prod man:** Allen K. Wood. **ass dir:** Robert E. Relyea. **r/t:** 152 minutes.

Cast: Natalie Wood (*Maria*), Richard Beymer (*Tony*), George Chakiris (*Bernardo*), Russ Tamblyn (*Riff*), Rita Moreno (*Anita*), Tony Mordente (*Action*), Tucker Smith (*Ice*), Simon Oakland (*Lieutenant Schrank*), William Bramley (*Officer Krupke*), Ned Glass (*Doc*), José De Vega (*Chino*), Sue Oakes (*Anybody's*), John Astin (*Glad Hand*), Penny Santon (*Madam Lucia*), Jay Norman (*Pepe*), Gus Trikonis (*Indio*), Robert Thompson (*Luis*), Eliot Field (*Baby John*), Larry Roquemore (*Rocco*), David Winters (*A-Rab*).

West Side Story begins even before the house-lights go down in the cinema. A long, low whistle fills the auditorium; the whistle is repeated; the lights go down and the film starts with a breathtaking aerial shot of Manhattan – a geometric display of crossing lines. Then the camera plunges to the streets below: a gang of youths walking along the road, clicking their fingers, keeping 'cool'; suddenly they freeze and move into a dance sequence. It is a daring and visually exciting opening to a film.

But more than that, these first few minutes establish a number of key elements: its location – the tenements and streets of Manhattan; its content – the rivalry between two gangs (one of white youths, one of Puerto Rican immigrants); and its form – a highly stylized musical. The opening prepares the audience for what is to follow.

West Side Story was conceived and developed for the stage by Jerome Robbins, who also choreographed and directed several of the dance routines. One of his early stage ballet hits was the choreography for Leonard

Bernstein's *Fancy Free* which later became the Broadway success *On the Town*. The film of *On the Town* (1949) had broken with tradition by attempting to integrate fully song, dance and dialogue into one continuous narrative, rejecting the often contrived excuses for breaking into song that had been a feature of previous musicals. However, it is relatively easy to do this when the plot of the film is nothing more than three sailors going ashore for 24 hours' leave, meeting three girls and returning to their ship.

West Side Story is a more difficult proposition. Loosely based on Shakespeare's *Romeo and Juliet*, it transposes the rivalry between the Capulet and Montague families to the tensions between racial groupings in New York, thus becoming one of the first musicals to deal with serious, contemporary issues – racialism and juvenile delinquency. The vigour and vitality of *West Side Story* owe a lot to its departure from the facile plots of *On the Town* or *Pal Joey* (1957) or the fantasy lives of *Seven Brides for Seven Brothers* (1954).

It presented Robbins and Robert Wise with the difficulty of how to carve out a modern style of presentation suitable for important problems. *West Side Story* found its style both by not trying to carry the plot forward in song and dance sequences – as *On the Town* did – and also by abandoning the hoedown set pieces of *Oklahoma!* (1955). Instead, the songs, at their best, add something more to the narrative, informing the audience about the atmosphere and details of the lives. The opening shots do this by economically establishing the territorial basis of the gangs' control. Later in the film, the aggressive and lively roof-top sequence 'America' is a hard-hitting proclamation of the disillusionment of immigrants with American society. On the other hand, the love song 'Maria' and the dance-hall routine, where the gangs challenge each other, are firmly part of the old tradition.

Of the criticisms ranged against the film, one concerns its combination of naturalism through location shooting and the obvious stylization of studio work. Whereas the beginning was actually danced on the streets of New York, the 'rumble' takes place in a studio-constructed set. And the choice of Natalie Wood as Maria – she had to have her singing voice dubbed and had difficulty looking Puerto Rican – has also been questioned as giving the film an unreal texture. But *West Side Story* does not aim to be realistic: it is a modern parable of what *could* happen in a racially divided society.

With its combination of innovatory and traditional elements, this was very much a transitional musical. Bob Fosse took the techniques of *West Side Story* further when he brought serious issues to *Sweet Charity* (1969), and combined them with biting satire in *Cabaret* (1972). Robert Wise went on to

46

Sharks (Puerto Rican immigrants) (2). Riff, the leader of the Jets, tries to persuade Tony, who founded the gang but has since drifted away, to go to the local dance.

Maria, the sister of Bernardo who leads the Sharks, is excited about her first dance. She goes with Chino, Bernardo and his girlfriend Anita. When they arrive, the two gangs display their rivalry through the dances they perform (3). Tony enters and sees Maria:

they are both entranced (4). When he asks her to dance, Bernardo warns her that Tony is a member of the rival gang. Riff uses the incident as an excuse to propose a 'rumble'.

Tony visits Maria on the fire-escape outside her room (5) and they realize that, despite the difficulties, they love each other. Returning to Doc's shop (where he works) Tony finds a war council in session. He persuades them to have a fair fist fight

between representatives from each side.

Telling Bernardo that she will be working late (6), Maria stays at the dress-shop until Tony arrives. She persuades him to try and stop the fight, but when he gets to the 'rumble' his offer of friendship is misunderstood. Bernardo kills Riff (7), and Tony kills Bernardo. When the police turn up, the gangs scatter (8).

Learning of her brother's death, Maria decides to stand by Tony,

and begs Anita to take a message to him. Anita goes to Doc's but is insulted by the Jets; she then lies when she tells them that Chino has killed Maria in anger.

Desolate, Tony roams the streets calling for Chino to come and get him. He sees Maria too late: he has already been spotted by Chino who shoots him. Both gangs appear, and Maria, crying, accuses them all of Tony's death (9). They take Tony's body off, for once united in tragedy (10).

THE LAST HEROES

Heroes were still heroic in the epic, the war film and the Western until doubt and cynicism began to creep in during the course of the Sixties

The Fifties saw the demise of the swashbuckling cycle which had been inaugurated at the end of World War II. Although many of these films had been produced on reduced budgets, some were able to match the lavishness of their pre-war counterparts by being filmed abroad, notably in Italy and Britain, where Hollywood production companies could utilize 'frozen' funds, cheap labour and ready-made castles. This cycle had also seen the return to swordfighting of many of the stars of pre-war swashbucklers. Errol Flynn, ageing and dissipated but still game, fenced and wooed his way through a series of modestly budgeted but engaging adventure films: *Against All Flags* (1952), *The Master of Ballantrae* (1953) and *The Dark Avenger* (1955); these were patterned on his Thirties' successes. Louis Hayward took over Flynn's old role of the pirate Captain Blood in *Fortunes of Captain Blood* (1950) and *Captain Pirate* (1952). Tyrone Power starred in a trio of rather stodgy epic-scale swashbucklers: *Captain From Castile* (1947), *Prince of Foxes* (1949) and *The Black Rose* (1950). Robert Taylor, now in dignified middle age, starred in three British-made chivalric romances from MGM: *Ivanhoe* (1952), *Knights of the Round Table* (1953) and *The Adventures of Quentin Durward* (1955).

But there were new, young adventurers arising to challenge the old stalwarts. In Hollywood, Universal-International and Columbia produced a stream of 'bread-and-butter' swashbucklers, economically made but generally done with verve and designed to showcase the riding, loving and fighting talents of their aspiring young actors. Universal's Tony Curtis, endearingly unabashed by his broad Brooklyn accent, performed with athletic grace and unflagging good humour in lively adventures both oriental, as in *The Prince Who Was a Thief* (1951) and *Son of Ali Baba* (1952), and occidental, as in *The Black Shield of Falworth* (1954) and *The Purple Mask* (1955). Columbia's John Derek, who combined the sensitive Italianate good looks of Tyrone Power with the fire and conviction of the young Errol Flynn, played the son of Robin Hood in *Rogues of Sherwood Forest* (1950), the first of a series of colourful swashbucklers. But for sheer style, no-one could beat Stewart Granger, whose virility, elegance and sardonic humour served him to good effect in such vintage swashbucklers as *Scaramouche* (1952), *Moonfleet* (1955) and *Lo Spadaccino di Siena* (1962, *Swordsman of Siena*) and in non-swashbuckling costume dramas such as *Young Bess* (1953) and *Beau Brummell* (1954), all for MGM.

Television inevitably spelled the decline of such films, for the small screen was crowded from the mid-Fifties onwards by a host of swashbuckling series, small-scale, black and white, often studio-bound, but well-acted, fast-moving and entertaining, typified by the long-running British *Adventures of Robin Hood*, starring former cinema swashbuckler Richard Greene. Hollywood turned instead to the epic in search of box-office crowd-pullers. Television could not recreate the glories of Babylon, Greece and Rome in wide screen format, in

colour and in stereophonic sound – even in the United States, colour TV sets were still quite rare at the end of the Fifties.

So D'Artagnan, Scaramouche and Captain Blood gave way to Alexander the Great, Ben-Hur and Cleopatra on the big screen, Vast budgets, armies of extras, teeming battle-scapes, huge reconstructions of ancient cities – these were now the order of the day. Cecil B. DeMille, who had definitely established the cinematic images of Cleopatra, Nero and the Crusaders in the Thirties, bowed out with *The Ten Commandments* (1956), which provided the new epic cycle with its greatest star, Charlton Heston. Heston went on to play the title roles in three of the greatest products of the cycle, *Ben-Hur* (1959), *El Cid* (1961) and *The War Lord* (1965). For a decade, the historical epic was to hold sway in the action and adventure field. The Bible, the classics and medieval legends were to be plundered for themes and stories.

Such films were generally derided by the critics, who enjoyed themselves enormously at the expense

Top: The War Lord *(Charlton Heston) of an 11th-century Normandy village rides in with, from left, his villainous brother (Guy Stockwell) and his faithful squire (Richard Boone), led by the village priest (Maurice Evans). The film's story of love and betrayal is set against a convincingly authentic background of druidic lore and ancient rural customs. Above: the Emperor of China (Robert Morley), seen here in an ornate oriental setting, schemes against Genghis Khan – but to little effect*

troubled, over-budget productions such as *Cleopatra* (1963); they pounced gleefully on factual errors and comic miscastings like the hilarious appearances of Robert Morley as the Emperor of China and James Mason as his buck-toothed ambassador in *Genghis Khan* (1965). But they wilfully ignored the visual splendours, mythic power, imaginative strength and sheer physical energy of the best of the epics. These films did not set out to create an impression of 'everyday life in ancient times'. They dealt with gods and heroes, great deeds and great men, the stuff of myth and legend. At their best the epics were awesome tributes to Hollywood's film-making skill and entrepreneurial enterprise.

Kirk Douglas starred in and produced two of the best, *The Vikings* (1958) and *Spartacus* (1960). Richard Fleischer's *The Vikings*, with its screeching falcons, proud dragon-ships, wolf-pits and muscular celebration of fighting, feasting and savage retribution, was the cinema's definitive depiction of

The fall of the American epic was mighty in cost to the producers

the barbaric Norsemen of popular legend. Stanley Kubrik's *Spartacus* was a slave-revolt epic of immense intelligence, which made up for the miscasting in some parts (John Gavin, Tony Curtis) by the wealth of talent employed to flesh out the major roles – Charles Laughton, Laurence Olivier, Peter Ustinov and Kirk Douglas himself.

Charlton Heston distinguished himself in the two finest chivalric epics that the cinema has yet produced: Anthony Mann's *El Cid* and Franklin Schaffner's *The War Lord*. Intelligently scripted and majestically staged, both films gave memorable cinematic life to that misty borderland between cultures and between epochs when chivalry and paganism, violence and tenderness existed uneasily side by side. Much less well-known is J. Lee-Thompson's *Kings of the Sun* (1963), a sweeping, surging, often inspiring saga about the fate of the Mayan civilization in Central America, with Yul Brynner and George Chakiris giving outstanding performances.

But the epic cycle came to an end with *The Fall of the Roman Empire* (1964), the last film from the Samuel Bronston organization, telling the almost symbolic tale of the collapse of the Roman Empire in the face of tyranny and extravagance within and barbarian assault from without. Staged by Anthony Mann on a massive, imperial scale, it embraced pitched battles, chariot races, triumphal processions and court intrigue, and Mann elicited sensitive and thoughtful performances from Alec Guinness as the Emperor Marcus Aurelius and

James Mason as a Christian philosopher. But it was seriously flawed by a lacklustre, unhistorical hero (Stephen Boyd), whose climactic refusal to occupy the throne and save civilization must have caused El Cid, King Arthur, Alexander the Great and Julius Caesar to turn in their epic graves.

The British film industry also climbed aboard the epic bandwagon in this period, particularly with Clive Donner's *Alfred the Great* (1969) and Ken Hughes' *Cromwell* (1970), films as absorbing and thoughtful as they were sumptuous and expansive. Particularly fruitful as a subject, however, was the British Empire, which had provided Hollywood with a memorable cycle of adventure films in the Thirties. A new Imperial cycle produced at least three major works, all filmed on location and all depicting the gallantry of a handful of outnumbered but never down-hearted Britons fighting against overwhelming odds. J. Lee-Thompson's *North West Frontier* (1959) recreated a hazardous train trip across rebel-infested India in 1905. Led by Kenneth More, the Imperialists emerged triumphant and vindicated. Cy Endfield's *Zulu* (1963) was an awe-inspiring re-creation of the battle of Rorke's Drift in 1879 when 105 men of the South Wales Borderers held an isolated mission station against 4000 Zulus. Basil Dearden's *Khartoum* (1966) was an impressive, in-depth study of General Gordon, superbly played by Charlton Heston.

A much less sympathetic view of British Imperialism was taken in Tony Richardson's *Charge of the Light Brigade* (1968), which exposed the squalid slum conditions, brutal army discipline and official corruption and mismanagement of mid-Victorian Britain, as a prelude to the heroic blunder of Balaclava. It featured two hilarious performances, from John Gielgud as the monumentally vague Lord Raglan, who was never sure whether he was fighting the Russians or the French, and from Trevor Howard as the cholerically Blimpish libertine and snob, Lord Cardigan. Richard Williams' delightfully funny jingoistic cartoon inserts were in the style of *The Illustrated London News*. In David Lean's *Lawrence of Arabia* (1962) Peter O'Toole made an enormous impact as the white-robed mystic who leads the Arabs to victory against the Turks but fails to secure their independence from the scheming British.

The serious war films of the late Forties and Fifties, such as *Twelve O'Clock High* (1949), *Paths of Glory* (1957) and *Pork Chop Hill* (1959), with their 'war is hell' message, gave way in the Sixties to big-budget, all-action, all-star military spectaculars, of which the only possible message was 'war is fun'. The style continued until the end of the decade, after which the impact of Vietnam finally produced a clutch of films marked by bitterness and cynicism: *M*A*S*H*, *Catch-22* and *Too Late the Hero* (all three 1970). But typical of the big-budget blockbusters was J. Lee-Thompson's *The Guns of Navarone* (1961).

Top left: David Hemmings as Alfred the Great in a battle scene. Top: Michael Caine is also embattled as an officer engaged in hand-to-hand combat in Zulu. Centre: Kirk Douglas as a Viking who has just lost the sight of one eye in The Vikings, a film dripping with spilt gore. Above: John Mills as Field-Marshal Sir Douglas Haig, who led the British forces in France during World War I, in Oh! What a Lovely War, which had a lengthy and star-filled cast list

Above left: Lord Cardigan (Trevor Howard) has a spot of bother in Charge of the Light Brigade. *Above right: inside the German fortress a couple of American soldiers (Lee Marvin and Charles Bronson) are helped out of their German uniform disguises in* The Dirty Dozen, *a film which proved that villainous heroes could also be popular if most of them died heroically. Opposite page, top left: Burt Lancaster and Lee Marvin as a pair of professional adventurers and Claudia Cardinale as a runaway wife in* The Professionals, *set during the revolutionary period in Mexico (and top right)* The Magnificent Seven *are, from left to right, Yul Brynner, Steve McQueen, Horst Buchholz, Charles Bronson, Robert Vaughn, Brad Dexter and James Coburn. Far right:* The Good, the Bad and the Ugly *features Lee Van Cleef as the bad guy and Eli Wallach as the ugly one, who survives the concluding shoot-out rich but stranded*

Right: the three-camera Cinerama was used to good effect in the Civil War episode of How the West Was Won, *directed by John Ford: a mother (Carroll Baker) says farewell to her elder son (George Peppard) as he sets off to fight on the Union side*

It was the first of a very profitable and popular series of films based on the works of Alistair MacLean. It bore all the MacLean hallmarks – preposterous plot, rudimentary characterization, all-star cast and non-stop action. In the same mould, *Where Eagles Dare*, *Ice Station Zebra* (both 1968) and many more, both war stories and adventure stories, followed in the Sixties and Seventies.

Genuine wartime episodes furnished the basis for other all-star spectaculars. Darryl F. Zanuck's production, *The Longest Day* (1962), re-created the D-Day landings, with John Wayne, Robert Mitchum and Henry Fonda leading the American forces and Richard Todd, Richard Burton and Kenneth More, the British. *Battle of the Bulge* (1965) restaged the last major German offensive of World War II, with Robert Shaw in good form as a ruthless blond Nazi tank commander. *Operation Crossbow* (1965) assembled yet more stars to play a host of cameo parts in the story of how Germany's V-2 rocket bases were identified and destroyed. The cycle did produce some impressive performances. George C. Scott deservedly won an Oscar for his virtuoso playing of the tempestuous General Patton in *Patton* (1970) and Laurence Olivier completely dominated another all-star epic, *Battle of Britain* (1969), with his quietly detached playing of Air Chief Marshal Sir Hugh Dowding. The major anti-war statement of the Sixties, Richard Attenborough's *Oh! What a Lovely War* (1969) was only intermittently successful in translating to the screen a concept that remained obstinately stage-bound.

Perhaps the key war film of the decade was Robert Aldrich's *The Dirty Dozen* (1967). It put to profitable use the idea of a bunch of assorted criminals recruited into the service of the Allies and employing their expertise at knifing, garrotting and dynamiting to knock out a vital Nazi target in France. With its virile anti-heroes cocking a snook at the Establishment while exercising their murderous talents, it proved enormously popular with the cinema's mainly youthful audiences. It inspired a whole series of imitations, including *Play Dirty* (1968) and *Kelly's Heroes* (1970), whose keynotes were violence, self-interest and increasing cynicism, which chimed well with the mood of the new generation.

As in epics and war films, so too in Westerns the rule was: size, scale, all-star action and no expense spared. The psychological Western of the Fifties was eclipsed by the likes of *How the West Was Won* (1962), a rambling chronicle of the expansion westwards of the United States, the first feature film in three-camera Cinerama. But the most trend-setting Western was John Sturges' *The Magnificent Seven* (1960). The group of outlaws (played by Yul Brynner, Steve McQueen, James Coburn, Charles Bronson, Robert Vaughn, Horst Buchholz and Brad Dexter) is hired to defend a Mexican village from bandits, but its members owe no allegiance to anyone or anything outside their group. This

central theme became a key idea in Sixties films. In Westerns, it led to no less than three sequels to *The Magnificent Seven* itself: *The Return of the Seven* (1966), *Guns of the Magnificent Seven* (1969) and *The Magnificent Seven Ride!* (1972); and to the reworking of the idea in *The Professionals* (1966), *The Wild Bunch* and, on a lighter level, the modish, whimsical *Butch Cassidy and the Sundance Kid* (both 1969).

The theme was also transferred to the war film. Significantly, Steve McQueen, James Coburn and Charles Bronson all turned up in Sturges' *The Great Escape* (1963). *The Dirty Dozen* used a similar but more numerous group. In real life, the idea of the tough, all-male professional group, with no loyalty to anything outside itself, found expression in the Nixon gang, exposed and broken up after the Watergate break-in.

There were other important themes which, taken all together, suggested that the American Western might have reached the end of the trail. There was a group of Westerns about modern-day cowboys, living anachronisms in a changing world: *The Misfits* (1961), *Lonely Are the Brave* (1962) and *Hud* (1963). With many of the major Western stars getting old, the theme of the ageing cowboy became common and there were jokes about John Wayne's age in several of his later Westerns, though he turned his girth and his years to good use in his rumbustious performance as the one-eyed US marshal Rooster Cogburn in Henry Hathaway's *True Grit* (1969). Joel McCrea and Randolph Scott, veterans of scores of low-budget Westerns, retired from the screen after making unforgettable appearances in Sam Peckinpah's *Ride the High Country* (1962). Echoes of that film's fierce elegiac pride can

lso be heard in *Will Penny* (1967) and *Monte Walsh* 1970).

Like the stars, the Western directors were growing older. The decade witnessed the retirement of three of the greatest. John Ford made his last masterpiece, *The Man Who Shot Liberty Valance* 1962), a moving, moody, meditative, wholly personal film, in which he decisively parted company with the tendencies of modern civilization. Then he got many of his old friends together for one last great trek, a flawed, all-star tribute to the fighting spirit of the Indians, *Cheyenne Autumn* (1964). Raoul Walsh bowed out with a characteristically risk and vigorous cavalry Western, *A Distant Trumpet* (1964). Howard Hawks, having distilled the quintessence of his world-view into the ultimate

The autumnal Westerns gave way to a new kind of stylized violence

Hawksian statement of beliefs and values, *Rio Bravo* 1959), twice reworked it, as *El Dorado* (1967) and *Rio Lobo* (1970).

The decisive new development in the Sixties took place not in the United States but in Italy, where Clint Eastwood established his reputation as the new superstar in a trio of Italian-made Westerns of which the characterizing features were stylized violence and tough cynicism: *Per un Pugno di Dollari* 1964, *Fistful of Dollars*), *Per Qualche Dollaro in Più* 1966, *For a Few Dollars More*) and *Il Buono, Il*

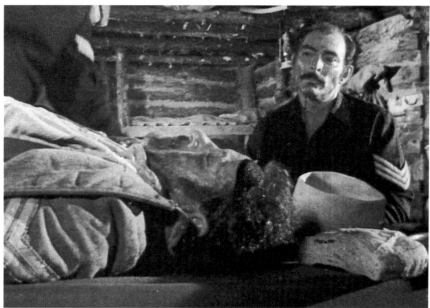

Brutto, Il Cattivo (1967, *The Good, the Bad and the Ugly*). The success of these films brought Eastwood back to Hollywood to make a direct imitation of them, *Hang 'Em High* (1968). But it was Sam Peckinpah, whose *Ride the High Country* had said an eloquent farewell to the old Western, who now celebrated the triumph of the new ethic in his epochal *The Wild Bunch*. Violence had now arrived as big box-office.

JEFFREY RICHARDS

"John Wayne, American"

John Wayne's long, final illness in the spring and summer of 1979 unleashed a tidal wave of American emotion. As the media constantly reminded everyone, Wayne was the man who carried 'true grit' over from the movie screen into real life: no self-respecting American could fail to be moved by the sight of the Duke, ravaged by 'Big C' but still a vast and imposing presence, looming up before the TV cameras at the 1979 Academy Awards ceremony. It *was* an awesome occasion:

'Oscar and I have something in common,' he said that night. 'Oscar first came to the Hollywood scene in 1928. So did I. We're both a little weatherbeaten, but we're still here and plan to be around for a whole lot longer.'

Two months later he was dead, but even as the old man slipped away Maureen O'Hara and Elizabeth Taylor fought desperately to win him a Congressional Medal of Honour, the highest tribute that can be paid to an American. It was the least President Carter could do, and the American people were able to take part in the medal-wearing too with the mass-minting of duplicate gold awards bearing the simple legend 'John Wayne, American'.

Above all others Wayne was the film star whom America had chosen as its symbol of strength, bravery, manliness, patriotism and righteousness in the post-war years. The film journalist Alexander Walker has persuasively argued in his book *Stardom* that Wayne 'was the most complete example of a star who has taken his politics into films and his films into public image'.

A Republican at Republic

The image of Wayne as the ultimate American fighting for right grew up during World War II when he played the war-hero in Republic's *Flying Tigers* (1942) and *The Fighting Seabees* (1944), and in the wake of Hiroshima when American military might was most in need of justification. In *Back to Bataan*, *They Were*

Above: the Duke in jovial mood on set for The Cowboys *(1972). Right: James Stewart, John Ford and Wayne pose for a publicity shot during the filming of* The Man Who Shot Liberty Valance. *Right, background: Colonel Marlowe waves farewell to his beloved after escaping from the Rebels by blowing up a bridge in* The Horse Soldiers

Marion Michael Morrison, a name to be conjured with – yet known by all. It is curious that women don't really take to him while men idolize him, and both will always see him sitting squarely on the back of a horse with a six-gun at his hip. However, given that as John Wayne he remained a superstar for over four decades, there must have been more to him than that . . . or must there?

Above left: pioneers (Marguerite Churchill and Wayne) take to The Big Trail *(1930) in a realistic Western with 'grubby' actors. Above: Oliver Hardy and Wayne in* The Fighting Kentuckian *(1949), a tale of two men's fight to help French refugees settle in Alabama. Below: Sergeant Stryker (Wayne) leads an attack in* The Sands of Iwo Jima

Expendable (both 1945), the fiercely jingoistic *The Sands of Iwo Jima* (1949), and John Ford's cavalry trilogy – *Fort Apache* (1948), *She Wore a Yellow Ribbon* (1949) and *Rio Grande* (1950) – he played war leaders who were tough, courageous, compassionate and *American*. Meanwhile, back at the Hollywood front Wayne, a staunch Republican and President of the Motion Picture Alliance for the Preservation of American Ideals, was taking an active part in running Communists out of the film capital – and colleagues out of their livelihood.

The films that also involved Wayne on the production side are those which most cohesively unite his movie and public images. *Big Jim McLain* (1952), which he co-produced, is pro-McCarthyist propaganda with Wayne as a

tough HUAC investigator pursuing 'pinkos'; in *The Alamo* (1960), his first film as director, he played Davy Crockett defending Texas against Santa Anna's Mexican army – a martyr for American freedom; *The Green Berets* (1968) was his second stab at direction and is a vituperative pro-Vietnam War film in which he plays a mercenary routing the Vietcong. As 'pro-American' propaganda this is strong, sometimes unpalatable stuff, and he even recorded an LP called 'Why I Love America' with Robert Mitchum. Now there is a hint of bathos in that title, as there is in the whole of Wayne's over-inflated image as the last American hero, and it would be feasible to suggest that Wayne was aware of it. His Republicanism and anti-Communism (he had read widely

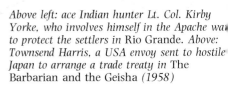

in Communist literature and in political science) were sincere, and he was a fervent supporter of Eisenhower, Goldwater and Nixon, but perhaps he knew too the power of talismans, bronze medals and movie images in the art of propaganda. Yet, strange as it may seem, in his greatest films Wayne's characters are not all that America would have them be.

South of the border . . .

If Wayne was and is a symbol of Americanism then, politically and socially, no other actor has done so much to undermine the self-righteous bluster of WASPish – White Anglo-Saxon Protestant – redneck values, both by espousing them and showing the neuroses nagging away at them. Wayne married three Spanish-Americans during his lifetime (so much for *The Alamo*) and eventually turned to Catholicism on his death-bed. If Ford, Hawks and the directors at Republic hadn't grabbed him for Westerns and war films in the late Forties and early Fifties, he might have been an effective star of *film noir*, so thoroughly ambiguous and troubled is his image when scrutinized. In fact Ford's *The Searchers* (1956) is a Western *film noir* with Wayne as a psychopath trapped in the alternatively light and dark landscape of his own mind. Even if Wayne *was* politically naive then surely he understood the dreadful frailty of his bloated, brow-beating characters and that the anger, insensitivity and spitefulness of Tom Dunson in *Red River* (1948), Sergeant Stryker in *The Sands of Iwo Jima* and Tom Doniphon in *The Man Who Shot Liberty Valance* (1962) showed the bully and the tyrant in the hero who defends his flag at all costs. These characters are tired, unhappy men, soured and warped by their own experiences and plunged into crises of conscience which they can only solve by blasting their way out.

For all their self-sufficiency and arrogant confidence Wayne's movie characters – his American heroes – are lonely, sulky, ill-

tempered and desperate. In good moods they tend to be bluff and patronizing – Wayne's grin is cracked, his eyes narrowed under his brow with suspicion. In bad moments they are monstrous; recall the incident in *Red River* when Dunson bounds across the trail, draws and shoots the cocky gunslinger without stopping his relentless march and lays into his young foster-son Matt (Montgomery Clift), a fury of flailing fists and mad temper. 'I never knew that big sonovabitch could act,' Ford said to Hawks after seeing *Red River*. As old men or neurotics Wayne was especially effective and knew exactly what he was about, as did Ford – his patron and mentor – and in *The Searchers*, *The Horse Soldiers* (1959), a wearied view of the Civil War, and *The Man Who Shot Liberty Valance*, they share the knowledge that the American Dream has become an American nightmare.

No Janet for John

On other levels Wayne's characters are equally ill at ease. It is significant that in many of his films he is essentially womanless. In *Red River* he leaves his girl behind (intending to return) but she is killed by Indians; *She Wore a Yellow Ribbon* finds him as a mawkishly sentimental widower who confides in his wife's grave; in *Rio Grande* he is estranged from his wife

Above left: ace Indian hunter Lt. Col. Kirby Yorke, who involves himself in the Apache war to protect the settlers in Rio Grande. *Above: Townsend Harris, a USA envoy sent to hostile Japan to arrange a trade treaty in* The Barbarian and the Geisha *(1958)*

because he burnt down her home in the Civil War; in *The Searchers* the woman he loves married to his brother; *The Man Who Shot Liberty Valance* sees him lose his girl to the man who also usurps his heroism. The Wayne persona inevitably engenders sexual disharmony. For such an American hero Wayne frequently cut an impotent, asexual figure – so colossal that he swamps mere masculinity. He was certainly no Gable – after all, how many women find the Duke attractive? – and this is surely not the way the American male likes to view himself.

Of course there is an escape clause, for Wayne is seldom just a tyrant. After Dunson and Matt have fought themselves into the ground in *Red River*, Tess Millay (Joanne Dru) comes up to them: 'Whoever would have thought that you two could have killed each other?' she chides, and the loving father-son relationship is re-established. 'Come on Debbie, let's go home,' Ethan (Wayne) says to his niece instead of killing her as he had set out

---

Filmography
1927 The Drop Kick (uncredited) (GB: Glitter); Mother Machree (ass. prop man; +extra). **'28** Four Sons (ass. prop man); Hangman's House (uncredited). **'29** Words and Music; Salute; Men Without Women. **'30** Born Reckless (ass. prop man); Rough Romance; Cheer Up and Smile; The Big Trail. **'31** Girls Demand Excitement; Three Girls Lost; Men Are Like That (GB: The Virtuous Wife); The Deceiver; Range Feud; Maker of Men. **'32** The Voice of Hollywood No 13 (short) (announcer only); Shadow of the Eagle (serial); Texas Cyclone; Two-Fisted Law; Lady and Gent; The Hurricane Express (serial); The Hollywood Handicap (short) (guest); Ride Him Cowboy (GB: The Hawk); The Big Stampede; Haunted Gold. **'33** The Telegraph Trail; The Three Musketeers (serial; re-edited into feature Desert Command/ Trouble in the Legion, 1946); Central Airport; Somewhere in Sonora; His Private Secretary; The Life of Jimmy Dolan (GB: The Kid's Last Fight); Baby Face; The Man from Monterey;

Riders of Destiny; College Coach (GB: Football Coach); Sagebrush Trail. **'34** The Lucky Texan; West of the Divide; Blue Steel; The Man from Utah; Randy Rides Alone; The Star Packer; The Trail Beyond; The Lawless Frontier; 'Neath Arizona Skies. **'35** Texas Terror; Rainbow Valley; The Desert Trail; The Dawn Rider; Paradise Canyon; Westward Ho; The New Frontier; The Lawless Range. **'36** The Oregon Trail; The Lawless Nineties; King of the Pecos; The Lonely Trail; Winds of the Wasteland; The Sea Spoilers; Conflict. **'37** California Straight Ahead; I Cover the War; Idol of the Crowd; Adventure's End; Born to the West (reissued as Hell Town). **'38** Pals of the Saddle; Overland Stage Raiders; Santa Fe Stampede; Red River Range. **'39** Stagecoach; The Night Riders; Three Texas Steers (GB: Danger Rides the Range); Wyoming Outlaw; New Frontier; Allegheny Uprising (GB: The First Rebel). **'40** The Dark Command; Three Faces West; The Long Voyage Home; Seven Sinners (GB reissue title; Café of the Seven Sinners); Melody Ranch

Above: Wayne as a rancher enlisting the help of even small boys in The Cowboys (1972). Above centre: a muddy reconciliation for McLintock! and estranged wife (Maureen O'Hara). Above right: Mattie (Kim Darby) and the marshal visit her father's grave in True Grit

do in *The Searchers*, and it was Jean-Luc Godard who pinpointed the secret of Wayne's appeal when he wrote, 'How can I hate John Wayne upholding Goldwater and yet love him tenderly when abruptly he takes Natalie Wood into his arms in the last reel of *The Searchers?*' Elizabeth Taylor was near the mark too when she said in that Congressional Medal plea, 'He was tough as an old nut and soft as a yellow ribbon'.

Wayne was capable of an extraordinary gentleness and chivalry and Ford was early to spot this when he cast him as Ringo, an outlaw who treats the whore Dallas (Claire Trevor) like a lady, in *Stagecoach* (1939). True, he was more accustomed to giving a girl a slap on the behind – most often Maureen O'Hara ('She's a big, lusty, wonderful gal . . . my kinda gal') who as the shrewish colleen of *The Quiet Man* (1952) warrants a playful smack and as the wife in *McLintock!* (1963) a thrashing with a shovel, but tenderness often undercuts his chauvinism. O'Hara seemed the only female

capable of bringing out the erotic in Wayne – caught bare-legged with him in a graveyard during the thunderstorm in *The Quiet Man* she charges the air between them with sexual electricity – despite his having made three films with Dietrich. In *Three Godfathers* (1948) and *The Alamo* Wayne also showed a familiarity with babies and toddlers, but those scenes are best forgotten. Tenderness and warmth are an acceptable part of the noble savage's make-up; allowed to be maudlin Wayne was embarrassing to watch.

Ford's *Stagecoach* had caught the right mixture of gentleness and toughness, and even gives a glimpse of the uncertainty in the Wayne hero. The opening shot of Ringo twirling his rifle over his arm saluted his arrival as a star, but in fact Wayne was already a well-known face, albeit in B pictures.

Shooting to stardom

He was born Marion Michael Morrison in Winterset, Iowa, in 1907, the son of a druggist who took the family West to Glendale, Los Angeles, when Marion was nine. In 1925 he won a football scholarship to the University of Southern California where the Western star Tom Mix saw him. Mix offered him a job shifting props at Fox and there Wayne met John Ford who employed him as a herder of

geese on the set of *Mother Machree* (1927). He appeared as an Irish peasant in Ford's *Hangman's House* (1928) and received his first screen credit as Duke Morrison for a bit-part in *Words and Music* (1929).

Then Raoul Walsh found him, changed his name to John Wayne and made him grow his hair long for the part of the wagon-train scout in the epic Western *The Big Trail* (1930). However, the film failed and despite a studio build-up, Wayne was consigned to B Westerns at Columbia, Mascot, Monogram (for whom he made a series as Singin' Sandy beginning with *Riders of Destiny* in 1933) and eventually Republic on Poverty Row. But he kept in with Ford and was finally bullied by him into a starring career that lasted for forty years.

By the Sixties Wayne had become an American institution, too formidable a presence for the good of his films except when working with Ford or Hawks. The long-awaited Oscar came for his portrayal of Rooster Cogburn, the one-eyed war-horse in *True Grit* (1969), but it was a tribute to Wayne's long career rather than to that particular performance. With his last film, *The Shootist* (1976), man and myth became inseparable: the movie begins with a sequence of clips from old John Wayne movies, a requiem for the character he is playing – an ex-gunfighter dying of cancer – and for himself.

The giant's shadow remains

As movie stars go John Wayne is pretty well indestructible, being the survivor of some two hundred films. Even the uncovering of the darker side of his image seems to inflate him all the more, as did the cancer he subdued for so long. 'I hope you die,' Martin Pawley (Jeffrey Hunter) shouts in rage at Ethan in *The Searchers*. 'That'll be the day,' Ethan grins back. Like Ethan, Wayne endures and is here to stay whether he is wanted or not; a dubious American hero but undoubtedly a remarkable screen presence.

GRAHAM FULLER

uncredited). '41 A Man Betrayed (GB: Citadel of Crime); Lady from Louisiana; The Shepherd of the Hills. '42 Lady for a Night; Reap the Wild Wind; The Spoilers; In Old California; Flying Tigers; Reunion in France (GB: Mademoiselle France); Pittsburgh. '43 A Lady Takes a Chance; In Old Oklahoma. '44 The Fighting Seabees; Tall in the Saddle. '45 Flame of the Barbary Coast; Back to Bataan; They Were Expendable; Dakota. '46 Without Reservations. '47 Angel and the Badman (+prod); Tycoon. '48 Red River; Fort Apache; Three Godfathers. '49 Wake of the Red Witch; The Fighting Kentuckian (+prod); She Wore a Yellow Ribbon; The Sands of Iwo Jima. '50 Rio Grande. '51 Operation Pacific; The Bullfighter and the Lady (prod. only); Flying Leathernecks; Jet Pilot. '52 The Quiet Man; Big Jim McLain (+co-exec. prod). '53 Trouble Along the Way; Island in the Sky (+co-exec. prod); Hondo (+co-exec. prod). '54 The High and the Mighty (+co-exec. prod). '55 The Sea Chase; Blood Alley (+exec. prod). '56 The Con-

queror; The Searchers. '57 The Wings of Eagles; Legend of the Lost (+co-exec. prod). '58 I Married a Woman (guest); The Barbarian and the Geisha. '59 Rio Bravo; The Horse Soldiers. '60 The Alamo (+dir; +prod). North to Alaska. '62 The Comancheros (+add. dir, uncredited); Hatari!; The Man Who Shot Liberty Valance; The Longest Day; How the West Was Won *ep* The Civil War. '63 Donovan's Reef; McLintock! (+exec. prod). '64 Circus World (GB: The Magnificent Showman). '65 The Greatest Story Ever Told; In Harm's Way; The Sons of Katie Elder. '66 Cast a Giant Shadow (+co-exec. prod). '67 El Dorado; The War Wagon (+co-exec. prod). '68 The Green Berets (+co-dir; +exec. prod); Hellfighters. '69 True Grit; The Undefeated. '70 Chisum; Rio Lobo. '71 Big Jake (+exec. prod). '72 The Cowboys; Cancel My Reservation (guest). '73 The Train Robbers (+exec. prod); Cahill – United States Marshal (+exec. prod) (GB: Cahill). '74 McQ. '75 Brannigan (GB); Rooster Cogburn. '76 The Shootist.

1

2

3

A brief introduction to *Butch Cassidy and the Sundance Kid* states: 'Not that it matters, but most of what follows is true'. The author was correct on both counts; the film *is* firmly based on the story of two outlaws at the turn of the century and it really does *not* matter that it is true, for it is one thing to base a script on real events and quite another to claim that the results are a 'true' representation of the facts.

The film is largely a vehicle for the Butch Cassidy (Paul Newman) and Sundance Kid (Robert Redford) relationship and the cinema has probably never produced a more endearing pair of villains. Butch is the thinker, a man who has vision 'and the rest of the world wears bifocals'. Sundance is the strong, more traditional type of Western hero who never uses two words when one will do. Together they rob banks and trains with such appealing politeness and ever-present incompetence that it is impossible not to like them.

For both actors it was an important film. Newman's previous major successes had been in roles where he was a rebellious loner – *The Hustler* (1961), *Hud* (1963), *Cool Hand Luke* (1967) – and his attempts at comedy are best forgotten.

You never met a pair like Butch and The Kid

They're Taking Trains...
They're Taking Banks
And They're Taking
One Piece Of Baggage!

20th Century-Fox presents

**PAUL NEWMAN
ROBERT REDFORD
KATHARINE ROSS**

BUTCH CASSIDY AND THE SUNDANCE KID

A George Roy Hill–Paul Monash Production Co-Starring STROTHER MARTIN, JEFF COREY, HENRY JONES Executive Producer PAUL MONASH Produced by JOHN FOREMAN Directed by GEORGE ROY HILL Written by WILLIAM GOLDMAN Music Composed and Conducted by BURT BACHARACH A NEWMAN-FOREMAN Presentation PANAVISION® COLOUR BY DE LUXE

6

Butch and Sundance, having extricated themselves from a card-game dispute (1), return to the Hole-in-the-Wall Gang's hideout (2) where Butch finds his leadership challenged by Harvey Logan (3). He re-establishes command but nevertheless accepts Harvey's idea of holding up the Union Pacific Flyer on successive runs.

After the first hold-up Sundance seeks out the attentions of teacher Etta Place and Butch demonstrates the wonders of a bicycle to the tune of 'Raindrops Keep Fallin' on My Head' (4).

The second Flyer hold-up is less accomplished than its predecessor; too much dynamite is used on the safe, and as the gang collects the scattered bank

notes (5) another train appears. It contains a Superposse which had been formed with the specific purpose of eliminating the menace of Butch and Sundance.

Several members of the gang are shot down, but Butch and Sundance escape. However, the pursuit is relentless (6) and they become faced with the choice between a hopeless shoot-out or

7

8

Yet his screen relationship with Redford belied what had gone before; he gave a relaxed, amiable performance with a faintly sarcastic humour failing to mask a genuine affection for his partner.

But if the film was a well-received step in a new direction for Newman, it was a major milestone for Redford. The Sundance Kid quite simply made him one of the cinema's great names. The role drew attention to his good looks and even though the script offered him few words, the lines were good enough for him to prove that he was a competent actor.

Although the stars' performances were universally acclaimed and gave the film its identity, the Oscars went elsewhere: to William Goldman for his screenplay, Conrad Hall for cinematography, and Burt Bacharach for his musical score and – with lyricist Hal David – best song, 'Raindrops Keep Fallin' on My Head'. There were nominations for Best Picture and Best Direction but the film lost out to John Schlesinger's Midnight Cowboy (1969) in both instances.

However, the awards it received were a reflection that the film sought to entertain – it looked and sounded good. The ideas were not always startlingly original, with several echoing Arthur Penn's Bonnie and Clyde released two years earlier, but they were executed with style. For example, the sepia shots that open the film, depict the New York sojourn of Butch, Sundance and Etta (Katharine Ross), and provide the final image of the shoot-out, are strikingly effective. The middle sequence makes use of over three hundred stills in the space of a few minutes, an exciting piece of cinema that deserved to work.

It is ironic that William Goldman won his award for a screenplay which had an economy of words bordering on the miserly, but he relied on a terse, witty repartee between the two outlaws to create a feeling of jaunty optimism, combined with occasional moments of perceptive seriousness which hint at the inevitability of the final slaughter. 'Dammit, why is everything we're good at illegal?' they ask. 'Who are those guys?' they wonder in desperation as the law, in the shape of the Superposse, tries to catch up with them.

Their conversation has a casual, wry humour which at times is so anachronistic as to be absurd, but which works nevertheless. During the chase Butch asks Sundance 'I think we lost 'em. Do you think we lost 'em?' and when the reply is 'no' continues 'Neither do I'.

The lively banter carries on to the end when, surrounded by what looks like the greater part of the Bolivian army, they debate the possibility of emigrating to Australia. By then the opposition has mounted to impossible odds and their words have a pathos which the humour cannot hide.

Goldman has been taken to task for the lack of realism in his script and his interpretation of the story, for there is a great deal of evidence to suggest that Butch Cassidy survived and returned to the United States where he opened a business making adding machines.

However, the film that represents the West as it really was has probably yet to be made, as the cult of the Western has long since eclipsed the reality of its subject matter. The cinema presents a stylized, often romantic view of an era that provided – as with Butch Cassidy and the Sundance Kid – rich story pickings which could be embellished and transformed into entertainment. JOHN THOMPSON

Directed by George Roy Hill, 1969

Prod co: Campanile Productions/20th Century-Fox. A Newman-Foreman presentation. **prod:** John Foreman. **sc:** William Goldman. **photo** (Panavision, De Luxe Colour): Conrad Hall. **ed:** John C. Howard, Richard C. Meyer. **art dir:** Walter M. Scott, Chester L. Bayhi. **mus:** Burt Bacharach. **song:** 'Raindrops Keep Fallin' on My Head' by Burt Bacharach, Hal David, sung by B. J. Thomas. **r/t:** 110 minutes.
Cast: Paul Newman (Butch Cassidy), Robert Redford (The Sundance Kid), Katharine Ross (Etta Place), Strother Martin (Percy Garris), Henry Jones (bicycle salesman), Jeff Corey (Sheriff Bledsoe), George Furth (Woodcock), Cloris Leachman (Agnes), Ted Cassidy (Harvey Logan), Kenneth Mars (marshal), Donnelly Rodes (Mason), Jody Gilbert (fat lady), Timothy Scott ('News' Carver), Don Keefer (fireman), Charles Dierkop ('Flat Nose' Curry), Francisco Cordova (bank manager), Nelson Olmstead (photographer), Paul Bryar, Sam Elliott (card players), Charles Akins (bank employee), Eric Sinclair (Tiffany salesman), Dave Dunlap (member of the gang), Percy Helton (old man).

---

a near-suicidal leap from a clifftop. They leap (7).

Worried by their growing notoriety and the posse's professionalism, Butch, Sundance and Etta head for South America (8) after a short stay in New York. Bolivia's banks are the new target, but life again becomes dangerous as their reputation spreads from town to town.

Etta decides to return to the United States (9), leaving Butch and her lover to 'go straight' as payroll guards. However, they are robbed, and after retrieving the money return to outlaw status. While eating at an inn they are recognized and a detachment of the Bolivian army surrounds the town. Escape is finally made impossible (10).

Born in 1925 in Cleveland, Ohio, Newman studied acting at the Yale University Drama School and at Lee Strasberg's Actors' Studio. After appearing in many live television dramas and on Broadway, he made his screen debut in *The Silver Chalice* (1955). After his second film, *Somebody Up There Likes Me* (1956), his stardom was assured, but Newman's major decade was really the Sixties when he created his four most memorable characters in *The Hustler* (1961), *Hud* (1963), *Cool Hand Luke* (1967) and *Butch Cassidy and the Sundance Kid* (1969), at the same time solidifying his clearly recognizable image.

This image was one of moody rebelliousness, rugged individualism, cool detachment and, above all, overpowering sex-appeal. Newman filled the vacuum created by the death of James Dean and decline of Marlon Brando. He ascended over others because he was best able to embody the alienation and restlessness of his era while possessing a traditional beauty that most of his contemporaries lacked. Paul Newman was simultaneously the perfect modern anti-hero and the link with a glamorous Hollywood that was rapidly fading into memory.

Dr Jekyll . . .

His screen persona and private personality have often been opposites. Like other Actors' Studio alumni, he considers himself a 'cerebral' actor and regards each role as an agonizing 'study session', yet he has played many spontaneous, uninhibited characters. He has also often portrayed supremely confident and charming types even though he is privately rather shy and insecure. Committed passionately to liberal and humanitarian causes, Newman has created a substantial gallery of men who are committed mainly to themselves, and although he has been married to one woman – actress Joanne Woodward – since 1958, his characters attack, insult and discard women, subordinating them entirely to male ambition.

Ambition is in fact a key aspect of the Newman image. Some of his characters are born on the wrong side of the tracks and pursue the American Dream of wealth and status, as in *The Young Philadelphians* (1959) and *Sweet Bird of Youth* (1962). Others are not necessarily interested in money – the goal may be winning a pool match in *The Hustler* or a motor race in *Winning* (1969), executing a mission such as helping Jewish refugees to enter Palestine in *Exodus* (1960), or excelling at music, the aim of Ram Bowen (Newman) in *Paris Blues* (1961) – but the means are similar. These men set aside considerations of love, family, humanity and morality, and push forward ruthlessly, alienating themselves from society in the process.

However, Newman's performances inspire identification with even his most arrogant and selfish characters' problems and obsessions. Many of his 'nasty' men at least have the

Right: Big Daddy (Burl Ives) learns he has cancer when his angry son (Newman) tells him during a confrontation in Cat on a Hot Tin Roof. *Centre right: ageing playboy Chance Wayne (Newman) and his lover (Shirley Knight) in* Sweet Bird of Youth.
Far right: private eye Harper *closes in on his quarry aided by Fay Estabrook (Shelley Winters)*

Paul Newman

First, the eyes; dazzlingly bright blue and seeming – as one columnist p[ut] it – 'as if they have just finished taking a shower'. Then, the classic profi[le] and sensual mouth, suggesting nothing less than a Greek statue [or] perhaps even Michelangelo's David. At the start, Paul Newman['s] success derived largely from his extraordinary looks and it took audience[s] – and critics – some time to discover the serious actor behind the façad[e]

having characteristic of recognizing their nastiness and turning it into charm; Newman's boyishness and sense of humour make them engaging. Of course this involvement is generated partly by his looks: he may characterize obnoxious, irresponsible, rough types, but his features usually suggest intelligence and sensitivity.

In addition, his portrayals of Brick in *Cat on a*

Left: the famous features that have helped ensure Newman's continuing success. Below: in The Sting he played an ingenious con-man out to trick a big-time gangster. Below right: as a pool shark in The Hustler, Newman scored one of his biggest hits

Hot Tin Roof, Billy the Kid in *The Left-Handed Gun* (both 1958) and Luke in *Cool Hand Luke* evoke sympathy because of the extreme loneliness that their actions bring them. A remarkable number of his characters are also humanized by having to undergo severe physical punishment: he has his thumbs broken in *The Hustler*; his face smashed in *Sweet Bird of Youth*; is dragged by a horse in *The Life and Times of Judge Roy Bean* (1972); and is continually and mercilessly tortured in *Cool Hand Luke*. The extreme degradation and pain creates an atmosphere of vulnerability that facilitates audience identification.

Perhaps the most important reason for the appeal of Newman's heroes and anti-heroes is

that they seem to have embodied the general moods of their times. In key Fifties roles, playing characters like Rocky Graziano (*Somebody Up There Likes Me*) and Billy the Kid, he slipped into the Brando/Dean mould – the confused, inarticulate rebel who strikes out at the world without knowing why. Rocky's alienation from his uncaring father and Billy's general difficulty with father-figures struck another responsive chord at the time, allying them with Dean's characters as well as with other troubled youths in Fifties cinema.

Rebel with a cause
In the Sixties, Newman's image evolved into that of the relatively *intelligent* rebel, more in

Profile of a winner

control of himself and better able to define his cause. 'Fast' Eddie (*The Hustler*), Chance Wayne (*Sweet Bird of Youth*) and Hud Bannon (*Hud*) *can* describe what motivates them and although they are hardly set on improving society their very ability to articulate may have made them connect with youth during the Kennedy era.

Ironically, Newman's stated intentions in playing these ruthless opportunists was to have the audience condemn them. He hoped to show that men who have everything impressive to fellow Americans – attractiveness, charm, virility, an ability to seduce women and to feel equally comfortable drinking with the guys – often have 'the seed of corruption' in them, and succeed only at the cost of their souls. Yet they were vibrant, magnetic, and audiences were drawn to them.

The quintessence was Hud, the amoral modern Texan who could have been a prototype for J.R. Ewing (Larry Hagman) of the popular television series *Dallas*; arrogant, opportunistic, Machiavellian, incapable of warmth or affection, rotten to the core – and yet completely captivating. Newman pulled out all the stops, bringing to perfection his familiar characteristics: the cynical, aloof manner; the nasty, contemptuous voice; the sly, insinuating smile; the icy stare; the insolent sexiness. The ads proclaimed, 'Paul Newman *is* Hud'. Their assumption may have been inaccurate, but for audiences Newman and Hud were one.

'Cool' in the coolers

In the later Sixties, perhaps as a reflection of society's growing cynicism, most of Newman's films abandoned even the attempt to condemn their amoral protagonists. Harper, the slightly

Above: Newman as Luke Jackson in Cool Hand Luke, *the story of a convict's two years hard labour on a chain gang and his eventual death. Below: in* Hud *he plays an amoral rancher whose debauched way of life finally drives his young nephew (Brandon de Wilde) away from the ranch*

Above: Newman with Joanne Woodward on the set of Rachel, Rachel, *in which she plays a repressed schoolmistress. Below:* The Life and Times of Judge Roy Bean *starred Newman as the Judge and Roddy McDowall as Frank Gass but the beer-drinking bear stole the limelight*

Right: Newman and Woodward shooting a scene for WUSA *as they 'speed' along, the back-projected scenery lending it authenticity. Below right: in an effort to escape his image, he played a foul-mouthed hockey-coach keeping a fading team together in* Slap Shot

orn, sardonic private eye in the 1966 movie the same name, was a perfect embodiment of xties 'cool': anti-heroic and brutally exploitative, he is the master of flippancy, nastiness and the new art of the 'put on'. Now audiences were meant to regard the character the hero, and they did, making Harper one Newman's most popular roles.

Moviegoers also responded enthusiastically *Cool Hand Luke*. Anti-establishment and nti-authority, Luke breaks the law not beuse of social deprivation – the excuse in most nirties' films – but because it gives him mething to do. The act of rebellion has come its own justification, making Luke an propriate anti-hero for the late Sixties. Here ewman had returned to the silent rebel type, ut unlike the Fifties rebel Luke chose to main silent. He is neither confused nor rectionless but is an intelligent individual

who elects to separate himself from the rest of humanity. Yet, as opposed to 'Fast' Eddie and Hud, he has no definite goal and unintentionally becomes a martyr.

Coping with comedy

As Luke, Newman gave his most relaxed performance so far, but in *Butch Cassidy and the Sundance Kid* he is even looser and more casual. Butch, a ludicrous, failed opportunist and hopeless romantic, is a fascinating comic version of Newman's ambitious dreamers. In previous attempts at comedy – such as *Rally 'Round the Flag, Boys!* (1958) and *A New Kind of Love* (1963) – Newman was stiff and forced, but here he is spontaneous and appealing. This derives partly from the fact that Butch is an easy-going, naturally funny fellow instead of an exaggerated comic character, and partly from the pairing with Robert Redford, which

creates an immensely attractive camaraderie that is rare in Newman's career. A huge success, the film had everything for contemporary audiences; hip cleverness, a casual attitude towards crime and violence, blundering anti-heroes instead of the traditional genre types, and good-natured but appropriately distanced relationships.

In the Seventies, Newman remained on the list of top box-office stars and two of his films, *The Sting* (1973) and *The Towering Inferno* (1974), far surpassed the grosses of *Butch Cassidy and the Sundance Kid*. Still, *The Sting*'s success may have been due more to the Newman/Redford partnership, or even to Redford's popularity alone, than to Newman's appeal, and *The Towering Inferno* did not seem to depend on the drawing power of its stars – the appeal of the disaster-movie being well established by then. Otherwise, Newman's only big hit since 1969 has been *Slap Shot* (1977), in which his late-career relaxation and sense of fun were strong contributions to his characterization of a hockey-coach.

His other Seventies work includes *The Drowning Pool* (1975) – a sequel to *Harper* that failed to recapture the original's magic – and several films in which Newman played such extremely unpleasant characters that audiences could not identify with them: a cynical, corrupt and thoroughly vicious opportunist in *WUSA* (1970); a stubborn reactionary in *Sometimes a Great Notion* (1971); and an exceedingly sadistic, violent man in *The Mackintosh Man* (1973).

His most challenging film in recent years has been *Buffalo Bill and the Indians . . . or Sitting Bull's History Lesson* (1976), a cynical exploration of show business in which Newman, adopting an ironic stance towards his character, seems to be exploring his own identity as a superstar. However, the film was so unremittingly bitter that it failed to find an audience.

New directions

During the late Sixties Newman decided to try his hand in another area and he has achieved some critical success as a director. *Rachel, Rachel* (1968) and *The Effect of Gamma Rays on Man-in-the-Moon Marigolds* (1972) are gentle, richly emotional and melancholy – yet never depressing – slices of ordinary people's lives. Both indicate a mature visual sensibility and feature excellent performances by Joanne Woodward who also appeared in the fourth film Newman directed, a television feature entitled *The Shadow Box* (1980). *Sometimes a Great Notion*, the story of the problems faced by a logging family, combined precise character portraits and vigorous outdoor adventure in the Howard Hawks mode.

The remainder of his acting career will be interesting to follow. In his mid-fifties he has retained his looks and physique and, like many traditional male stars, is enduring as a leading man well into his later years; his romances with women quite a few years his junior in *The Mackintosh Man* and *When Time Ran Out . . .* (1980) are surely in the Gable/Cooper/Grant tradition. On the other hand, he has always wanted to be a character actor and since this will undoubtedly be forced upon him by age, he may enjoy the opportunity. Judge Roy Bean, a combination of leading man – attractive, gentle, charming a young woman – and character personality – grizzled, gruff, befriending a bear – is a suitable point of departure.
MICHAEL KERBEL

Filmography
1955 The Silver Chalice. **'56** Somebody Up There Likes Me; The Rack. **'57** The Helen Morgan Story (GB: Both Ends of the Candle); Until They Sail. **'58** The Long Hot Summer; The Left-Handed Gun; Cat on a Hot Tin Roof; Rally 'Round the Flag, Boys! **'59** The Young Philadelphians (GB: The City Jungle). **'60** From the Terrace; Exodus. **'61** The Hustler; Paris Blues. **'62** Sweet Bird of Youth; Hemingway's Adventures of a Young Man/Adventures of a Young Man. **'63** Hud; A New Kind of Love; The Prize. **'64** What a Way to Go!; The Outrage. **'65** Lady L (USA-FR-IT). **'66** Harper (GB: The Moving Target); Torn Curtain. **'67** Hombre; Cool Hand Luke. **'68** The Secret War of Harry Frigg; Rachel, Rachel (dir; +prod. only). **'69** Winning (+co-exec. prod); Butch Cassidy and the Sundance Kid (+co-exec. prod). **'70** King . . . a Filmed Record: Montgomery to Memphis/Martin Luther King (doc) (co-narr. only); WUSA (+co-prod). **'71** They Might Be Giants (co-prod. only); Sometimes a Great Notion (+dir; +co-exec. prod) (GB: Never Give an Inch). **'72** Pocket Money (+co-exec. prod); The Effect of Gamma Rays on Man-in-the-Moon Marigolds (dir; +prod. only); The Life and Times of Judge Roy Bean (+co-exec. prod). **'73** The Mackintosh Man (GB); The Sting. **'74** The Towering Inferno. **'75** The Drowning Pool (+co-exec. prod). **'76** Silent Movie (guest); Buffalo Bill and the Indians . . . or Sitting Bull's History Lesson. **'77** Slap Shot. **'79** Quintet. **'80** When Time Ran Out . . .; Fort Apache, the Bronx. **'81** Absence of Malice. **'82** The Verdict.

In the early Sixties the American cinema was obsessed with size – epic themes, wide screens, three-hour running times, all-star casts. Genre spectaculars – *The Guns of Navarone* (1961), *El Cid* (1961), *How the West Was Won* (1962) – lured audiences away from their TV sets in huge numbers.

The Great Escape is a typical product of this inflationary period, scarcely justifying its length, but zestfully directed by John Sturges. The script – a watered-down version of Paul Brickhill's largely factual account – is an anthology of genre clichés established in many British prisoner-of-war camp dramas of the Fifties, except that here there is a formidable American presence.

The British films, such as *The Wooden Horse* (1950) and *The Colditz Story* (1955), consciously strove to create a microcosm of England behind barbed wire, where attitudes of class could maintain morale and discipline. The deprivations and dangers of incarceration were minimized to strengthen the point about British resilience and the known outcome of the war; eccentricity and xenophobia became patriotic attributes, and quips like 'See you at Simpson's' served to promote a nostalgia that was fast fading.

The Germans were rarely cast as loathsome villains, but tended to be characterized as 'goons' – incompetent and obsequious. But as the Cold War developed, with Germany divided and suddenly the frontline of Allied defence, war films began to make distinctions between ordinary soldiers and officers who merely acted under orders, and the sadistic and fanatical SS men.

The Great Escape simply spreads this judicious blend of political diplomacy and Allied fervour on an unusually broad canvas, using an extensive and superbly designed set built on location in Bavaria. As with *The Guns of Navarone*, it is essentially an adventure drama, only incidentally a war film, with sharply defined characters played by charismatic stars.

Significantly, the film kills off the entire British contingent (Richard Attenborough, Donald Pleasence, Gordon Jackson, David McCallum) whilst the more resourceful and independently-minded Americans (the more expensive actors) survive. The massacre of Attenborough and his countrymen is shown and then forgotten in the closing images that pay tribute to Steve McQueen's star presence.

The film is in some ways a re-working of *The Magnificent Seven* (1960), having an equally memorable thematic score by Elmer Bernstein, and starring three of the 'seven': McQueen, Charles Bronson (playing a Pole) and James Coburn (playing an Australian). The fourth American is the amiable James Garner, and as a star vehicle the film is brilliantly organized.

Garner plays a versatile scrounger, Hendley – a humanized version of William Holden's Sefton in

1

2

The MIRISCH COMPANY Presents
Steve McQUEEN · James GARNER · Richard ATTENBOROUGH

A GLORIOUS SAGA OF THE R.A.F

JOHN STURGES'

COLOUR BY DE LUXE
PANAVISION®

THE GREAT ESCAPE

JAMES **DONALD** · CHARLES **BRONSON** · DONALD **PLEASENCE** · JAMES **COBURN** · JOHN **LEYTON** · Produced & Directed by JOHN **STURGES** · Screenplay by JAMES **CLAVELL & BURNETT** · Based upon the book by PAUL **BRICKHILL**
Music by ELMER **BERNSTEIN** A MIRISCH-ALPHA PICTURE

Stalag 17 (1953). He puts his illicit 'general store' to good use, applying the Americanized hard-sell to a timid and stupid German called Werner who is terrified of being sent to the Russian front. Hendley's growing loyalty to the blind and feeble Blythe marks him as the American with heart – a soft-skinned cynic. Bronson's Danny Velinski represents bulging muscles and a neurotic mind – the conscience of the audience. James Coburn's Sedgwick is an irresistible image of stoicism whose outlandish suitcase upsets the bureaucratic British-run escape routine, but does not prevent his peaceful and picturesque jaunt on a stolen bicycle to neutral Switzerland.

But most noteworthy is Steve McQueen as Hilts, the quizzical, independent tough-guy who dominates the film, playing off superbly against Attenborough's stiff-upper-lip Squadron Leader Bartlett. Attenborough arrives at the camp preceded by his reputation as a fearless fighter and staunch ally, but it

is the expectations aroused by Hilts that generate most tension. *The Great Escape* strongly confirmed McQueen's stardom, and it ingeniously cheats its audience by regularly sending him into solitary confinement, away from the action. And yet McQueen's constant tossing of a baseball in his cell increases the tension within both

himself and the audience. When the escape finally comes, the film indulges McQueen's love of speed by granting him a cathartic motor-cycle chase across open fields. His final crash into a barbed wire barrier – possibly a foretaste of the Iron Curtain – sensibly prevents him from turning into a comic strip hero.
ADRIAN TURNER

Directed by John Sturges, 1963
Prod co: Mirisch/Alpha. **prod:** John Sturges. **ass prod:** Robert E. Relyea. **sc** James Clavell, W.R. Burnett, based on the book by Paul Brickhill. **phot** (De Luxe, Panavision): Daniel Fapp. **col:** De Luxe. **sp eff:** Paul Pollard. **ed** Ferris Webster. **art dir:** Fernando Carrere. **cost:** Bert Henrikson. **mus:** Elme Bernstein. **sd:** Harold Lewis. **ass dir:** Jack Reddish. **prod man:** Allen K. Wood **r/t:** 173 minutes.
Cast: Steve McQueen (*Hilts*), James Garner (*Hendley*), Richard Attenborough (*Bartlett*), James Donald (*Ramsey*), Charles Bronson (*Danny Velinski*), Donald Pleasence (*Blythe*), James Coburn (*Sedgwick*), John Leyton (*Willie*), Gordon Jackson (*MacDonald*), David McCallum (*Ashley-Pitt*), Nigel Stock (*Cavendish*), William Russell (*Sorren*), Angus Lennie (*Ives*), Tom Adams (*Nimmo*), Robert Desmond (*Griffith*), Lawrence Montaigne (*Haynes*), Jud Taylor (*Goff*), Hannes Messemer (*Von Luger*), Rober Graf (*Werner*), Harry Riebauer (*Strachwitz*), Robert Freytag (*Posen*), Heinz Weiss (*Kramer*), Til Kiwe (*Frick*), Hans Reisser (*Kuhn*), George Mikel (*Dietrich*), Ulrich Beiger (*Preissen*), Karl Otto Alberty (*Steinbach*).

3

4

6

8

9

In 1942 Squadron Leader Bartlett arrives at Stalag Luft North, a top security German prisoner-of-war camp. He contacts Ramsay, the senior British officer, and proposes a mass breakout of 250 men. A nucleus of experts is assembled but an American –

Hilts – says he is breaking out next day (1). Testing a blind-spot between two watch-towers (2), Hilts is spotted and sent to the 'cooler' for solitary confinement, where he passes the time playing compulsively with a baseball.

Meanwhile, Bartlett's plan goes ahead and three tunnels – nicknamed Tom, Dick and Harry – are started. On his release Hilts volunteers to escape and be recaptured, after having memorized the surrounding countryside. Hilts has his day of freedom and is returned to the cooler. Another American, Hendley, scrounges special equipment from the Germans by bribing them with cigarettes and chocolate; Blythe forges identity papers; a Pole, Velinski, supervises the digging; others make civilian clothes and act as look-outs.

Hilts is released and starts an illicit distillery, and during impromptu Fourth of July

celebrations (3) the Germans discover Tom. Bartlett orders that all work be concentrated on Harry, and although Blythe begins to go blind, and Velinski suffers from claustrophobia (4), the tunnel is finally made ready. But because Harry is several yards short of the trees, the Germans discover the escape-in-progress (5) and only 76 men get away, travelling by train, plane, boat and on foot (6).

Hilts leads the Germans on a hair-raising motor-cycle chase, but crashes (7) and is arrested; Blythe is killed in a plane crash (8); Velinski and a few others manage to cross the border. Bartlett is recaptured after a chase in a village (9) and is summarily executed along with 50 others. As the Commandant leaves the camp in disgrace, some prisoners are returned – including Hendley and Hilts, the latter being thrown his baseball as he walks towards the cooler (10).

The Steve McQueen Affair

'Speed is incredible and beautiful. Slip-streaming around a turn in the middle of a pack is what separates the men from the boys. If you can't cut in you may have to back out. It's as simple as that.' The words of Steve McQueen, talking about his love for race-driving and perhaps about his career as a film actor, are the words of the most realistic of superstars. Tough, laconic, and independent, McQueen always seemed likely to win the race . . .

The career of Steve McQueen seems a classic example of the American Dream made real, of a small-town boy triumphing over adversity – broken home, poor education – to become one of the richest and most sought-after superstars in the world. He was a man who finally found the love he never knew as a child in the adoration of the millions of fans who flocked to almost every action-packed screen adventure graced by his rugged, tanned but quizzical good looks. His shocking early death at 50 from cancer robbed the cinema of an exceptional personality who had been steadily maturing into an actor of a wider range and sensitivity

than his scripts demanded, and one keenly interested in all aspects of the productions in which he starred.

The Indianapolis kid

Terence Stephen McQueen was born into a farming family in Indianapolis on March 24, 1930; his father left before the baby was six months old and never saw his son again. His mother was only 19 and went to work in California, entrusting her child to his great-uncle, who raised him on his farm and saw that he had a basic education in the local one-room school. When he was nine, he was taken

back to Indianapolis by his mother, a move that seems to have propelled him into delinquency. He joined small gangs, took to petty thieving and the kinds of minor hooliganism shown in Fellini's *I Vitelloni* (1953, *The Spivs*) a film McQueen admired for its accurate depiction of teenagers hanging around on street corners whistling at girls. His mother remarried and took Steve to Los Angeles but he had become an unruly, rebellious youth and had to be sent to a reform school – Chino where he spent two years – when he was not playing truant. The school's tough regime made a valuable impression, however and in later years McQueen often revisited it talk to the boys and present awards he had endowed, also regularly keeping in touch with former inmates and helping them when in trouble.

After a brief unsuccessful reunion with his mother, McQueen ran away to sea on a tanker and took several odd jobs before enlisting in the Marine Corps at 17; he worked as a tank-driver and mechanic, which prompted a life-long interest in vehicles, especially motorcycles and racing. In 1950 he went to live in the bohemian Greenwich Village district of New York where, between low-paid casual jobs as a bartender and TV repair-man, he was first introduced to acting by a girlfriend. Through her he met Sanford Meisner, director of the Neighbourhood Playhouse drama-school, who enrolled him after an audition, immediately recognizing his tough and yet strangely child-like qualities. Meisner found McQueen his first professional part, a one-line role in a Yiddish play on Second Avenue which paid $40 a week. He subsequently won a scholarship to the Uta Hagen-Herbert Berghof Dramatic School in Manhattan, and two years later was selected as one of five out of five thousand applicants to the Actors' Studio, the famous 'Method' workshop run by Lee Strasberg. About this time a diving accident impaired his hearing but he overcame this hardship and embarked on a modestly successful theatrical career, acting in summer stock, appearing in several television dramas and eventually making it to Broadway in 1956 – replacing Ben Gazzara as the young drug-addict in *A Hatful of Rain*.

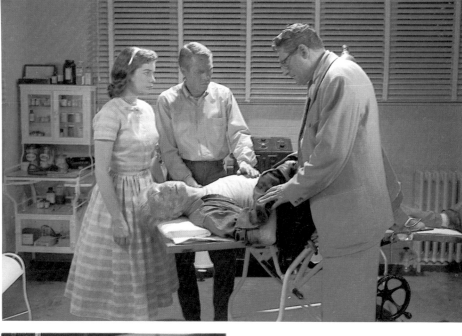

A wanted man

After his marriage to actress and singer Neile Adams, McQueen moved to Hollywood and won his first film role as a $19-a-day extra in Robert Wise's *Somebody Up There Likes Me* (1956), the life-story of boxer Rocky Graziano. In 1958, billed as Steven McQueen, he played the lead part of a Jewish law student – with John Barrymore's son Drew cast as his Catholic, criminal friend – in a confused Harold Robbins melodrama, *Never Love a Stranger*. He received better notices in an independently produced, low-budget thriller, *The Great St Louis Bank Robbery* (1959), and had turned in the most natural performance in a near-classic science-fiction B movie, *The Blob* (1958), combatting a carnivorous jelly from Outer Space

Left: Hilts 'the Cooler King' finally comes to grief in The Great Escape. *Above right: an early part for McQueen in* The Blob. *Right: publicity shot for* The Cincinnati Kid *with Ann-Margret and Tuesday Weld. Below: with Faye Dunaway in* The Thomas Crown Affair

and some equally ludicrous dialogue.

McQueen's break into stardom came, in fact, not in the cinema but on television, thanks to his creation in 1957 of the role of bounty-hunter Josh Randall in the CBS Western series *Wanted – Dead or Alive*. McQueen managed to make the character sympathetic – a man doing his job, however sordid, as best he could. It was a part he was to repeat, with variations, in several of his films. The director John Sturges saw McQueen in *Wanted – Dead or Alive* and subsequently gave him the scene-stealing part of a cheeky, scrounging soldier (originally meant for Sammy Davis Jr) in his war film *Never So Few* (1959). The production was designed as the Hollywood launch for Gina Lollobrigida and also starred Frank Sinatra and Peter Lawford, but it was McQueen who caught the eye with the deft timing of a practised comedian – a very different characterization from the moody men of action he was usually to portray.

Sturges probably did most to further McQueen's film career. He brilliantly cast him as one of *The Magnificent Seven* (1960), his outstandingly successful Western remake of Kurosawa's *Shichinin No Samurai* (1954, *Seven Samurai*). McQueen immediately caught the public's imagination as a deadly gunfighter, cool and calculating but with sufficient wry touches to offset the playing of the film's established star Yul Brynner. He was quickly hailed as the successor to James Dean, and his offscreen behaviour – his rebelliousness, independence and idiosyncrasies in speech and dress – helped project a hell-raising image.

Into top gear

After *Never So Few*, McQueen's only other out-and-out comic role was as another larcenous but lovable man in uniform, a peacetime navy lieutenant in *The Honeymoon Machine* (1961) who uses his warship's computer to break the roulette bank at Venice and nearly provokes a Russian attack in the process. But he seemed more at ease in straight war dramas – such as Don Siegel's *Hell Is for Heroes* (1962) – and confirmed his impact with critics and millions of moviegoers with his daredevil motorcycle stunts in *The Great Escape* (1963), in which

Sturges co-starred him with James Garner and Richard Attenborough as one of the Allied prisoners-of-war tunnelling to freedom from Stalag Luft North. As 'the Cooler King' (who constantly tries to break out alone and is thrown into the 'cooler' when recaptured), McQueen had a part completely in character – and himself suggested the famous chase sequence when he makes his getaway, though, as in his later pictures, he actually performed less of the exploits than meet the eye, reluctantly accepting a double for the most dangerous takes. He still won the Best Actor award at the Moscow Film Festival, however.

In his next couple of films McQueen strengthened his appeal to female audiences with romantic roles for the director Robert Mulligan – partnering Natalie Wood in *Love With the Proper Stranger* (1963), where he played a footloose musician reluctant to marry his pregnant girlfriend, and appearing as the violent hillbilly with Lee Remick as his wife in *Baby, the Rain Must Fall* (1965), an offbeat drama unsure of its convictions. McQueen had by this time earned enough to invest in several small businesses and start his own production

companies to buy or develop film projects. But he took a year's holiday with his family before beginning his next film, Norman Jewison's suspenseful *The Cincinnati Kid* (1965), the story of a young stud-poker player pitted against a champion card-sharp played by Edward G. Robinson, whose very presence managed to upstage even McQueen's delicately judged performance.

In 1966 he worked again with director Robert Wise in *The Sand Pebbles*, this time a costly and elaborate reconstruction of an incident involving an American gunboat blockaded on the Yangtze River during the Chinese Civil War in 1926. Although the cumbersome production went down like the Titanic in cinemas all over the world, McQueen clearly

Below: the climax of Nevada Smith *with McQueen – a young version of the character played by Alan Ladd in* The Carpetbaggers *(1964) – about to take his revenge on the men who murdered his father and Indian mother. Right: as the ex-convict who, unreformed, gets together with his wife (Ali McGraw) and robs a bank in Sam Peckinpah's violent crime thriller* The Getaway

revelled in his well-observed role as the gunboat's chief mechanic. 'He dominates every foot of the film on which his image is imprinted', the director commented, and the star was subsequently nominated for an Academy Award for his magnetic portrayal of the decent but doomed sailor.

Crowning moments

This stage of his career saw McQueen able to choose his own roles and, with the backing of his own company Solar, ensure that any picture would adequately showcase his talents. For Henry Hathaway and Solar he played the title-role in *Nevada Smith* (1966) a latter-day revenge Western inspired by a character in Harold Robbins' novel *The Carpetbaggers*; his rifle-toting, Christ-like pose for the film's publicity became a popular icon. Solar also co-produced *The Thomas Crown Affair* (1968), a well-liked thriller flashily directed by Norman Jewison, which gave McQueen some memorably erotic scenes with Faye Dunaway, cast as the insurance investigator using all her charms to counter his suave and sexy crooked businessman. 'He's the most difficult actor I ever worked with' Jewison later remarked.

Racing remained a ruling passion of McQueen's life, despite the fears of his wife and the studios' insurance agents, and it was one he persisted in pursuing on the screen – with unforgettable results in *Bullitt* (1968), which might have been an ordinary police thriller but for its amazing car chase up and down the steep streets of San Francisco, but with a notable lack of success in *Le Mans* (1971). This is a dull, near-documentary re-creation of the 24-hour French race that had become an obsessive goal for McQueen but proved less engrossing for his public. Its box-office failure contributed to a spell of self-doubt for the actor, who found the demands of stardom an increasing burden. But working twice in 1972 for Sam Peckinpah, a kindred unruly spirit, brought him a different, more mature type of role – as the declining rodeo rider in *Junior Bonner* – and a new wife (Neile had left him in 1970) in Ali McGraw, co-star of *The Getaway*, a violent and amoral robbery-and-chase movie.

Around this time McQueen joined with Barbra Streisand, Sidney Poitier and Paul Newman in their First Artists Production (FAP) company and remained one of the world's most highly paid performers throughout the Seventies, though his films became less frequent. He took the title role in *Papillon* (1973), the blockbuster adaptation of a real-life escape from Devil's Island, and played the fire-chief hero of *The Towering Inferno* (1974), the disaster movie that proved far from disastrous at the world's box-offices. But McQueen was not at all satisfied with the way his career was going and tried to strike out into more intellectual movies.

Million dollar McQueen

Living as a virtual recluse, he turned down many pictures after *The Towering Inferno* and even refused the lead in *Apocalypse Now* (1979) by demanding $3 million for three weeks work, an unheard-of sum in 1976 when production began (though he earned more than that on *The Hunter* (1980).

He returned to the screen after an absence of nearly four years in a modest and valiant version of Ibsen's play *An Enemy of the People* (1977), in which he was a heavily bearded and almost unrecognizable as the doctor fighting hypocrisy in a small Norwegian spa. Poorly released and critically undervalued, it was nevertheless a fine, impressive enterprise and suggested new avenues for McQueen to explore. Indeed, he planned to film Harold

Below: McQueen as a tired and grizzled bounty-hunter in Tom Horn. *Bottom, from left to right: as a brooding American racing driver in his pet project* Le Mans, *a virtually plotless, semi-documentary re-creation of the big race; as* Papillon, *the prisoner who escapes from a nightmare existence on Devil's Island; in his final film* The Hunter *as the man who tracks down crooks who jump bail*

Pinter's play *Old Times*, but a bitter lawsuit with FAP obliged him to make *Tom Horn* (1979), another Western about a bounty-hunter, instead.

The hunter and the hunted

He was already ill during the making of *The Hunter*; this final film, though not especially distinguished, shows a tender, rueful quality amid the knockabout heroics and McQueen's instinctive feel for comedy gives an appealing edge to the true story of a modern bounty-hunter and his crazy capers.

After the rare lung disease mesothelioma was diagnosed late in 1979, the actor characteristically tried to fight off the cancer for a year, undergoing strenuous exercise, diet and medication in a controversial treatment which at first seemed to work. He died of a heart attack after a stomach operation, on November 7, 1980, in a Mexican hospital, with his third wife model Barbara Minty and his two eldest children at his side.

It was a tragic end for a star whose life had celebrated manly virtues and whose youthful high-spirits and deep-rooted insecurity had matured into courage and determination, both on the screen and off. His death was the sadder in view of his frustrated efforts to use his star status to better effect. At the height of his fame he had no illusions about his role as a star and was never convinced that acting was a thing for a grown man to be doing.

PHILLIP BERGSON

Filmography
1956 Somebody Up There Likes Me (uncredited). '58 Never Love a Stranger; The Blob. '59 The Great St Louis Bank Robbery; Never So Few. '60 The Magnificent Seven. '61 The Honeymoon Machine. '62 Hell Is for Heroes; The War Lover (GB). '63 The Great Escape; A Soldier in the Rain; Love With the Proper Stranger. '65 Baby, the Rain Must Fall; The Cincinnati Kid. '66 Nevada Smith; The Sand Pebbles. '68 The Thomas Crown Affair; Bullitt. '69 The Reivers. '71 On Any Sunday (doc); Le Mans. '72 Junior Bonner; The Getaway. '73 Papillon. '74 The Towering Inferno. '77 An Enemy of the People (+exec. prod). '79 Tom Horn (+exec. prod). '80 The Hunter.

I think *Dont Look Back* (1967) is about Bob Dylan. About a folksinger and songwriter coming to a turning point in his career. It may be about music. It may even be about myself. Dylan called it 'Pennebaker by Dylan'.

The idea for a film like this had been in my head for a long time. Not necessarily about Dylan but about an artist trying to stay on top of an extraordinary talent in the face of adulation and disapproval.

I think the first time I thought about it was when reading Peter Quennell's book 'The Pisan Chronicles', a collection of letters to, from and about Byron during the tumultuous years he spent in Pisa with Percy and Mary Shelley. By listening to each character, as it were, through their writing, I had a sense, unlike anything I had read before, that I was there in Pisa watching them create the legend that was to dominate literature for the next two-hundred years. That seemed like a film worth doing. All it needed was finding the right person at the right moment. A film for history; perhaps instead of history.

Meeting Dylan

That's the movie I want to make when Albert Grossman, Dylan's manager, walks into our studio. He wants to know if my partner, Richard Leacock, and I would be interested in

Looking back on

D. A. Pennebaker, along with film-makers like Richard Leacock, the Maysles brothers, Robert Drew and others, changed the face of the American documentary. Here Pennebaker recounts the shooting of *Dont Look Back*, a visual record of the 1965 British tour of folk-singer and songwriter Bob Dylan – a key film in the evolution of 'direct cinema' and one that led the way to the making of pop-music festival films like *Monterey Pop* (1968) and *Woodstock* (1970) in the late Sixties and early Seventies

filming Dylan on his forthcoming English concert tour. Ricky wants to know who Bob Dylan is. It's going to be my project.

I meet Dylan at the Cedar Tavern. He's with Bob Neuwrith, who's going to be the road manager. We stand awkwardly at the bar. He and Neuwrith are both dressed in black leather jackets, like motorcyclists. I'd read that he rode a motorcycle. I wonder if he has one outside.

I think that I'd better figure out how to raise some money because I'd like to film this trip.

I listen to 'Subterranean Homesick Blues' and call people I know in the television business . . . or *any* business. Either they don't know who Dylan is or they don't think much of his music; at least they don't think it will play on television.

By taking only one person, sound man Bo Van Dyke, and using a couple of Dylan friends, Howard and Jones Alk, we figure t make the film on our own. The deal is that w put up the production costs and Dylan puts u himself and we split the profits 50/50. The was no contract. We shook hands on it.

We arrive in England in the early spring 1965 with folksinger Joan Baez (who clain she is only along for the ride). From then on it a month of carrying heavy equipment, loadin cameras and trying to get film to labs early i the morning after being up all night, an wondering how to shoot the concerts. An there is the problem of sticking with Dyla who is under a number of pressures, includin those from Joan Baez (personal) and th

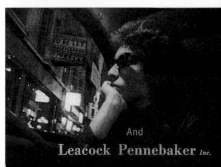

Dont Look Back

with the music, pulling it through by hand, but the material is so simple that it cuts itself. I feel like an audience simply watching it go by.

Ed Emshwiller, the Underground film-maker, has sent me over a piece of film he's shot of Dylan down in Greenwood, Mississippi during a civil rights rally. It sits over my editing bench for months. Now I'm into the film, I come to a place where the BBC correspondent looks hungrily at Bob and says: 'How did it all start for you Bob, how did it all begin?' I can't think what to cut to. I'm stuck. Then I remember Ed's roll of film. I attach it to the BBC man, pull it through the viewer to see what it's like. I never take it out of the film. I never even cut it.

The first screening takes place in Hollywood about six months later. It is a disaster. Afterwards Dylan turns around to the hundred or so strangers who have sneaked into the screening room and says: 'Well now, it's got to have a lot of changes. Tomorrow we'll just run it again and I'll make a list of what we have to do.' Despair!

The next day the screening room is even more packed with total strangers, all Hollywood Dylan freaks. I am mute with paranoia. This screening is worse than the first and ends up completely out of sync. I am thinking seriously of giving up film-making and going back to engineering. It's the worst screening I have ever had to sit through. The lights go on. The room is quiet. Dylan has a big pad of yellow paper. He holds it up – it's empty. 'Well', he says, 'that's it. It's fine the way it is.'

After nearly a year of being turned down by every distributor, we release it ourselves with the aid of a West Coast porno chain hoping to upgrade its image. And we do everything ourselves – ads, radio spots. A low-budget film release if ever there was one.

By the time it arrives in New York for the grand opening we have a 35mm print, so we no longer have to mention the words 16mm or documentary. We have convinced everyone that it's just another movie – Bob Dylan's first, and a littly fuzzy and grainy, but a regular movie.   D. A. PENNEBAKER

ncerts (public). I have to take it on faith the m will not be a series of press conferences and tting in and out of concert halls. Little by tle, as always happens, Dylan and I draw oser. I start to relax.

Then one day I almost blow it. And it is not en my fault. I was shaken for the rest of the m. Coming back from Liverpool, Joan and I d some others are following Bob's car. He ps the car and starts talking to some gypsies. an says 'Stop the car!' and gets out. 'Come ', she calls to me. 'Bring your camera.' I pick the camera but for some reason don't shoot. feel Dylan's anger before I see his face. He rns on Joan. As I get closer I hear him saying . . my people. Don't you know that they're t part of some folk movie. I've lived with ople like these all my life. What the hell are u trying to do?' He looks at me suddenly. 'I'd e to punch out the cameraman!' Then he rns and gets in the car.

With Bob Van Dyke recording every concert

from beginning to end, I film as the impulse strikes, driving from packed hall to packed hall, everything sold out without so much as a poster up on the wall.

Disaster . . . and success

It becomes clear that Dylan is going through some kind of change, and I know that if I can stick with him I'll see something of it. I realize that it's what a lot of others want to see too. That's what makes a theatrical film. But the hardest part about making a theatrical film is getting it into theatres.

I return from England tired and very broke. Dylan is playing with The Band now. 'Like a Rolling Stone' is all over the radio. I keep picturing the last Albert Hall concert in London, cutting to The Band setting up for a concert or getting into 'Mr Jones'. I have trouble believing that the shooting is finished. Albert Grossman is talking about going over next year and making a television special for ABC. Maybe it will never be finished – I have films like that.

Then one day, to the relief of everyone in my studio, I sit down and begin to edit. I use a viewer and a synchronizer as I can work faster with them than on a moviola. It's a little hard

r left: the Emshwiller footage Pennebaker ed in Dont Look Back *showing Dylan in ississippi. Left: four shots from the credit quence showing Beat poet Allen Ginsberg bove) and Dylan (below)*

Below: more shots from the film – Dylan cues the lyrics to 'Subterranean Homesick Blues', and with friends Joan Baez (bottom left) and Alan Price (bottom right). Below: passing the time away on the road between concerts

Through Canadian Eyes

The National Film Board of Canada came into being by Act of Parliament on May 2, 1939. But since the NFB's first films appeared during World War II, many people have had the impression that its existence was *caused* by the war. Not so. The 'uniqueness' that René Clair spoke about is largely the result of a far-seeing, practical and politically acceptable plan, carefully worked out by John Grierson, the British documentary producer, in peacetime after much research and study, in response to the Canadian government's request. He was to develop that plan richly during the six war years that followed, in his post as Commissioner.

The result was an organic whole, embodying production, distribution, administration and all necessary technical services under one roof. The Board is independent of government departments, reporting directly to Parliament through a cabinet minister. Its purpose and mandate is:

'. . . to initiate and promote the production and distribution of films in the national interest and in particular . . . films designed to interpret Canada to Canadians and to other nations.' This general statement allows the Board to be flexible in its response to the changing times.

The war years at the Board were a period of recruiting inexperienced young Canadians and training them on the job while films were being turned out. From Britain, Grierson brought over Stuart Legg, Stanley Hawes, Raymond Spottiswoode and J. D. Davidson, all experienced producer/directors. For the most part, the film styles and formats of the war period naturally followed the British prototypes.

But NFB wartime films were innovative in one field particularly – the compilation film. It was most important to develop a series of public information shorts on international themes and subjects affecting Canada, but time and money and war conditions prevented original shooting in many parts of the world. In his series for cinemas, *The World in Action*, Stuart Legg developed a highly distinctive and dynamic style of film editing, combined with sophisticated historical and political commentary, which rendered his releases on international subjects competitive with *Time-Life-Fortune*'s *March of Time* in the United States. His film *Churchill's Island* (1941) won the Board's first Hollywood Academy Award in 1941. *The Gates of Italy* (1943) was one of his finest compilations, tracing the rise of Italian fascism.

Meanwhile, in spite of pressures to concentrate only on war subjects, Grierson managed to produce non-theatrical films of Canadian industry, labour, agriculture, natural resources, native and immigrant peoples, health, community problems, frontier development, the arts – *and* a notable animation programme under Norman McLaren. All these were distributed by a new network of rural, industrial and educational circuits of travelling NFB projectionists, which revolutionized film distribution in Canada.

It was largely the success of this over-all system that saved the NFB from extinction after the war, when Grierson and his British producers had gone away, as they always said they would. Certain interests argued that the Board was an expensive wartime propaganda agency, which the government could now easily and economically dispense with.

Under this pressure, the young Canadian film-makers, now on their own, were trying to develop peacetime projects, never knowing from year to year if the government would renew their funding. Staff was reduced from the high of 787 at the end of the war to 550, without serious loss of morale. Ross McLean succeeded Grierson as Commissioner after having been his deputy.

In spite of the difficulties of those years, some notable advances were made in the film programme. The *Mental Mechanisms* series of popular psychiatric films was developed by Robert Anderson and Stanley Jackson, and sponsored by the Department of National Health and Welfare. A number of major films were made about and for the United Nations and its agencies; and new ground was broken by Gudrun and Morten Parker and Stanley Jackson in the field of community life and education. In films such as *Look to the North* (1943), *Listen to the Prairies* (1945) and *Kitchen Come True* (1948), we in Canada began to see images of people and the land that were no longer perceived through imported or borrowed eyes, but which struck us as something fresh and distinctly 'Canadian' by nature.

By 1950 all the forces and counter-forces had come to a head. The government, struck by the support of educational experts and public users but bowing to the pressures of press and critics, decided finally to confirm the NFB as a permanent institution with a new building of its own, but dropped Ross McLean as Commissioner and replaced him by a journalist, Arthur Irwin, editor of *Maclean's Magazine*. The press, rallying behind their ex-colleague, considered the NFB to be acceptable at last.

In the new and positive atmosphere of the early Fifties, fresh creative forces were liberated. It was the era of Norman McLaren's *Neighbours* (1952) and *Blinkity Blank* (1954). Under McLaren's training and encouragement, a group of new and versatile animators began to bloom. Wolf Koenig's *The Romance of Transportation in Canada* (1953) appeared. Some of the animators added actuality to their palette. The *Faces of Canada* series, designed to discover new talent, gave out small grants for films about interesting Canadian characters in typical jobs and backgrounds; one such was *Paul Tomkowicz – Street Railway Switchman* (1953). *Corral* (1954) was another notable live-action film of this period, in similar vein.

On his appointment as Commissioner, Irwin had decided that the NFB should be moved from under the political eyes of Ottawa to Montreal, then a bilingual city and a cultural centre of both French and English. But it was to take six years before the new building was ready. After the move to Montreal, two trends already present began to accelerate: films for television and French-language films.

The French side of the Board burgeoned strongly, culminating in 1964 in a separate and independent French Production Branch parallel to the English Production Branch. The needs of television now stimulated the start of the *Candid Eye* series, Canada's contribution to the invention of *cinéma-vérité*, characterized by a general sharing in the functions of shooting, editing, directing and producing. Roman Kroitor and Wolf Koenig drew around them a multi-talented team that variously included Terence Macartney-Filgate, Stanley Jackson, John Spotton, the musician Eldon Rathburn and others. They turned out such films as *Day Before Christmas* (1958), showing busy Montreal in winter; *The Back-Breaking Leaf* (1960) about the Ontario tobacco harvest; and *Lonely Boy* (1961), a portrait of pop singer Paul Anka. On the French side the pioneering was shared by Michel Brault, Gilles Groulx, Georges Dufaux and Marcel Carrière. In 1968, the anthropologist and documentary film-maker Jean Rouch wrote in *Cahiers du Cinéma*:

'All that we've done in France in the area of *cinéma-vérité* came from the National Film Board. It was Brault who brought a new technique of shooting that we hadn't known and that we have copied ever since.'

Two other landmark films of the period affected film-making elsewhere. *City of Gold* (1957), about the Klondike gold rush, was one of the earliest and most successful attempts to use stills cinematically. *Universe* (1960), which used animation to represent outer space, appeared just at the time when the Russians first launched a sputnik into space. The technique of *Universe* were studied by Stanley Kubrick and its optical expert hired for work on *2001: A Space Odyssey* (1968); even its narrator, Douglas Rain, was adopted for the voice of Hal, the computer.

In the Sixties the world-wide youth movement and counter-culture influenced the NFB considerably. This led for the first time to an emphasis on *personal* films. The inner world of the psyche became the subject-matter of experimental films. Arthur Lipsett, Derek May, Mort Ransen and Ryan Larkin contributed to this movement.

The expansive period that began in 1950 was still going full speed as the country headed

'This National Film Board for which you are working is something absolutely unique in the world. And this is not a mere compliment, it is simply the truth.'

René Clair in 1961

owards the peak year of 1967 – the year of Canada's Centennial and the year of Expo '67, the World's Fair that came to Montreal. The FB's single most successful production in its history was *Labyrinthe* for Expo '67. This was a eparate pavilion in which two highly original multi-screen theatres and a sound-and-light naze' were combined with architecture, music, sculpture and other crafts to form a memorable 'experience', based on a modern endering of the Greek legend of Theseus and the Minotaur. This production was so popular hat people waited in line as long as six and a half hours to see it.

Such a technical achievement draws atten- on to the Board's own creative Technical esearch Department. Besides its major contri- ution, *Labyrinthe*, it has developed the three- ght additive colour printing process; 3-D for Norman McLaren at the Festival of Britain in 951; the first use in the world of the then-new 5mm Eastman Colour negative stock; an nvention for *City of Gold* permitting delicately ontrolled camera movements over still photo- raphs (long before computerized animation); light-weight location sound system which nade the *Candid Eye* operation feasible; and the design of an underwater communication ystem and under-sea-ice lighting system for hooting in the Canadian Arctic.

After the euphoria of 1967 came winds of hange. Unionization, previously forbidden in overnment, was introduced compulsorily in 968. The government also cut back budgets rastically. Staff cuts had to be made, reducing r stretching services to the limit. Concern for ocial, economic, political and cultural ques- ions came to the fore once again. The cultural ifferences in interests and aims between nglish- and French-speaking film-makers vere apparent, but both groups shared in an nnovative programme of social action called *Challenge for Change*. The Fogo Island pilot roject in Newfoundland developed the haracteristic method of two-way communi- ation, in which not only did the government peak to the people but, through film and ideo, the people were enabled to speak dir- ctly to the government and be heard sym- athetically. This programme was shared by even key government departments which ointly provided half the budget. *Challenge for Change* personnel worked much with com- munity groups directly, training them in video echniques.

The other main innovation of the period ince 1967 has been the regionalization of roduction – Distribution has been regional-

Above: the old NFB building in Ottawa had once been a lumber mill and housed the NFB from 1941 to 1956. Above right: the team that made The Romance of Transportation in Canada *– left to right, Eldon Rathburn (composer), Tom Daly (producer), Wolf Koenig (animator), Colin Low (director) and Robert Verrall (designer). Below: John Grierson in*

1944 (left), the British Documentary producer who developed the NFB from 1939. Below: production shot of Chamber I of the Labyrinthe *pavilion at Expo' 67, showing two CinemaScope screens at right angles, using 70mm film. Bottom: this portrait of Norman McLaren, taken in 1967, wittily imitates the style of his live-animation* Pas de Deux (1967)

Above left: Paul Anka with some Atlantic City fans in Lonely Boy, *a portrait of the pop singer. Above: Jean-Paul Ladouceur and Grant Munro as* Neighbours *who kill each other for a flower. Left: Jean Duceppe as the local undertaker and Jacques Gagnon as his nephew in* Mon Oncle Antoine. *Bottom: Colin Low works on the model animation for* Universe

ized from the beginning. English-language regional Production offices exist in each of the four main geographical areas outside Quebec province. French Production has branches in Ontario, Manitoba and New Brunswick, where the French-speaking population is sufficiently numerous. The flow and tension between the regional offices and headquarters is helping to keep the Board more in touch.

The NFB's feature-film production has not been large or particularly impressive. Funds for features have always been very limited at the Board; and even the best documentary film-makers do not easily become ideal writers or directors of feature films with actors.

NFB features have used both documentary and fictional approaches. The first feature, *Drylanders* (1963), was a standard fictional drama. *Nobody Waved Goodbye* (1964) broke new ground, using candid-camera shooting techniques with actors improvising lines to a pre-planned story outline. *Pour la Suite du Monde* (1964, *The Moontrap*) was a candid camera documentary following a real-life story. *Prologue* (1969) had a mainly scripted story and incorporated key actors who took part in the actual political events associated with the 1968 Democratic Convention in Chicago. But perhaps the most celebrated of NFB fiction features have been *Mon Oncle Antoine* (1971, *My Uncle Antoine*) and *J. A. Martin, Photographe* (1976, *J. A. Martin, Photographer*), both emanating from the French Production group, and nostalgically depicting Quebec life.

But if fictional drama has followed an uncertain course at the Board and never reached the heights, the creative fictional spirit is alive and well in the NFB's Animation Department which has been one of the leading lights of the Film Board throughout its history. The variety, quality and value of its output, both humorous and serious, both free and sponsored, remain astonishing. The state of health of the Animation Department closely reflects that of the National Film Board as a whole.

TOM DALY

NOTHING BUT THE TRUTH

The documentarists of *cinéma-vérité* (cinema truth) tried to capture life as it happened, photographing and recording real people in real-life events and situations

was some years after the death, debt-ridden and neglected, in 1951 of Robert Flaherty, the pioneer documentarist, that the seeds planted in his *Nanook of the North* (1922) began to flower in an emerging independent cinema, called by the French '*cinéma-vérité*' and often referred to in the United States as 'direct cinema'. It has come to be labelled as the characteristic documentary of the Sixties, probably because historians sought to include it in the riotous movements of revolutionary ferment that surfaced in that period; but it was clearly descended from developments of the Forties and Fifties, particularly the technical improvements that in fact shaped the work of film-makers to as great a degree as did their cinematic talents or revolutionary ideas.

The standard wartime newsreel camera had been the Bell & Howell Eyemo, a handwound 35mm camera that was capable of filming for only ten to fifteen seconds at a time. This tended to make most American war films a collection of tiny shots with no character continuity or substantial visual line. When Louis de Rochemont made *The Fighting Lady* (1944), a wartime propaganda film about an aircraft carrier, he used 16mm colour for all the cameras that recorded the combat scenes. The effect of not using the old handwound 35mm cameras was that for the first time he was able to record long runs both for deck combat shots and for interior shots of his characters. This gives the film a sense of situational reality that is missing from John Huston's otherwise far superior battle reportage, *San Pietro* (1945).

In the Fifties, Lionel Rogosin was trying to make enacted drama into documentary. In *Come Back, Africa* (1959), filmed clandestinely in South Africa, he mixed enacted scenes with real ones. Of course, Flaherty had staged the seal hunt in *Nanook of the North* and cut the igloo in half to get lighting; but that was not the same as casting Nanook as an actor. That is what the enacted documentary came up against: certain liberties were allowed, and it was not exactly clear what the rules were. But there was a line that could not be crossed, and it seemed to require that the film-maker be present when things actually began to happen. As long as there was a real event, documentary had to go along on the real thing and, in effect, take chances. So true documentary was a risky kind of film to make and required a whole new kind of apparatus.

That apparatus was just beginning to appear: portable tape recorders; faster film stock; lenses that allowed for shooting in natural light; and, an almost overlooked development, the zoom lens. This lens allowed the cameraman to get rid of the turret full of lenses that he formerly had to carry, and to use one that could be adjusted to anything he wanted. It could move objects closer or further away. It could begin to suggest that peculiar flexible quality of the human eye, which combines peripheral vision and the equivalent of telephoto, overlapping and intermingling constantly, unlike the fixed view of a normal camera lens. It meant that a scene could be

filmed in real time with successively different eye perceptions, and not require editing afterwards except perhaps for shortening. With the zoom the cameraman could select the material as he shot, in a continuous camera-edited take, without changing the real-time sequence of events.

A film-maker could take a hand-held camera and sound recorder almost anywhere. As people discovered their own subjects and made films about them, the role of the film-maker began to emerge as no longer the one-way glass through which an audience watched unobserved; the relationship between filmer and filmed began to take a part in

Above left: Nanook of the North *told of life among the Canadian Eskimos, generally minimizing the impact of modern civilization and emphasizing man's struggle with the elements. Above:* The Fighting Lady's *director of photography was Edward Steichen, who insisted on colour. Below: Haskell Wexler's* Medium Cool *(1969) mixed fiction with fact in telling of a newsreel cameraman (Robert Forster), seen here with his soundman (Peter Bonerz), who gets involved in the Chicago Democratic Convention of that stormy year 1968*

Top: Woodstock *recorded the music event that brought together the world's largest-ever crowd for three days in upper New York State and is said to have resulted in about ten thousand marriages. Top right: Richard Leacock's* Chiefs *(1970) is a tongue-in-cheek view of a police chiefs' convention in Hawaii. The police chiefs liked the film until they realized that audiences of hippies were enjoying it as a skit. Above: cameraman-director Albert Maysles (right) with his younger brother David and Charlotte Zwerin. This team made* Salesman *and* Gimme Shelter

the film. Unlike all previous forms of communication, film had the ability to show what had happened at a particular event, even show simultaneous views that no one participant could have seen. The documentary, unlike the narrative film, could show a real world without the necessary pre-arrangements of the screenplay-writer's mind. The documentary was still a work of the imagination. But it was to develop its own 'playwrights' and its own regulations as it moved forward gathering momentum. Often the initial concept was laid down in the camera, intact and in full heat. Editing further intensified it. The visual language of this kind of film was unique.

Among the first of the new documentaries was *Primary* (1960). It was made by *Life* magazine as part of an experiment, soon dropped, to help programme their newly purchased television stations. It was about John F. Kennedy and Hubert Humphrey squaring off for the Democratic nomination in the 1960 presidential campaign. It was the first released film of the *Time-Life*/Drew Associates series and was made by Robert Drew, Richard Leacock, Albert Maysles, Terence Macartney-Filgate and D.A. Pennebaker. The film was exciting to audiences anxious to know what kind of person the new President was. In *Primary* Kennedy emerges as a reality and not a political contraceptive. Actually, much of *Primary* is the same old commentated voice-over documentary that had been around for years. But such was the vitality of the real Hubert Humphrey arranging his own television show and of Kennedy strategizing in his hotel room that the unfamiliar bits were taken for the whole, and the film was immediately seen as something new. The French called it *cinéma-vérité* (cinema truth) when it appeared at the Pagode in Paris.

The new material for this kind of film drama would be events and persons of the real world, who were in principle available free of charge and required no written script. The Drew unit went on to make a large number of such films. Some, including *Yanki No* (1960), went on network television. Others, such as *Eddie* (1960) and *Jane* (1962), had a minor cinema release; and the rest – *David* (1961), *The Chair, Susan Starr* (both 1962) and others – fell into limbo and were syndicated throughout the United States on various television stations.

The idea of a camera operating unobtrusively within a delicate situation seemed impossible. Yet it was discovered that there was almost nowhere that a camera could not be taken, provided the operators were sufficiently sensitive to the complex psychological dynamics involved and the subjects were truly willing – not simply bought or pressured into a mood of camera acceptance. Albert and David

Maysles' early film *Showman* (1962) was a touching but superficial portrait of movie impresario Joseph E. Levine; Levine did not wholeheartedly accept the freedom of the film-makers to depict him and refused permission for the film to be shown in the United States. The Maysles brothers later *Salesman* (1969) resulted from a year-long engagement with four Bible salesmen, the least successful of whom is particularly featured. *Salesman* demonstrates the greater depth possible when the film-makers can genuinely enter the lives of the protagonists. It was one of the first films to crash the barrier of cinema distribution and ran for 12 weeks in a New York first-run house.

By then, too, independent distributors had emerged, often motivated by social conscience as much as by profits. Bruce Brown's California surfing film *The Endless Summer* (1966) appeared at a long-established porno house and ran for six months. Documentary was no longer a dirty word when it came to the box-office. Another film produced by Drew Associates, *Crisis: Behind a Presidential Commitment* (1963), which concerned the integration of

'Direct cinema' had no regular access to television and needed cinema release for real success

the University of Alabama under pressure from President Kennedy and Attorney General Robert Kennedy, despite the opposition of Governor Wallace, had opened at the New York Film Festival in 1963, and might have played in cinemas had not the ABC network decided to run a slightly censored version on the air. This was the last time for a decade that an independently produced political confrontation film was allowed to go out on network television.

Richard Leacock's incisive portrait of a small Midwestern town agonizing over the birth of quintuplets, *A Happy Mother's Day* (1963), was intended for cinemas but it came too early and the film was too short. As a result it has never had much exposure in the United States although it ran on BBC television in Britain. What became apparent by the middle of the Sixties was that the only outlets for independents were cinemas, colleges and film groups. Films made both money and reputation in cinemas; but it was necessary to rid the cinema owners of a long-term bias against 16mm film.

When *Dont Look Back* was completed in 1966 it was shown to every cinema distributor in the United States. It was in black and white, about an unknown singer called Bob Dylan, and mainly shot in 16mm, so it aroused no interest. When it opened

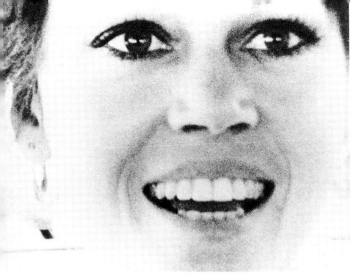

t the Presideo in San Francisco, an ex-porno ouse, there was no 35mm blow-up as yet. For that ntire run no mention was made either of documntary or of the narrow gauge. It was treated in eviews as if it were a regular film. By the time it eached New York there was a 35mm print but that o longer mattered. When *Monterey Pop* (1968) pened in 1969, the issue was dead. Within a year *Woodstock* was out, blown up from 16mm to huge creen size, followed by the Maysles brothers' *Gimme Shelter* (both 1970).

Meanwhile, Fred Wiseman, an ex-law professor oncerned with social institutions, had teamed up vith film-maker John Marshall to produce *Titicut ollies* (1967), a fearsome investigation of instiutional life in a hospital for the criminally insane, ollowed by *Law and Order* (1969) and *Hospital* (1970). Allan King with Dick Lieterman in Toronto ade *Warrendale* (1967), an institutional film about motionally disturbed children which was parcularly interesting in that King, an ex-BBC docuentarist, broke with the time-honoured tradion of putting all possible information into the ommentary and instead opted for a narrationless rama, with much of the medical aspect unxplained.

The Canadians were busy all through the Fifties nd Sixties – the existence of the National Film oard had given them a big start over other ountries in developing documentary imaginately. In the Sixties the French section of the Board, elatively quiet throughout the earlier years, began show more and more energy. With works like *our la Suite du Monde* (1964, *The Moontrap*) by ichel Brault and Pierre Perrault, a study of uebec rural life, the French-Canadians began to atch in style and passion such earlier *cinémarité* films as Terence Macartney-Filgate's *Blood nd Fire* (1958), about the Salvation Army, and *The ack-Breaking Leaf* (1960), about the tobacco harest in southern Ontario. A forerunner of *Dont Look ack* was Wolf Koenig and Roman Kroitor's *Lonely oy*, a *cinéma-vérité* portrait of the Canadian popnger Paul Anka made in 1961.

During this period a number of shorter works ppeared in Europe and the socialist countries, here length was a less critical issue. Joris Ivens, ie Dutch communist, continued his world-wide ocumentary explorations. For the Government of apua New Guinea, Gary Kildea and Jerry Leach ade a wonderfully funny and irreverent film on ie Trobriand Islanders called *Trobriand Cricket* 976). Amidst the amiable remarks of the Oxfordraduate tribesmen, two of the tribal cricket teams ay out an elaborate ceremonial game, based on nglish cricket, in which the host always wins and ie ritual aspects of the game are paramount.

After the incredible thrust of the years dominated

by John Grierson, the Scottish producer, and then the burst of energy of Lindsay Anderson, Karel Reisz and Peter Watkins, Britain fell into a sort of torpor during much of the Sixties, possibly brought on by the economic pressure of imported American television. The work of Watkins is an exception: his stunning *Culloden*, shown by the BBC in 1964, and the more ambitious *The War Game* (1965) were both much admired in the United States; his *Punishment Park* (1971), about the United States in the Sixties, aroused much controversy but never achieved very wide cinema showing.

Otherwise most of the documentary work was limited to festival screenings and occasional noncinema release. The few English distributors of documentary were by and large not interested in British films. Television ran many documentaries but they tended to be expressions of journalistic opinions and were almost never produced by independents. One interesting exception was the series commissioned by Granada which consisted of several series-length documentaries by Roger Graef, an American resident in England; one of these was entitled *Decision: Steel* (shown on television in 1976) and followed the inner workings of management during a critical corporate decision.

In France, which had given impetus to the whole movement, Jean Rouch, a research ethnographer specializing in Africa, and Chris Marker, a radical writer/director and founder of a film-making cooperative, both continued to make film after film, mainly on anthropological and political themes that made them less interesting for cinema release than to a more specialized or scholarly audience. *Chronique d'un Eté* (1961, *Chronicle of a Summer*), an investigation into whether people in Paris were happy, made by Rouch in collaboration with Edgar Morin, a well-known sociologist, is as widely distributed in the United States as in France, as are many of Rouch's later films.

It is unfortunate that Rouch and Marker never achieved the glory that Godard and Truffaut and the other feature-film makers received, when much of their perception and directness was picked up and used to such great avail by the *nouvelle vague*. For instance, they borrowed the use of direct interviews, hand-held cameras, non-actors as actors and even the use of actors as real people in Godard's *La Chinoise* (1967, *The Chinese Girl*), for which a small group of actors lived for a time in a kind of Maoist commune, in much the same way as the characters in the film.

Yet because they spoke first, or perhaps because of the efforts of Henri Langlois to make the *Cinémathèque* in Paris the home of all documentary the world over, the French will probably be forever known as the originators of the Sixties documentary, *cinéma-vérité*. D.A. PENNEBAKER

Top left: Jane *follows an up-and-coming actress called Jane Fonda in a new play from out-of-town tryouts to disastrous Broadway opening. D. A. Pennebaker shot the Fonda footage. Top: President Kennedy takes stock of the situation while his power is challenged by a State Governor in* Crisis. *Above:* Warrendale *was a controversial film about a treatment centre for young people. Below:* Gimme Shelter *showed the Rolling Stones concert at Altamont, California, which led to violence and an on-camera murder*

Miklós Jancsó-Hungarian rhapsodies

Jancsó's brilliant directorial style, often using extended and elaborately choreographed camera takes, has sometimes obscured the essentially political message in his sweeping views of history, with their strongly implied hopes for a Utopian future of ecstatic communal bliss

Miklós Jancsó was the first Hungarian director to achieve world-wide fame without permanently leaving his country. In view of his fame, surprisingly few of his films are known outside Hungary. Hardly anyone has seen his entire output of over thirty shorts and, by 1981, eighteen feature films. Of his features, fourteen were made in Hungary, including one Soviet and one French co-production. Of the four films he made in Italy, three were little seen; the fourth, *Vizi Privati, Pubbliche Virtù* (1976, *Private Vices, Public Virtues*) had the widest distribution of any Jancsó film so far.

Jancsó often says that tyranny and oppression were the formative experiences of his life. Born in 1921, he reached military age during World War II. Soon after, the high hopes of 1945–48 were choked off by the *coup d'état* of Mátyás Rákosi, who practised the worst Stalinist excesses for the next six years. From 1954 to 1956, while Jancsó worked his way from newsreels towards documentaries, Khruschev tried to repudiate Stalinism. The Hungarian

uprising of 1956 found Jancsó very far away from home: he was filming a dance group's tour of China.

He directed his first feature film in 1958; but he prefers to forget about it. His first proper feature *Oldás és Kötés* (1962, *Cantata*) was about the self-searchings of a young surgeon. The peasant-born doctor's preoccupations and inner crisis were shared by most Hungarian intellectuals in the Sixties, but in form the film owed much to Antonioni.

The idea of revolution

Jancsó's transition from the private to the panoramic, from psychology to history, can be traced in *Így Jöttem* (1964, *My Way Home*), which tells of a young Hungarian soldier taken prisoner by the Soviet army at the end of World War II. (Since *My Way Home*, Jancsó's screenplays have been written in collaboration with Gyula Hernádi in Hungary and Giovanna Gagliardo in Italy.) With *Szegénylegények* (1965, *The Round-Up*) Jancsó revealed the full

originality of his talent. Still shot in black and white, with the sharpest possible contrasts of sunshine and shadow, *The Round-Up* introduced many of the stylistic features which are characteristic of but not essential to Jancsó. Whether his stylistic devices are praised for their originality or condemned as gimmickry, Jancsó himself is always more concerned with the content of his films.

A Jancsó film could be described as an analysis of oppression, revolution, counter-revolution and even the contentious idea of permanent revolution. Of course, these cannot be separated; their juxtaposition causes the dramatic conflict in the historic situations which trigger off each film. Oppression is frequently shown as the outcome of a counter-revolution. In *The Round-Up*, the chief mechanism of oppression is treachery; in *Csend é. Kiáltás* (1968, *Silence and Cry*), it is compounded by the complicity of a demoralized peasantry. *La Tecnica e il Rito* (1972, *Technique and Rite*) explored the working of the 'cult of

personality' as used by the young Attila in recruiting and training his storm-troopers, grabbing leadership from his elder brother and creating myths about his supernatural powers.

Socialist faith

Revolution, in the broad sense of a popular uprising, appears in various historical settings. In *Fényes Szelek* (1969, *The Confrontation*), the young and rather crass idealists who resemble the Peoples' College groups of 1945–47 fall victim to manipulation by Party professionals. This, together with the totally fluid construction, makes *The Confrontation* seem like the apotheosis of 1968, the Paris student riots and the Dubček reforms in Czechoslovakia. The subject is reinforced by an historic irony: while Jancsó was shooting this, his first colour film, the Soviet troops were evacuating their nearby camp and moving along the road in the film crew's line of vision; but no-one knew as yet that those tanks were rolling towards Prague. In *Még Kér a Nép* (1972, *Red Psalm*), Miklós Jancsó choreographs a peasant uprising of the 1890s, though as in all his films since *The Round-Up* time and place are abstract and notional. The strikers are butchered and defeated, but their spirit symbolically survives. *Red Psalm* was Jancsó's least ambiguous statement of socialist faith and his most widely praised work since *The Round-Up*.

Counter-revolution has many faces. In *The*

Round-Up reprisals were the aftermath of the unsuccessful 1848 revolution against the Austrian Empire. Both *Csillagosok, Katonák* (1967, *The Red and the White*) and *Égi Bárány* (1971, *Agnus Dei*) take place after the Bolshevik revolution was attacked by freshly grouped counter-revolutionary armies, who were defeated in Russia but who conquered in Hungary. The leftists are shown in both films as a motley, ill-equipped and loosely organized gathering of brave civilians and army deserters, while the Right are always represented by officers, elegant in their frogged uniforms and indulging their autocratic whims between bouts of killing. Furthermore, in *Agnus Dei* there is an alliance between a perverted Church and the oligarchy.

Just before this, Jancsó had made *Sirokkó* (1969, Winter Sirocco) where a Serbian paramilitary organization hides its training camp across the border, in Hungary. It is likely that Jancsó was already searching for a formula that would be more powerful than over-smart uniforms, devotion to rank and ritual, and homosexual and psychopathic overtones to suggest the perversion that National Socialism and fascism bring to the political life of a country. Besides, right-wing terrorism has taken on a completely different image from the Sixties onwards; this was foreseen by Jancsó all too accurately in his first Italian-made film, *La Pacifista* (1971, The Pacifist). Here, a small group of right-wing terrorists, without any

r left: a portrait of Jancsó at work. Above: an ...borate evening ritual of cleansing from ...legro Barbaro (named after a piece of music ... Béla Bartók); the rite combines the elements ... earth, air, fire and water. Right: in Silence ...d Cry, set in 1919, the right-wing soldiers ...etend to give suspects a chance to escape, but ...oot them down on an open hillside. Below: ... Way Home tells of the brief friendship ... tween a Hungarian prisoner and his Soviet ...ard, who is mortally wounded

clear ideas or principles, commit acts of urban violence: they intimidate, threaten and murder, but the police are too busy putting down left-wing student riots to attend to the real crimes.

Choreographing history

The idea of permanent revolution infuses *Szerelmem, Elektra* (1975, *Elektreia*), in which Orestes persuades his sister Elektra to shoot him; but he springs up from his bier, resurrected: a Redeemer cannot die. As Jancsó's films became more stylized, moving from epic story-telling to choreographed ritual, his films became more poetic. Literary scholars have stressed ambiguity as a constituent element of poetry and this is borne out by the increasingly ambiguous, not to say contradictory, effect of Jancsó's films. For instance, when an unarmed left-wing popular movement behaves more like a folk-group at a dance festival than a revolutionary force, as in *Red Psalm* or *Elektreia*, Jancsó's indulgence of their holiday mood is not without irony. Similarly, the counter-revolutionaries are always well-tailored, handsome young men, sometimes in love with death and destruction, but manipulated by wily politicians. This becomes almost exaggerated in *Magyar Rapszódia* (1979, *Hungarian Rhapsody*) and *Allegro Barbaro*

Above left: in Private Vices, Public Virtues *a prince defies his father and is regularly unfaithful to his strictly virtuous wife. Above right: in* The Confrontation *students in a Catholic school are challenged by a group of Communist youths*

(1979), two parts of a projected trilogy, where instead of sweeping destructively through the countryside in vengeance, the White officers are shown at an orgy which ends in mass suicide.

In his Italian films, Jancsó is sending oblique and ironic messages to Western youth. To focus attention on content rather than just his style of long takes lasting several minutes, in *Private Vices, Public Virtues* he chopped up each long take into quite short snippets. But his aim was still to fuse political ideas with emotionally meaningful forms of myth, fable and ritual. While *Elektreia* was based on Greek myth, *Private Vices, Public Virtues* is a parody of a Viennese operetta, including even a court ball. The film begins as a summer frolic, and it hardly matters whether it moves through a night and a following day, or through the months into an elegiac autumn. Like all his films, *Private Vices, Public Virtues* must be understood on several levels at once. The rebel prince is romanticized, but also shown as a

naive fool; the beauty of sexual freedom i advocated, but shown to be an empty, childish charade when those who indulge themselve are manipulated and eventually destroyed b the authorities.

Towards Utopia

When he returned to Hungary after about fou years' absence, Jancsó embarked on hi version of the 'megafilm', spanning the cen tury – like Bernardo Bertolucci's *Novecent* (1976, *1900*) or Volker Schlöndorff's *Di Blechtrommel* (1979, *The Tin Drum*). He plan ned a trilogy, ending in 1956, loosely based o the biography of a Hungarian politician wh changes from being a right-wing, nationalis officer to becoming a self-appointed leader of disaffected peasantry. The hero's motives ar doubted by the peasants in the commun which he allows to flourish on his own estate although he protects them through his statu within the oppressive regime. Jancsó returns i *Hungarian Rhapsody* and *Allegro Barbaro* from group choreography to an epic narration, bu he avoids a plodding depiction of Hungary slide into fascism by presenting the period fron

Filmography
1951 Kezünkbe Vettuk a Béke Ügyét (short) (co-dir); Szovjet Mezőgazdasági Küldöttek Tanításai (short) (co-dir). '52 A Nyolcadik Szabad Május 1 (short). '53 Választás Előtt (short); Arat az Oroshází 'Dózsa (short); Közös Úton (short) (co-dir). '54 Egy Kiállítás Képei (short); Galga Mentén (short); Éltető Tisza-Víz (short); Emberek! Ne Engedjétek! (short) (co-dir); Ösz Badacsonyban (short). '55 Emlékezz, Ifjúság! (short); Angyalföldi Fiatalok (short); Egy Délután Koppánymonostoron (short); Varsói Vit I-II-III (short). '56 Móricz Zsigmond 1879–1942 (short); Kína Vendegei Voltunk (short); Dél-Kína Tájain (short); Peking Palotái (short); Színfoltok Kínából (short). '57 A Város Peremén (short). '58 Derkovits Gyula 1894–1934 (short). '59 A Harangok Rómába Mentek; Halhatatlanság (short); Izotópok a Gyógyaszatban (short). '60 Az Éledés Müvészete (short) (co-dir); Három Csillag (USA/GB: Three Stars) (one *ep.* only). '61 Az Idö Kereke (short); Alkonyok és Hajnalok (short); Indián Történet (short). '62 Oldás és Kötés (GB: Cantata)

(+sc). '63 Hej, Te Eleven Fa . . . (short). '64 Így Jöttem (GB: My Way Home) (+co-sc). '65 Jelenlét (short) (+sc); Szegénylegények (USA/GB: The Round-Up). '66 Közelről: A Vér (short). '67 Csillagosok, Katonák (+co-sc) (HUNG-USSR) (USA/GB: The Red and the White). '68 Csend és Kiáltás (+co-sc) (USA/GB: Silence and Cry); Kameraval Kosztromaban (doc) (appearance as himself only). '69 Fényes Szelek (USA/GB: The Confrontation); Sirokkó/Sirocco d'Hiver (+co-sc) (HUNG-FR). '70 Füst (short); Tanulmány (doc) (appearance as himself only). '71 Égi Bárány/Agnus Dei (+co-sc); La Pacifista (+co-sc) (IT-FR-MONACO). '72 La Tecnica e il Rito (+co-sc) (IT) (shot as TV film but shown in cinemas); Még Kér a Nép (+co-sc) (USA/GB: Red Psalm). '73 Roma Rivuole Cesare (+co-sc) (IT-HUNG) (USA: Rome Wants Another Caesar). '75 Szerelmem, Elektra (USA/GB: Elektreia). '76 Vizi Privati, Pubbliche Virtù (IT-YUG) (USA/GB: Private Vices, Public Virtues). '79 Magyar Rapszódia (+co-sc) (USA/GB: Hungarian Rhapsody); Allegro Barbaro (+co-sc).

Above: in Agnus Dei, *set in 1919, the victims of terrorism abase themselves before a mysterious executioner (Daniel Olbrychski).*
Left: the original title of Red Psalm *means 'That people still demand . . .', reflecting the optimistic tone of its revolutionary message*

Below: Elektreia *combines ancient myth and invented rites with modern dress and technology, including the use of a mobile camera – the film contains only 11 shots.*
Bottom: Hungarian Rhapsody, *named after the musical composition by Franz Liszt*

1927 to 1944 as a vision, dreamed by the hero. Are revolutions merely dreams, then? Or are they exactly as real as the nightmare cruelties of the Nazis?

Perhaps the only firm principle which emerges from Jancsó's films is that there are no private acts: even in love, sex and family relationships, people respond to, or rebel against, the current social order. No human being can avoid taking part in the power-struggle, either as the tool of a manipulator or as his victim; even the most passive person is a political unit – especially as the passive are all prospective victims. Jancsó's films should be seen in this perspective. To enjoy his films, it is not necessary to accept his ideas – only to be aware of them. Besides, the glittering sensuous beauty of his films is an unalloyed enjoyment. Jancsó's dream of human equality, which is the touchstone of his morality, has nothing puritanical about it. Perhaps some of his ambiguity comes from showing even evil and destruction with seductive loveliness, while at the same time creating dream images of singing, dancing, sharing and loving communal Utopias.   MARI KUTTNA

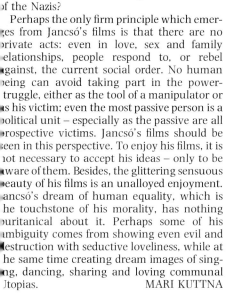

A Shop on the High Street

Directed by Ján Kadár and Elmar Klos, 1965

Prod co: Československý Film. **sc:** Ladislav Grosman, Ján Kadár, Elmar Klos, based on a story by Grosman. **photo:** Vladimír Novotný. **art dir:** Karel Škvor. **mus:** Zdeněk Liška. **r/t:** 128 minutes. Released in Czechoslovakia as: *Obchod na korze*. Released in USA as *The Shop on Main Street*.

Cast: Ida Kamińska (*Rozálie Lautmannová*), Jozef Króner (*Tono Brtko*), Hana Slivková (*Evelina Brtková*), František Zvarík (*Markus Kolcocký*), Helena Zvaríková (*Rose Kolckocká*), Martin Holly (*Imro Kuchár*), Martin Gregor (*Katz, the barber*).

A Shop on the High Street, the first Czech feature film to win an Academy Award, was the seventh film collaboration of Ján Kadár (1918–79) and Elmar Klos (b.1910), who had been working together since 1952.

The story of this directorial tandem typifies the fate of talented, socialist-minded, engaged artists in Central Europe in the years following World War II. Klos had started his film career in the Thirties, establishing a studio to make publicity films for the BATA shoe empire, and had studied new techniques in Hollywood. During the war he proved himself a talented documentary director.

Kadár, a Hungarian-Slovak Jew, emerged from a Nazi labour camp in 1945 and two years later became an assistant in the new Bratislava film studios. Both he and Klos had been converted by their wartime experiences into dedicated communists. They came together as a creative team in Prague, where Kadár settled after political criticism of his first, independently directed feature, *Katka* (1951).

Separately or together, the two seemed destined to displease the authorities. Their first collaboration *Unos* (1953, *Kidnapped*) was intended as Cold War political propaganda, but was considered too realistic; nor was *Hudba z Marsu* (1955, Music From Mars), a musical comedy satirizing bureaucracy in high places, any more likely to please. They seemed on safer ground with a realistic, poetic and ostensibly non-political story of ordinary people, *Tam na konečné* (1958, The House at the Terminus), but were immediately in trouble again with *Tři přání* (1958, *Three Wishes*). The film's exposure of corruption and opportunism horrified the authorities; it was shelved and Kadár and Klos were banned from the studios for two years.

In 1963 they returned with what is probably their best film, *Smrt si říká Engelchen* (Death Is Called Engelchen), an unsparing contemplation of the horror of the war which at the same time discovered contemporary lessons in past history. In an atmosphere cautiously becoming more liberal they made *Obžalovaný* (1964, The Defendant), a socially critical fictional account of the trial of a group accused of 'economic' crimes; and then *A Shop on the High Street*. This is based on a story, *The Trap*, by Ladislav Grosman, which Kadár and Klos said:

'. . . aroused our interest because of its rather unusual treatment of the theme in relation to factual evidence and tragi-comedy, intensified through the humane approach of the author. The tragedy of the story rests on a single pair of characters and is a unique case of seeing fascism from within.

'*A Shop on the High Street* is one episode of a great tragedy. Basically it is a parable, though depicting realistic situations. Not even the most tragic scenes are deprived of a share of humour, but the audience knows it is a matter of life and death . . .'

Compared with the innovatory work from the new school of Czech directors that emerged in the Sixties, Kadár and Klos' film was conservative, even old-fashioned. In a perceptive review written at the time, Kenneth Tynan remarked that their 'self-denying respect for the script may well prevent them from ever becoming fashionable.'

A Shop on the High Street is for all that a considerable *tour de force*. With deftness and precision it balances with the brutal horror of the situation, a tone of intimate, everyday human comedy, exemplified in the misunderstandings of the exasperated Tono and the imperturbably uncomprehending old lady. From this balance emerges the point that the humankind that is capable of committing such monstrous deeds as are witnessed on the screen is individually composed of small, weak human beings. Tono is quite a pleasant, friendly, even well-meaning man, for whom fascism happens to offer a convenient economic way of life. Even his shrewish wife and fascist brother-in-law are the grotesque minor villains that are most frequently found in bucolic comedy.

Critics of the time, indeed, charged the film with taking things too lightly, by indulging in such whimsies as the coda. Behind the gentle exterior, though, lay a contemporary message, as the directors pointed out:

'The same thing could clearly take place anywhere, even today . . . We feel that no-one may be excluded from the society in which he lives, and no-one may be robbed of his rights as a human being. As soon as something like that can happen, anything can happen, thanks to the indifference of the bystanders. All that is needed is a little bit of cowardice, of fear.'

The message of the film was clear enough for *A Shop on the High Street* to be unacceptable to the new regime that followed the Soviet invasion of Czechoslovakia in 1968. Kadár and Klos made one last film, *Hrst plná vody* (*Adrift*), released in 1969, but after the events of 1968 Klos was to be definitively banished from film-making. Kadár emigrated to North America and made three moderately successful films before his death: *The Angel Levine* (1970), *Lies My Father Told Me* (1975) and *Freedom Road* (1979). The first of these featured Ida Kamińska, the great star of the Warsaw Jewish Theatre and the actress who played Mrs Lautmannová in *A Shop on the High Street*. Ironically enough, Kamińska was herself driven from Poland by the wave of anti-semitism in the years 1968–69.

ANTONIN LIEHM

6

A small town in wartime Slovakia in 1943. Tono Brtko, the impoverished local carpenter (1), and his wife find it hard to make ends meet, so Tono cheerfully accepts his fascist brother-in-law's offer (2) of a job as 'Aryan controller' (3) of a Jewish-owned button shop. The job does not provide the rewards Tono had hoped for: the shop has been losing money for years; the proprietor, Rozálie Lautmanrňová (4), is quite deaf, blissfully unaware of the true facts of the situation, and takes Tono for a voluntary assistant whom she pampers like a son (5). The local Jewish community, which has long supported the old lady, now extends its charity to Tono.

When the order to deport the Jews comes (6, 7), Mrs Lautmannová's name has been forgotten. The old lady has a momentary comprehension (8): she murmurs, out of painful old memories, the single word 'pogrom'. Tono is faced with a terrible dilemma – either he exposes her, or hides her and risks the consequences of concealing a Jew. In panic (9) he thrusts her down into a cellar and locks the door. He opens it again, when the danger has passed, only to find her dead. He hangs himself.

In a coda, the ghosts of Tono and Mrs Lautmannová drift through the town, dressed in the finery of her happy past (10).

9

10

Towards the Prague Spring

Czechoslovak cinema came to the international forefront in the Sixties, winning Oscars and worldwide screenings. But when the popular movement that led to greater political freedom in the Prague Spring of 1968 was crushed by the Soviet invasion, the cinema went into retreat for several years

In the late Fifties, a number of important films were produced which can be considered fore-runners of the Czechoslovak 'New Wave'. Directors making their debuts included Vojtěch Jasný, František Vláčil, Karel Kachyňa, Zbyněk Brynych and Ladislav Helge. With older directors such as Václav Krška and the team of Ján Kadár and Elmar Klos, they produced a body of work that challenged the conventions of the Fifties. The challenge took two forms: an attempt to look honestly at contemporary society; and a revival of Czech lyricism applied to a basically humanist subject-matter. A number of the films were examined at a special conference in 1959, as a result of which five were banned and the head of the Barrandov studios sacked. But all of the directors went on to make a major contribution in the Sixties, notably Kadár and Klos with their Oscar-winning *Obchod na korze* (1965, *A Shop on the High Street*).

The first breakthrough of the Sixties came with the Slovak film by Štefan Uher, *Slnko v sieti* (1963, Sunshine in a Net), a complex, poetic account of the problems of contemporary youth which was accused of containing a coded political message. In 1963 a number of new directors made their first films and were stimulated by a desire to reflect society in a non-stereotyped fashion, to focus on the 'look' of everyday life and to examine the lives of non-heroes. They included Jaromil Jireš, Miloš Forman and Věra Chytilová. All in different ways were influenced by the fashion for *cinéma-vérité*.

Forman and friends

The one group which remained faithful to the realist tendencies of 1963 consisted of Forman and his two friends and collaborators, Ivan Passer and Jaroslav Papoušek. Together they developed a recognizable style of film-making,

with both Passer and Papoušek becomi directors in their own right. In their preferen for non-actors, focus on everyday enviro ment, functional use of camera and casu approach to narrative, they owed much to t example of neo-realism in Italy.

The social criticism of their early fil remained oblique. Forman's *Černý Petr* (196 Peter and Pavla) dealt with the problems o not very bright boy, who cannot even co with his job in a supermarket; his *Lásky jed plavovlásky* (1965, A Blonde in Love) looked the love affair of a factory girl who had on attempted suicide because her parents we divorced. Both leading characters were from the kind of uplifting examples required socialist-realist morality. Of course, their pro lems were merely the pretext for a study wider issues, but the film-makers escap censure because the films were regarded merely comedies. The final film directed Forman before he left Czechoslovakia, *Hoři, n panenko* (1967, The Firemen's Ball), was mu more controversial and consciously pointe Ostensibly a comedy about the failure of firemen's committee to organize a dance in small village, it was actually a satire on socie and its institutions.

Other directors worked alongside Formar

Left: Věra Chytilová, foremost woman director of the Czech 'New Wave'. Above: her Czech-Belgian co-production Ovoce stromů rajských jíme *had only limited distribution in the West. Top right: her* Daisies *starred two non-professionals, Ivana Karbanová (left) and Jitka Cerhová. Right: Magda Vašáryová played the title role in* Markéta Lazarová *and František Velocký portrayed her seducer. Bottom: a prisoner humiliated in* Žert

group, in a form derived from the tradition of critical realism. Although the approach to narrative was more conventional and professional actors were used, the criticism offered was frequently more analytical and overt. Films by Jireš and, particularly, Evald Schorm can be placed in this category. In *Každý den odvahu* (1964, Everyday Courage), Schorm dealt with the consequences of Stalinism and provided a not unsympathetic portrait of a party dogmatist who ended up a lonely and bewildered man. Schorm's next film, *Návrat ztraceného syna* (1966, Return of the Prodigal Son), was a compelling study of alienation, the story of an intellectual contemplating suicide. His problems lie in a refusal to adapt and accept compromise even if it is 'consecrated by a great cause'. Rather cleverly, the film reveals the unsatisfactory nature of the lives of those who have compromised and the way in which the hero's problems are central to society as a whole.

The cultural revival of 1963–65 ushered in a new interest in literature and the avant-garde traditions of the Thirties. Notable films based on pre-war works included two adaptations from Vladislav Vančura: Vláčil's impressive historical epic *Markéta Lazarová* (1967), set in thirteenth-century Bohemia, and Jiří Menzel's bitter-sweet story of strolling players in a small town, *Rozmarné léto* (1968, Capricious Summer). Jireš made a late entry with his visually elaborate version of Nezval's surrealist vampire novel, *Valerie a týden divů* (1970, Valerie and a Week of Wonders). The influence of the novelist Franz Kafka was apparent in a number of films, most notably Pavel Juráček's *Postava k podpírání* (1964, Josef

Kilian), where the absurd was linked to a world of bureaucracy lost without its Stalinist supports. Perhaps the best films based on contemporary novels were Menzel's Oscar-winning version of Bohumil Hrabal's *Ostře sledované vlaky* (1966, Closely Observed Trains), a comic account of how a lovesick young station guard accidentally becomes a martyr during World War II, and Jireš' version of Milan Kundera's *Žert* (1969, The Joke), about the attempted revenge of a young man who had been sent to a labour camp for writing 'Long Live Trotsky' on a postcard to his humourless Communist girlfriend.

New forms, new content
The film-makers most interested in formal innovation were Jan Němec and Věra Chytilová. Němec made three deliberately 'un-realistic' features, two of them almost without dialogue. In *Démanty noci* (1964, Diamonds of the Night), he portrayed the visions and hallucinations of two youths escaping from a Nazi

profound spiritual crisis. The examination of contemporary society or of personal morality characterized nearly all of the films, regardless of differences of approach.

From spring to winter

The Warsaw Pact invasion of 1968 was a relatively swift reaction to the Prague Spring inaugurated by the reform leadership of Alexander Dubček. The proposal to introduce a 'socialist democracy' was seen as a threat to the leading role of the Communist Party and the division of Europe established by the Yalta and Potsdam agreements of 1945. Following the invasion, the degree of repression required under the policy of 'normalization' was not immediately apparent. Dubček remained in office until April 1969 and was not expelled from the Party until mid-1970. However, the 'expulsion' of 70,000 Party members and the 'removal' of a further 400,000 indicated the extent of the crisis. The film industry was relatively untouched until its reorganization in 1969 but, in mid-1970, ten films were banned and a number stopped in mid-production. The early Seventies saw an abject fear not only of honest comment but also of possibly dangerous allegorical themes.

Directors chose historical subjects and children's films while veterans produced some dire imitations of Fifties socialist realism. In this unpromising climate, Jireš turned out one of the few convincing 'committed' works, *a pozdravuji vlaštovky* (1972, And My Love to the Swallows). The story of the unswerving convictions of a wartime resistance heroine, it caused a minor ripple since her relatives had supported the Sixties reforms. Forman, Passer, Kadár, Jasný, Němec and others left the country and most of the 'New Wave' filmmakers were unable to work.

It was not until 1976 that there was some sign of revival with the return to the studios of Menzel with *Na samotě u lesa* (1976, Secluded, Near Woods), Chytilová with *Hra o jablko* (1977, The Apple Game), Vláčil with *Dým bramborové natě* (1977, Smoke on the Potato Fields) and Hanák with *Růžové sny* (1977, Rose-tinted Dreams). While all the films were bland by the standards of the Sixties, *The Apple Game* became another *cause célèbre* and provided some abrasive feminist comedy, and *Růžové sny* used a fantasy framework to touch on the controversial issue of the treatment of gypsies. Vláčil's form of poetic humanism seemed best fitted to survive and his next film *Stíny horkého léta* (1978, The Shadows of a Hot Summer) was rewarded with the Grand Prix at the Karlovy Vary Film Festival in 1978.   PETER HAMES

death train, while his *Mučedníci lásky* (1967, Martyrs of Love) presented a dream world drawing heavily on pre-war traditions of Surrealism – a homage to silent films, sentimental ballads and sad heroes. The influence of absurdist theatre, such as the dramas of Ionesco and Beckett, can be found in his *O slavnosti a hostech* (1966, The Party and the Guests), the most politically controversial of all the Czech films. It is the story of a lakeside celebration or feast to which guests are escorted by an ominous assortment of secret police. The real subject is the process of accommodation and self-deception by which the guests adapt to an ideological tyranny.

Věra Chytilová's characteristic combination of feminism and experiment was already apparent in her first film, *O něčem jiném* (1963, Something Different). It juxtaposed the unrelated lives of an ordinary housewife (filmed as fiction) with that of a world champion gymnast (filmed as semi-documentary). In *Sedmikrásky* (1966, Daisies) she produced a complex, non-narrative film based on the destructive antics of two teenage heroines who decide that, since the world has been spoiled, nothing really matters. Her attraction, and that of her husband and cinematographer Jaroslav Kučera, to the visual in its own right was even more apparent in *Ovoce stromů rajských jíme* (1970, The Fruit of Paradise), an amazingly

Top left: the allegorical overtones of The Party and the Guests *were politically critical. Top right: the lesbian trend of female vampires was treated as fantasy in* Valerie and a Week of Wonders. *Above: a rural scene from* Secluded, Near Woods

rich, beautiful film with a deliberately ambiguous narrative in which 'nothing is as it seems'. Chytilová's objectives were to make any single interpretation of her films impossible and to force a conclusion that what has been seen forms only part of the truth.

At the end of the Sixties, after so much development in the Czech part of the country, the focus again shifted to Slovakia, where a number of new directors made their first films. These included Juraj Jakubisko, Elo Havetta and Dušan Hanák. Before the shutters came down in 1969, Jakubisko made a notable impact with his apocalyptic and comic vision of the horrors of war, *Zbehovia a pútnici* (1968, The Deserters and the Nomads), which drew its inspiration from Slovak folk art and perhaps also from the example of the Armenian director Sergei Paradzhanov.

While the economic issues of the early Sixties played a key role in the crisis of the Novotný regime and the coming to power of the reformers, the cinema throughout the Sixties was concerned with the even more

TRANSATLANTIC RAINBOWS

British films in the Sixties seemed to have found an American pot of gold to revive the industry but in the end it proved to be only Hollywood tinsel

The years 1958–63 witnessed the first stages of a profound social and cultural revolution in British life. It swept aside accepted traditions and conventions and it released all the pent-up energies and aspirations of youth, which found expression in a whole new world of music, fashion and sexual mores. Alongside the other developments came a renaissance in British film-making, often described as the 'New Wave'. A new and talented generation of film directors, many of them nurtured in the Free Cinema documentary movement, brought to the screen the frustrations, limitations and aspirations of working-class youth. Films such as *Room at the Top* (1959), *Saturday Night and Sunday Morning* (1960), *A Taste of Honey* (1961), *A Kind of Loving* and *The Loneliness of the Long-Distance Runner* (both 1962) were all accompanied by melancholy, dissonant jazz and were shot in black and white on genuine north-of-England locations; they explored this strange new world with sober realism and bleak compassion. In the main, these films were produced by small independent companies, raising money where and how they could – from National Film Finance Corporation loans, from deferred fees, from small American investments. Pre-eminent among them was Woodfall, founded by Tony Richardson and John Osborne and for a short time involving the Canadian financier Harry Saltzman. But alongside them were Joseph Janni's Vic Films, Bryanston – a consortium of 16 independent producers headed by Michael Balcon – and the enterprising Beaver Films of Bryan Forbes and Richard Attenborough.

Forbes and Attenborough perfectly exemplified the new method of film financing when they took no salary for producing *The Angry Silence* (1960), the controversial but highly praised film about the ostracism of a lone worker by strikers. Later they joined forces with Michael Relph and Basil Dearden, Jack Hawkins and Guy Green to form Allied Film-Makers, pooling their talents to produce a polished and popular 'caper' thriller, *The League of Gentlemen* (1960). Under this banner, Forbes and Attenborough went on to produce a series of sensitive, meticulously crafted off-beat dramas which

brought them deserved critical acclaim – *Whistle Down the Wind* (1961), *The L-Shaped Room* (1962) and *Seance on a Wet Afternoon* (1964).

But when Woodfall proposed a colour film of *Tom Jones*, Henry Fielding's classic eighteenth-century novel of a young man's growth to maturity, they were unable to raise the money from British backers and approached an American company, United Artists, for financial support. United Artists' decision to invest in the film and the enormous international success of *Tom Jones* (1963) were to change the face of British film-making. Bawdy, funny, uninhibited, *Tom Jones* celebrated a previous permissive age of gusto, gourmandizing and joyous free-living. It caught the mood of the moment. The Labour election victory in 1964 ended 13 years of Conservative rule with the promise of '100 days of dynamic action'. Censorship, prudery and convention were in retreat. Swinging London was born. It was a frenzied saturnalia, a cult of the new and the now, a world of colour supplements, pirate radio, glamorous television commercials, dolly birds, discos and boutiques, exciting music and freedom of thought and expression.

In the early Sixties United Artists also backed the desire of producers Harry Saltzman and Albert R. ('Cubby') Broccoli to bring Ian Fleming's chic spy

Above: Tony Richardson directing Charge of the Light Brigade, *a satirical look at the inefficiency and brutality of the Victorian military establishment. Below: in* What's New, Pussycat? *a sociable young man (Peter O'Toole) joins a suicidal American stripper (Paula Prentiss) in a routine at a fashionable Paris night-club. Below left: as* Isadora, *Vanessa Redgrave plays an American dancer who establishes a dancing school in the Soviet Union*

Above: in The Jokers *Michael Crawford (centre) at a party as an alibi while 'borrowing' the crown jewels. Above right: Michael Caine as Alfie with two of his girlfriends, Annie (Jane Asher, left) and Gilda (Julia Foster). Below: Lynn Redgrave as a northern girl trying to succeed as a pop singer in* Smashing Time *(1967). Bottom: Spike Milligan and Michael Hordern as survivors of nuclear war in* The Bed Sitting Room *(1969)*

thrillers to the cinema screen. The result was *Dr No* (1962). This film and its immediate follow-ups, *From Russia With Love* (1963) and *Goldfinger* (1964), all starring Sean Connery, created another cult hero – secret agent 007, James Bond, 'licensed to kill'. The films were an unbeatable blend of conspicuous consumption, brand-name snobbery, colour-supplement chic, comic-strip sex and violence, and technological gadgetry. Above all, the films were cool, stylish and knowing, and these were the prized characteristics of the Sixties.

The almost simultaneous success of Connery as James Bond and Albert Finney as Tom Jones with American and international audiences convinced American film companies that a bonanza awaited them in the United Kingdom. Britain had become the music and fashion centre of the world and, with the young, 'Britishness' was in. Overhead costs were lower in Britain than in the United States and there were reserves of acting, directing and technical talent to be tapped too. So American companies began to announce big British production programmes. Paramount, Columbia, Warner Brothers, Universal and the other major studios poured money into their British operations and were joined by leading American independents, including Joseph E. Levine's Embassy Films and Martin Ransohoff's Filmways. The independent British companies which had characterized the 'New Wave' were simply unable to compete.

By 1966, 75 per cent of British first-features were American-financed; in 1967 and 1968 that proportion had risen to 90 per cent. The last gasp of the native industry came with the sale of British Lion, the company which had released the bulk of the 'New Wave' films. Since the National Film Finance Corporation had a controlling interest in it, the government decided to sell off the company in 1964. After an unsavoury scramble by a variety of groups, a consortium headed by Michael Balcon acquired it, aiming to launch a viable programme of film-making independent of the American companies. But the lack of guaranteed circuit release, difficulties in raising capital and boardroom squabbles combined to defeat the venture and British Lion never became the projected 'third force' in British film-making.

The 'New Wave' had spent itself by 1964. Swinging London was now the theme, encouraged and financed by the Americans. Sober realism and earnest social comment gave way to fantasy, extravaganza and escapism; black-and-white photography and north country locations were superseded by colour photography and the lure of the

metropolis. Stars and directors who had made their names in 'New Wave' films forsook grim industrial landscapes and the pressures of working-class living. Tony Richardson and Albert Finney, the director and actor originally most associated with the 'New Wave', set the transition in motion with *Tom Jones*. Perhaps significantly Richardson, with the exception of the flawed *Charge of the Light Brigade* (1968), was never again to make a film of any consequence, critically, artistically or commercially. Karel Reisz, who had directed Finney in *Saturday Night and Sunday Morning*, went on to make *Morgan, a Suitable Case for Treatment* (1966), emphasizing fantasy in the story of a social and psychological misfit who identifies with a gorilla, and *Isadora* (1968), a lengthy and indulgent celebration of the American dancer Isadora Duncan, one of the dotty darlings of the Twenties, an earlier age of 'bright young things'.

Lindsay Anderson, whose *This Sporting Life* (1963) had been one of the crowning achievements of the 'New Wave', turned fantasy to good effect in his devastating *If. . . .* (1968), combining the dream of youthful revolt and sexual liberation with a comprehensive assault on the public-school system and the hierarchical society of which it was a microcosm. John Schlesinger, who had made his feature-film debut with the delicate and moving *A Kind of Loving* (1962), laid bare the essential hollowness of Swinging London in *Darling . . .* (1965), the story of a key icon of the age, the glamorous fashion model, played here by Julie Christie.

Just as Richardson, Reisz, Anderson and Schlesinger had been the characteristic directors of the 'New Wave', so the celebrants of the new style were Richard Lester, Clive Donner and Michael Winner. Lester's style, fragmented and breathtakingly fast-moving, was an amalgam of influences from television commercials, comic-strips and Goon Show surrealism. He was at his best in *A Hard Day's Night* (1964) and *The Knack* (1965), both of them photographed in black and white and set in highly stylized, dazzlingly designed decors. *A Hard Day's Night* enshrined the myth of the decade's greatest cult figures, the Beatles. *The Knack*, in which a simple young man played by Michael Crawford raced around trying to find out the secret of making out with girls, was an inextinguishable celebration of the London of Carnaby Street and the pirate radio station Radio Caroline.

Clive Donner's *Nothing But the Best* (1964) was the new era's equivalent to *Room at the Top*, redone as a black comedy in lavish colour. This time working-class aspirant Jimmy Brewster, played by

Alan Bates, jokily cons and murders his way to the top, in stark contrast to the earnest and painful ascent of Joe Lampton. *Here We Go Round the Mulberry Bush* (1968) took up the theme of *The Knack*, that of an inexperienced youth trying to lose his virginity. But this time the story was filmed in colour, set in Stevenage New Town and told with engaging humour, truthfulness and charm. Rather more in the Sixties mainstream was the frantic knockabout of Donner's *What's New, Pussycat?* (1965), in which actor/writer Woody Allen gave a first taste of his distinctive vision of the neurotic outlook and sexual hang-ups of modern urban man.

Michael Winner's films, particularly *You Must Be Joking* (1965), *The Jokers* and *I'll Never Forget What's-'is-Name* (both 1967) encapsulated the joky, cynical, remorselessly flip humour of the day. But perhaps most typical of the money-spinning American-backed British successes of the decade were Paramount's *Alfie* (1966), directed by Lewis Gilbert, charting the ruthless amatory progress of a cockney Casanova, and Columbia's *Georgy Girl* (1966), directed by Silvio Narizzano, a Cinderella story about the romantic misadventures of a lumpish provincial girl loose in London.

Amidst all the fun and frenzy a few films remained valiantly out of step with the mood of the times: Bryan Forbes' *The Whisperers* (1967) was a haunting study of loneliness and old age; and

---

Once again expensive productions for international markets failed too often at the box-office

---

Kenneth Loach's *Kes* (1969) was a moving and truthful account of a working-class lad's escape from his environment through his training of a kestrel.

Foreign directors produced some distinctive work in British studios. François Truffaut's *Fahrenheit 451* (1966), a science-fiction fantasy about a book-burning society of the future, was accounted one of the less successful efforts. But Antonioni's *Blow-Up* (1966) utilized the contemporary London scene and one of its key symbols, the fashion photographer, played by David Hemmings, for a characteristically opaque and multi-layered study of the relationship between illusion and reality. Roman Polanski, the Polish director, also found Britain a congenial setting for his own peculiar phantasmagoric visions of sexuality and instability, as expressed so powerfully in *Repulsion* (1965) and disturbingly in *Cul-de-Sac* (1966). Even Joseph Losey, the expatriate American long resident in Britain and the director

of a trio of films, scripted by the playwright Harold Pinter, which brilliantly and definitively laid bare the complexities of the British class system – *The Servant* (1963), *Accident* (1967) and *The Go-Between* (1971) – succumbed to the prevailing mood. On the one hand, he directed a brace of impenetrable baroque extravaganzas, *Boom!* and *Secret Ceremony* (both 1968), revelling in their decorative qualities at the expense of sense or meaning, and on the other, he turned out the comic-strip-inspired spy story *Modesty Blaise* (1966); it was in many ways the characteristic film of the period, a film for insiders, cultish and chic.

But it could not last. The bubble eventually and inevitably burst. Universal poured some £30 million into Britain in three years, 1967–69, producing a dozen films, few of which made any profit at all, and some of which were simply expensive fiascos. Despite the involvement of such directorial talents as Jack Gold, Joseph Losey, Peter Hall, Karel Reisz and even Charlie Chaplin, Universal produced failure after failure: *A Countess From Hong Kong* (1967), *Charlie Bubbles, Work Is a Four Letter Word* (both 1968), *Three Into Two Won't Go* (1969) and, to cap it all, the ludicrously titled *Can Hieronymus Merkin Ever Forget Mercy Humppe and Find True Happiness?* (1969), arguably the last word in self-indulgence. But more conventional film titles also failed at the box-office, including such hugely expensive British-made musicals as *Dr Dolittle* (1967), *Star!* (1968) and *Goodbye Mr Chips* (1969), and epics such as *Alfred the Great* (1969).

By 1969, almost all the Hollywood film companies were heavily in debt, the taste for 'Britishness' had passed and the films that were making money were such all-American works as *The Graduate* (1967) and *Butch Cassidy and the Sundance Kid* (1969). Their remedy was simple. They pulled out, virtually altogether and virtually all at once. By 1970 only Columbia had any sort of production programme in Britain at all. The British film industry collapsed. Symptomatic of its plight was the rapid dashing of the attempt to fill the vacuum when EMI took over Associated British Pictures in 1969, appointed Bryan Forbes as production chief and announced an ambitious production schedule. But the first three films released almost simultaneously failed and although *The Railway Children* (1970) and *Tales of Beatrix Potter* (1971) proved successful, Bryan Forbes had by then resigned and the experiment had been abandoned. With the Seventies, London stopped swinging, the butterfly culture of the Sixties flew away and, as economic recession, stagnation and unemployment loomed, there was a return to traditional values with the re-election of a Conservative government. The British film industry meanwhile lay flat on its back.

JEFFREY RICHARDS

Top: Cyril Cusack as the Captain of the book-burning firemen in Fahrenheit 451. *Above: Edith Evans as an isolated old lady who hears voices whispering about her from the radio, the water-pipes and the walls in* The Whisperers. *Below: the Beatles inspired a feature-length cartoon,* Yellow Submarine *(1968). Below left: an Old Etonian (Denholm Elliott) selects an old school tie for an ambitious man (Alan Bates) in* Nothing But the Best

The whole world loves **Tom Jones!** X

ALBERT FINNEY · SUSANNAH YORK
HUGH GRIFFITH · EDITH EVANS
JOAN GREENWOOD · *"Tom Jones"*
also starring
DIANE CILENTO

GEORGE DEVINE and the guest appearance of DAVID TOMLINSON · JOHN OSBORNE · TONY RICHARDSON · EASTMAN COLOUR · A WOODFALL PRODUCTION

Directed by Tony Richardson, 1963
Prod co: Woodfall (United Artists). **prod:** Tony Richardson. **exec prod:** Alan Kaplan. **sc:** John Osborne, based on the novel by Henry Fielding. **photo** (Eastman Colour): Walter Lassally. **2nd unit photo:** Manny Wynn. **ed:** Antony Gibbs. **art dir:** Ted Marshall, Ralph Brinton. **mus:** John Addison. **sd:** Don Challis. **prod sup:** Leigh Aman. **prod man:** Roy Millichip. **narr:** Micheál MacLiammóir. **r/t:** 128 minutes.
Cast: Albert Finney (*Tom Jones*), Susannah York (*Sophie Western*), Hugh Griffith (*Squire Western*), Edith Evans (*Miss Western*), Joan Greenwood (*Lady Bellaston*), Diane Cilento (*Molly Seagrim*), George Devine (*Squire Allworthy*), Joyce Redman (*Jenny Jones*), David Warner (*Blifil*), David Tomlinson (*Lord Fellamar*), Rosalind Knight (*Mrs Fitzpatrick*), Peter Bull (*Thwackum*), John Moffatt (*Square*), Patsy Rowlands (*Honour*), Wilfrid Lawson (*Black George*), Jack MacGowran (*Partridge*), Freda Jackson (*Mrs Seagrim*), Julian Glover (*Lt Northerton*), Rachel Kempson (*Bridget Allworthy*), George A. Cooper (*Fitzpatrick*), Angela Baddeley (*Mrs Wilkins*), Avis Bunnage (*landlady*), Rosalind Atkinson (*Mrs Miller*), James Cairncross (*Parson Supple*), Redmond Phillips (*Lawyer Dowling*), Mark Dignam (*lieutenant*), Lynn Redgrave (*Susan*), Jack Stewart (*MacLachlan*), Michael Brennan (*jailer*).

'The whole world loves Tom Jones!' proclaimed the posters hopefully, showing the title character with arms joyously outstretched as several scantily clad ladies worship at his feet. The slogan proved prophetic. Although it failed originally to obtain a circuit booking, *Tom Jones* broke box-office records when it opened at the London Pavilion – a success repeated when it was finally distributed across Britain and internationally. The film ultimately picked up four Oscars (for Best Film, Direction, Screenplay Adaptation and Music), as well as a host of festival and British Academy awards, and was universally received as one of the undisputed film delights of 1963.

Such commercial and critical acclaim might initially seem surprising. The film was based on one of those eighteenth-century literary classics more widely esteemed than read. Henry Fielding's comic novel contains much lively detail and emphasizes the contrast between country and city – offering visual opportunities that the film wholeheartedly embraces. But its episodic structure and digressive narrative style pose interpretative problems, and such unwieldy literary originals often spawn servile screen adaptations that sink under the weight of their own reverence.

Here, however, the treatment is at the hands of writer John Osborne and director Tony Richardson, and reverence is not a quality immediately associated with either of them. Osborne had rejuvenated the English stage in the late Fifties with plays such as *Look Back in Anger* and *Luther* – both celebrations of the rebel hero. Richardson had brought prestige to the British cinema with grim film versions of *A Taste of Honey* (1961) and *The Loneliness of the Long-Distance Runner* (1962). Whilst these truly abrasive personalities could not

be expected to match faithfully Fielding's urbane humour, it was fair to anticipate a sympathy with the unconventional hero and an identification with the novel's criticism of hypocrisy and humbug. Such expectations were amply fulfilled.

The film's success can be attributed to a combination of acting prowess, technical felicity and fortuitous timing. Certainly the film was fortunate in its cast, who all threw themselves into the period with energy and style. Also, if the distributors were dubious about the commercial potential of a period romp in a film era more noted for social realism, in retrospect it seems that it was precisely this novelty that attracted world audiences. *Tom Jones* brought colourful extravagance back into the British cinema – recalling the painterly style of Fielding's friend Hogarth – with its vigorous feeling for landscape and costume, while pointing out (in the celebrated stag-hunting scene) some of the century's lingering bestiality and barbarism.

This latter scene in particular reassured the critics. Even in period costume, Richardson and Osborne had not lost their cutting edge. Indeed, in some ways the film seemed to sharpen it, and Richardson found a perspective and wit sometimes absent from the dramas of British contemporary life made by him and other directors of the time. Tom Jones was Joe Lampton (ambitious working-class hero of *Room at the Top*, 1959) with a sense of humour: the underprivileged boy with sexual as well as social aspirations, shown in a way that reflected the increasingly liberated morality of the time – the England of 1745 and 1963 had suddenly come together. And in a strictly sexual

sense Tom Jones was a kind of rural James Bond. His appearance coincided with the emerging popularity of Bond, and the depiction of the hero's amorous appetites seemed to reflect a contemporary mood. The saucy sex comedy was hot property in 1963: if people could not get in to see *Tom Jones*, they went to see *Irma la Douce*.

The film was applauded for bringing a modern style – slapstick comedy, captions, narration asides to the camera, speeded-up action – to a period classic: creating comedy out of the incongruity. Once the contemporary modishness had worn off, however, it became more common to claim that this style had little thematic justification. Also, as Tony Richardson's reputation subsequently declined, retrospective doubts were inevitably cast over his earlier achievements.

But if the whole world no longer loves *Tom Jones*, its impact at the time was enormous. It also blazed a trail of frankness and good cheer into the international market, epitomizing for many the sparkle and exuberance of swinging Britain in the Sixties. Its confidence and élan would be hard to reproduce today and there is a whole world of difference between the jolly tread of Richardson's *Tom Jones* and the poisonous progress, a decade later, of Kubrick's *Barry Lyndon* (1975), also a dazzling re-creation of the eighteenth century, but which narrates the downfall of its eponymous social upstart with suave relish.
NEIL SINYARD

Tom Jones, abandoned as a baby in mysterious circumstances, is brought up by Squire Allworthy. Resented by Allworthy's legitimate heir Blifil, Tom grows into an amiable rascal, fond of poaching (1), hunting (2) and the fair sex. He loves Squire Western's daughter Sophie (3), but when discovered by his tutors with a local girl Molly, he gives them a thrashing (4) and is banished by his benefactor. After numerous adventures he reaches London and embarks on an affair with the wealthy Lady Bellaston (5) whom he meets at a masque (6).

Meanwhile, Squire Western's sister has arranged a marriage between Sophie and Blifil (7). Horrified, Sophie escapes to London, meeting up with her cousin Mrs Fitzpatrick, who is also running away from her husband. Mr Fitzpatrick follows them and suspects Tom of having seduced his runaway wife.

Discovering Tom in London, Fitzpatrick involves him in a brawl (8). Tom wounds Fitzpatrick and is sentenced to be hanged (9) . . . largely on false evidence arranged by Blifil. However, Allworthy has discovered the truth about Tom's birth, concealed from him by Blifil – that Tom, though illegitimate, is the child not of a servant, but of Allworthy's sister Bridget. Tom is saved from the gallows and joyfully reunited with Sophie (10).

O ANDERSON!

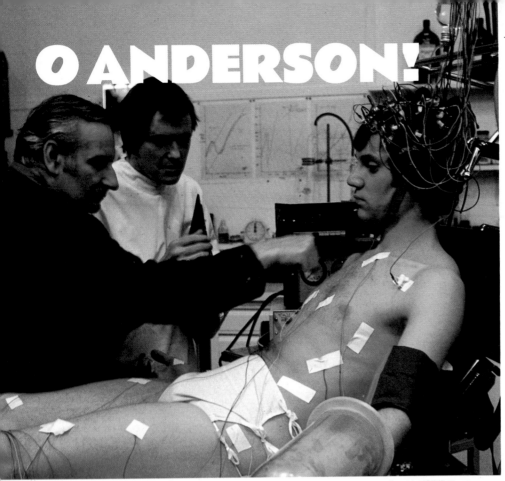

British cinema's most uncompromising son

Lindsay Anderson has been a dominant creative figure in British cinema for thirty years. From the late Forties, when he co-founded the magazine *Sequence*, he was a crusading critic. He went on to become the father of Free Cinema; to create a body of films more innovative and personal than those of any other native director; to break down barriers between theatre and film. As a writer – of scripts or of social and aesthetic criticism – he has exceptional perception.

Yet critical recognition of Anderson has been notoriously grudging in his own country – even allowing for the ordinary national tendency to undervalue home-produced art. Anderson's frankness about displaying his emotions disturbs critics who are inhibited about revealing their own. His passionate anger is dismissed as 'prickly'. His demanding, uncompromising professionalism makes him 'difficult'.

Surveying the reaction of forty years to his films shows how critics, evidently alarmed by their sheer force, have created a code to deal with them. His ferocity is called 'spleen'; his generous humanism and unrepentant romanticism are 'sentimentality'; his irony is 'cynicism' and his directness is 'simplistic'. Anderson's most revolutionary contribution to British cinema was to persuade film-makers to look outside London, to perceive the importance of the real and the dignity of ordinary people. This was labelled 'bleak' and 'drab' by the critics of the Fifties.

If not exactly serenely, Anderson has survived his critics; and his films will outlive their criticism. All of them, in the end, tell us about ourselves, about our fears and inhibitions, about Britain. Above all they are about human possibility and hope; for alongside Anderson's anger there is an equal optimism and faith, confidence in the human kind and in the search for the wisdom to live.

In the following portrait of Lindsay Anderson, one of his most important collaborators, the actor Malcolm McDowell, describes the experience of working with him.
DAVID ROBINSON

In 1966, I was a young actor in England. One winter afternoon, I went to the Shaftesbury Theatre to an open audition for a film whose working-title was *Crusaders*. I arrived late for the audition because I was rehearsing a play, *Twelfth Night*, at the Royal Court Theatre. I had run all the way. I was almost denied the reading but finally found myself on stage, out of breath, squinting across the footlights at the director of the film, Lindsay Anderson.

Good auditions are painfully elusive to most actors and this one had certainly not begun well. But Lindsay came up onto the stage and somehow put me at ease. We had a good ol' gossip about the Royal Court. The reading itself seemed to sneak up on me before I had time to get nervous or, as I was sometimes inclined to be at auditions, angry and on the defensive. Two weeks and one audition later, I was cast as Mick Travis in what later became *If . . . .* (1968), and my experiences with the great director had begun.

Lindsay is one of the very few directors that actually *likes* actors. He is like a psychiatrist in that he directs every actor in a totally individual style. For some, he is patient and gentle. He can also be very firm. Somehow when he is in rehearsals for a play or film, he brings the best out of the people around him. He expects contributions and likes to work in the spirit of collaboration with his team. He is also a marvellous technician, although he often pretends not to understand some of the more complicated aspects of film-making. I have seen him arguing with his superb cameraman, Miroslav Ondříček telling him where to put the camera for a particular shot, and

her picture. Lindsay marched over to her, grabbed her by the arm, threw her through the doors into the cinema saying, 'Go on – get in there! You're late!'

After the screening Warner Brothers was celebrating its fiftieth anniversary with a banquet which was a complete fiasco. The speeches were very long and boring. The lady, who was brought out at great expense, no doubt, to serve as the mistress of ceremonies, got everybody's name wrong – even introducing James Coburn as Charles Coburn! Lindsay got so fed up with all these goings on that, during the speech from the Chairman of the Board, he climbed down under the table, black tie and all, and proceeded to fall soundly asleep.

While I was in Hollywood making *Time After Time* (1979), Lindsay came out to discuss various development deals with the studios. He loved it for the first two weeks, doing the rounds of parties, lying by the pool in the sun. He even acquired a perfect southern California accent. My Hollywood image of him is Lindsay standing in the swimming-pool, telephone in hand, saying, 'Gee, thanks! You have a great day too!' But of course the honeymoon was short-lived. Hollywood is a great place for making deals, but not such a great place for constructive collaboration. Still, Lindsay did manage to return to England with five development deals and his apartment in West Hampstead was for a short time the virtual centre of the British Film Industry.

Lindsay was my first film director and in my naive way I thought all films were made with the same dedication and love that he puts into all *his* work. I was in for a few surprises. I will always be grateful to him for letting me share some of his magic.   MALCOLM McDOWELL

Filmography
1948 Meet the Pioneers (doc. short) (+sc; +co-ed; +narr). '49 Idlers That Work (doc. short) (+sc; +narr); Out of Season (doc. short) (narr. only). '52 Three Installations (doc. short) (+sc; +narr). '53 O Dreamland (doc. short) (+sc). '54 Trunk Conveyor (doc. short) (+sc; +narr); The Pleasure Garden (short) (prod; +act. only); Thursday's Children (doc. short) (co-dir; +co-sc). '55 Green and Pleasant Land (doc. short) (+sc); Henry (doc. short) (+sc; +act); The Children Upstairs (doc. short) (+sc); A Hundred Thousand Children (doc. short) (+sc); £20 a Ton (doc. short) (+sc); Energy First (doc. short) (+sc); Foot and Mouth (doc. short) (+sc; +narr). '56 Together (co-ed. only). '57 Every Day Except Christmas (doc. short) (+sc). '59 March to Aldermaston (doc. short) (co-dir; +co-sc; +co-ed). '61 Let My People Go (doc. short) (co-sponsor only). '62 Der Schwur des Soldaten Pooley (E. GER/GB) (narr. only on GB release version only: The Story of Private Pooley). '63 This Sporting Life. '65 Obchod na Korze (CZECH) (titles only on GB release version only: The Shop on the High Street; Le Ciel, la Terre (FR) (narr. only on GB release version only: The Threatening Sky). '67 Mučednící Lasky (actor only) (CZECH) (GB: Martyrs of Love). '68 The White Bus (short) (+prod); Raz, Dwa, Trzy (short) (+sc) (POL) (GB: The Singing Lesson); Inadmissible Evidence (actor only); Abel Gance – The Charm of Dynamite (narr. only) (shot as TV film but shown in cinemas); About the White Bus (short) (appearance as himself only); If . . . . (+co-prod). '70 Hetty King – Performer (doc. short) (narr. only); '72 75 years of Cinema Museum (doc) (narr. only); A Mirror From India (doc) (narr. only). '73 O Lucky Man! (+co-prod; +act). '75 In Celebration. '81 Chariots of Fire (actor only). '82 Britannia Hospital.

urse being proved right at the rushes. When directs actors, there is never a feeling of ing 'directed', since he generates an nosphere where everyone can *create*.

It was during the shooting of *If* . . . . that he roduced me to the documentaries of mphrey Jennings. They helped me understand something about Lindsay's style, his etry and his sense of the epic. He is not red to be sentimental in the right way. I nk that only a man who loved his school d loved England could have made a film like . . . .

He encouraged me to write my adventures a coffee salesman, giving me three books to uence the direction of the script – Voltaire's ndide, Franz Kafka's *America* and Thornton lder's *Heaven's My Destination*. Later, when scriptwriter, David Sherwin, and I were

sitting in the pub trying to think of a title for the script, we came up with 'Lucky Man'. When we, in our excitement, told Lindsay the idea, there was a long pause after which he said 'O Lucky Man!', and grinned sardonically. With one word, Lindsay had given us a magical *epic* title for our film which took it out of the bounds of naturalism altogether.

If Lindsay has acquired a reputation for having a spiky temperament, it is because he cannot abide fools. He tends to overpower and intimidate people who are not sure of their ground. When *O Lucky Man!* (1973) was being shown at the Cannes Film Festival, Lindsay and I were on the steps of the cinema after having seen the audience into their seats for the beginning of the film. A young starlet, arriving late, was posing and smiling at a photographer who was clicking away taking

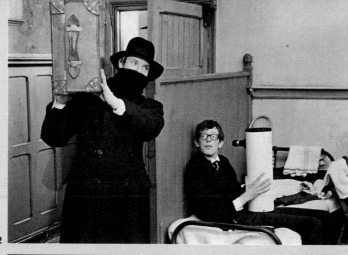

1

2

6

Which side will you be on?

if....

A MEMORIAL
ENTERPRISES FILM
Directed by
LINDSAY ANDERSON
Screenplay by
DAVID SHERWIN
Produced by
MICHAEL MEDWIN &
LINDSAY ANDERSON
Colour

ARTHUR LOWE · PETER JEFFREY · MONA WASHBOURNE · GEOFFREY CHATER · ANTHONY NICHOLS
MALCOLM McDOWELL · RICHARD WARWICK · CHRISTINE NOONAN · DAVID WOOD · ROBERT SWANN

PARAMOUNT the cinema FROM THURSDAY
downstairs DECEMBER 19TH
PICCADILLY CIRCUS Tel: 839.6494

Appearing when it did, at the end of a year of youthful dissidence and revolt, *If . . . .* has often seemed to be a film made purposely to reflect the revolutionary fervour of the late Sixties. The truth is quite different.

Sometime in 1966, I had a telephone call from a friend of mine, the director Seth Holt. Seth asked if I would be interested in the idea of directing a film with him as producer. He explained that John Howlett, a young writer with whom he had been working, had shown him a script about life in an English public school. John had written it with David Sherwin with whom he had shared horrific years at Tunbridge School. Seth had not felt competent to undertake such a subject as he had not been to public school himself.

I responded to the story, then entitled *Crusaders*, because I approved of its romantic and rebellious spirit, and because there was so much of my own experience that could relate directly to the subject; and not just my experience of school but my experience of society in the years that had followed. So from the beginning the making of *If . . . .* was a warmly and intimately personal experience.

I met John and David and liked them. As soon as they realized that I had no wish to 'tone down' their story, they were responsive to my ideas.

It was David who undertook the work of revising the script with me. He and I took *Crusaders* to pieces, invented some new characters,

new incidents and a new structure. We decided that we wanted to make a film in 'epic' style which would aim consciously at the dignity and importance of a general theme. I had early on started elaborating the idea of an apocalyptic finale, but as the script developed we were anxious from the beginning *not* to appear to be reflecting revolutionary student action in France or America. The only element of contemporary iconography to be seen in the film is a poster of Che Guevara: it had been pinned up on the wall by a boy at the school where we were shooting. I did not have the heart to take it down.

Seth Holt did not in the end produce the film. His own director's career suddenly reanimated itself — and anyway I do not think he really liked the direction in which David and I took the script. This was away from naturalism and towards a style which I would certainly claim to be realistic ('realism' implying a concern with essences rather than with surfaces) and poetic rather than 'fantastic'.

I am often asked how we managed to find the actors for *If . . . .*, and particularly Malcolm McDowell. At first I thought that perhaps the script called for boys of exactly the age of the characters. But after some experiment, I realized that youth for the screen was a matter of temperament and character rather than of literal years. I remember vividly Malcolm's second audition on the stage of the Shaftesbury Theatre,

when he and Christine Noonan improvized with a marvellous, reckless intensity their love-hate scene in the Packhorse Café. They cast themselves in an instant.

Other key talents in *If . . . .* brought the blessing of familiarity. Arthur Lowe had given a fine performance in *This Sporting Life* (1963) and I had worked with Mary MacLeod, Graham Crowden and Jocelyn Herbert, the art director, at the Royal Court Theatre. Miroslav Ondříček, whom I had first met shooting for Miloš Forman when I visited Prague in the early Sixties, had been my cherished collaborator on *The White Bus* (1968).

It was hard to get the money to make *If . . . .*; it has always been

hard to get money for any British film of originality and risk. Eventually Albert Finney and Michael Medwin, who had started their own production company, Memorial Enterprises Ltd, out of Albert's rewards for *Tom Jones* (1963), managed to impress Charles Bluhdorn, the idiosyncratic head of Paramount Pictures, and we secured his backing. It was generally imagined by everyone that our subject was 'too English' to appeal outside the British market. In the event, although the picture was enthusiastically received by the British critics, it did only averagely decent business in this country. It was abroad that it made its chief impact, in the United States, in Europe, and even behind

92

4

5

College House. Return. College reassembles for the Winter Term. The boys of College House inspect lists, find their places and unpack their things. New boys, like Jute and Biles, are 'scum'. Authority among the boys is represented by four prefects known as 'whips' (1) including the impeccable Rowntree and the puritanical Denson. Mick Travis, a senior boy, arrives wearing a scarf to hide the moustache grown in the holidays (2). He and his friends, Johnny and Wallace, have little respect for tradition.
College. College settles down to a routine. Chapel. Learning.

Games. Jute is grilled until he is word-perfect in the obligatory slang. Mick covers his study walls with images of freedom and violence. Dreaming, he listens to primitive music on his record-player. Biles is hunted, captured (3) and strung upside-down in the lavatory.
Term time. Bobby Philips, Rowntree's attractive scum, serves tea to the whips. In his study, Johnny leafs through magazines while Wallace peers into the mirror for symptoms of decay and Mick writes notes for a philosophical credo. 'Violence and revolution are the only pure acts' (4).
Ritual and romance. Bobby is repelled by Denson's yearning for him. Enthralled, he watches Wallace perform on the horizontal bar in the gym; a friendship is formed. During a College match, when they should be 'cheering loudly', Mick and Johnny escape downtown, pinch a motor-bike, and ride off to adventure and excitement with the girl at the Packhorse Café (5) (a black-and-

white sequence).
Discipline. Mick, Johnny and Wallace are told by Rowntree that they have become a bad example to the House. They are beaten (6).
Resistance. The pressures of authority mount. The three boys mingle blood in a ceremony of solidarity.
Forth to war. During a College Cadet Corps field exercise, Mick shoots and bayonets the chaplin. The Headmaster gives the rebels a last chance: the Privilege of Service. They discover a forgotten stack of ammunition while clearing out lumber from under the stage (7).
Crusaders. Speech Day. General Denson is addressing boys and parents when the hall goes up in smoke. The assembly pour out into the Quad (8), to be met by a hail of bullets. The rebels have installed themselves, with automatic weapons, on the roof. Bravely, the Headmaster steps forward. 'Trust me! . . .' he cries (9). The girl takes steady aim. The Establishment counter-attacks. Mick continues firing (10) . . .

Directed by Lindsay Anderson, 1968.
Prod co: Memorial Enterprises Ltd. **prod:** Michael Medwin, Lindsay Anderson. **sc:** David Sherwin, from a story by David Sherwin, John Howlett. **photo** Eastman Colour): Miroslav Ondříček. **ass photo:** Chris Menges. **ed:** David Gladwell. **art dir:** Jocelyn Herbert. **mus:** Mark Wilkinson. **sd:** Christian Wangler. **ass dir:** John Stoneman. **r/t:** 111 minutes.
Cast: Malcolm McDowell (*Mick*), David Wood (*Johnny*), Richard Warwick (*Wallace*), Christine Noonan (*the girl*), Rupert Webster (*Bobby Phillips*), Robert Swann (*Rowntree*), Hugh Thomas (*Denson*), Michael Cadman (*Fortinbras*), Peter Sproule (*Barnes*), Peter Jeffrey (*Headmaster*), Anthony Nicholls (*General Denson*), Arthur Lowe (*Mr Kemp*), Mona Washbourne (*matron*), Mary MacLeod (*Mrs Kemp*), Geoffrey Chater (*Chaplain*), Ben Aris (*John Thomas*), Graham Crowden (*History teacher*), Charles Lloyd Pack (*classic master*), John Garrie (*music master*). Tommy Godfrey (*school porter*), Guy Ross (*Stephans*), Robin Askwith (*Keating*), Richard Everitt (*Pussy Graves*), Brian Pettifer (*Biles*), Michael Newport (*Brunning*), Charles Sturridge (*Markland*), Sean Bury (*Jute*).

it had its greatest impact and greatest effect. If only the British distributors could understand that it is not necessarily by 'international elements' in casting or in a script that a film can transcend the limitations of provincialism or parochialism. It is by the vitality of emotional impulse, the urgency and importance of what needs to be said. This is a truth which Americans seem to recognize, alas, much more readily than the English. But then, Americans are less scared and more stimulated by challenge.
LINDSAY ANDERSON

9

10

Losey takes all

Left: Elizabeth Taylor and Losey at work on a scene from Boom!, *in which she plays a dying millionairess. Above:* The Boy With Green Hair *(Dean Stockwell) is looked after by his grandfather (Pat O'Brien) after his parents' death – the cause of the boy's 'greening'*

By the time Joseph Losey settled in Britain he was already a well-known figure in both theatre and cinema. His enforced exile from America did not make him into an insular film-maker, nor did it make him into a European director; indeed, he was possibly the first completely cosmopolitan director – even if that was not entirely a matter of his own choosing

Born in 1909 in La Crosse, Wisconsin, Losey was a drama-critic from adolescence and went on to become a director and adaptor of several stage plays. In 1935 he made his first visit to Western Europe and the Soviet Union and on his return became a promoter of a production entitled *Living Newspaper* – a total theatre extravaganza in which he directed no less than one hundred actors. He never forgot this rigorous stage apprenticeship, and in recent years there have been nostalgic traces of those 'total' productions – as in his stage presentation of *Galileo* and his film of Mozart's *Don Giovanni* (1980).

In 1938 Losey broke into cinema as an editor and, in effect, a writer of scientific films for the Rockefeller Foundation. After the interruption of the war he took up a career in cinema and in 1946 he was awarded an Oscar for his first short fiction film, *A Gun in His Hand* (1945). Three years later, helped by RKO's liberal boss Dore Schary, he made an anti-rascist apologia entitled *The Boy With Green Hair*,

which Losey had the good sense to turn into a poetic ballad rather than a sermon or harangue. His post-Hollywood films come within the genre of detective movies, but he transformed them into accounts of the experience of growing-up and evocations of human solitude – of which *The Big Night* (1951) is the most convincing on both counts.

Leftist Losey looses out

Then Losey made the mistake of agreeing to direct the ageing Hollywood star Paul Muni in an Italian co-production, *Imbarco a Mezzanotte* (1952, *Stranger on the Prowl*), with no firm financial guarantees. Despite enjoying the cultural climate in Italy, the shooting proved disappointing and Losey could not agree with either the star or the producers. Their discussions held up the work and – as the crowning misfortune – Losey suffered because of his reputation for being left wing once the film was completed. The threat that Losey had hoped to escape by being in Italy became more

acute, for while he had been away from Hollywood the HUAC anti-communist witchhunt was stepped-up and his name subsequently figured on the blacklist for 'refusal to reply' to a convocation from the McCarthy commission. The film was released and first distributed in Europe, but it had been cut, re-edited and the scriptwriter Ben Barzmann – who had also been blacklisted – had his name removed from the credits along with Losey's.

In September 1952 Losey found himself in London; out of work and short of money. Moreover, at that time British production was too heavily dependent on American distribution networks and American funding for him to be able to work under his own name – *Stranger on the Prowl* had been credited to Andrea Forzani, one of the producers who had not even been present during shooting. In Britain Losey wrote scenarios for shorts, directed countless advertising commercials and finally two full-length features – *The Sleeping Tiger* (1954), accredited to the producer Victor Hanbury, and *The Intimate Stranger* (1956) accredited to the obvious pseudonym Joseph Walton – Walton being Losey's other forename.

Lands of hope and glory

In 1957 some young British independent producers enabled him to make *Time Without Pity* under his own name. Whereas the two preceding films were notable as sketches or 'roughs' for his later work, *Time Without Pity* was a key film in Losey's development. Although the film is a melodramatic suspense story in which David Graham (Michael Redgrave) trys to save his son (Alec McCowan) from hanging, it allowed Losey to comment on capital punishment and alcoholism. For the first time he brought the dramatic resources of his previous films to their peak. *Time Without Pity* found its warmest reception in France (where Losey's name had come to the notice of moviegoers as early as 1952) and a propaganda campaign

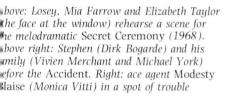

Above: Losey, Mia Farrow and Elizabeth Taylor (the face at the window) rehearse a scene for the melodramatic Secret Ceremony *(1968). Above right: Stephen (Dirk Bogarde) and his family (Vivien Merchant and Michael York) before the* Accident. *Right: ace agent Modesty Blaise (Monica Vitti) in a spot of trouble*

was subsequently launched in support of the director. From then onwards Losey's standing in international cinema was beyond question.

Losey's view of Britain – exemplified by some excellent films such as *Accident* (1967), the story of an Oxford don infatuated with a rich young student, and *The Go-Between* (1971), an adaptation of L.P. Hartley's classic novel in which a young boy takes love letters from an upper class girl to her farm-hand lover – is no different from his view of America despite his being an exile, and in fact he has himself admitted that being an exile has possibly offered him greater freedom for social observation – as demonstrated by the wealth and 'class' distinctions in *Blind Date* (1959). Furthermore, it is to Losey that Britain owes the discovery of English actors such as Dirk Bogarde and Stanley Baker.

Excelling in exile

But if his stay in Britain gave him the opportunity to perfect many details of his working method, that method – mostly the fruit of his personal experiences – does not demonstrate anything specifically British. No matter where he may be 'exiled', Losey bases his cinema on the reconciliation of two opposing principles; observation of externals and determined concentration on the most violent and innermost emotional dramatic moments.

Losey's is essentially a cerebral cinema. Certainly he manages to include emotion and even a straightforward perception of the surrounding physical world (as with the inserts of flowers and animals in *The Go-Between*, things not having any direct symbolic value), but

whatever the subject he is dealing with – excepting *Modesty Blaise* (1966), a folly which shows no trace of the Losey touch – the predominating factor in his cinema is, at first glance, the 'seriousness' of a man for whom general concepts exist, concepts of social critique and even concepts of metaphysics. This does not mean that Losey is at pains to prove theories or propose solutions. For him, as with all the great American directors, a film is essentially the spectacular presentation of character conflicts. Therefore his taste for

debating ideas never spills over into the schematic development of the film. It is only when an excess of emotion threatens to destroy a facial expression that he opts for a certain coldness at the close of a film.

The shooting on *Mr Klein* (1976), the story of an art dealer in Occupied Paris who fears he has a Jewish double, ended in a fever of creative activity with Losey cutting short the shooting schedule and simplifying the problems. It resulted in one of the most successful works by a scrupulous craftsman, and a

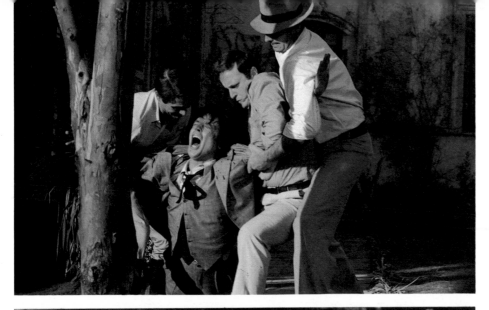

the very proposition of despair on its head.

Losey's visual style – the ease with which he directs his actors and integrates technical advances into a readily recognizable 'handwriting' – and his aggressive desire to always set his sights high, have made him one of the greatest living film-makers.

GERARD LEGRAND

Translated from the French by David Roper

---

certain amount of improvisation became possible, even though Losey remained faithful to the technique of 'pre-designing' which he has used extensively. This work is as indispensable to him as breathing, something that allies him, curiously enough, with the 'old-school' American directors. Doubtless it is a balance to check his deep-seated pessimism; for some twenty years he has given the impression of only talking about failures or decay – as in *Eve* (1962), in which a novelist is ruined by a money-seeking *femme fatale*, and *The Servant* (1963), in which a rich young man is eventually brought down by his manservant. But despite the fact that the flavour of happiness is only fleetingly apparent in his films – as in certain details in *Accident* and at the end of *Blind Date* – it would be wrong to identify the director with any of his characters. Usually they are motivated by ambition or a desire for learning. Losey described *The Servant* as being a 'new version of the Faust story'. The hero is implicated in a test of endurance which, whilst always carrying the threat of destruction, nevertheless enables him to discover his true identity. However, this discovery often

turns out to be pointless, causing a fatal wound or even provoking a disaster for someone else as in *Boom!* (1968) – a wealthy lady dies after a young man exposes her self-congratulatory existence.

The art of aesthetics

Losey's attention to decor and to the relationship he builds up between the characters have stood out since *Time Without Pity*, and these two elements explain – in an aesthetic dimension – the maturity of his subsequent work. Although essentially a self-confessed Puritan, Losey introduces into his films a dream of finding salvation by virtue of works of art as with the sculptures of *The Damned* (1962), the statues in *The Servant* and *Boom!* Venice in *Eve* and – in one sense – the celebrations at the villa in *Don Giovanni*.

However, the stories are often ambiguous and all that survives of the 'dream of life' is the impression of man turned into an object in a world of objects. For instance, the camera wanders around Klein's empty apartment which the Nazis – incarnations of inhumanity – have sealed up. To avoid despair Losey turns

Filmography
1939 Pete Roleum and his Cousins (short) (+prod; +sc) (USA). **'41** A Child Went Forth (short) (co-dir; +co-prod; +sc) (USA); Youth Gets a Break (short) (co-dir; +sc) (USA). **'45** A Gun in His Hand (short in Crime Doesn't Pay series) (USA). **'48** The Boy With Green Hair (USA). **'50** The Lawless (USA) (GB: The Dividing Line). **'51** The Prowler (USA); M (USA); The Big Night (+co-sc) (USA). **'52** Imbarco a Mezzanotte (under pseudonym) (IT-USA) (USA: Stranger on the Prowl; GB: Encounter). **'54** The Sleeping Tiger (under pseudonym) (GB). **'55** A Man on the Beach (short) (GB). **'56** The Intimate Stranger (under pseudonym; +act) (GB) (USA: Finger of Guilt). **'57** Time Without Pity (GB); The Gypsy and the Gentleman (GB). **'59** Blind Date (GB) (USA: Chance Meeting). **'60** First on the Road (short) (GB); The Criminal (GB) (USA: The Concrete Jungle). **'62** The Damned (GB) (USA: These Are the Damned); Eve (+act) (FR-IT) (USA: Eva). **'63** The Servant (+co-prod) (GB). **'64** King and Country (+co-prod) (GB). **'66** Modesty Blaise (GB). **'67** Accident (+co-prod) (GB). **'68** Boom! (GB); Secret Ceremony (GB). **'70** Figures in a Landscape (GB). **'71** The Go-Between (GB). **'72** The Assassination of Trotsky (+co-prod) (IT-FR-GB). **'73** A Doll's House (+prod) (GB-FR). **'74** Galileo (+co-sc) (GB-CAN). **'75** The Romantic Englishwoman (GB-FR). **'76** Mr Klein (FR-IT); Comment Yukong Déplaça les Montagnes (co-sc. only on English language version only) (USA/GB: How Yukong Moved the Mountains); Resistance (doc) (appearance as himself only) (GB). **'78** Les Routes du Sud (+co-sc) (FR-SP) (GB retitling for TV: Roads to the South). **'80** Don Giovanni (+co-sc) (IT-FR-GER).

JOHN SCHLESINGER
dreams and reality

Left: Schlesinger in the Munich Olympic stadium during filming for his section of the compilation film Visions of Eight *(1973). Above: one of Schlesinger's best-loved British films is* Billy Liar, *starring Tom Courtenay as the undertaker's clerk living in a fantasy world*

peras, plays, documentaries, films of stark realism and gh fantasy. John Schlesinger is a director with many rings to his bow and as if to emphasize his versatility s latterly been as successful in the United States as he d previously been in Britain

he many gifted film-makers who emerged ing the burst of creativity in British cinema he late Fifties and early Sixties, none has red a straighter or more consistent course John Schlesinger. His 30-minute docum-ary *Terminus* won him instant critical ac-m in 1961 and many of the qualities which vided the fabric of his later, more ambitious s were apparent in this spirited evocation day at Waterloo Station: his wry, affec-ate eye for the quirks of personal be-iour; his sympathy with human frailty and atience with pomposity and affectation; his verent sense of humour; his tremendous ing for cinema rhythm.
chlesinger was born in 1926, the eldest of

the five children of a Berkshire doctor. He was film and stage-struck from childhood and as a student at Oxford he took part in stage shows and shot two 16mm films. He made his trans-ition from enthusiastic amateur to enthusias-tic professional with almost obsessive determi-nation. He was first a bit-part actor, then a researcher on documentary films and eventu-ally, by persistently battering on doors, he broke into television as a director.

Monitoring his progress
Schlesinger's outstanding work on the arts programme *Monitor* attracted the attention of Edgar Anstey, then head of British Transport Films. This resulted in *Terminus* – and the

Golden Lion Award at the Venice Film Festival.

His *Monitor* films, in particular one about Italian opera, also caught the eye of the Italian producer Joseph Janni who gave him the chance to make his first feature film *A Kind of Loving* (1962). Janni and Schlesinger con-tinued to work together for many years.

In most of his films Schlesinger has been concerned, in one way or another, with the difference between the way people would like to behave and the patterns of behaviour forced on them by the moral, social and cultural values of their specific environments. His flair for pin-pointing small but telling background details is thus essential to the foreground drama. In *A Kind of Loving* the inhibiting force is Northern upper-working-class Puritanism which, combined with the housing shortage, cripples the relationship between a disorien-tated young couple (Alan Bates, June Ritchie) who are more or less forced into marriage. In *Billy Liar* (1963) popular images of a machismo hero dominate the mind of a mixed-up lad (Tom Courtenay) frustrated by small-town life. A casual encounter with a free-spirited young woman (Julie Christie) offers him his single chance of escape.

This was Julie Christie's first important screen role – one of the earliest British film characterisations of a comparatively liberated woman – and the beginning of a very reward-ing association with Schlesinger. She came brilliantly into her own in *Darling . . .* (1965) as a young model fecklessly climbing the social ladder in search of new experiences and find-ing emptiness at every level. Schlesinger's sardonically comic observations on various forms of self-indulgence among the wealthy emphasize the false jet-setting values which have destroyed the girl's chance of genuine self-fulfillment.

Although his first three films belonged firmly to the Sixties trend for socially critical realism, Schlesinger stood a little apart from

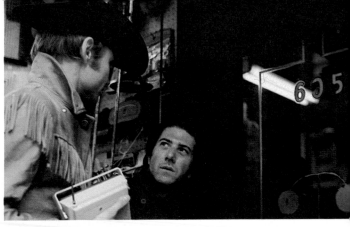

keen observational light on an alien scene – the streets, hotels, cafés and back-alleys of New York – revealing an undercurrent of corruption and violence. The two main characters can be seen as opposite sides of down-beat American life. Joe (Jon Voight) is a thick-headed Texan youth in flash cowboy gear who has a totally deluded image of himself constructed from the macho heroes of Western and commercialized culture. Ratso (Dustin Hoffman), who offers Joe back-street shelter when his plans to make his fortune as a stud go violently and pathetically awry, is a gutter realist dying of consumption. The big change in the grudging relationship between them – and the most poignant moment in the film – comes when Joe pawns his transistor radio in an effort to save Ratso's life. Separated from the continual stream of canned music that had helped to feed his illusions he at last begins to shed them – one of Schlesinger's rare recognitions of regeneration rather than compromise.

The radio in *Midnight Cowboy* is an example of Schlesinger's frequent use of everyday objects as natural symbols. In *Sunday, Bloody Sunday* (1971), perhaps his most personal and deeply felt film, the key symbol is the telephone – the disembodied voice substituting for physical contact among people cut off from mainstream London suburban life by the nonconformist nature of their sexuality. Delightfully observed episodes of middle-class conformity under its various guises run counterpoint to a complex emotional drama between a trendy, bisexual sculptor (Murray Head), a gentle homosexual doctor (Peter Finch) and an independently minded heterosexual (Glenda Jackson). The love-making scenes between the two men are handled with sensitivity, and the film undoubtedly pushed back the boundaries of censorship in its time, as had *A Kind of Loving*, with its engaging episode about shopping for contraceptives, ten years earlier.

The way the cookie crumbles

Schlesinger has often ruefully remarked that a director is only as 'bankable' as his last picture. After the dazzling box-office success of *Midnight Cowboy* he could have made anything he wanted to; after the relative failure of *Sunday*,

the other key directors of the period – Karel Reisz, Lindsay Anderson, Tony Richardson. His characters were victims of society rather than rebels against it. There was, in fact, a kind of fatalism about his work – which is probably why he was drawn to the novels of Thomas Hardy.

Bathsheba (Julie Christie), the central character in *Far From the Madding Crowd* (1967), is a typical Schlesinger heroine: an impoverished but high-spirited country girl enters the male-dominated world of business when she inherits a farm, but she is unable to resolve the conflict between her own sexual and emotional desires and her received notions of 'womanly' behaviour. With his eye for detail remaining as sharp in period reconstruction as it had previously been in contemporary location work, Schlesinger vividly evoked the rugged life-style of the villagers and the rigid class distinctions and moral values of the times. With his strong sense of rhythm he matched the mounting human passions with the moods of the changing seasons.

An urban cowboy

For his first Hollywood film, the Oscar-winning *Midnight Cowboy* (1969), Schlesinger shone his

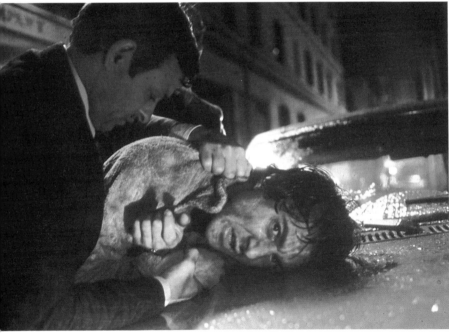

Freeway – an all-American comedy-fantasy with 14 principal characters, 103 speaking parts and a veritable army of cars, lorries and zoo animals – was financed by the British company EMI. It is a tragedy for British cinema that its own film industry has forced its best indigenous film-makers to work mainly in television or else, as with Schlesinger, to opt for Hollywood and the super-budgets and broad canvasses that it can offer.

In the less pressurized world of theatre, however, Schlesinger continues to work in Britain and has been an associate director of the National Theatre since 1973. In 1980 – some twenty years after the *Monitor* opera film sparked off his film career – he produced the opera *The Tales of Hoffman* for Covent Garden.

The CBE awarded to him in the 1970 Honours' List was a well-deserved tribute, but the opportunity to continue to make British films would have been a more fitting and longer-sighted accolade. NINA HIBBIN

Left: the Yanks *receiving a rousing send-off from the British. Below: Schlesinger's latest film, a British-backed fantasy extravaganza. Below left: the bewildered student (Dustin Hoffman) recaptured after escaping from the sadistic dentist in* Marathon Man

EMI FILMS presents A John Schlesinger Film "Honky Tonk Freeway" A Don Boyd Production Starring in alphabetical order: au Bridges · Hume Cronyn · Beverly D'Angelo · William Devane · George Dzundza · Teri Garr · Joe Grifasi · Howard Hesseman · Paul Jabara aldine Page · Jessica Tandy · Screenplay by Edward Clinton · Directed by John Schlesinger · Produced by Don Boyd and Howard W. Koch

ody Sunday – it was popular in Britain but s so in America – nobody, for a time, wanted know. He tried and failed to get backing for a g-standing ambition – an all-British screen sion of *Hadrian VII* – and he and his nerican co-producer Jerome Hellman had to nt hard to set up *Day of the Locust* (1975). This Nathanael West novel about Holly-od in the Thirties offered the basis for yet other variation on the Schlesinger theme; a ung artist/designer arrives at the film city of hopes and illusions which are gradually ttered by the realities behind the Holly-od dream. In many of his films Schlesinger ludes scenes of crowds running amok – vild party or a sudden outburst of violence. *Day of the Locust* such explosive episodes ne thick and fast, culminating in a mind-wing scene of chaos as a hotel burns, an lized child star is kicked to death and the b runs wild. By intercutting this terrifying nax with scenes of mass hysteria in Nazi rmany during the Thirties, Schlesinger

boldly points up the destructive power of mass manipulation, whatever its roots.

The anti-Nazi theme is implicit in his two subsequent films – *Marathon Man* (1976), a taut political thriller, and *Yanks* (1979), about Americans in wartime Britain. In both films, however, there are signs of deviation from the straight line between *Terminus* and *Day of the Locust*. *Yanks*, with its underlying themes of conflicting loyalties and clashing life-styles provoked by a British/American romance, reflects the changes in Schlesinger's own life – the pressures and problems faced by an international film-maker commuting between two cultures.

It was a scandal that the producer Joseph Janni could find no British finance forthcoming for *Yanks* which is a totally American film. At one stage Schlesinger was urged to 'remove its Englishness', a devastating requirement for a director celebrated for his sensitivity towards the nuances of British life. Ironically, the film that he began working on in 1980, *Honky Tonk*

Filmography

1948 Black Legend (co-dir; +co-prod; +co-sc; +photo; +act). '51 The Starfish (co-dir; +co-prod; +co-sc). '53 Single-Handed (actor only) (USA: Sailor of the King). '55 Oh, Rosalinda!! (actor only). '56 The Battle of the River Plate (actor only) (USA: Pursuit of the Graf Spee); Sunday in the Park (short) (co-dir; +co-prod; +co-sc). '57 Brothers-in-Law (actor only); Seven Thunders (actor only) (USA: The Beasts of Marseilles). '61 Terminus (short) (+sc). '62 A Kind of Loving. '63 Billy Liar. '65 Darling . . . (+co-sc). '67 Far From the Madding Crowd. '69 Midnight Cowboy (+co-prod) (USA). '71 Sunday, Bloody Sunday. '73 Visions of Eight *ep* The Longest (+sc) (USA). '75 Day of the Locust (USA). '76 Marathon Man (USA). '79 Yanks (USA). '81 Honky Tonk Freeway.

Karel Reisz belongs to the post-World War II generation of intellectuals who substantially influenced film criticism and film-making in the Fifties and early Sixties. Reisz was one of the forces behind Britain's Free Cinema group which, if it did not have the international impact of the French *nouvelle vague*, did change the character of the British cinema.

He was born in Czechoslovakia in 1926, but came to Britain as a child. He first wrote criticism for the magazine *Sequence*, where many of the ideas that inspired Free Cinema were first formulated. Becoming programme planner at the National Film Theatre, he continued to write criticism for *Sight and Sound* magazine. He also wrote a book on the techniques of film editing. The first films Reisz directed were a part of the Free Cinema programme. With Tony Richardson he co-directed *Momma Don't Allow* (1955), a short documentary about a London jazz club. He followed this with a longer and more ambitious documentary about a London youth club, *We Are the Lambeth Boys* (1959). Both films can be seen as a continuation of the British documentary tradition established by John Grierson and his associates in the Thirties, despite the fact that the Free Cinema critics had been unsympathetic to Grierson's work. Crucially, Reisz (along with Richardson and the other Free Cinema film-makers) shared with Grierson, Paul Rotha, Arthur Elton and Edgar Anstey the aim of realism. Where the Free Cinema films differ from those of the Thirties is in their subject matter. The earlier documentaries were concerned with the world of work, especially its transformation by technical innovation. The Fifties documentaries dealt with the world of leisure, especially that of young people.

Everybody loves Saturday Night

The first feature film Reisz directed, *Saturday Night and Sunday Morning* (1960), was a key film for British cinema. It marked, first, the emergence of a new generation of film-makers; second, through the performance of Albert Finney, the emergence of a new generation of film actors; and thirdly, and most importantly, the refurbishing and up-dating of the tradition of realism within British feature cinema, which by the late Fifties, had become coy and archaic. To gain a proper historical perspective on *Saturday Night and Sunday Morning* it should be seen with a film like Ealing's *The Titfield Thunderbolt* (1953), for example. Through its acknowledgment of sexuality and violence, and through its careful observation of a working-class world being transformed by increased wealth, *Saturday Night and Sunday Morning* destroyed the coyness and showed it was possible for the cinema to be responsive to contemporary social developments.

Although Reisz had moved from documentary to feature films, *Saturday Night and Sunday Morning* belongs in many ways with *Momma Don't Allow* and *We Are the Lambeth Boys*. All three films were part of the Free Cinema

Above right: production shot taken by Frank Connor of Meryl Streep and Karel Reisz on location for The French Lieutenant's Woman *(1981). Right:* We Are the Lambeth Boys, *a documentary about youth in South-West London. Far right: life with the Seatons (Albert Finney, Frank Pettit and Elsie Wagstaffe) in* Saturday Night and Sunday Morning

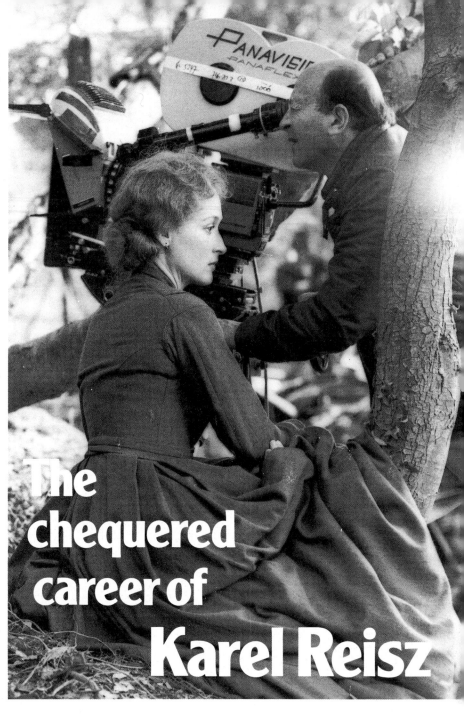

The chequered career of Karel Reisz

In over twenty years of film-making Karel Reisz has only made eight films. Yet, despite his limited output, he has substantially influenced the direction of British cinema which he helped to revitalize in the Fifties, before going to America to continue his career

Left: in Night Must Fall, *Danny (Albert Finney) ingratiates himself with the wealthy Mrs Bramson (Mona Washbourne). Below left: David Warner plays the anarchic hero of* Morgan, a Suitable Case for Treatment. *Bottom left: Isadora Duncan (Vanessa Redgrave) with Bugatti (Lado Leskovar) minutes before her death in* Isadora

struggle to revitalize realism: all three deal sympathetically with young people in the context of the social change that was coming to be known as the 'affluent society'; and all three are careful to avoid sensational effects.

If Reisz's work is to be distinguished from that of his Free Cinema associates it is by the sharper and slightly more distanced nature of his observation. An emblematic sequence in this respect is the cricket match in *We Are the Lambeth Boys.* The distance from which the meeting of working-class and public-school boys on a sports field is observed gives this sequence a wry humour.

Suitable cases for film treatment

Reisz's next three films, *Night Must Fall* (1964), *Morgan, a Suitable Case for Treatment* (1966), and *Isadora* (1968), can also be conveniently grouped together. Although they reveal the same interest in the observation of social context, the central characters are more dominant in the narrative. Their behaviour is also more extravagant and unconventional. The hero of *Night Must Fall* is a murderer; Morgan in *Morgan, a Suitable Case for Treatment* leads an anarchic and uncontrolled social life; the heroine of *Isadora* is disastrously ambitious in both her artistic and her personal life.

Along with this change in the conception of the central figures went a change in film-making technique. The technique of *We Are the Lambeth Boys* and *Saturday Night and Sunday Morning* is sensitively orthodox. Generally the editing is invisible and its rhythms controlled, the lighting is balanced and camera positions unobtrusive. This orthodoxy, if not completely overthrown in the later group of films, was considerably loosened up.

In accordance with one of the central tenets of realism – the artist should be a neutral observer – the presence of the director was not made obvious in Reisz's earlier films. In his later films the director's presence was more discernible. This development in Reisz's work highlighted one of the contradictions in the Free Cinema position. A central demand was that the cinema should be a medium where personal expression was possible; a film director should have the same creative scope that novelists, poets, composers and painters were supposed to have. But the demand for realism limited that freedom since the director was necessarily constrained by the nature of the world he was trying to represent.

Where the realist commitment had been dominant in Reisz's earlier films, the commitment to authorial freedom became dominant in the succeeding ones. Reisz was responding to the changed character of film-making brought about by the work of the *nouvelle vague.* Unencumbered by realist intentions, Jean-Luc Godard, François Truffaut, Claude Chabrol and their associates could pursue the goal of authorial freedom in an unrestrained way. The success of films like *Les Cousins* (1959), *A Bout de Souffle* (1960, *Breathless*) and *Tirez sur le Pianiste* (1960, *Shoot the Pianist*)

101

Filmography
1955 Momma Don't Allow (doc) (co-dir; + co-sc).
'57 Every Day Except Christmas (doc) (co-prod.
only). '59 We Are the Lambeth Boys (doc); March
to Aldermaston (doc) (assoc. prod. only). '60
Saturday Night and Sunday Morning. '63 This
Sporting Life (prod. only). '64 Night Must Fall
(+co-prod). '66 Morgan, a Suitable Case for
Treatment. '68 Isadora (USA: The Loves of
Isadora). '74 The Gambler (USA). '78 Who'll Stop
the Rain? (USA) (GB: Dog Soldiers). '81 The
French Lieutenant's Woman.

Reisz clearly has a place in the history of the British cinema for his work in revitalizing realism in the late Fifties and early Sixties. Even if that revitalization was shortlived within the British cinema it had an important effect on television, helping to create the climate out of which came the work of Ken Loach and Tony Garnett, a television series like Z Cars and the plays of David Mercer, Dennis Potter and Trevor Griffiths.

In terms of overall achievement, it is hard to make a substantial judgment of Reisz's films. In many ways he is a displaced figure, a Czech who became an Englishman, a British director who became an American one. It might even be claimed that he is an 'art' director masquerading as a mass-entertainment director. Certainly his films have the kind of ambition and artistic awareness that mark out the art cinema. But his ambition has always been to create intelligent mass entertainment. An estimate of his success in doing so depends on drawing a fine line between work that is sympathetically ambitious and work whose pretentions outstrip its achievements.

However that success might be estimated, there ought to be a place for artists with Reisz's ambitions and qualities in any worthwhile form of mass entertainment. It is one of the major failures of the British cinema that it has not been able to find a place for them.

ALAN LOVELL

influenced film-makers both in the United States and Europe to pursue the same goal.

Of Reisz's films, *Morgan, a Suitable Case for Treatment*, with its speedily paced narrative, over-exposed photography and intercut clips from old Tarzan films, most obviously shows the signs of the *nouvelle vague* influence. *Saturday Night and Sunday Morning* was made representative of the 'kitchen sink' era in the British cinema. Because of the change in technique, *Morgan, a Suitable Case for Treatment* was made representative of the 'swinging London' era. Reisz has undoubtedly always been sensitive to changes in cultural atmosphere.

Taking a gamble

The most recent films Reisz has made, *The Gambler* (1974) and *Who'll Stop the Rain?* (1978), known in Britain as *Dog Soldiers*, indicate another change in his career. Both of these films were financed by American companies, are set in the United States, and deal with subjects rooted in American life – *Who'll Stop the Rain?* is about such a sensitive area as some of the consequences of the Vietnam war. For somebody who was a part of the Free Cinema movement, with its preoccupations with creating a socially relevant British cinema, the move to the United States seems an important one. Reisz says that working there was not a free decision on his part but one forced upon him by the conservatism of the British film industry. In trying to set up films that were not just run of the mill he found American producers were much more responsive.

Reisz claims that his two American films are ostensibly different from his British ones. He feels that the organizing principle of the British films was a character portrait of the central figures, which meant that the narratives were necessarily loose – *Isadora* is the most obvious example of this. With *The Gambler* and *Who'll Stop the Rain?* he wanted to 'tell a story' and consequently the narratives are more tightly organized. Certainly both films have aspects in common with the American thriller. Yet they seem closer to the cinema of *Saturday Night and Sunday Morning* than they do to that of *Morgan, a Suitable Case for Treatment*. Because of the concern with telling a story, the central characters are not so dominant, the film-making technique is less obtrusive and there is the same kind of careful observation and presentation of the social contexts in which the action takes place.

Although he has now been making films for over twenty years, Reisz's output is not a substantial one. In total it amounts to two documentary films and six features. He explains this limited number as the result of his own rhythms of work, but the overall decline in film production during the period he has been active must have had an effect as well. This decline has been particularly marked in Britain – so much so that a British feature cinema hardly now exists. Reisz is effectively a director without any kind of native national film industry to work within.

Above left: The Gambler, Reisz's first American film, is about a man (James Caan) whose attraction with gambling is losing.
Below: Ray Hicks (Nick Nolte) prepares a shot of heroin in front of a bemused Marge (Tuesday Weld) in Who'll Stop the Rain?

007

The James Bond films, combining wit and high technology with sex and violence, were box-office hits for two decades

With hindsight, it is amazing that the James Bond books took so long to arrive on the screen – nor was it for want of trying. The creator of James Bond, Ian Fleming, began writing the books with the possibility of filming very much in mind, and at least one of them, *Thunderball*, published in 1961, was originally conceived as a film scenario. Fleming probably had no idea what a goldmine he had struck upon when he wrote the first one, *Casino Royale*, in 1953, and the film rights were disposed of for a modest sum soon after publication. It was to be followed by another James Bond book regularly as clockwork every year until Ian Fleming's death in 1964.

Little by little the books built up their sales until their success on screen was a foregone conclusion. They are all efficiently constructed thrillers; normally Bond spends about two-thirds of the story making his way into the exotic arch-villain's clutches and the rest rather simple-mindedly fighting his way out of them, destroying his adversary in the process. James Bond, agent 007, with a licence to kill on her Majesty's secret service, is a 14-year-old schoolboy's fantasy of sophistication. The ideals he embodies are to do with preserving one's cool and knowing about food and wine, even while behaving as the perfect sportsman towards miscellaneous foreign cads and bedding a succession of indistinguishable girls resembling lush *Playboy* centrefolds.

From book to film

In 1962, a British production company called Eon – consisting of Harry Saltzman and Albert R. ('Cubby') Broccoli – acquired the rights to all the Bond books except *Casino Royale* and gingerly activated the first adaptation, of Fleming's sixth Bond novel, *Dr No*. There was a lot of talk about who would be the screen Bond, and various big stars were mentioned, among them Richard Burton, Peter Finch and Trevor Howard, before the choice finally fell on a relative unknown, a young Scottish actor called Sean Connery, who was at least husky and cheap to employ. The whole film, in fact, was done on the cheap, and emerged without any major fanfare. But after a slow start it proved to be a spectacular instance of the public itself making a film into a success; the ingredients were so right that word-of-mouth publicity soon made it fifth in the list of British box-office champions for 1963.

A second film was immediately put into production, *From Russia With Love* (1963). This time the budget was large, the locations in Venice and Istanbul spectacular, the action highlights very well integrated (by Terence Young, who had also directed *Dr No*) and the

Licensed to Kill

Above: the familiar logo that introduces a James Bond film is usually accompanied by Monty Norman's evocatively menacing musical theme. Below: James Bond (Sean Connery) encounters Honey (Ursula Andress) on the beach at Crab Key in Dr No

supporting cast easily the best of any Bond movie: for once there was one heroine who went all through the story, attractively played by Daniela Bianchi, with villainy well represented by Robert Shaw and Lotte Lenya. Sean Connery had annexed the character to himself by this time, bringing to it a happy irony which forbade taking all the nonsense any more seriously than he did.

Gadgets and gimmicks

The next two films, *Goldfinger* (1964) and *Thunderball* (1965), were in many respects a falling off from their predecessor, not so well plotted or played and relying increasingly on visual gimmicks and disconnected action highspots to pep up rather sluggish narratives (Ken Adam was responsible for the elaborate production design). Everyone remembers the

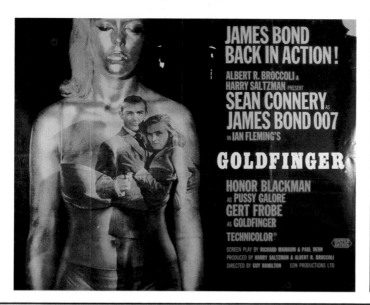

Sean Connery

Sean Connery's presence added lustre to the image of James Bond, yet his talent and ambition led him to other roles, more varied and more mature. Not all of his later films were successes; but he demonstrated that he could go it alone – without Bond

increasingly discontented with the limitatio Bond imposed on his career. He got excelle notices on his own account with The I (1965), a tough military drama, and A F Madness (1966), an eccentric comedy set New York about an iconoclastic Dyla Thomas-like poet. He made another Bond fil You Only Live Twice (1967), and several i distinguished films plus one, The Anders Tapes (1971), a robbery thriller, which w excellent of its kind and a great success wi the public.

After another Bond movie, Diamonds A Forever (1971), Connery had grown rea tired of wearing a toupee; he wanted to matu and play roles with more character. In wha ever way his Seventies' films as a whole mig be judged, there is no possible doubt th anyone who could steal the all-star Murder the Orient Express (1974) from a dozen maj international attractions, or match Micha Caine in effortless ease and authority in Jol Huston's The Man Who Would Be King (197 or play an ageing Robin Hood in the bitte sweet Robin and Marian (1976) with su delicacy and truth has to be a star for seasons.   JOHN RUSSELL TAYLC

Out of Bondage

While it may well be true that Sean Connery was the definitive James Bond, it has become increasingly clear that James Bond was not the definitive Sean Connery.

He was born in Edinburgh in 1930, and had from the start the noticeable Scottish accent which he has never since managed (or perhaps tried) to shed completely. He played his first major lead with Lana Turner in Another Time, Another Place (1958), and was the human scaffolding for a lot of Disney film trickery in Darby O'Gill and the Little People (1959). By 1962, when the role of James Bond needed casting, he had the advantage of being very cheap – for Dr No (1962) he received a mere £5000. But when Ursula Andress came out of

the sea in a minimal bikini his natural virility really made the sparks fly on screen; so he was cast again in the second and best of the series, From Russia With Love (1963). He then insisted on doing two films right away from the Bond image: A Woman of Straw (1964), with Gina Lollobrigida, was negligible; but Marnie (1964) used Connery's unique combination of fine intelligence and unselfconscious masculinity to devastating effect, and Hitchcock considered Connery one of his most satisfactory leading men ever. With his third Bond film, Goldfinger (1964), the Bond boom was nearing its peak, and arrived there with Thunderball (1965). Connery had become a top box-office star in Britain and America for 1965, but he was

Filmography
1957 No Road Back; Time Lock; Hell Drivers; Action of the Tiger. '58 Another Time, Another Place. '59 Darby O'Gill and the Little People (USA); Tarzan's Greatest Adventure. '61 The Frightened City; On the Fiddle (USA: Operation Snafu). '62 The Longest Day (USA); Dr No. '63 From Russia With Love. '64 A Woman of Straw; Marnie (USA); Goldfinger. '65 The Hill; Thunderball. '66 A Fine Madness (USA). '67 You Only Live Twice. '68 Shalako. '69 The Bowler and the Bonnet (doc) (dir. only). '70 The Molly Maguires (USA); Krasnaya Palatka/La Tenda Rossa (USSR-IT) (USA/GB: The Red Tent). '71 The Anderson Tapes (USA); Diamonds Are Forever. '72 The Offence. '74 Zardoz; Murder on the Orient Express. '75 Ransom (USA: The Terrorists); The Wind and the Lion (USA); The Man Who Would Be King. '76 Robin and Marian (USA); The Next Man (USA). '77 A Bridge Too Far (USA). '79 The First Great Train Robbery (USA: The Great Train Robbery); Meteor (USA); Cuba (USA). '81 Outland; The Time Bandits. '82 Five Days One Summer (USA); Wrong Is Right (USA) (GB: The Man with the Deadly Lens). '83 Never Say Never Again.

ar left: Shirley Eaton plays a girl done to *ath with gold paint by the villainous *oldfinger (Gert Frobe), who plans to rob Fort *nox. Left: James Bond (Sean Connery) seems * be down, if not out, in a lift when attacked

with a piece of jagged glass in Diamonds Are Forever. Above left: Bond (George Lazenby) marries Tracy Draco (Diana Rigg) in On Her Majesty's Secret Service; but the bride is murdered before the honeymoon. Above:

Bond (Roger Moore) uses a little persuasion on Rosie (Gloria Hendry) in Live and Let Die. Below: elaborate technology features alarmingly in The Man With the Golden Gun, in which Britt Ekland stars with Roger Moore

Above: as a prisoner in a North African military camp bestriding The Hill as a punishment. Left: as Daniel Dravot, out to impress, in The Man Who Would Be King. Below: as Robin Hood with Audrey Hepburn in Robin and Marian

gadgets, the specially equipped cars and custom-built weapons, and the occasional bizarre incident, like the girl killed by being gilded all over, but few can remember how they fit into the plots or, after a while, which come in which film. As was cannily pointed out at the time, the Bond films were the first to understand intuitively the new sort of audience-reaction engendered by television, where the attention span is minimal, so plot coherence counts for nothing, and all that matters is the ability of the material to hook back wandering viewers every ten minutes or so with a mini-climax of some sort.

Goldfinger took more than $20 million in the American market alone, and *Thunderball* rapidly hit $27 million, thereby becoming one of the all-time box-office champions up to that date. Those who owned the rights to *Casino Royale* decided to film that novel as a wild spoof of the genre, with half-a-dozen directors and as many pseudo-Bonds. The whole enterprise was a disaster, offering when it came out in 1967 no challenge of any sort to the legitimate heir, *You Only Live Twice*.

All the same, *that* dipped noticeably in box-office takings. Moreover, Sean Connery wanted out, and felt that if he stayed with the role he was worth more to the movies than he was being paid. The producers went ahead with a substitute Bond, an Australian model called George Lazenby, for their next production, *On Her Majesty's Secret Service* (1969), which served only to confirm Connery's view.

Things were quickly patched up to get him back into the role for *Diamonds Are Forever* (1971), which racked up a suitably gigantic take and indicated that he was the definitive James Bond, since the film had little else to recommend it. Deciding, perhaps, to quit while he was ahead, Connery did not make another Bond film until 1983.

Forging a new Bond

His departure left the producers with several valuable properties and a desperate need to fill the role adequately. The choice fell upon Roger Moore, a one-time MGM player but best known for his long-running television series *The Saint*. Moore was at least amenable, cheerfully (and properly) denigratory about his acting abilities, and decidedly nearer to Bond as originally written than Connery. With him as star the series has worked its way through Fleming's remaining Bond novels: *Live and Let Die* (1973), *The Man With the Golden Gun* (1974), *The Spy Who Loved Me* (1977) and *Moonraker* (1979), which moves Bond a few steps towards Superman territory. The films continue to perform satisfactorily at the box-office; but undeniably Roger Moore's lack of that extra big-star charisma which Sean Connery brought to the role has debilitated them, and the reliance on gimmickry and rather childish sexual innuendo becomes ever more obvious. Essentially James Bond in the cinema was a creation of the Sixties.

JOHN RUSSELL TAYLOR

When Hollywood became bored with its own stars, the only thing to do was to borrow from Europe. Some of these turned out to be talented and popular, and fame soon followed. Others proved of little interest to an American public. But as Hollywood's make-or-break influence palled, the international star became a respectable and desirable commodity

Hollywood's gamble on European talent began in 1920 when New York audiences went wild over Pola Negri in *Madame Dubarry* (1919, *Passion*). She was besieged with contracts, and though the country as a whole did not endorse New York's opinion, it became standard practice for the American studios to test and possibly sign the most popular European stars. The biggest success was Garbo, and she was the only major continental player to vault with ease the Hollywood transition to the talkies. That event had halted the importation of foreign talent, but when, with sound, Garbo proved a bigger draw than ever, and when Marlene Dietrich also became a box-office attraction, Hollywood talent scouts poured again into Europe – though mainly looking for sophisticated sex sirens. Two other continental stars who became big Hollywood names of the Thirties were Charles Boyer and Maurice Chevalier. Boyer stayed on, but Chevalier turned his back on the film capital at the instant his popularity seemed to be slipping.

Sound with motion

A number of actors unable to work in the German film industry were well received, including Peter Lorre and Paul Henreid, and the glamorous Hedy Lamarr was briefly popular; but the enforced Hollywood stays of French stars Jean Gabin and Michèle Morgan did not provide the right vehicles. Mlle Morgan was later to say that the one thing in her career that she had wanted was to be a Hollywood star. Because of the great success in the United States of Sweden's Ingrid Bergman, after the war producer David O. Selznick brought over Alida Valli from Italy, but all the publicity making of her a new Garbo could not disguise the fact that in English this superb actress became somewhat immobile. There were to be too many such well-publicized failures, and by the early Fifties all but one of the Hollywood studios had lost interest in foisting them on an unwilling public.

That exception was MGM. It had become clear that Europeans could no longer be played

by Americans (or Britishers) assuming accents, and thus Pier Angeli appeared as an Italian war bride in Fred Zinnemann's *Teresa* (1951), and Leslie Caron made *An American in Paris* (1951) – to such acclaim that MGM was pleased to have both under contract. But in Angeli's case her freshness went as quickly as her youth.

Vittorio Gassmann arrived from Italy in 1953, but neither he nor MGM were satisfied with his four American films. Since the play of *The Rose Tattoo* (1955) by Tennessee Williams had been written with her in mind, Anna Magnani was invited to do the film version, for which she won an Oscar; Hal Wallis at Paramount promptly invited her back for *Wild Is the Wind* (1957), but in both that and *The Fugitive Kind* (1960) she was simply too overwhelming.

A taste of Europe

There was at this time, however, a new impetus in Hollywood's poaching of European talent. Television had seriously begun to eat into American audiences, and it was therefore essential to bolster foreign takings with the presence of stars popular in their home territory – particularly as some local audiences, almost for the first time, were tending to prefer their own films to those sent across from the United States. Also, the American public itself was beginning to develop an appetite for foreign films, if not to the extent of offering ompetition to Hollywood. Hence, the studios ecided to capitalize on the interest engen- ered in the United States by the new European ex symbols – Brigitte Bardot, Gina Lollob- igida and Sophia Loren. Bardot signed a Iollywood contract, but one that allowed her o film in France and in French. Loren did go on o an international career, but Lollobrigida – in uch films as *Trapeze* (1956) and *Solomon and heba* (1959) – simply did not connect with the American public, though her popularity in Europe kept her in English-speaking films for a ew more years. Their ample bosoms were hought to be the cause of American interest in Lollobrigida and Loren – a fact which brought emporary stardom to a former Swedish model and Hollywood bit-player, Anita Ekberg, in Artists and Models* (1955) and *Hollywood or Bust* (1956). But fame did not arrive until she vas making a cloak-and-sandal epic in Italy, vhere Fellini saw her and put her into *La Dolce Vita* (1959, The Sweet Life). She was welcomed back to Hollywood by Frank Sinatra and Dean Martin, who thought it might be fun to team hemselves with her and the equally voluptu- ous Ursula Andress in *Four for Texas* 1963) . . . it was not. Ekberg returned to Italy, and a weight problem contributed to her ading from the film scene. It was from the

Far left: never less than majestic, Ursula Andress appeared in She *as a voluptuous demon- queen. Above left: the 1959 remake of* The Blue Angel *saw Dietrich replaced by May Britt, originally a Carlo Ponti discovery. Left: a galaxy of stars shone together in* Fanny (1961) *– Charles Boyer, Lionel Jeffries, Horst Buchholz, Maurice Chevalier, Raymond Bussières, Leslie Caron. Below: suave Oskar Werner on board a* Ship of Fools *(1965) with Simone Signoret. Below right: the rather bedazzling Raquel Welch playing a fantasy temptress in* Bedazzled *(1968). Below, far right: Omar Sharif as Doctor Zhivago*

Italian film industry that the Swiss-born Andress had come, though like Lollobrigida she had had an early, fruitless period in Hollywood before success. In her case, that turned out to be brief, at least as an inter- national actress, and she is best remembered as the first of the James Bond girls – in *Dr No* (1962) – and in the title-role of *She* (1965).

Italian exports
The Italian producer Franco Cristaldi chose Claudia Cardinale to replace Loren and Lollo- brigida in his films, and later married her. She came to international prominence in two films by Visconti – *Rocco e i Suoi Fratelli* (1960, *Rocco and His Brothers*) and *Il Gattopardo* (1963, *The Leopard*) – and was considered useful for the European market in such American-financed films as *The Pink Panther* (1963), *Circus World* (1964) and *Blindfold* (1966). Indeed, she made English-language movies throughout the Six- ties, but when it became clear that her popu- larity would never rival that of Loren, her activity began again to be confined to her home ground. Another Italian sex-star who failed abroad was Silvana Mangano: beautiful but cold, she disliked filming, and retired early. She has been more effective in the films she has made since her come-back, notably for Vis- conti, in *Morte a Venezia* (1971, *Death in Venice*) and *Ludwig* (1973). She certainly seemed earthy when she started, in provocative roles in *Riso Amaro* (1948, *Bitter Rice*) and *Anna* (1952), but she failed to come across in three co-productions with Hollywood – *Mambo* (1954), *La Diga sul Pacifico* (1958, *The Sea Wall*) and *La Tempesta* (1958, *The Tempest*) – all produced by her husband Dino Di Laurentiis, who, like Carlo Ponti, would eventually move his company to the United States.

Quinn spins in
It was De Laurentiis who persuaded Kirk Douglas to cross the Atlantic for *Ulisse* (1954,

Ulysses), but both Ponti and De Laurentiis were to profit from the discovery that many less successful players were prepared to do so, led by Anthony Quinn, whose career was revitalized by the move. Mexican-born Quinn had had a profitable career in supporting roles in Hollywood, to the extent of winning an Oscar for *Viva Zapata!* (1952); but he wanted to be a star, and thus accepted some good roles in Italy, notably the title-role in *Attila Flagello di Dio* (1955, *Attila the Hun*) and that of the strong man in Fellini's *La Strada* (1954, The Road). This last re-awakened Hollywood interest, and he was able to win another Best Supporting Oscar for his portrayal of Gauguin in *Lust for Life* (1956), which led to starring roles in American films. But whenever his popularity in the United States seemed on the wane, he headed back to Europe, playing a variety of nationalities in both local productions (usually in English) and American-backed films. Indeed, there is no star more international than Quinn, though in the last twenty years his popularity in English-speaking countries has been limited to one film – *Zorba the Greek* (1964) – and some would call that a depressing experience.

That is also a description which fits *Der Besuch* (1964, The Visit) which Quinn made with Ingrid Bergman, from a play by Friedrich Dürrenmatt, directed by Bernhard Wicki, a German-Italian-French-American co-produc- tion. It has a companion piece in the Italian- French *I Sequestrati di Altona* (1962, *The Condemned of Altona*) since that also does no justice to a good play (by Jean-Paul Sartre), a fine director (Vittorio De Sica) and an interest- ing cast. The cast, incidentally, indicated the pitfalls of the 'international' film, since it was difficult to believe that there was any con- ceivable way in which one German family could comprise Fredric March, Sophia Loren, Robert Wagner, Maximilian Schell and the French actress Françoise Prévost.

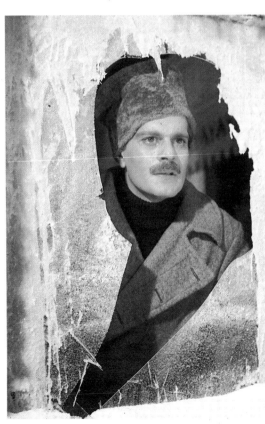

Mistaken identities

Maximilian Schell (b.1930) is one of the most interesting actors of the international scene, winning a well-deserved Oscar for his playing of the foxy defence lawyer in *Judgement at Nuremberg* (1961). His own judgment proved faulty when he chose to do a number of routine films, eventually turning director with such movies as *Geschichten aus dem Wiener Wald* (1979, Tales From the Vienna Woods). Virtually every film he has made as an actor has featured stars of many countries, but he did manage to be in two of the best – Jules Dassin's *Topkapi* (1964) with Melina Mercouri, Peter Ustinov, Robert Morley and Akim Tamiroff, and Sidney Lumet's *The Deadly Affair* (1967), with Simone Signoret, James Mason and Harriet Andersson, both films proving that assorted nationalities can work when relevant to the plot. Since the Swiss-born Schell is German speaking, he has played a number of German officers in the expensive re-creations of World War II that marked the Seventies, including *A Bridge Too Far* (1977) – presumably for a large fee, since he once said that he loathed such parts. Similarly trapped from time to time is Hardy Kruger (b.1928), who in fact made his foreign debut as an escaped German POW in the British *The One That Got Away* (1957). His 'international' films include one of the most opportunistic – the American *Hatari!* (1962), which also gathered in a Frenchman (Gérard Blain) and an Italian (Elsa Martinelli) with no reason given why this group of jungle scientists – which included John Wayne – were of differing nationalities.

Far from home

In the early Sixties Germany's teenage favourite Romy Schneider (1938–1982) was appearing in a series of candy-coated confections, including three films in which she played the young Empress Elizabeth of Austria. To escape her image Schneider went to Italy to play a young wife with sex on her mind in Visconti's episode of *Boccaccio 70* (1962), and to France to play a prostitute in Welles' *Le Procès* (1962, The Trial). She thus became another actress with whom Hollywood flirted, appearing in *The Victors*, *The Cardinal* (both 1963) and *Good Neighbour Sam* (1964), among others. More recently she was seen in *Ludwig*, again as Elizabeth of Austria, and in *Bloodline* (1979), while consolidating her position in France, where she is a major star. She has twice won the César – the French Oscar – for *L'Important C'Est d'Aimer* (1974, The Main Thing is to Love) and *Une Simple Histoire* (1970, Simply a Story), indicating that the French find in her qualities which disappear when exported.

One of the characteristics of international casting is its inappropriateness. Schneider's presence in *Good Neighbour Sam* was supposed to help a Hollywood comedy in Europe – often a difficult market for the genre. Despite complete failure as a comedienne, the star, Jack Lemmon, cast Virna Lisi from Italy to play with him in *How To Murder Your Wife* (1965), with equally poor results. Since musicals are risky in Europe, Jean Seberg – a star in France – was brought back to the United States for *Paint Your Wagon* (1969), and Sophia Loren – an unusual, though not unwise choice – was cast in *Man of La Mancha* (1972). Similarly, Petula Clark's continental popularity was expected to help both *Finian's Rainbow* (1967) and *Goodbye*

Chips (1969), while Barbra Streisand was
ned in *Funny Girl* (1968) by Omar Sharif,
d in *On a Clear Day You Can See Forever*
970) by Yves Montand.

Unhappy uprooting

e casting of Sharif in that particular film was
d – an Egyptian playing a Jewish American –
t since making his English-speaking debut in
Lawrence of Arabia (1962) Sharif (b.1932) has
not been easy to cast: he played an Armenian
prince in *The Fall of the Roman Empire* (1964), a
Spanish priest in *Behold a Pale Horse* (1964), a
Yugoslav peasant in *The Yellow Rolls Royce*
(1964), a Mongol conqueror (the title role) in
Genghis Khan (1965), a Russian (the title role)
in *Doctor Zhivago* (1965), a German officer in
The Night of the Generals (1967), a Spanish
prince in *C'Era una Volta* (1967, *Cinderella –
Italian Style*) and an Austrian one in *Mayerling*
(1968). No one in the international field had
better chances than Sharif, but he threw them
away, as is clear from his statement on the set
of *Mayerling*:

'If a director wants Omar Sharif to play a
part he gets Omar Sharif, not the reincarnation
of some nutty prince . . . All I care about is
getting to the studio on time and remembering
my lines.'

Thus the engaging actor of *Lawrence of
Arabia* gradually became so cardboard that the
important film roles began to die out.

Even more difficult to cast is Japan's magnificent Toshiro Mifune, which is perhaps why his
films away from his home ground have been so
disappointing. Max Von Sydow and Liv
Ullman – from Ingmar Bergman's stock
company – have simply been unlucky away
from Sweden. And for the superb Raf Vallone
(b.1917), international stardom came a little
too late. A former journalist, he was one of the
most virile and attractive Italian leading men
from his debut in *Bitter Rice*, but he was in his
early forties by the time he was widely seen
abroad – in *La Ciociara* (1961, *Two Women*) as a
cheerful truck driver, or in *El Cid* (1961) as
Charlton Heston's rival. He was a Mafia boss in
The Italian Job (1969) and a Neapolitan police
chief in *The Human Factor* (1979), with John
Mills; he also plays priests and high-ranking
officers, and turned up as a Mexican entrepreneur in a Western with Kirk Douglas – *A
Gunfight* (1971). Too many of the films he has
made in recent years are poor, but he is one of
the justifications for the international star: no
matter where he crops up, the film will be
better for his presence.   DAVID SHIPMAN

109

Best Sellers

Although primarily a comic and mimic of exceptional ability, Peter Sellers found himself in films at an early stage in his career and went on to act in a vast number of movies from the Fifties to his death in 1980. Always appearing as 'Peter Sellers in costume with a funny accent', he nevertheless carried the audience with him and his best performances were outstanding.

When, after a severe heart attack, Peter Sellers died in London on 28 July, 1980, the tragic inevitability of the announcement did not relieve the shock or the grief. The wide coverage of his funeral and memorial service, the numerous tributes on radio and television and the hasty revivals in cinemas were evidence of his popularity and the affection in which he was held both in Britain and abroad. His heart condition had put him into hospital many times but he continued to work relentlessly, even recklessly, as if he knew he was living on borrowed time.

Sellers was born in Southsea on 8 September, 1925, and took a traditional path to stardom. His parents ran a seaside variety theatre and he became a comedian and impressionist; later he joined the Entertainments National Service Association (ENSA). At the end of the war he played the Windmill Theatre in Soho. His gift for vocal mimicry led to a few radio appearances and in 1949 the entertainer and novelist Harry Secombe introduced him to comedy writers Spike Milligan and Michael Bentine, with whom he devised *The Goon Show*. The BBC radio programme ran for seven years and its anarchic and surrealist humour rapidly became a cult.

During this time Sellers began to receive film offers and appeared in many supporting roles until the enormously successful *I'm All Right Jack* (1959) made him a leading star of the British cinema. By the mid-Sixties he had become an international star and celebrity, a position he was only able to maintain in the Seventies by reviving The Pink Panther series which had begun in 1964. His obituary in *The*

Times of London was headlined 'Comic genius of the cinema screen', but his reputation is not borne out by his filmography; it has more than its fair share of mediocre and terrible films.

Labouring for laughter

By all accounts Sellers was a difficult man to live and work with. Like many 'funny men' he had serious misgivings about his talent, was prone to periods of deep depression, but worked with tireless enthusiasm; according to those close to him he only came alive when in costume and make-up. He had built his career gradually but suddenly it ran away with itself and instead of channelling his power into challenging projects he squandered it. He directed himself once only – in *Mr Topaze* (1961) – but lacked the discipline and the self-awareness to join the ranks of Jacques Tati, Woody Allen or Mel Brooks as an *auteur*. There was no such thing as a Sellers *character*, only a bewildering array of Sellers' *performances*.

His great weakness was a lack of judgment, the ability to see beyond the specific demands of his own role. He was betrayed by too many screenwriters and directors who failed to harness his talent or provide a grand enough context for it. Unlike Orson Welles, with whom Sellers shared an understanding of radio, Sellers' presence in shoddy material did not lend it weight, authority, fascination or irony. Welles' magnified persona is compulsive even in dross because Welles is an actor who does not require a context in which to flourish. Sellers, on the other hand, never cultivated a forceful enough ego to transform dressing-up into autobiography.

Guinness was good for him

Another useful comparison is with Alec Guinness, who was Sellers' idol. Guinness is the very opposite of Welles because he has no identity outside his roles. Of course, Guinness is regarded as an actor rather than a comedian but to see him in his Ealing films – *Kind Hearts and Coronets* (1949), *The Man in the White Suit* (1951), *The Lavender Hill Mob* (1951), *The Ladykillers* (1955) – is to witness an actor creating a complete character without resort to self-indulgence or technical display. Sellers' early performances are clearly influenced by Guinness' restraint, but as the scripts became worse so the 'international' Sellers became a show-off. The audience is always conscious of watching Peter Sellers in costume and speaking with a funny accent.

Sadly, many of his films were too conventional and conservative to contain him and it is interesting to speculate on how Michael Powell, Luis Buñuel or Billy Wilder might have used him. Sellers could also be swamped, as in the frantic *What's New, Pussycat?* (1965) or the mindless *The Prisoner of Zenda* (1979), and although he paid great attention to detail he let himself be cast in slapstick, a genre of obvious gestures and effects. In a sense, Sellers was a miniaturist, at his most brilliant in scenes that emphasized subtlety over action. His nervous

telephone call to the Soviet premier in *Dr Strangelove, or How I Learned to Stop Worrying and Love the Bomb* (1964) is arguably his finest moment because of its close-up clarity and its perfectly realized context.

The best of the rest

His bad films are perhaps best forgotten. Fortunately there are several good and outstanding ones that secure him a place in film history. His spiv in *The Ladykillers* is an adroit cameo of cheap nastiness, a forerunner of his East End gangster in *The Wrong Arm of the Law* (1963). His drunk and doddery cinema projectionist in *The Smallest Show on Earth* (1957) explores both the absurdity and the pathos of the character as his beloved fleapit collapses about him. His triple-role in *The Mouse That Roared* (1959) – as duchess, prime minister and straight-laced hero – showed his range and his taste for satire. *I'm All Right Jack* was perhaps too satirical, attacking all targets with buckshot, but Sellers' aggressive shop steward

110

was an immaculate conception, part parody yet always dignified.

His best films are *Lolita* (1962) and *Dr Strangelove*. In the former he portrays the dual-personality of Quilty with a fine sense of grotesquerie and pretension, acting the paranoid pursuer of a young girl with disturbing menace and the suburban intellectual with sickly charm. His three roles in *Dr Strangelove* – eccentric but sane RAF officer, incompetent American president, mad ex-Nazi scientist – are all superb characterisations, rich in detail and with a nightmarish quality. None of his subsequent films touched Sellers' potential for dramatic or horrific comedy and his rare excursions into 'straight' roles, such as *The Blockhouse*, were rarely released.

From Goon to goon

With *The Pink Panther* (1963) Sellers created

Inspector Clouseau, the clumsy and ineffectual French detective. The first film is a character study with an incidental plot. However, when the series was revived in the Seventies Clouseau had become a parody rather than an eccentric and believable character, a slapstick cut-out with an accent that drew attention to itself as a gimmick.

Being There (1979) gave Sellers his best opportunity since *The Pink Panther* and *Dr Strangelove*. As the simpleton gardener who becomes a White House aide and presidential candidate, Sellers gave one of his most subtle performances, the kind of performance that Alec Guinness might have been proud of. *Being There* should have marked a new era for Sellers but he mugged shamelessly in *The Fiendish Plot of Dr Fu Manchu* (1980) and was preparing yet another Pink Panther at the time of his death.
ADRIAN TURNER

Left: Inspector Clouseau sheds light on the subject. Below left: shop steward Fred Kite (Sellers) and his wife (Irene Handl) engage in battle over the tea while an aghast Stanley Windrush (Ian Carmichael) looks on in I'm All Right Jack. *Below right: Pearly Gates (Sellers) and members of his gang (Dermot Kelly and Bernard Cribbins) meet to hatch a plot in* The Wrong Arm of the Law

Top right: the gardener who little knows he is on his way to the White House in Being There. *Right: a man constantly distracted by pretty girls consults a psychiatrist (Sellers), who in turn is similarly afflicted in* What's New, Pussycat? *Bottom right: Sellers and Goldie Hawn as a big-headed TV personality and the trouble-making girl he picks up in* There's a Girl in My Soup *(1970)*

Filmography
1951 Let's Go Crazy (short); Penny Points to Paradise; Burlesque on Carmen (short) (narr. only); London Entertains (short) (as himself). **'52** Down Among the Z Men. **'53** The Super Secret Service (short). **'54** Malaga (dubbed voices only for USA release version only: Fire Over Africa); Orders Are Orders. **'55** John and Julie; The Ladykillers. **'56** The Case of the Mukkinese Battlehorn/Gone Goon (short) (+co-sc); The Man Who Never Was (voice only) (GB). **'57** The Smallest Show on Earth; Insomnia Is Good for You (short); The Naked Truth; Dearth of a Salesman (short); Cold Comfort (short). **'58** Up the Creek; Tom Thumb. **'59** Carlton-Browne of the FO (USA: Man in a Cocked Hat); The Mouse That Roared; I'm All Right Jack; The Battle of the Sexes. **'60** Two Way Stretch; The Running, Jumping and Standing Still Film (short) (+co-prod;+co-sc); Climb Up the Wall (as himself); Never Let Go; The Millionairess. **'61** Mr Topaze (+dir) (USA: I Like Money); Only Two Can Play. **'62** Lolita (USA-GB); The Road to Hong Kong (guest) (USA-GB); Waltz of the Toreadors; The Dock Brief (USA: Trial and Error). **'63** The Wrong Arm of the Law; Heavens Above!; The Pink Panther (USA). **'64** Dr Strangelove, or How I Learned to Stop Worrying and Love the Bomb; The World of Henry Orient (USA); A Shot in the Dark (USA-GB). **'65** What's New, Pussycat? (USA-FR). **'66** Birds, Bees and Storks (short) (narr. only); The Wrong Box; Caccia alla Volpe (IT-GB-USA) (USA/GB: After the Fox). **'67** Casino Royale; The Bobo; Woman Times Seven (FR-USA). **'68** The Party (USA); I Love You, Alice B. Toklas (USA). **'69** The Magic Christian (+co-sc). **'70** Hoffman; Simon, Simon (short); There's a Girl in My Soup. **'72** Where Does It Hurt? (USA); Alice's Adventures in Wonderland. **'73** The Blockhouse (unreleased); The Optimists of Nine Elms (USA: The Optimists); Soft Beds, Hard Battles (USA: Undercover Hero). **'74** The Great McGonagall. **'75** The Return of the Pink Panther; Gift of Laughter (short) (as himself). **'76** Murder by Death (USA); The Pink Panther Strikes Again. **'78** Revenge of the Pink Panther. **'79** The Prisoner of Zenda (USA); Being There (USA). **'80** The Fiendish Plot of Dr Fu Manchu (USA).

The Italian Cinderella

The real-life fairy story of Sophia Loren: from poverty in a war-torn Italian village, to the luxury of life as one of the world's most admired, individual and stunningly beautiful actresses

'Sophia is perhaps the only movie star who has never forgotten where she came from', a close acquaintance of the actress once observed – and in a profession where origins are often deliberately obscured or fabricated by publicists for popular consumption the details of Loren's early background do carry a rare stamp of truth. It is a background that has always informed her best work, be it in her lusty Neapolitan comedies or dramas set in the war-racked years when Southern Italy bore the brunt of bombings, famine and disease. Loren was, moreover, illegitimate and it is to her mother's eternal credit that she refused to place her daughter in an orphanage but prefered to face the ignominy and disgrace that would inevitably be their lot in the intensely moral, small town of Pozzuoli where they lived. The father, however, did consent to give the child his name and thus she was christened Sofia Scicolone. The year was 1934.

During the war, when the tide of fortune began to turn in the Allies' favour, the bombings became more and more persistent and after the last train to Naples had passed through, the inhabitants of Pozzuoli repaired nightly to a stinking tunnel where, starving and riddled with particularly virulent lice, they would remain until the first morning train was signalled. And when living in Naples the young Sofia and her mother witnessed the most horrendous atrocities as the street urchins banded together to harass the Germans, often sacrificing themselves in order to set fire to German tanks and trucks.

Curtain calls

Sofia's mother always had a fierce determination that her daughter should make her own way in life, and this probably stemmed from an early bitter disappointment of her own, when she had won a competition for the closest resemblance to Garbo. The prize was a trip to Hollywood and a screen test at MGM, but her parents had refused to let her go, owing to the prevalent Italian rumour that Valentino had been murdered by the New York Mafia – a fate that, in their eyes, must await all Italians bent on a Hollywood career. Sofia was a skinny child who had always been referred to derisively by her schoolmates as 'The Toothpick', but at the age of 14 she began to blossom and

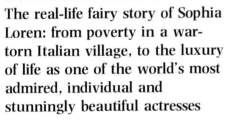

Far left: Loren as first seen by a wider international audience in The Pride and the Passion, which co-starred Cary Grant. Bottom left: a publicity shot from their next film together, Houseboat. Left: Loren gave an Oscar-winning performance in Two Women,

directed by Vittorio De Sica. Above left: she acted with De Sica in La Bella Mugnaia (1955, The Miller's Wife). Above: Loren with husband, the producer Carlo Ponti; after Heller in Pink Tights (right) failed they left Hollywood for Italy and superior roles

her mother entered her in a Naples beauty contest which she won in a dress improvised from the living-room curtains. The prize was a mixed bag of blessings: a railway ticket to Rome, a table cloth with matching napkins, some rolls of wallpaper and about thirty-five dollars.

Their first introduction to a film studio came when Sofia heard a rumour that hundreds of xtras were needed for a film in Rome. This was enough for the mother to pack their bags and they both secured four days' crowd work in director Mervyn LeRoy's Quo Vadis (1951). But no more work was forthcoming. Moreover, they received news that Sofia's young sister – a second illegitimate child by the same father who this time had refused to give the child his name) – was ill in Pozzuoli. Sofia was left alone in Rome in the reluctant charge of some distant cousins. She found work being photographed for the popular cheapjack newspaper serial stories – fumetti – and it was not until she entered another beauty contest, in which she was placed second, that she came close to the cinema again, for the jury was composed entirely of movie people.

Her pride and passion

One in particular favoured her – his name was Carlo Ponti. During the course of the next year, Ponti arranged several screen tests for Sofia whose name had now been changed by the fumetti producer to Sofia Lazzaro. All the tests were negative and the cameramen's complaints all the same: her mouth was too wide, her nose too long, her hips too wide – a far cry from the modish film star's face of the period. In despair Ponti suggested that she have a nose operation, but she declared, in an unusual burst of self-confidence for her at the time, that she preferred to stay as she was.

Back in Rome, Sofia's mother was tireless in her search for work for her daughter and the result was a series of unremarkable bit parts during the course of which a producer decided

to change her name yet again to Sophia Loren. Her first leading role was Aida (1953), mouthing the words to the voice of the reigning operatic star, Renata Tebaldi. The million lire that she earned from this sufficed to buy her father's permission for his second daughter to assume his name legally. At this point, Sophia met the second great influence on her professional life, Vittorio De Sica.

De Sica did not forget their encounter and eventually offered her a part in one of the six episodes in L'Oro di Napoli (1954, The Gold of Naples). In this fellow-Neapolitan Loren found a director whom she could trust; their understanding was instinctual and immediate and she was able to release her emotions as never before, secure in the knowledge that he would dexterously control her performance. As the wife of a pasta vendor Loren made a hit, not only in Italy but abroad. During that year and the next she was to appear in four films with De Sica as an actor and was also to act with Marcello Mastroianni; thus the Neapolitan trio, who were to work so often together in the future, was forged.

Loren was by now under exclusive contract to Ponti who was already aiming to place her in American movies. In between takes and at every available moment she was subjected to a crash course in English. Before she was really at ease with the language he had secured her the leading role in director Stanley Kramer's The Pride and the Passion (1957) with Cary Grant and Frank Sinatra.

Lost in Hollywood

Hollywood has a blemished record in dealing with Italian actresses. Even the great Anna Magnani, despite winning an Oscar for The Rose Tattoo (1955), failed to find subsequent material to match her earthy, explosive talent and soon returned to Italy. Loren fared little better; and the remarkably wide range of material in which she played seems to indicate that no-one – not even Ponti – knew quite

what to do with her. Early on, she appeared in Legend of the Lost (1957), a rubbishy piece with John Wayne about the discovery in the desert of an archaeological treasure, and she was also saddled with director Delbert Mann's artificially lit, studio-bound production of Eugene O'Neill's play Desire Under the Elms (1958), cast opposite that most introspective of actors, Anthony Perkins. Two films during this period came near to revealing a relaxed, jokey Loren: Houseboat (1958) with Cary Grant (the actress's strong personal attachment to Grant must have lent her confidence), and a bizarre Western, Heller in Pink Tights (1960), directed by George Cukor, whose imaginative flair for bringing out the best in his leading ladies from Judy Holliday to Hepburn and Garbo, is legendary. But Loren did not appeal to a large public as a blonde-bewigged leading lady in a group of travelling players who gambles her virtue in a game with a killer. The actress seemed to have lost her way. In England she fared only marginally better, playing the world's richest woman, opposite Peter Sellers as the doctor who eludes her advances, in *The Millionairess* (1960). The film was based on George Bernard Shaw's play but her performance and Anthony Asquith's direction lacked the necessary panache to allow Shaw's dialogue to sparkle. She needed to return to Italy and De Sica to discover her full potential.

Move over Magnani

La Ciociara (1961, *Two Women*) was originally intended as a vehicle for Magnani. Alberto Moravia's story of a mother and her daughter in war-time Italy who, while making their way back to their native village, are raped by marauding Moroccan troups, was set in an emotional climate that Loren vividly remembered.

Magnani was to play the mother and Loren the daughter but Magnani obstinately refused this casting. Finally the roles were adapted for Loren to play the mother with a much younger daughter. Under De Sica's perceptive direction she rose superbly to the challenge. She had now become mature enough as an actress to draw inspiration from her early memories and re-create them with exceptional artistic strength. She had learnt to act with her whole being and when she was awarded the Oscar for her performance – the first time it was ever given for a performance in a foreign-language film – it must have seemed like a vindication for the predominantly second-rate material she had been offered in her American productions.

The next 13 years showed Loren in more misses than hits. On the credit side were: *El Cid* (1961), which saw Loren, under Anthony Mann's direction, sandwiched between a spectacular single-handed combat and a final impressive battle; *Le Couteau dans la Plaie* (1962, *Five Miles to Midnight*), a modest thriller

in which she was well cast, for once, as the Italian wife of an American in Paris: and *Arabesque* (1966), which saw her give a delightful performance as an oil magnate's mistress opposite Gregory Peck as a linguistics expert. Ponti was also wise enough to bring Loren back to her native scene in two films by De Sica, *Ieri, Oggi e Domani* (1964, *Yesterday, Today and Tomorrow*) and *Matrimonio all'Italiana* (1964, *Marriage Italian Style*). In both films she was reunited with Marcello Mastroianni and although some British critics found the films too salacious and brash for comfort the director and his stars marvellously evoked the spirit and rhythm of the raffish, warm and defiant Naples they all knew so well.

On the debit side were such dead losses as Anthony Mann's *The Fall of the Roman Empire* (1964), Daniel Mann's *Judith* (1965) with its stilted script by Lawrence Durrell, and the screen version of the American musical success, *Man of La Mancha* (1972) with Peter O'Toole, misguidedly shot in the Rome studios instead of the Spanish countryside. There was also the fiasco of the last Chaplin venture, *A Countess From Hong Kong* (1967) in which the actress starred with a Brando who acted as if he wished he were miles away.

A special role

It was not until 1977 that Loren found a vehicle that fully revealed once again her characteristic warmth and humanity which not even the appallingly dubbed version

Above right: Loren in I Girasoli *(1970, Sunflower). Right: with Michel Albertini in* Verdict *(1974). Below right: a production shot from* A Special Day *with Marcello Mastroianni. Below: with a moody Marlon Brando in* A Countess From Hong Kong

Above: some reflected glory in Arabesque *in which Loren plays the exotic mistress of a fetishistic Arab oil magnate (Alan Badel). Left: Marcello Mastroianni and Sophia relax during the making of* La Moglie del Prete *(1970, The Priest's Wife)*

shown in England could subdue. Director-screenwriter Ettore Scola's *Una Giornata Particolare* (*A Special Day*), shot in muted tones which perfectly evoked its World War II setting, presented Loren as a mother of six children who chances to meet an outcast homosexual, played by Mastroianni, in a deserted block of flats whose inhabitants are all attending a monster rally in celebration of Hitler's visit to Mussolini's Rome. Their brief encounter and subsequent inevitable separation was beautifully, bleakly traced with never

a false emphasis.

Was it out of a desire to counter the incessant calumnies to which the Ponti-Loren ménage has been constantly submitted through the years (particularly by the Italian press and the Vatican which, for some years branded him as a bigamist and her as his concubine, refusing to accept his Mexican divorce as legal) that they decided to make a $3 million television version of her life based on the book *Sophia: Living and Loving* which she wrote with A. E. Hotchner? Perhaps; but the project presented a big producer's problem: was it wise to keep your superstar waiting in the wings while three other actresses portray her early years until she herself takes over at the age of 23? The solution was beautiful in its simplicity: Loren also plays her own mother.

DEREK PROUSE

Filmography

Films as Sofia Scicolone unless otherwise specified: **1950** Cuori sul Mare (IT-FR) (USA); Le Sei Mogli di Barbablù. **'51** Quo Vadis (extra) (USA); Era Lui, Sì, Sì (as Sofia Lazzaro); Io Sono il Capataz; Milano Miliardaria; Il Voto. **'52** E'Arrivato l'Accordatore (as Sofia Lazzaro); Anna (as Sofia Lazzaro); Mago per Forza; Il Sogno di Zorro. *All remaining films as Sophia Loren*: **'52** La Tratta delle Bianche (USA/GB: Girls Marked for Danger reissued as The White Slave Trade). **'53** Africa Sotto i Mari; Aida; Ci Troviamo in Galleria; Due Notti con Cleopatra; La Favorita. **'54** Carosello Napoletano (USA: Neapolitan Carousel; GB: Neapolitan Fantasy); La Domenica della Buona Gente; Un Giorno in Pretura (USA: A Day in Court); Miseria e Nobiltà; L'Oro di Napoli *ep* Pizze e Credito (USA: Gold of Naples; GB: Every Day's a Holiday/Gold of Naples); Il Paese dei Campanelli (IT-FR); Tempi Nostri *ep* La Macchina Fotografica) (USA: Anatomy of Love; GB: A Slice of Life). **'55** Attila Flagello di Dio (IT-FR) (USA: Attila; GB: Attila the Hun); La Bella Mugnaia (USA: The Miller's Beautiful Wife; GB: The Miller's Wife); La Donna del Fiume (IT-FR) (USA/GB: Woman of the River); Pane, Amore e . . . (USA/GB: Scandal in Sorrento); Peccato che Sia una Canaglia (USA/GB: Too Bad She's Bad); Pellegrini d'Amore; Il Segno di Venere (GB: The Sign of Venus). **'56** La Fortuna di Essere Donna (IT-FR) (USA/GB: Lucky to be a Woman). **'57** The Pride and the Passion (USA); Boy on a Dolphin (USA); Legend of the Lost (USA-PAN-IT). **'58** Desire Under the Elms (USA); Houseboat (USA); The Key (GB); The Black Orchid (USA). **'59** That Kind of Woman (USA). **'60** Heller in Pink Tights (USA); A Breath of Scandal/Olympia (USA-IT-A); It Started in Naples (USA); The Millionairess (GB). **'61** La Ciociara (IT-FR) (USA/GB: Two Women); El Cid (USA-IT). **'62** Boccaccio '70 *ep* The Raffle (IT-FR); Madame Sans-Gene (IT-FR-SP) (USA: Madame); I Sequestrati di Altona (IT-FR) (USA/GB: The Condemned of Altona); Le Couteau dans la Plaie (FR-IT) (USA/GB: Five Miles to Midnight). **'64** Ieri, Oggi e Domani (IT) (USA/GB: Yesterday, Today and Tomorrow); The Fall of the Roman Empire (USA-IT); Matrimonio all'Italiana (IT-FR) (USA/GB: Marriage Italian Style). **'65** Operation Crossbow (GB-IT); Lady L (FR-IT); Judith (USA-IS). **'66** Arabesque (USA-GB). **'67** A Countess From Hong Kong (GB); C'Era una Volta (IT-FR) (USA: More Than a Miracle/Once Upon a Time/Happily Ever After; GB: Cinderella – Italian Style). **'68** Questi Fantasmi (IT-FR) (USA/GB: Ghosts, Italian Style). **'70** I Girasoli (IT-USSR) (USA/GB: Sunflower); La Moglie del Prete (IT-FR) (USA/GB: The Priest's Wife). **'71** La Mortadella (IT-FR) (USA: Lady Liberty); Bianco, Rosso e . . . (IT-FR-SP) (USA: White Sister/The Sin). **'72** Man of La Mancha. **'74** Il Viaggio (IT) (USA/GB: The Voyage/The Journey); Verdict (FR-IT); La Pupa del Gangster (IT-FR). **'77** The Cassandra Crossing (GB-IT-GER); Una Giornata Particolare (IT-CAN) (USA/GB: A Special Day); Angela (CAN). **'78** Brass Target (USA). **'79** Fatto di Sangue Fra Due Uomini (IT) (USA/GB: Blood Feud); Firepower (GB).

1

2

3

A LOVE CAUGHT IN THE FIRE OF REVOLUTION

Turbulent were the times and fiery was the love story of Zhivago, his wife... and the passionate, tender Lara.

METRO-GOLDWYN-MAYER PRESENTS A CARLO PONTI PRODUCTION

DAVID LEAN'S FILM OF BORIS PASTERNAK'S

DOCTOR ZHIVAGO

STARRING

GERALDINE CHAPLIN · JULIE CHRISTIE · TOM COURTENAY
ALEC GUINNESS · SIOBHAN McKENNA · RALPH RICHARDSON
OMAR SHARIF (AS ZHIVAGO) · ROD STEIGER · RITA TUSHINGHAM

SCREEN PLAY BY ROBERT BOLT · DIRECTED BY DAVID LEAN · IN PANAVISION® AND METROCOLOR

WINNER OF 6 ACADEMY AWARDS!

6

David Lean's film of *Doctor Zhivago* is at once an instance of old-style movie-making in the tradition of *Gone With the Wind* (1939) and the beginning of a new phase in the history of the epic. By the mid-Sixties the vogue for biblical epics had waned. The Roman Empire had indeed fallen and the financial debacle of *Cleopatra* (1963) effectively sealed the fate of the cloak and sandal spectaculars. That broad, sweeping canvas of history needed changing again and the Russian Revolution, with its explicit theme of the old order giving way to the new and its cinematic potential for blending costume drama with a more up-to-date historical theme, seemed an ideal proposition. When

the rights to Boris Pasternak's Nobel prize-winning novel were offered by producer Carlo Ponti to MGM, the film of *Doctor Zhivago* began to make economic sense, even in a Hollywood baffled at the loss of its own Midas touch.

When the project was begun, the book was high in the best-seller lists, the scandal by which the Soviet authorities had denied Pasternak permission to accept his prize was still fresh in people's minds, and David Lean – with the Oscar-winning *The Bridge on the River Kwai* (1957) and *Lawrence of Arabia* (1962) under his belt – was among the most bankable directors in the business.

Lean set up his production base

on a ten-acre site near Madrid airport, as Spain was proving more economical than Hollywood for the shooting of big-budget movies. Even so *Doctor Zhivago*'s original budget of $7.5 million was doubled by increased production costs.

In their meticulous re-creation of the Moscow streets (carefully altered to denote the passage of time) nearly eight hundred craftsmen worked for more than two years to create one of the most elaborate sets ever erected outside Hollywood. John Box, the production designer, had worked with Lean on *Lawrence of Arabia* as had the other key technicians.

Lean's casting reflected his preference for familiar faces such as Alec Guinness and Ralph Richardson, though there were people in Hollywood who felt that risks were being taken with the then little-known Omar Sharif and Geraldine Chaplin. Equally important to the director's conception was the authenticity of the film's many exterior scenes. Accordingly, the entire unit was moved to a location in Eastern Finland not far from the Russian border. Here, in temperatures of 30°C below zero, local people made daily appearances as extras in the re-staging of the great retreat from the Eastern Front, a scene which, like many in the movie, captured in the long shot of the Panavision 70

frame the epic nature of the narrative.

The first six months of *Doctor Zhivago*'s world-wide release proved that Hollywood could still make the old epic formula work: MGM were $18 million happier despite the lukewarm response of the critics. Reviewers, especially those in Britain, felt that Pasternak's 'difficult and elusive' novel had been betrayed and the much-repeated question seemed to be: 'How could an American studio film a Russian classic anyway?'.

The answer depended on what image of a Russian classic – and specifically what account of the Russian Revolution – would be widely acceptable to Western audiences. With the Cold War and the

8

4

5

Yuri Zhivago is in love with and later marries Tonya Gromeko (1), whose family brought him up after his parents died. While studying medicine in Moscow he meets and is attracted to Lara (2), the daughter of a dressmaker. When Komarovsky, her mother's lover, seduces and humiliates Lara, she shoots and wounds him at a party (3). Taking this action to be a gesture of political revolt in a climate of violent demonstrations (4), Pasha, a committed revolutionary, escorts Lara from the party (5) and they are later married.

During World War I, when Zhivago is working as a doctor at the front he again meets Lara who has become a nurse (6). Back in Moscow Zhivago finds the city transformed by the Revolution and himself under suspicion for the poetry he has published. Yevgraf, his half-brother and a Bolshevik police commissar (7),

urges Zhivago to flee Moscow with the family and stay at their country estate (8). Zhivago discovers that Lara is living nearby and he visits her frequently until his capture by Red Army partisans.

For a while Zhivago serves as a doctor but later deserts and makes his way to Lara's house. The Gromeko family have been deported to France and Zhivago and Lara elect to stay in Russia and live on the estate, where they enjoy a brief spell of happiness (9) before Komarovsky returns and persuades Lara to flee. Years later, still searching for Lara, Zhivago dies on a Moscow street and Lara disappears into a labour camp. Their daughter, however, has survived and is discovered by Yevgraf working on the construction of a hydro-dam. He completes the story of her parents for her (10).

Cuban Missile Crisis over, the new tone of East-West relations was characterized by the word 'thaw'. What better reflection of this mood than a warm and glowing love story set against the snowy wastes of icy, inhospitable Russia? When Lean cuts from Zhivago and Lara's love-making to a field of spring daffodils blooming after the long winter, the ideology of the film becomes most transparent – human values, such as love and passion, are represented as more enduring than political systems. In the same way, the 'survival' of Zhivago's artistic talent through his daughter is essential to the film's argument, even if the final shot of a rainbow over the newly completed dam stretches credibility into cliché.

For all the seductions of its setting and story, *Doctor Zhivago* has two potentially troublesome themes. The story turns on an adultery in which the two protagonists are allowed to indulge, and the outcome of the historical events is the modern Soviet state. What remains fascinating about the film is the way in which it negotiates these twin 'problems', first by stressing the poetic and artistic side of Zhivago's character which legitimizes his 'immorality', and second by focusing attention on a small group of wholesome individuals who are given added depth by being set against the drably-dressed and brutalized mass of Pasternak's people.

MARTYN AUTY

Directed by David Lean, 1965

Prod co: Carlo Ponti. **exec prod:** Arvid Griffen. **prod:** Carlo Ponti. **sc:** Robert Bolt, from the novel by Boris Pasternak. **photo** (Eastman Color, print by Metrocolor. Panavision 70): Freddie Young. **sp eff:** Eddie Fowlie. **ed:** Norman Savage. **art dir:** Terence Marsh, Dario Simoni. **cost:** Phyllis Dalton. **mus:** Maurice Jarre. **sd:** Winston Ryder. **2nd unit dir:** Roy Bossotti. **2nd unit photo:** Manuel Berenguer. **ass dir:** Roy Stevens, Pedro Vidal. **prod man:** Augustin Pastor, Douglas Twiddy. **r/t:** 193 mins.
Cast: Omar Sharif (*Yuri Zhivago*), Julie Christie (*Lara*), Geraldine Chaplin (*Tonya*), Rod Steiger (*Komarovsky*), Alec Guinness (*Yevgraf*), Tom Courtenay (*Pasha/Strelnikov*), Ralph Richardson (*Alexander*). Siobhan McKenna (*Anna*), Rita Tushingham (*the girl*), Jeffrey Rockland (*Sasha*), Tarek Sharif (*Yuri age 8*), Bernard Kay (*the Bolshevik*), Klaus Kinski (*Kostoyed*), Gérard Tichy (*Liberius*), Noel Willman (*Razin*), Geoffrey Keen (*medical professor*), Adrienne Corri (*Amelia*), Jack MacGowran (*Petya*), Mark Eden (*engineer at dam*), Erik Chitty (*old soldier*), Roger Maxwell (*Colonel*), Wolf Frees (*delegate*), Gwen Nelson (*female janitor*), Lucy Westmore (*Katya*), Lili Murati (*the train-jumper*), Peter Madden (*political officer*), Mercedes Ruiz (*Tonya age 7*).

9

10

FOR A FEW MILLION MORE

The megamovies cost x million dollars apiece, were glossy, star-filled and international in funding as well as in their intended appeal – and nearly ruined Hollywood

The kindest way to approach the great, glossy movies of the Sixties is with a clear understanding that the industry which produced them had gone mad. Hollywood was on a spending spree – investing twice as much each year as it could possibly hope to get back from the box-office worldwide. Cold-eyed bankers saw the seeds of destruction, but the studios could not afford to pause. They owed too much money and made too little profit.

The logic of making supermovies – of spending $12 million on a thin slapstick comedy such as Blake Edwards' *The Great Race* (1965) at Warners, for example – was threefold. Big movies, at big ticket prices, might earn big money fast. Sometimes the theory worked: for instance, MGM stayed afloat in the late Sixties largely on the high earnings of David Lean's *Doctor Zhivago* (1965) and the reissue profits from *Gone With the Wind* (1939). Big movies at high ticket prices, with deals that made cinemas send back a high proportion of their take, would probably bring back a big cash flow, so staving off problems with the banks – at least there would be money passing through which, with a little creative accounting, could be represented as a real business asset. And big movies were supposed to have international appeal – bloody wartime action, broad comedy, parades of stars, a sense of gloss and luxury.

Hollywood still thought in terms of movies that could not be seen on television. Such movies were meant to glitter more, cost more, look like more money than anything television could offer; and their stars were hired either to broaden the market or to guarantee the interest of foreign distributors. Hollywood, for the first time in its history, was drawing more than half of its income from outside America; and simultaneously the United States had been knocked out of first place in film production. Movies for all the globe, so Hollywood thought, were the necessary product in the Sixties.

Other, more general factors pushed the studios towards the big movies. It was easier to borrow money for a relatively accessible, explainable project than for smaller stories which bankers might not understand; it was easier to borrow to make another big gamble than to find the cash to service existing debt. The studios, to stay credible, had to keep borrowing – and the big movies were often the easiest way.

At the same time, the old managements of the studios were breaking up. Darryl F. Zanuck had returned to 20th Century-Fox, but he would barely survive the Sixties; MGM was torn apart by management feuds; Jack L. Warner would sell out of Warner Brothers in 1967 to Seven Arts. The authority of the studio heads had all but dissolved, and the conglomerates understood the real psychological crisis in Hollywood. What was missing was confidence. In 1966, Paramount would be sold to Gulf and Western for less than the conservatively estimated value of its backlist of marketable movies.

Hollywood was trapped – so troubled and so anxious that it felt a great need to minimize risk by making familiar sorts of film on a bigger scale with more stars; so financially disordered that it needed to take huge risks to have a chance of breaking through to survival. Out of that madness and uncertainty came the megamovies.

Their international character was partly a question of markets and partly a matter of production costs. The moguls had seen labour costs in California rise alarmingly, and they felt they could drive a harder, better bargain outside America. They could also use the movie subsidies in more than one country. This logic led to such films as *Cleopatra* (1963): by 1964 it was lying fourth in the list of America's all-time top-grossing movies, and it was still nowhere near turning a penny of profit – an international, glossy, money-spinning disaster.

Mike Todd has to take the blame. *Around the World in 80 Days* (1956), that hugely glossy confidence trick, was at first rejected by the Hollywood establishment. When the movie opened, Todd's cheques were bouncing in spectacular fashion. Much of United Artists' investment went to settle payrolls on which Todd was about to default. Once

Top left: David Lean directing a crowd scene for Doctor Zhivago, *his epic story of the Russian Revolution. Top: Elizabeth Taylor and Richard Burton as two of The VIPs, playing a couple whose marriage is on the verge of breaking up. Above: Jack Lemmon as the comically sinister Professor Fate and Peter Falk as his timorously loyal assistant in* The Great Race

Above: Anthony Quinn plays an Arab leader during World War I in Lawrence of Arabia. *Above right: Ethel Merman as a mother-in-law dumped with the trash in* It's a Mad, Mad, Mad, Mad World. *Below: Gordon Jackson as a Scottish competitor in the London-Paris air race, running into trouble in* Those Magnificent Men in Their Flying Machines

released, though, the movie coined money. Its production costs were around $6 million, twice the original budget – it is difficult, more with Todd even than with other producers, to be exact. By 1968, that $6 million had earned United Artists $23 million in American rentals and $18 million in the rest of the world. The formula seemed solid.

Darryl F. Zanuck, making his black-and-white *The Longest Day* (1962), was asked by his staff how the public would know the movie was not a newsreel. 'We'll have a star,' he said, 'in every reel.' Routine products such as *The VIPs* (1963) and *The Yellow Rolls Royce* (1964), both well-crafted and sluggish movies by Anthony Asquith that belied the high intelligence of his *Orders to Kill* (1958), were among the top ten movies of their respective years when they appeared in America, and sold largely on their stellar casts. The formula owes something to such earlier MGM star vehicles as *Grand Hotel* (1932) and Cukor's *Dinner at Eight* (1933), but with this twist: stars were now introduced, as in the Mike Todd movie, virtually as cabaret turns, playing characters closely resembling themselves. So Frank Sinatra was a crooner in Todd's film; and Richard Burton and Elizabeth Taylor were impossibly chic VIPs stranded at London's Heathrow airport in the Asquith film.

Along with top-heavy casts, the studios of the

Sixties were also prepared to pay for top-heavy production values. Blake Edwards' *The Great Race*, a heavily stylized comedy of snow-white hero (Tony Curtis) and melodramatic villain (Jack Lemmon) locked in deadly rivalry, cost a staggering $12 million, including $200,000 for antique cars, newly built. Its set-pieces actually misfire because of their sheer scale. A custard-pie fight in 70mm risks diverting audience attention every which way; it is almost impossible to focus on the single, funny incident when about thirty identical events are happening across the open prairies of the wide screen.

High budgets and gloss made commercial sense only when they were entrusted to the sort of project David Lean pursued – a rather Victorian romanticism, lushly and cleverly presented. Lean's *The Bridge on the River Kwai* (1957) was hugely successful, both critically and commercially; his *Lawrence of Arabia* (1962), despite ten months' shooting in the Jordanian desert and nineteen months of work for its star Peter O'Toole, was also hugely successful. *The Bridge on the River Kwai* was shot on difficult locations, with the centrally important bridge built simply to be blown up and a train hauled across jungle terrain for its starring role. At the time such devices seemed extravagant, and yet the total production cost was barely $3 million; the film was

sold to US television in 1966 for $2 million, after its highly profitable career in cinemas.

Lean's triumph – although there is room for debate about its quality – was *Doctor Zhivago*, a quite extraordinarily ambitious project. Lean read the book, Carlo Ponti had done a clever side-deal with its Italian publisher and the result was the salvation of MGM during its most difficult years. Lean deliberately concentrated on the people rather than the political background, the landscapes of the earth rather than of the mind.

In very important ways, Lean did not follow the rules of the megamovies. His casts often had a generous sprinkling of distinguished names, but the leads went to actors (Peter O'Toole, Omar Sharif, Julie Christie) who were in Hollywood terms 'unknown'. While megamovies were still tied to 'bankable' stars – of whom there were fewer and fewer – Lean had freedom to cast for something other than marquee value.

His first epics, *The Bridge on the River Kwai* and *Lawrence of Arabia*, also benefitted from the intelligence of the producer Sam Spiegel, who rarely made publicity about high budgets, an unusual discretion; he combined determination (the rights to T. E. Lawrence's book *The Seven Pillars of Wisdom* took years to acquire) with Hollywood credibility to raise studio cash. He was essentially an unrefusable monster in a Hollywood dominated by men who wished that they were like him – other moguls. He had, according to the novelist and screenwriter Budd Schulberg, 'unmitigated gall plus unmitigated charm plus unmitigated taste.'

Less distinguished than Lean was Ken Annakin, journeyman director of *Those Magnificent Men in Their Flying Machines* (1965) and *Quei Temerari Sulle Loro Pazze Acatenate Scalcinate Carriole* (1969, *Monte Carlo or Bust!*), known in America inevitably, as *Those Daring Young Men in Their Jaunty Jalopies*.

Hollywood producers could no longer feel sure that biggest was best – or most profitable

---

Annakin's solid, professional, characterless output was utterly without distinguishing themes or viewpoint. Such thin entertainments were successful because Annakin had the art of allowing his star turns to perform effectively. The only characterization permitted was casting according to type: a Gert-Frobe-like Germanic villain, played by Gert Frobe, brought overtones of every other villain Frobe ever played; a cad played by Terry-Thomas was exactly like every other Terry-Thomas cad. With the particularly enthusiastic backing of Daryl F. Zanuck, Annakin's films did make money.

That was more than Stanley Kramer's *It's a Mad, Mad, Mad, Mad World* (1963) could promise.

Kramer assembled stars from the silent era and later, all for the purpose of denouncing human greed. The result made much less money than expected.

The megamovies left a legacy. Although the financial logic of the early specimens had involved the availability of several subsidies in different countries, and varied sources of finance, encouraging co-productions on a grand scale, the most successful ones were made by a full-time studio employee – Jennings Lang, one-time head of the talent agency MCA's television film company and later a major figure at the MCA-owned Universal studios. Lang will have a place in Hollywood history for two reasons: he was the man shot by the producer Walter Wanger in a quarrel over Wanger's wife, Joan Bennett, perhaps the most famous Hollywood shooting of them all; and he was responsible for the making of *Airport* (1970). When it appeared, *Airport* seemed heavy-handed, literal, old-fashioned. Yet the movie, with two sequels, cost a total of $25 million to make and earned $225 million in rentals. Lang had revived the old-style narrative movie, complete with heroics, a gorgeously hokey drama which stuck close to the cardboard figures of Arthur Hailey's novels.

There were danger signs in all this megalomania. Little movies grossed almost as much as the big ones: *Easy Rider* (1969) in its first year almost squelched *Chitty Chitty Bang Bang* (1968) in the American top ten; *To Sir, With Love* (1967) grossed almost as much in one year as *Around the World in 80 Days* had in a dozen; Mark Rydell's botched version of a D. H. Lawrence story *The Fox* (1967) almost matched *2001: A Space Odyssey* (1968) at the box-office. The profits, of course, except with such a long-lived classic as *2001: A Space Odyssey*, were infinitely greater from the smaller movies. Hollywood's sense of spectacle was actually taking away from its sense of the business aspects.

Spectacle was hardly likely to be a useful response to the odd turbulences of the late Sixties, when the heroic and mass-produced stereotypes of warfare turned into the angry music-hall routines of Richard Attenborough's *Oh! What a Lovely War* (1969) and Richard Lester's black comedy *How I Won the War* (1967), with John Lennon; or when drug experience became commercial in such movies as *The Trip* (1967); or when political unrest required some reflection, some resonance in movies.

Hollywood by that time was perfectly insulated. Studios owed too much money to listen to the world. instead, they listened to the banks – who dreamed, as did the moguls, of the great hit that would heal all the fundamental problems of the movie industry. The great hit never came; the problems took over; Hollywood changed, and the violence of the change was largely due to the insulation that megamovies had offered for a few lucrative years in the mid-Sixties. MICHAEL PYE

Above: Billy (Dennis Hopper) pauses during his cross-country motorcycle trek in Easy Rider; *Hopper also directed and co-wrote the film. Below: Caractacus Potts (Dick Van Dyke) is an eccentric inventor in* Chitty Chitty Bang Bang, *which was based on stories by Ian Fleming. Bottom left: two faces of the bisexual Ellen March (Anne Heywood) in* The Fox, *produced by Raymond Stross, Anne Heywood's husband. Bottom right: a music-hall singer (Maggie Smith) entices young men to take the King's shilling, enlisting for World War I, in* Oh! What a Lovely War

UNDERGROUND USA

The Underground film-makers of New York and elsewhere formed a resistance movement against the domination of Hollywood, and yet Hollywood films images continued to fascinate them

'Underground film' was a term the press coined to describe the independent film activity that reached its peak in the Sixties in the United States and particularly in New York. Until the end of the Sixties, most states and cities had direct censorship of all films that were publicly exhibited, and often charged film-makers heavily for viewing and judging their work. This system was not changed until all film censorship was declared unconstitutional by the United States Supreme Court in the late Sixties.

The Underground movement was not united by the type of film-making but by the necessity for film-makers to stand collectively against the harassment of police raids and the mockery of the press. This togetherness provided the very essential social relationships which made up an audience, as well as the physical exchange of film-making equipment and even actors – many film-makers acted in each other's films. Most of them came to film from other art disciplines; the essential motivating force was self-expression and the use of film was another, and new, medium in which to express and explore individual concerns. In this they followed the example of the Dadaists and Surrealists, some of them also film-makers, who shocked the establishment European art world of the Twenties.

The new forms, images and content appeared as a sort of rebellion that was confronted by the usual reaction against the new, as well as the more political confrontation with the censorship that made it 'illegal' to have public showings of unsensored films or to charge admission. Working on and showing films had to function much as the 'underground' resistance did during the war – signs and markings on lamp posts, word of mouth of the new film-making community and empty warehouses as cinemas. An additional factor was that after the war years, film material and equipment became cheaper and accessible to more people, so it was suddenly easier for an artist to acquire a camera and make films.

Prior to the many Underground films of the Sixties, there were individual attempts to free cinema expression, notably by Maya Deren, a dancer, whose first film, *Meshes of the Afternoon* (1943), attempted to express her own personal sense of duality, sometimes by showing two images of her simultaneously on the screen. Deren also began to lecture and write about the personal or individual film. She hired a small theatre, the Provincetown Playhouse in downtown New York City, to show her films and with the money received from the screenings helped other independent film-makers, including Stan Brakhage and Kenneth Anger.

In 1957 the Californian film-maker Robert Pike decided to distribute his own films, since no other distributor would handle them. He also distributed the films of other West Coast film-makers, including the Whitney brothers' 'motion graphics', Jordan Belson's new animation, Bruce Conner's film collages made from 'found footage' and Curtis

Above left: Maya Deren was influenced by Surrealism in her Meshes of the Afternoon, but her own image in the film is at times almost Pre-Raphaelite. Above: Jack Smith's Flaming Creatures *featured an orgy involving transvestite men and a few women; the shots of limp penises inflamed the wrath of the New York police. Below: Kenneth Anger's* Scorpio Rising *fetishistically portrays motorbikes and their leather-clad riders*

Above: avant-garde musician Tony Conrad shooting The Flicker *with the assistance of Beverly Grant. Above right: Stephen Dwoskin's* Alone (1964) *concerned a favourite theme of his early films, the individual's relation or lack of relation to others, portrayed through women. Below: a child's cry is depicted by the emergence through its torn face of a tiny crying child in Stan Brakhage's* Dog Star Man

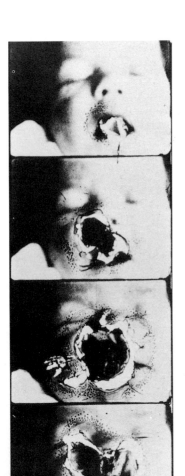

Harrington's filmic drama poems.

These attempts, small as they might seem, laid the groundwork for the most important initiative for the presentation and distribution of independently made films, the formation of the New York Film-Makers Cooperative. This cooperative was the gathering together of many film-makers, not only for film production but also to handle the exhibition of their work. For its time, the unity and the collective policy of the New York cooperative were unique, for it not only challenged the censorship laws but also introduced a policy allowing all films, of any content or style to be supported, screened and distributed without bias. There was no pre-selection policy and the organizational matters and labour were handled by film-makers themselves.

Its moving spirit, Jonas Mekas, was a poet, writer and film-maker. His own films were in a free diary-like style: *Circus Notebook* (1966) or *Reminiscences From a Journey to Lithuania* (1972). Mekas also wrote for the widely read and influential newspaper *The Village Voice* and his weekly column, reviewing the new independent films, drew considerable attention to the new film movement. Along with his brother Adolfas, also a film-maker, Jonas Mekas founded in 1955 the first serious magazine to deal with all aspects of cinema, *Film Culture*.

By the Sixties, the break from conventional Hollywood film became clearer. The battle had begun when the Underground films began to be shown by the New York Film-Makers Cooperative. One of the most memorable film screenings was the first showing of Jack Smith's *Flaming Creatures* (1963), a glorious film of fantasy in a dream-like transvestite orgy, in a warehouse in downtown Manhattan. *Flaming Creatures* became so notorious that the United States Customs and the New York police destroyed any prints they could find. Years later it was the same film, brought before the United States Supreme Court, that finally led to the abolition of censorship.

Most of these Underground films were made without any assistance from grants or large public funding bodies. Personal expression was allowed in painting and poetry, but in terms of film it was highly criticized as not being properly film at all, much less serious cinematic expression. On another level, film was considered a mass medium used for communication, entertainment and propaganda, and was predominantly used as such. The notion of film in the hands of individuals or political groups presented a threat to the control of any establishment in society.

Kenneth Anger's films inhabited the same arena of homosexual concerns and the frustrations of a suppressed group as *Flaming Creatures*. In his firs film *Fireworks* (1947) and later in *Scorpio Risin* (1963), Anger brilliantly and freely portrayed th rituals and dilemmas of the male homosexual. Jea Genêt, the French novelist, made *Un Chant d'Amou* (1950, A Song of Love) in which, as in Jea Cocteau's *Le Sang d'un Poète* (1930, *The Blood of Poet*) and *Le Testament d'Orphée* (1959, *Testament o Orpheus*), the personal concerns of sexual self expression produced strong films as well. Genêt' film, like *Flaming Creatures* but even more explicit was raided and prints burned for years in a continuing witch hunt.

Kenneth Anger combined his personal world with a deep interest in what he called 'Magick' an its rituals and was very influenced by the writings o the English magician Aleister Crowley. His film *Kustom Kar Kommandos* (1965) and *Invocation of M Demon Brother* (1969) are superb examples. So is th more ambitious *Inauguration of the Pleasure Dome* describing a wild party that is also a quasi-religiou

Underground films exploited the properties of the film medium as we as improprieties of conduct

rite and made in three different versions betwee 1954 and 1966.

The films made moved across many terrain More than thirty years after Maya Deren's *Meshes the Afternoon* attempted to express the role of woman in society, Yvonne Rainer, another dance continued the theme in her *A Film About a Woma Who . . .* (1975). Another area seriously explore by film-makers was the formal notion of 'film a film', in which the film material itself or the physica presence of film and light became the subject. On example of this style is apparent even in the title *Film in Which There Appear Edge Lettering, Di Particles, Sprocket Holes, Etc.* (1965). Almost ever film-maker of this type thought of film as film stoc or as light, or as time, or as any combinatio leaving no aspect untouched.

Tony Conrad's *The Flicker* (1966) simply con sisted of clear and dark frames, arranged in pa terns, causing the sensation of a changing b calculated strobe-effect. In a similar vein, in whic the metric rhythm becomes an essential in gredient along with light and dark, is the Vienne Peter Kubelka's *Arnulf Rainer* (1960), but instead a strobing effect, a greater rhythmic beat is create Kubelka pursued this metric effect mainly throug

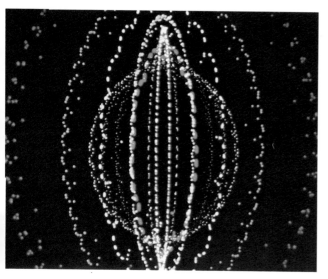

the editing process – Conrad did it through the camera process – and this rhythmic editing is best exemplified in *Unsere Afrikareise* (1966, Our Trip to Africa) which uses images rather than pure black-and-white frames. Another scrutiny of the filmic material can be found in *Tom, Tom, the Piper's Son* (1969) by Ken Jacobs, in which an old short film based on the nursery rhyme, made by D. W. Griffith's cameraman Billy Bitzer in 1905, was subjected to a process of reframing, slowing down and other effects, to make up a whole new film in which every primary element of the cinema is explored.

Structuralism was a movement in French thought that emphasized the structure of relationships between parts rather than the parts themselves. *Wavelength* (1967), made by the Canadian Michael Snow, was unquestionably most influential in establishing the notion of structuralism in film. The film had the power to embrace filmic time, movement, colour and sound into a single unit, and those same elements were the content of the film itself. Snow, being both a sculptor and a musician, was able to bring into film in a pure state the ingredients of these other arts. Snow continued to explore these concepts in his films ⟷ (1969, also known as *Back and Forth*) and *La Région Centrale* (1971, The Central Region), shot on a mountain in Quebec. *Wavelength*, however, remained the most influential; viewers attributed to the film the notion of 'real time' (the length of time a film takes to view being equal to the time in which it was shot) because the film appeared to be a continuous zoom through a large room when, in fact, it was not continuous and often the 'real time' was broken.

It was the painter Andy Warhol who actually used 'real time'. This is best seen in *Empire* (1965), eight hours from dusk to dawn of the Empire State Building in New York. Warhol also made films which played off Hollywood stories, as in the Western parody *Lonesome Cowboys* (1968); or reading of scripts as in *Kitchen* (1965); or a take-off of multi-screen epics as in *The Chelsea Girls* (1966), set in New York's Chelsea Hotel and intended for showing on two screens simultaneously. This pop-art aspect, involving a love-hate relationship with the commercial Hollywood film, has been apparent throughout the Underground movement from the beginning.

Pull My Daisy (1959) might be called the first Underground film. This came from the 'Beat' generation of artists, with script and voice-over by the novelist Jack Kerouac and with Allen Ginsberg playing the Poet; the film was made by Robert Frank and the painter Alfred Leslie. Ron Rice's films

brought together the parody and fantasy elements in *The Flower Thief* (1960), *Senseless* (1962), *Chumlum* (1963). The Kuchar brothers made films which were like Bronx backyard versions on minimal budgets of Hollywood pseudo-dramas, using such titles as *Hold Me While I'm Naked* (1966) and *Eclipse of the Sun Virgin* (1967).

In this era, the most important aspect of all was the freedom and independence of personal choice and individual imagery, the enormous output and wide-ranging attitudes. There was animation done by such people as Stan VanDerBeek or the lifelong work of Harry Smith's epic and magical animation *Heaven and Earth Magic* (1962, released 1965 as *No 12*) and the enormous output of Robert Breer. There were continuous developments in computerized film imagery in, for example, the works of the Whitney brothers, such as *Lapis* (1966), which contributed subtle kinetic imagery to the later development of video.

On the other end of the scale was 'free documentary' from such groups as 'Newsreel' as well as more specifically political films by Emile De Antonio, including *In the Year of the Pig* (1969), concerning the Vietnam War. The collage films of Bruce Conner not only utilized collage and 'found footage', material previously shot by other people for other purposes, but they were looped and structurally put together in such a way as to make a statement: for instance, *A Movie* (1958) and *A Report* (1965) comment on the commercial dramatization of news events. Social issues were also explored by Shirley Clarke in *The Cool World* (1963), about young blacks in Harlem, and in *Portrait of Jason* (1967), an interview with a male prostitute. John Cassavetes independently pursued social issues as well as using improvisation and an imitation of the *cinéma-vérité* style, simultaneously with the French *nouvelle vague*, in *Shadows* (1960), dealing with the relationships between the members of a black family in New York.

In the field of personal and poetic expression many worked and explored areas: the diary films of Mekas, the freedom of sexuality in the work of Jack Smith, the poetics of Bruce Baillie, emphasizing the effect of physical sensation, and of the most prolific film-maker in this area, Stan Brakhage. Brakhage's work, made over many years, includes *Dog Star Man* (1964), in which a man chopping down a tree is haunted by visions of his own past, *The Art of Vision* (1965) and a series called *Songs* (completed in 1969) as well as a relentless array of other films dealing with his own life, the world of nature, birth and death, and with the very nature of film and seeing.

STEPHEN DWOSKIN

Top left: Permutations *(1967), John Whitney's abstract animation. Top right: Adolfas Mekas' 1963 film was widely shown. Above: Emile De Antonio's film (1969) showed McCarthy's presidential hopes in 1968. Below: Sylvia Miles in a film about Hollywood, Paul Morrissey's* Heat *(1972), from Warhol's Factory*

European immigrant family) in 1930. There were two seminal influences on his childhood. The first was his grandmother, who had been a costume mistress in silent films, and who played a decisive role in forming the boy's tastes and interests, especially in occultism. The second was his appearance – at the age of five – in the Max Reinhardt-William Dieterle version of *A Midsummer Night's Dream* (1935). He played the Indian princeling, and spent the movie riding a unicorn and being seized alternately by Oberon and Titania. His upbringing in Hollywood was later acidly reflected in his book of scandals *Hollywood Babylon* (published 1975), first released in French as a series of articles in the magazine *Cahiers du Cinéma*.

Playing with fire

He began making films at a very early age: he recalls shooting a version of *Ferdinand the Bull* with his troupe of cub-scouts at the age of seven. He continued making short films through his early teens, but it was not until he made *Fireworks* (1947) at the age of 17 that he seriously set about seeking an audience for his work. He found that audience not in America but in Europe: after submitting *Fireworks* to the Festival des Films Maudits in Biarritz in 1949, he received not a prize but a letter of warm encouragement from Jean Cocteau, who had sat on the Festival jury. Before long, he was travelling Europe, showing his films and trying to make new ones; he returned to California to shoot *Inauguration of the Pleasure Dome* (1954), but did not settle back in the United States until 1962. He has since divided his time between San Francisco, New York and London, and has spent the last decade working intermittently on a major film called *Lucifer Rising*, planned as his first feature.

Fireworks marked one of the most incandescent debuts of the post-war cinema. It is a psycho-drama – a form introduced to art and film circles in California by the film-maker Maya Deren – framed as a violent fable of homosexual initiation. Anger himself plays the lead, a young man who dreams of a rough encounter with a group of sailors, and emerges from the nightmare with a longed-for lover.

Anger Rising

Kenneth Anger has been in the forefront of the Underground film movement since he released his first film in 1947. From one point of view, his prominence is surprising: he has released only 9 films, none of them longer than 40 minutes, and he has never associated his work with any particular school or style of film-making

Although film-making was instituted as an industrial process in the United States earlier than anywhere else, there is a parallel tradition of non-commercial film-making in America that dates back at least to the Twenties. In the early years, it was known as 'film poetry'. When it acquired notoriety in the early Sixties, it was dubbed 'Underground film'. In the polemics of the late Sixties, it identified itself as 'New American Cinema'. Finally, in the all too placid Seventies, it gained academic respectability as 'the independent avant garde'. Both the films and the organizations around them have changed enormously over the years, but Kenneth Anger remains a unique figure – and not just in the American context.

Anger was born in Los Angeles (into a

bed. The film's sexual candour was striking the period, and it remains shocking for ny audiences today, but the film cannot be uced to a 'mere' homosexual wish-ilment. Anger was indebted to Cocteau's *Le g d'un Poète* (1930, *The Blood of a Poet*) for ne of his imagery, and to Eisenstein's early us for some of his montage experiments, but overall rhythms and cadences were orig-l enough to make the film famous as a binger of a new generation of American ependents.

xual symphonies

as *Fireworks* which also introduced what s to become Anger's most enduring theme: relationship between an individual and a up – often phrased as a fantasy of some sort ith the group ultimately being assimilated the individual by some uniquely cinematic osis. This theme reappears in Anger's two t-known films, *Inauguration of the Pleasure ne* and *Scorpio Rising* (1963). *Pleasure Dome* n extended fantasia about a party, where polysexual host adopts a different persona d costume) to welcome each of the guests. guests, for their part, represent a heteroge-us set of mythologies – from Hollywood (a ilyn blonde) to ancient Greece (the writer üs Nin as Astarte) by way of German ressionism (Cesare the somnambulist from

Das Kabinett des Dr Caligari, 1919, *The Cabinet of Dr Caligari*, played by director-to-be Curtis Harrington). *Scorpio Rising*, on the other hand, begins as a quasi-documentary on a Brooklyn motorcycle gang, and gradually turns into a bizarre Hallowe'en ritual which rhymes hero-worship with blasphemy, and speed with death. Scorpio, the solitary central character, is seen desecrating a church, and is contrasted successively with Brando (in *The Wild One*, 1953), Christ and Hitler. Intricate cross-cutting links him with a group of other bikers, one of whom finally crashes and dies, apparently at Scorpio's bidding.

Magic moments

The strong currents of fantasy and eroticism that run through these films come together in Anger's fascination with the 'sex Magick' of the English occultist Aleister Crowley, a re-negade from 'The Hermetic Order of the Golden Dawn', who published copious vo-lumes of occult lore. Anger has insisted in interviews that Crowley is central to his work; others might argue that the elements of occult-ism are peripheral to more substantial ques-tions of sexuality, morality and culture.

Anger is half aesthete, half maker of popular culture. At their best, his films subversively tease out undercurrents in the society around him, while at the same time marking daring

advances in film aesthetics. *Scorpio Rising* finds all manner of disquieting implications in its soundtrack of 1962 pop songs and its images of comic-strips, pin-ups and leather fetishism. *Puce Moment* (1949) sardonically takes the 'divinity' of a screen goddess of the Twenties literally, endowing the figure of Barbara La Marr with frivolous magic powers. *Eaux d'Artifice* (1953) is a brilliant variation on the celebrated cream-separator sequence from Eisenstein's *The General Line* (1928), which preserves the abstract visual poetry of the original while conjuring a half-hidden narrat-ive from the movements of a solitary figure and the play of jets of water from fountains. *Kustom Kar Kommandos* (1965) has the last word on car fetishism with its images of a Californian blond polishing his prized hot-rod with a powder puff.

Growing Anger

Capsule descriptions of Anger's films risk making them sound pretentious or outlandish. Although consistently innovative, the films are never obscure: each is designed to work first and foremost as a sensual experience, articulated through colour, surreal juxtapo-sition and, above all, humour. Anger tirelessly reworks his films to heighten their impact or reassess their meaning. He has recently tigh-tened *Scorpio Rising* from 31 minutes to 28. *Pleasure Dome* has been through many ver-sions: it was shown in Brussels in 1959 with a 3-screen climax (on the lines of Abel Gance's *Napoléon*, 1927), and the current version (1966) accumulates layer upon layer of super-imposition as it proceeds, to delirious effect. *Rabbit's Moon* (1970), a self-mocking fantasy about a young man's infatuation with a magic-lantern, was shot in the early Fifties in Paris as a *commedia dell'arte* fable, *La Lune des Lapins*, but finally turned into a wry parable about self-deception.

Lucifer Rising – when released – may well force a complete reappraisal of Anger's cinema. In the meantime, his short films stand as monuments to an independence of means, thought and strategy. In them, the power of imagination flies high.   TONY RAYNS

125

ANDY WARHOL ..... FACTORY WORKER

Andy Warhol – poet of kitsch and high-priest of camp – is now more famous as a cult hero than as a film-maker. His cinematic vision and the output of his art Factory nonetheless were a radical and disturbing prelude which influenced the structuralist Seventies

Andy Warhol is the leading post-war avant-garde film-maker in the West. Born Andrew Warhola in 1928 of a Czech immigrant proletarian family, Warhol studied at Carnegie Institute as a painter, and became well known for his commercial illustrations in the early Fifties. He is best known for his paintings and films, but his activities – in all their diversity and volume – have included producing the rock group the Velvet Underground, designing record albums (notably for the Rolling Stones) and writing books including a serious philosophical treatise *From A to B and Back Again*.

From the late Fifties until 1968 – when he was near fatally shot by Valeria Solanas for reasons that have never been clearly ascertained – most of his output flowed from the Factory, the name given to his silver-papered studio in Manhattan. Since then, when he stopped making films but continued painting he has worked and gone 'public' at a huge Union Square loft/business-office, which also houses the magazine *Interview*. After 1968 the films were made by Paul Morrissey, with the exception of *Women in Revolt* (1972) which was filmed by Warhol . . . and it shows!

No more easels
Warhol's fame was established by his silkscreen pictures of Campbell soupcans and other commercial imagery. Images came from films – often of Elvis Presley, Marilyn Monroe

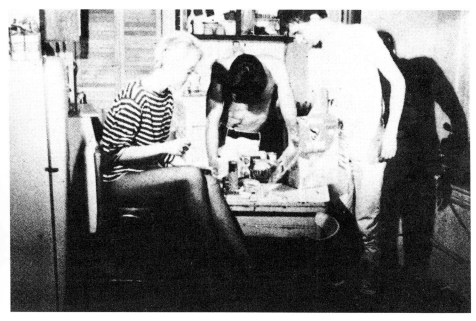

appeared about 1963, often using similar subject matter as he used for the paintings. *Kiss* (1963) shows Rufus Collins and Naomi Levine kissing for the full 100-foot reel of 16mm film. The $2\frac{1}{2}$ minutes projection time was elongated by the use of silent speed to $3\frac{1}{2}$ minutes, then looped for 40 minutes, emphasizing the duration, the unstoppable machineness of the camera stare.

This is one of the main radical moves of Warhol's early cinema: a re-investigation of the basics of the film apparatus. No sound and one camera set-up emphasize the apparatus by the very insistence of avoiding editing, avoiding camera and lens movement, avoiding narrative, avoiding synchronous sound to fill in the meaning of the image. Essentially the early work is a cinema of negation. It functions simply and ineluctably to question the illusionist mechanisms of dominant cinema, whilst at the same time forming a different – an avant-garde – cinema of its own. Warhol's avant-garde work disclosed its procedures and processes constantly and in full view. It is never possible to escape the ineffable stare of the camera in its relentlessness. Thus the film is about film, the way avant-garde writing is about writing and language.

In the early Fifties Warhol worked with a Brechtian theatre group which performed plays as well as building the sets for them, and this belies the commonly held (and self-perpetuated) notion of Warhol the passive intellect or anti-intellectual. In fact, like most avant-garde artists this century, Warhol is primarily an intellectual, if that term means that the work he produces raises questions within its own context, and makes reference to those questions insistently, and that each work takes up positions which a previous work dealt with inadequately or too briefly. In that sense a historical line can be extended back from Warhol's interrogatory intellect to Gertrude Stein, Bertolt Brecht, Sergei Eisenstein, Dziga Vertov and Jean-Luc Godard.

Housework

By 1965 Warhol had begun working with sound film: in *Kitchen*, with its tableaux shot with static camera for two half-hour segments, the actors have a basic script by Ronald Tavel, who wrote many plays for Warhol's middle-period films (1964–66). The script is essentially a hilarious Freudian grotesque, with several characters named Joe (both men and women) and lines such as: 'Which Joe were you having sex with in the shower?' Reply: 'You don't have sex with a name,' and so forth. All along, while the Freudian repartee goes on and on and on, and washing machines go on and off (making much of the speech inaudible for

Above left: Warhol faces the camera during shooting of Lonesome Cowboys *(1968). He himself is no stranger to the lens, and some would say his media image may now have suffered from overkill. Top: Naomi Levine and Rufus Collins in* Naomi and Rufus Kiss *(1964) – one sequence from the more ambitious* Kiss, *40 minutes of cinematic labial congress. Above: how to turn suburban routine into subculture epic –* Kitchen *is a comedy of manners starring Edie Sedgewick as the Underground version of a Hollywood vamp. Below: Warhol's unmistakable image of Marilyn – screen-printed in countless colour variations as a consumer product, it is a perfect symbol of pop-art styles*

car crashes, lynchings and other social-historical incidents – and were then transferred mechanically from the original photographs (or dupes) to the silkscreen web, then applied to paper or canvas.

It is not easy – nor is it necessary – to separate totally the painterly, artistic works of Warhol from the film work, as the two overlap not only in his practices but also in the dominant culture through which we formulate meaning through representation.

The popular, commercial images used for his silkscreens were a challenge to normal notions – in form and content – of fine art. The same goes for his films when they first

Top: *Warhol's superstar Viva!* with one of the Lonesome Cowboys. *Top right: filming* The Chelsea Girls *in the Factory. Above:* Bike Boy *(1967) with Ingrid Superstar and bikeboy Joe Spencer. Right: Candy Darling seems to have found her man in* Women in Revolt

several minutes on end), actress Edie Sedge-wick is sitting on a chair dangling her long legs in a parody of Hollywood, and doing her nails and playing with a mirror which starts to reflect and draw attention to the out-of-scene crew and the audience. Then she speaks to those behind the ostensible camera, breaking the accepted illusion of only representing naturalistic space.

At the same time we are engaged by the disjointed quality of the speaking, by the actors' obvious forgetting of lines, falling into improvisation, picking up hidden copies of the script, etc . . . and all the while, people are running in and out of scene, breaking up whatever pathos the grotesque *mise-en-scène* had for a few moments allowed. So there are constant interruptions, an emptying-out of any level of communication in the usual sense. What such film work does – apart from forcing great laughter – is to undermine any realism in actors' projections, and to leave the viewer with only a series of excuses for language, gesture, movement. In normal Hollywood cinema – as in the 'high' art cinema of Europe – the labour process, the film process, the mechanisms used, are always effaced or sup-pressed to create the 'suspension of disbelief' that is the basic tenet of such cinema involve-ment. But Warhol's is a cinema that makes cinema as illusionistic experience problematic, whilst at the same time dealing materialistically with problems of representation, realism, truth, narrative: showing the mechanics of the whole process, the material qualities of film-making.

Filmography

Many of the Factory films remain unshown publicly, and those that were screened often received 'premieres' up to two years after com-pletion. For Factory movies, direction is usually attributed to Warhol up until the late Morrissey features.

1963 Tarzan and Jane Regained . . . Sort Of; Eat; Sleep; Kiss/Andy Warhol Serial; Andy Warhol Films Jack Smith Filming 'Normal Love' (short); Dance Movie/Roller Skates; Haircut. **'64** Blow Job; Batman Dracula; Empire (co-dir); Naomi and Rufus Kiss (short) (*ep* of Kiss); Henry Geld-zahler; Salome and Delilah (short); Soap Opera/The Lester Persky Story (co-dir); Couch; Shoulder (short); The End of Dawn (short); Mario Banana; Pause; Apple; Messy Lives; Lips; Harlot; 13 Most Beautiful Women; 13 Most Beautiful Boys; 50 Fantastics and 50 Personalities; Taylor Mead's Ass; Award Presentation to Andy Warhol (short) (appearance as self). **'65** Ivy and John (short); Suicide; Screen Test No.1; Screen Test No.2; The Life of Juanita Castro; Drunk; Horse; Poor Little Rich Girl; Vinyl; Bitch; Res-taurant (short); Kitchen; Assassination; Prison; Face; Afternoon; Beauty No.2; Space; Outer and Inner Space; My Hustler; Camp; Hedy/Hedy the Shoplifter/The Shopper/The 14-Year-Old Girl; The Closet; More Milk, Yvette/Lana Turner; Lupe; Paul Swan; Andy Warhol (short) (appear-ance as self). **'66** Bufferin/Gerard Malanga Reads Poetry (short); Eating Too Fast/Blow Job No.2; The Velvet Underground and Nico; Whips; The Chelsea Girls; The Gerard Malanga Story †; Hanoi Hanna (Queen of China) †; The Pope Ondine Story †; Their Town †; The Bed †; The John †; The Trip †; The Duchess †; Roy Lichten-stein and Andy Warhol (TV film) (short) (appear-ance as self). **'67** ****/Four Stars; International Velvet (short); Alan and Dickin‡; Imitation of Christ‡; Courtroom‡ (short); Gerard Has His Hair Removed With Nair‡ (short); Katrina Dead‡ (short); Sausolito‡ (short); Alan and Apple‡ (short); Group One‡ (short); Sunset Beach on Long Island‡ (short); High Ashbury‡ (short); Tiger Morse‡ (short); Withering Sights; I, A Man; Bike Boy; Nude Restaurant; The Loves of Ondine; The Illiac Passion (appearance only); Bleu Comme Une Orange (appearance only) (FR); Andy Warhol Super Artist (appearance as self); Andy Warhol's Exploding Plastic Inevitable (appearance as self); Joan of Arc (short) (appear-ance only). **'68** Lonesome Cowboys; Blue Movie/Fuck/Viva and Louis; San Diego Surf/Surfing Movie; Flesh (prod. only); Andy Makes a Movie (appearance as self). **'70** Trash (prod. only); Andy Warhol and His Clan (appear-ance as self) (W.GER). **'72** Women in Revolt/Sex/Andy Warhol's Women (co-dir. only); Heat (prod. only); L'Amour (co-dir. only); Painters Painting (appearance as self). **'73** Andy Warhol's Frankenstein/Flesh for Franken-stein/The Frankenstein Experiment ('presented by' only) (IT-FR). **'74** Andy Warhol's Dracula ('presented by' only) (IT-FR) (GB: Blood of Dracula); Identikit (appearance only) (IT) (USA: The Driver's Seat). **'77** Andy Warhol's Bad (prod co. only). **'79** Cocaine Cowboys (appearance only). **'80** Model (appearance as self).

Andy Warhol has been the subject of, or else has appeared in numerous arts documentaries and under-ground shorts. The films mentioned probably repre-sent only a small proportion of these.

† original sequence from *The Chelsea Girls*
‡ original sequence from ****/*Four Stars*

Film addiction

In *The Chelsea Girls* (1966), a 3½ hour double-screen film – probably Warhol's best-known and most important – the usage of the machinery is different from the early period. A set of instructions comes with the film, and the first 5 minutes with sound come up on one screen, while the other reel is being laced onto the projector, then a switch and 25 minutes with sound on the other, and so on. The half-hour reels are all single takes, and within the given duration the camera takes up a position and varies wildly from scene to scene in the way it is operated: constant zooming, focusing, swivelling (both of the camera and the microphone) create an effect of equalizing the weight of the given subject matter and the apparatus which is supposedly communicating this subject matter. A radical requestioning is taking place, even in the way the viewer is here positioned. There is no narrative; when any does occur it does not last long enough for the viewer to identify or involve him or herself (even unconsciously) as in a conventional narrative with its seamless flow of images.

A scene from *The Chelsea Girls* with several women speaking to one another and also at various times on the 'phone is shown on the left screen, whilst another reel of another time of the same people doing the 'same' things is screened on the right. The break in linear, logical, rational time is disconcerting, and forces the viewer to attempt (and fail) to read out some coherence, or to respond to a different set of questions from those normally, if unconsciously, posed by cinema. And those different questions would be to do with cinematic truth, with naturalism: how does this illusionist mechanism give a truth, how can any interpretation be taken to be truth, as if communicated adequately by the apparatus 'cinema'? In fact, what is given is a process.

Other reels in *The Chelsea Girls* are different: this is the only example of left screen and right screen following similar subject matter. All other juxtapositions are entirely of different spaces and different times. In one scene (on one screen) Brigit is shooting up heroin and talking on the 'phone, while the whole time talking to, acting to, the camera, the unseen presence of the crew and the audience. The status of narrative story is undercut by such acting techniques, and the viewer's focus is brought to the machine, the camera which some actors even remark on: 'When is that fucking thing gonna stop?' The nihilism, the working down to an end, the emptying out of meaning are all part of such a cinematic enterprise.

Sex is sex

The constant emphasis in Warhol's work is on sexuality. Sexuality is always given as produced, as an ideological position, and not as some preordained biological necessity. Stereotypes of femaleness and maleness are always challenged. When a woman overacts, camping it up as Edie does in *Kitchen*, or when a man in drag camps it up in *The Chelsea Girls*, or when in *Women in Revolt* women and transvestites enact other people's fantasies of what 'the feminine' is, then we, as viewers, are always placed in a position of non-acceptance of the dominant cultural archetypes. These gestures, these ways of speaking, these enactments are always seen as precisely that – enactments.

Thus the notion of 'the natural', and the

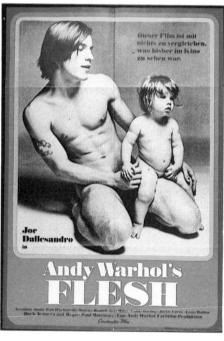

When Paul Morrissey came to direct most of the later films, the Factory's product became notably more commercial – though this did not prevent Flesh *(above) and* Trash *(top) being closely associated with Warhol. Both movies, together with* Heat *featured the ambivalently macho qualities of Joe Dallesandro*

oppression which causes and results from that, is radically opposed by Warhol's work. His films are in that sense less patriarchal, less misogynist, less anti-feminist than any others. This is not to radicalize Warhol, the person, but it is to see his work as radical. The fact that certain contradictions in the life of any artist may prove productive, and find in the work different resolutions, is another matter. Avant-garde art problematizes contemporary cultural issues – economy, history, sexuality, politics – and Warhol's work is in the foreground of that problematization. Although his film work ended in 1968, that same concern now operates in his painting.

Cash for trash

Since 1968 Paul Morrissey's work – *Flesh* (1968), *Trash* (1970), *Andy Warhol's Frankenstein* (1973) and *Andy Warhol's Dracula* (1974) etc. – has attempted to cash in on the fame which society accorded to Warhol's persona. Produced by Warhol, they are more or less straightforward high-art films – some, like *Heat* (1972) very funny, others merely pretentious, with a 'Warhol style'. This often amounts to long-held shots, people walking out of frame, slight emphasis on the acting over the pertinence of the particular story, but essentially a watered-down stylistic of the processes which Warhol's early and – in cinema terms – highly unpopular work was doing. The films fetishize the working-class and lower middle-class characters who were merely one aspect of the process in previous Warhol works, and brought a different social class to the movies, so to speak, but at the same time the old Catholic morality, condescension, narrative suspension of disbelief, and high-art formalism became evident again. Morrissey films are thus a different *genre* in all respects.

At this stage, the many films Warhol made from 1963 till 1968–9 are locked in a vault, and it is extremely difficult to get at them, which unfortunately mythologizes them unduly. What is, however, certain, is that the works – both through viewing and being written about – form the basis for the last 20 years of film-making that went much further along the same route . . . in the direction of structural/materialist film and in the investigations into narrative which are now taking place.

PETER GIDAL

Little Darlings

They may be smart, precocious, cheeky, appealing or even appalling; they may have famous parents or come from 'nowhere'; they may go on to greater things or disappear from the public gaze forever. They are today's child stars

Until the mid-Fifties, the major child performers in Hollywood and Britain embodied a basic innocence. However, former juvenile star Natalie Wood's brilliant portrait of troubled adolescence in *Rebel Without a Cause* (1955) heralded a transition from innocence to experience among screen youngsters over the next five years. America dominated this territory, with Elvis Presley in the vanguard. Britain, at the decade's end, could only offer Cliff Richard as a pale reply.

At the beginning of the Sixties, however, the balance unexpectedly shifted. Only a few transatlantic children made their mark. Patty Duke, as the deaf-and-dumb Helen Keller in *The Miracle Worker* (1962), achieved a *tour de force* of grimacing, madly wilful pathos, combining rage and helplessness with happiness, charm and shy, silent love. Tippy Walker and Merri Spaeth in *The World of Henry Orient* (1964)

provided a fresh depiction of adolescent friendship: their first meeting, when they exchange trivial personal details in Central Park, establishes a spontaneous flavour and a later conversation allows Spaeth's homely, pensive face some touching reactions.

Sugar and spice . . .

But it was from Britain, where the Swinging Sixties were soon to erupt, that the pioneering young star of the era came. Hayley Mills made her debut as the witness to crime in *Tiger Bay* (1959) and in Walt Disney's 1960 remake of the old Mary Pickford vehicle *Pollyanna*, she exhibited absolute informality and lack of sentimentality, as well as a genuine comic sense. Back in Britain for the whimsical religious fable *Whistle Down the Wind* (1961), she found herself upstaged by a highly amusing, hoarsely stammering, beadily suspicious little

boy named Alan Barnes. However, reunite with Disney for *The Parent Trap* (1961), when she played twin sisters, she was permitted fa greater freedom of expression. Her manne isms seemed legitimate and neatly calculate rather than synthetic or obtrusive: the wrink ling of forehead, eyes and nose; the eagerly o thoughtfully licking lips and tongue; the fir gers unconsciously, meditatively pulling at lapel; the mischievous or disconcerted litt cough; the eloquently rolling eyes; the suc denly convulsive, squawking tantrums an ghoulish mugging for humorous effect.

In a later Disney picture, *Summer Mag* (1963), she tasted the dreams, joys and pang of youthful romance; her appealing histrion tricks and quirks were toned down and re placed by a relaxed and restrained confidenc Admittedly confidence was not quite enoug for total success in a more ambitious, trag comic role in *The Chalk Garden* (1964). Neve theless, her soliloquy of would-be-materna and lonely tenderness to a doll emerged as th movie's single fully realized episode. Durin the rest of the Sixties, Hayley Mills rang othe agreeable changes on adolescent pleasure an pain in films like the romantic romp *The Trut About Spring* (1965) and the wry north country comedy *The Family Way* (1966). Bu gradually her vehicles became less satisfac tory. Pieces such as the tiresome 1967 film o the Noel Coward story *Pretty Polly* and th distasteful shocker *Twisted Nerve* (1968), di her little good; and the uneasy screen versio

of Kingsley Amis' *Take a Girl Like You* (1969) foreshadowed the decline of her promise.

Girls will be girls

In retrospect Hayley Mills' personality and talent appeared more at home in the old traditions of pert wholesomeness than in the tough, knowing new Sixties trend for youthful sophistication. In contrast, another notable young British actress, Pamela Franklin, progressed from her part as the eerie child in *The Innocents* (1961) – an adaptation of Henry James' story *The Turn of the Screw* – to a vivid portrayal of tomboyishness in the big-game-hunting adventure *The Lion* (1962), and an even more telling sketch of flirtatiousness in the thriller *The Nanny* (1965). In a melodrama about orphans, *Our Mother's House* (1967), she admirably conveys a girl's quasi-incestuous desire for her supposed father, and if the weird crime tale *The Night of the Following Day* (1968) requires her merely to sob and/or scream, she seized a much richer opportunity in the film of Muriel Spark's idiosyncratic school yarn *The Prime of Miss Jean Brodie* (1969). As a provocative pupil, she adopts an impassively enigmatic facial and vocal technique, leaving the exact degree of virtue and vice in her character an ambiguity. Apart from a striking performance as a medium in the paranormal extravaganza *The Legend of Hell House* (1973), most of her subsequent work has been for American TV.

Far left: Ryan and Tatum O'Neal in Paper Moon. *Above left: Helen Keller (Patty Duke) and her teacher (Anne Bancroft) in* The Miracle Worker. *Above: Hayley Mills as a child getting the better of her abductor (Horst Buchholz) in* Tiger Bay. *Below right: Elizabeth (Jane Asher, left) catches a thief in* The Greengage Summer. *Below left: the governess and her charge (Deborah Kerr and Pamela Franklin) in* The Innocents

After a faintly sententious early role in the emotional drama *The Greengage Summer* (1961), Jane Asher developed swiftly in the Edgar Allan Poe fantasy *The Masque of the Red Death* (1964), but attained her peak at the start of a new decade in *Deep End* (1970), the Polish director Jerzy Skolimowski's extraordinary depiction of sleazy London. In one sequence she brought ferocious conviction to a superbly contemptuous, hysterical monologue ending in the dismissal of her older, married lover (not surprisingly, perhaps – for the scene was written by her). During the Seventies, however, Asher gravitated increasingly towards television and theatre.

A calm in Britain

The remainder of Britain's youthful acting record is distinctly fragmentary. A powerful version of William Golding's allegory of child castaways, *Lord of the Flies* (1963), featured a remarkable vignette from Hugh Edwards as Piggy, the prim, pompous, yet endearing 'fat boy' who is the tragic butt of bullies. In another distinguished literary transposition, an adaptation of Richard Hughes' *A High Wind in Jamaica* (1965), Deborah Baxter persuasively suggested a teenager's capacity to ensnare a pirate chief.

The Seventies spectacularly accelerated the Sixties tendency towards street-wise adolescence in the cinema, besides restoring the U.S. to supremacy in that field. True, there was a handful of noteworthy British newcomers: Dominic Guard was vulnerable yet dogged as the boy enmeshed in adult traumas in *The Go-Between* (1971); and a more lasting impression was made by Jenny Agutter, who matured from the delightful period family saga *The Railway Children* (1970) and the grimmer Australian parable *Walkabout* (1971), to grown-up stardom in movies like the elaborate psychiatric study *Equus* (1977).

Near the decade's end Toyah Wilcox – following a graphic cameo as the heartless tease in George Cukor's television version of *The Corn is Green* (1978) – turned to the big screen in Derek Jarman's punk epic *Jubilee* (1978) and unconventional *The Tempest* (1979).

Yet the lion's share of juvenile talent has come from the United States. Cukor directed one of these new hopefuls, Cindy Williams, in *Travels With My Aunt* (1972), a beguiling and

underpraised adaptation of Graham Greene's serio-comic novel in which she plays a hippie sharing a brief, witty, yet affecting semi platonic rapport with a staid Englishman. Williams moved on to appear as the touching rather drab 'steady' girlfriend of a stud in *American Graffiti* (1973), the nostalgic chronicle of Sixties teenage morals, and as the nervily guilt-ridden lover spied on in *The Conversation* (1974). Since then she has found her greatest public as Shirley in the American television series *Laverne and Shirley*.

Ugly ducklings . . .

In the same year as *American Graffiti* a more sensational stir was generated by a very young performer. In Peter Bogdanovich's Depression era comedy *Paper Moon*, nine-year-old Tatum O'Neal shared a splendidly funny father daughter relationship with her real-life dad Ryan – creating a faultless rendering of bratty, surly, foul-mouthed, yet winning childishness, unmarred by any strenuously coy pseudo refinement. When she lights a cigarette, inhales, blows the smoke out and gazes disenchantedly at her outraged pa, she looks a battle-scarred, bored adult – but also the kid she actually is. When her po-faced hostility abruptly melts into a dawning, half suppressed grin, coupled with a quick, sidelong glance at her 'poppa' – or when she turns on a full-strength beam of infantile delight – her appeal is irresistible.

Added to this, her delivery of scornful implacable one-liners is flawless: witness the moment at the fun-fair when her father asserts that he possesses scruples, she witheringly retorts 'Whatever they are, I bet they don't belong to you'. Largely retaining her freshness in the baseball jape *The Bad News Bears*, and the homage to silent movies *Nickelodeon* (both 1976), O'Neal found the upper-middle-class English horse-training atmosphere of *International Velvet* (1978) less congenial, and often lapsed into arch ecstasy or schmaltzy melancholy.

. . . and budding swans

The teenage sex-satire *Little Darlings* (1980) saw her out-acted by a newcomer from TV.

Top left: watchful Piggy (Hugh Edwards) and Ralph (James Aubrey) in Lord of the Flies. *Top right: Toyah Willcox as Miranda in* The Tempest. *Above left: a note passes between Leo (Dominic Guard) and Marion (Julie Christie) in* The Go-Between. *Left: Bobbie (Jenny Agutter), Phyllis (Sally Thomsett) and Peter (Gary Warren) worry about their Russian refugee (Gordon Whiting) in* The Railway Children

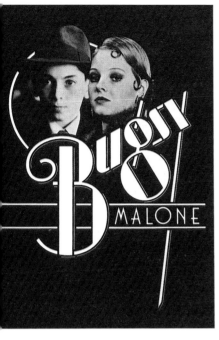

Above: Scott Baio and Jodie Foster star in Alan Parker's gangster spoof. Above right: possessed by the devil – Linda Blair in The Exorcist. Above, far right: Linda Manz as a girl who leaves Chicago for the wide open spaces in Days of Heaven. Right: father and son (Jon Voight and Ricky Schroder) look for 'mum' in the crowd in The Champ, and (below right) father and son (Dustin Hoffman and Justin Henry) think about her in Kramer vs Kramer

the abrasive but moving Kristy McNichol. In one sequence – where she confesses the loss of her virginity – McNichol poignantly communicates the character's momentary inability to be truthful, tears starting to her eyes as her face works in tremulous smiles, her head turning away for an instant as she steels herself to the revelation.

With her mixture of street-smart poise and underlying sensitivity, Kristy McNichol resembles Jodie Foster, who surely remains the strongest prospect of the crop of Seventies' children, and fully demonstrated her powers in Echoes of a Summer (1975) and The Little Girl Who Lives Down the Lane (1977). In the former, as an eleven-year-old doomed to die of a heart ailment, she is stoically witty and piercingly sad, as captured in her nocturnal venture with her father; her sardonic gags and Southern drawl in a discussion with her doctor; her fierce rejection of her stern governess' Christian faith; her scenes with a young male chum, in which she makes him hold her hand as an emblem of the sexual fulfilment she is never to have; and the sequence where she plies her mother with queries about adult life and love, then voices the longing to be twenty-five for a day and have 'a secret date with a married man'. She was even more unerring as The Little Girl Who Lives Down the Lane, whether in her cautiously budding amorous harmony with a lame youth, or in her glacial disclosures of her deathly past.

Earlier she had etched a cherishable vignette in Alice Doesn't Live Here Anymore (1974) and then came Taxi Driver (1976), where as a juvenile whore she achieves a bitter-sweet sense of the character re-awakening to her untainted self, laughing to hide her hurt when

the cabbie reveals that her 'ponce' has cruelly termed her a 'piece of chicken'. And as a gangster's moll in *Bugsy Malone* (1976), she delivers cracks like 'Why don't you smear my lipstick a little?' with utter aplomb.

By comparison, Foster's next two Disney pictures were bound to be anti-climactic. *Freaky Friday* (1976) sees her as a girl who magically assumes her mother's brain, and Foster marvellously transmits – by use of facial expression and vocal intonation – her jealous appraisal of a predatory female secretary. In *Candleshoe* (1977), as a delinquent with a conscience, she is touchingly brusque – 'I'm no good at goodbyes', she says to the old lady played by Helen Hayes. Foster's two most recent movies, *Foxes* and *Carny* (both 1980), signal the next phase of a potentially fruitful career.

Among the other transatlantic juveniles of

the Seventies, the principal girls include Linda Blair, the diabolically possessed victim in *The Exorcist* (1973); Linda Manz, throaty narrator of the farming epic *Days of Heaven* (1978); Quinn Cummings as the perky daughter in *The Goodbye Girl* (1977), and Lisa Lucas as a more serious daughter in *An Unmarried Woman* (1978); Diane Lane, one of the young lovers in *A Little Romance* (1979); and Brooke Shields, playing an adolescent prostitute in Louis Malle's stylish evocation of a New Orleans bordello, *Pretty Baby* (1978).

Enter the snails and puppydog tails!
Of the boys Jackie Earle Haley has singled himself out as the bizarre child in the Hollywood drama *Day of the Locust* (1975), and then in more orthodox roles in films such as *The Bad News Bears* and *Breaking Away* (1979); Justin Henry in the divorce drama *Kramer vs*

Above: an adolescent girl (Tatum O'Neal, right at summer camp urges her friends to spy on the boys in Little Darlings. *Below: Brooke Shields and Susan Sarandon in* Pretty Baby

Kramer (1979); Ricky Schroder in the remake of the boxing soap-opera *The Champ* (1979) and the aristocratic weepie *Little Lord Fauntler* (1981); and Jeremy Levy as one of the mixed *Rich Kids* (1979).

Levy's female co-star, Trini Alvarado, went on to appear in the teenage picture *Times Square* (1980) with Robin Johnson, a newcomer of 15. Johnson goes further than even Jodie Foster or Kristy McNichol in gritty acerbic insurrection, perhaps only lacking their subtlety of emotion. All the same she clearly one of the great hopes for the future and as such warrants serious attention.

DOUGLAS McVA

lent movies dictated that kids
hould be seen but not heard.
When sound came along they
ill didn't protest much at the
ay cinema and society pushed
hem from pillar to post. But in
he Fifties Lolita, James Dean and
heir brothers and sisters at last
egan to turn the screws on
heir elders and betters . . .

the mid-Fifties, Andy Hardy had gone badly
tray. In real life he was Mickey Rooney on
e wrong side of 30, a former child star
gulfed in divorces, money problems and
erior pictures. On screen in 1958, Rooney
ed to revive memories of tranquil com-
unities and stable families in *Andy Hardy
mes Home*, but there was no audience left for
ch wholesomeness – the kids preferred Sal
neo or Presley, and the parents stayed at
me with TV. Even for Rooney, the film was a
version; the last hurrah for Andy Hardy was
ndwiched between *Baby Face Nelson* (1957)
d *The Last Mile* (1959), apocalyptic B movies
out punks who turned their hatred and their
ns on a stupid, hypocritical society.

Louis B. Mayer, who had died in 1957,
uld have been aghast But just as his MGM
bes, Rooney and Judy Garland, had found
aster and dismay as adults, so Hollywood's
ealization of childhood could no longer stand
to the facts of life. The plight of the unloved
ld in art is as old as *Oliver Twist*, and movies
e *The Kid* (1921) and *The Champ* (1931) had
derstood that orphanhood, separation and a
ild's distress could be milked for pity so long
the child was eventually restored to a
mfortable home, high-key lighting and a
cure future. Even *Oliver Twist* ends with the
ndling in a nice home so that its readers
ay forget the nightmare of Fagin and Bill
kes.

ildhood in ruins

t to think of the David Lean film of *Oliver
vist* (1948) is to recall its gloomy city and the
rid evil of the underworld characters. Dic-
ns' London was relevant in 1948 because so
any cities were wastelands after the war and
many children homeless and lost. Italian
o-realism frequently observed the effects of
cial breakdown on children. Who could

*Above: Jackie Coogan – the orphan befriended
by Chaplin in* The Kid – *still wearing his lost,
unwanted look three years later in* A Boy of
Flanders *(1924). Below: Oliver (John Howard
Davies) at the mercy of a vicious Bill Sikes
(Robert Newton) in* Oliver Twist

forget the thorough plotting of the road from
delinquency to death in De Sica's *Sciuscià*
(1946, *Shoeshine*) or the woeful countenance of
the son in *Ladri di Biciclette* (1948, *Bicycle
Thieves*)? Most eloquent of all was Rossellini's
Germania, Anno Zero (1947, *Germany, Year
Zero*), in which a little boy is seen as the seed of
fresh fascism in the rubble of post-war Berlin.
Fred Zinnemann's *The Search* and Joseph
Losey's *The Boy With Green Hair* (both 1948)
showed that Americans too were aware of how
grimly the war had dealt with children. In
Losey's film, the pained face of Peter (Dean
Stockwell) seems to be looking at mankind's
final abandonment of hope or charity.

Bombed homes meant shattered families. So
few pre-war movies had mentioned divorce, let
alone the havoc it could leave in children's
lives – yet in the Fifties society saw rapid
increases in marital instability, as well as
widespread prosperity, changed attitudes
about sex and birth control, and a rising tide of
rebellion among teenagers. Most of those
strains need to be invoked to explain the
impact of James Dean and rock'n'roll in the
middle of the decade. Dean, in his early
twenties, played a schoolboy in *Rebel Without a*

Cause (1955), but the movie reflected the confusing mixture of frustration, self-pity and independence in the young middle-class.

Lo and behold

After Dean's death, *The James Dean Story* (1957) – directed by the then unknown Robert Altman – used a mournful theme song, 'Let Me Be Loved', as if the single most marketable aspect of Dean was that the kid had been unloved. Ten years later, when the Rolling Stones howled about the dearth of satisfaction they were getting, it was apparent that love had become a more carnal preoccupation. But psychology was insisting that even infants had a sexual awareness, and the key novel of the Fifties – Nabokov's *Lolita* – concerns the seduction of an articulate, adult, would-be seducer by the plastic spirit of American childhood. Kubrick's 1962 movie of the novel nudges the love story into a 'respectable' student-professor affair: the movies still faced limits of censorship, and so we had to put up with Sue Lyon as Lo. Not until Jodie Foster played a pubescent hooker in *Taxi Driver* (1976) did the screen find an actress worthy of Nabokov's nymphet. Still, around 1960 there were many films sensitive to the dilemmas of children, and several that saw children as just young adults, sometimes as malign and wayward as their elders. The safeguards of sentimentality were being discarded, and no-one can have much hope of their being adopted again.

Young devils

In 1956, as if the system had suddenly glimpsed the sham of reiterated innocence and loveliness in children, it spewed up a picture - Mervyn LeRoy's far-fetched but nevertheless effective *The Bad Seed* – about a little witch (Patty McCormack), who kills anyone threatening to deprive her of an idiot mother's love. *Psycho* (1960) is a much better film, if no more believable. But at a mythic, psychological level, it depicts Norman Bates (Anthony Perkins) as an arrested child who has preserved his mother as a doll and as a She-who-must-be-obeyed. The notion that the child can harbour wickedness and be destructive has been very influential in movies: *The Exorcist* (1973) and *The Omen* (1976) constitute a reverse sentimentality in which the child has become a monster.

Linda Blair as the possessed girl in *The Exorcist* is as great a distortion as Shirley Temple. The best thing about the years around 1960 was the number of films that discovered children as human beings, less the emotional centres of their worlds than troubled observers of it. François Truffaut's *Les Quatre Cents Coups* (1959, *The 400 Blows*) was a key work in the French *nouvelle vague* and a reflection of Truffaut's own unhappy upbringing. Antoine Doinel (Jean-Pierre Léaud), the boy in the film, hardly realizes he is unloved, and Truffaut never lets him become an object of easy pathos.

Left: she's asleep – but what is she dreaming about? Patty McCormack as the young murderess in The Bad Seed. *Above left: James Mason as Humbert Humbert and Sue Lyon as the child-woman of his dreams –* Lolita. *Top: the legacy of war – bombsite boy Karel (Ivan Jandl) looks for his mother in* The Search *(left); Jean Seberg as a teenager pampered by her playboy father (David Niven) in* Bonjour Tristesse *(right)*

He is an ordinary kid – sly, cocky, bewildered, abject – all within the space of a moment. It is too good a picture to bear an obvious social moral – it knows that chance decides so many lives untouched by school or family. But when it ends with a freeze-frame of the boy, escaped from reform school but imprisoned in his problem, the face stares out into the cinema as if Truffaut wondered about lonely kids (like himself) growing up in movie theatres and shaped by the screen's illusions of romance and transformation.

In Charles Laughton's *Night of the Hunter* (1955), two children from a Grimm fairy tale flee across a surreal landscape pursued by a demon preacher (Robert Mitchum). Jean Seberg plays a teenager in *Bonjour Tristesse* (1958), who knows the turmoil of not being able to give up her father for loves of her own. The children in *Imitation of Life* (1959) suffer from the ambitions and lies of their mothers. In *All Fall Down* (1962) and *Hud* (1963), Brandon De Wilde was very touching as a boy who cannot decide which of his elders to believe in. *The Courtship of Eddie's Father* (1963) introduced Ronny Howard – still earning a living playing kids in the late Seventies – as the child who has to deal with the loss of a parent. *To Kill a Mockingbird* (1962) is a liberalizing view of Southern bigotry rendered through the eyes of children.

The Miracle Worker (1962) portrays a great American heroine, but in the hands of Patty Duke and Arthur Penn, who directed her as the young Helen Keller, it is also the study of a handicapped child poised between primitive instinct and enlightenment. Hayley Mills made her name in *Tiger Bay* (1959), where she befriends a killer, and in *Whistle Down the Wind* (1961), where she believes an escaping murderer is Christ. From Japan, Nagisa Oshima's *Shonen* (1969, *Boy*) shows a family that uses its son as the 'victim' in fraudulent accident claims. In *Mouchette* (1967), Robert Bresson chose a young girl to represent the human spirit confronted by suffering and resignation. *A High Wind in Jamaica* (1965) – from the Richard Hughes novel – shows kidnapped children proving more cold-blooded than pirates.

Spoonfuls of sugar

Of course there was also *Mary Poppins* (1964) and *The Sound of Music* (1965), both triumphant at the box-office and loyal to the Victorian, paternalistic view of children. But an audience needs such reassurances, especially if it is learning how quickly the legendary innocence of children can turn into the tribal fury of *Lord of the Flies* (1963). Film had freed children from many restrictions: they could be victims now, beyond the reach of happy endings or comfortable explanation. But, in recompense, they had acquired a new energy that could sometimes rebuke and victimize the older world.   DAVID THOMSON

Right: there is no escaping the look of accusation – the unloved Billy (David Bradley) and his only solace, the kestrel hawk he tends and trains, in Kes *(1969). Above right: Alan Barnes, Diane Holgate and Hayley Mills as the children who bring food to a convict hiding in a barn, believing him to be Jesus, in* Whistle Down the Wind. *Top right: Tetsuo Abe as the victim of selfish, merciless parents in Oshima's* Boy *– a harsh indictment of family traditions*

THE GRIP OF TERROR

The roots of terror lie deep in the psyche, but psychological analysis of films can cast some fascinatingly vivid light into the primitive darkness

The 'terror' film is not easy to define, since it occupies an area bounded on the one side by the horror film and on the other by the thriller. The horror film relies heavily on the supernatural and the creation of monsters to create apprehension and anxiety in the audience, and the thriller requires intricate plots and mechanics for the provision of similar effects. The terror film exploits certain fundamental characteristics of the cinema to produce effects that are based much more explicitly in the manipulation of psychology and psychopathology. The cinema of terror is the cinema of madness, sadism and voyeurism located in human beings rather than in vampires or criminal conspiracies. Its true power lies in its premise that the agents of terror are apparently ordinary people. Hence the fascination of films that compel the audience to confront uncanny forces that are both repulsive and familiar.

In his famous essay on 'The Uncanny' in 1917, Freud seized on this combination of repulsion and familiarity to explain the potency of terror by suggesting that it represented the eruption into adult life of the most powerful and primitive infantile wishes and fantasies. These fantasies – of violent murder, torture and suchlike abominations – hold their sway on the adult mind because they strike profound resonances with aspects of the psyche that, although repressed from babyhood, live within everyone.

The very nature of the cinema itself is higly conducive to the invocation of these infantile fantasies. Like the infant, the audience is passively watching scenes over which it has no control. The physical size of the screen presents the audience with characters far larger than life. But above all the audience is gazing; just as the baby gazes at the spectacle of the world over which it has little control, so the audience is constantly entrapped by the lures of the world on the screen. Both the child and the audience are passive voyeurs captivated and seduced by a world on to which their identifications and fantasies are projected. The mechanisms of the cinema provide a most potent structure for the evocation of infantile terror.

A central feature of all films of terror is voyeurism. The Sixties started with two masterpieces of voyeuristic cinema, Hitchcock's *Psycho* and Michael Powell's *Peeping Tom* (both 1960). In *Psycho*, as in so many of Hitchcock's films, voyeurism is implicit from the start. The camera gradually moves in on and peers into a seedy hotel room where Marion Crane (Janet Leigh) lies half-undressed with Sam Loomis (John Gavin). But it is frustrated voyeurism that is exploited until the famous scene of the murder in the shower. Just as Norman Bates (Anthony Perkins) fails to get a full view of Marion's naked body as he spies on her in the motel, so the audience is also denied full voyeuristic satisfaction and obtains a sense of sadistic relief when she is killed. It is as if she is being punished for being tantalizing but inaccessible. Hitchcock here succeeds in putting the audience in exactly the same

psychological position as her killer, Norman Bates. This leads rapidly to identification with the murderer, though his guilt is as yet unknown to the audience on first viewing. As Bates anxiously watches Marion's car fail at first to become fully submerged in the swamp where he is hiding it, the audience prays that the car will be fully engulfed.

Peeping Tom was almost universally vilified when it was first released, since it was explicitly concerned with the voyeurism that underlies all films of terror. Its hero is a young man who derives sexual satisfaction from filming women as he murders them with the spiked end of his camera tripod. The entire film is a metaphor for the cinema of terror and the audience's relationship with the screen. Just as the hero is captivated and aroused by the cinematic murders he commits, so too is the audience. There is simply no escaping from the fact that a large part of the fascination of films of terror lies in the opportunity they give to re-experience primitive infantile desires. Powell made this quite

Top: Charlotte (Bette Davis) is tricked into shooting a scheming doctor with blanks as part of a plot to get her certified; later on, she does kill him and go mad in Hush . . . Hush, Sweet Charlotte. *Above: can the blind girl (Audrey Hepburn) get out of this tight spot in* Wait Until Dark *and kill the bad guy (Alan Arkin)? She can indeed*

anxieties about the supernatural are thus tamed in a way not dissimilar to what happens in *The Wizard of Oz* (1939). In Hiroshi Teshigahara's *Suna No Onna* (1964, *Woman of the Dunes*), an entomologist finds himself trapped in a hut at the bottom of a gigantic sandpit and is initially terrified and desperate. But trapped along with him is an attractive widow and the film proceeds to depict the ever-increasing erotic pleasures of their shared captivity. The hero's earlier helpless terrors have given way to an immersion in Oedipal bliss.

Not surprisingly the taming and mastery of neurosis is another common feature of the terror film. John Huston's *Freud* (1962), although not strictly a film of terror, ends with Freud's deciphering a terrifying dream about his mother and realizing that neurosis can be explained and overcome. In Hitchcock's *Marnie* (1964), one of the commonest of all neurotic complaints, a phobia, is finally cured. Marnie's phobia is based on a fear of blood and is cured at the emotion-releasing climax of the film in which Marnie relives the traumatic experience of killing a sailor to protect her mother. Although this dramatic cure may bear little relationship to actual psychiatric practice, it proves to the audience that the very neurosis masterfully exploited by Hitchcock throughout the film can be conquered.

Not all neurosis or psychosis can be tamed, and some films of terror operate by reasserting the

Above: Michael Powell's Peeping Tom *was treated with critical contempt when it first appeared, despite its knowledgeable references to film-making and film criticism; now it is considered a masterpiece. Top: Harry (Peter Vaughan) in* Fanatic *attempts to kill his wife's boss, Mrs Trefoile – but she will turn the tables on him. Top left: in* Onibaba *a woman (Nobuko Otowa) finds that the stolen mask she uses to frighten her errant daughter-in-law has stuck to her face, rotting the flesh. Left: two mutually jealous Hollywood sisters destroy their own lives and each others' in Robert Aldrich's* What Ever Happened to Baby Jane?

overt, thereby incurring critical wrath; but *Peeping Tom* remains the most sophisticated film ever made about the psychological fascination of terror.

Films of terror do not operate solely in terms of the voyeuristic reliving of childish desires and fantasies, and the fantasies involved are not purely those of a murderous kind. Other forms of infantile anxiety can be exploited and then mastered. Such basic anxieties as fear of the dark, the unknown and things that go bump in the night may evoke infantile terrors which can then be written off when the evil is vanquished or the inexplicable is explained. Terence Young's *Wait Until Dark* (1967) presents the fears of the blind Susy Hendrix (Audrey Hepburn) as those of an infant terrorized by a bogey-man, Roat (Alan Arkin). The terror that pervades the film reaches its climax when the crazed Roat literrally jumps out of a cupboard. But this terror is quickly dissipated as Susy kills her assailant and survives. Both she and the audience have, at least temporarily, mastered their fear of the dark.

Similar taming and mastery techniques operate in Kaneto Shindo's *Onibaba* (1965), one of a number of Japanese terror films that were distributed in the West during the Sixties. In *Onibaba*, a series of apparently demonic murders is shown to be the work of two women rather than of devils. Infantile

Childhood fears and passions can be aroused and also eased in the safety of the darkened cinema

power of infantile forces, refusing to reassure the audience that mastery over madness is possible. The ending of *The Birds* (1963) is scarcely encouraging for those with animal phobias, since the characters are allowed to escape from Bodega Bay only because of the inexplicable and uneasy truce established by their victorious persecutors. Even more strikingly, the journalist hero of Samuel Fuller's *Shock Corridor* (1963) ends driven into madness by the forces of the corrupt mental institution that he seeks to expose.

In many terror films infantile desires and fantasies are not expressed as neurosis or any formal kind of madness, but are rather represented by characters embodying the cruel and sadistic aspects of a child's emotional life. These murderous tendencies can be contained or vanquished in various ways. At the very crudest level, this can be accomplished by the villainous character's being caught, tamed or killed. The very fact that the villain gets his come-uppance must inevitably lead to a certain easing of the infantile fantasies and anxieties that have been engendered in the audience by the film.

Throughout the Sixties the British cinema produced a series of films featuring crazed, homicidal villains whose main function was to commit primitive acts of violence and then to be punished for them. For example, Hammer turned out *Maniac*, *Paranoiac* (both 1963) and *Fanatic* (1965), all using the standard trappings of ominous music, creaking floorboards and slowly turning doorknobs and all based on the premise that the beast could be tamed. Unfortunately the beasts in question were portrayed with little in the way of psychological interest or understanding to support them, and so the films merely provided a few predictable shocks.

A more interesting category of beast is that provided by early fantasies about bad parents or wicked siblings. It is such figures that are exploited in Robert Aldrich's Grand-Guignol Californiangingerbread masterpieces *What Ever Happened to Baby Jane?* (1962) and *Hush . . . Hush, Sweet Charlotte* (1964). In *What Ever Happened to Baby Jane?*, Bette Davis as Baby Jane is the embodiment both of the feared bad mother who feeds the child dead rats instead of food and also of the resented villainous sibling who persecutes her crippled and disadvantaged sister, played by Joan Crawford. The major psychological pleasure produced by the film is the audience's infantile delight in seeing these archetypally terrifying beasts vanquished as Baby Jane receives her just deserts. The revenge of the wronged child is even more radically treated in *Village of the Damned* (1960) and in its sequel, *Children of the Damned* (1964). In both these films, all-powerful children terrify the adults surrounding them, and although they are finally defeated the

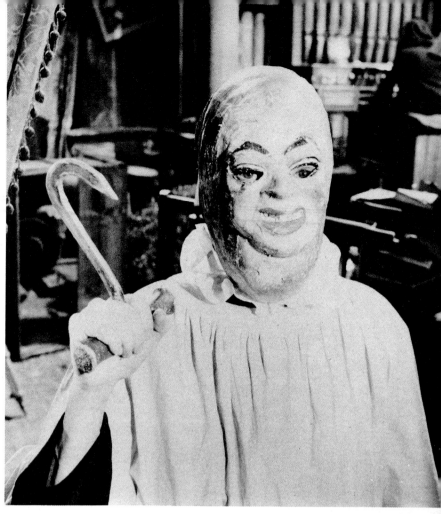

children act out, in the most graphic way, the infant's desire to turn the tables on malignant parental figures. This theme is further explored in Seth Holt's *The Nanny* (1965), a much underrated film in which Bette Davis once again portrays an archetypal bad mother-figure who gets her punishment at the hands of her charges. Even bad parents can be mastered.

Understanding, like Hitchcock, the infantile and neurotic roots of the film of terror, Roman Polanski is a talented exploiter of a potent neurosis, claustrophobia: the fear and horror that can be engendered by enclosed spaces, with anxieties to do

with being trapped or impinged upon, can be traced back to early infancy. The darkened cinema provides an excellent site in which to exploit these fears. Polanski combined his manipulation of claustrophobia with a profound loathing and contempt for mankind, and both features are prominent in his early Polish film *Nóz w Wodzie* (1962, *Knife in the Water*). It was with *Repulsion* (1965) that Polanski brought these elements together in his first terror film. In tracing the descent of Carol (Catherine Deneuve) into homicidal madness, Polanski not only extracts every ounce of claustrophobic terror from the flat in which the film is mostly set but he also infuses the scene with primitive Oedipal fears and resentments. As Carol overhears her sister in bed with a lover, Polanski strikingly evokes the terrors of the Primal Scene, Freud's term in describing the child's terror at the apparently violent implications of parental sexual intercourse. As Carol's paranoid psychosis begins to erupt, the audience is confronted with its own repressed memories of the first impingement of sexuality.

Another study of infants' fears was Blake Edwards' *Experiment in Terror* (1962), an extremely accomplished work in which Kelly Sherwood (Lee Remick) is pursued by a criminal while the FBI stands back helpless to intervene because he holds a hostage. Edwards puts the audience in the woman's place as she is threatened and harassed from a distance. The film brilliantly conveys Kelly's sense of infantile helplessness in a situation where quasi-parental intervention (from the FBI) cannot help her. The film's most chilling scene results from her having to hide herself amongst rows of mannequins as the killer tries to track her down – a scene so successful that a variant of it appeared in Michael Crichton's *Coma* (1978).

On the other hand, William Castle's *Homicidal* (1961) was a most crass attempt to capitalize on a

Above: cold-blooded radioactive children are secreted in the cliffs near Portland Bill in The Damned *(1962). Top: Harriet (Sheila Burrell) attacks an inquisitive detective to protect her insanely murderous nephew in* Paranoiac. *Left: schoolgirl Toby Sherwood (Stefanie Powers) is kidnapped as a hostage to force her sister to rob the bank where she works in* Experiment in Terror; *but the girl is rescued in time*

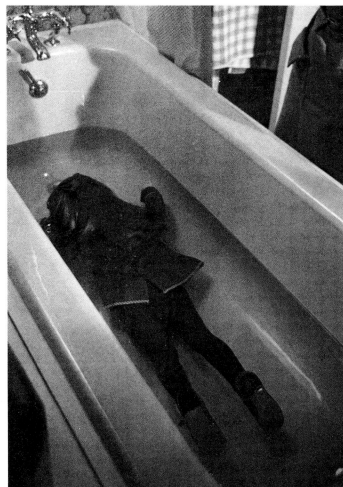

bove: Cathy (Constance Towers) ~ars that Johnny (Peter Breck), a ~urnalist, is being driven mad by ~s undercover investigation of a ~urder in an asylum in Shock ~orridor. *Top right: The Nanny* ~Bette Davis) *is mysteriously ~volved in the drowning of a little ~rl, and it is no wonder that her ~ther charge, ten-year-old Joey, is ~spicious and resentful of her. ~endy Craig, who played the ~ildreñ's mother, was later ~erself to become a nanny in a ~ritish television series*

major hit. It was a transsexual version of *Psycho* with the fact of the villain's transsexuality not being revealed until the climax, with an accompanying pseudo-psychiatric explanation. Outrageously derivative on all counts, the film had a certain primitive charm. Towards the end of the Sixties Castle became considerably more artistically respectable and was the producer of Polanski's superior horror film *Rosemary's Baby* (1968).

If the content of the terror film is replete with infantile fantasies of a voyeuristic and sexual nature, the style and technique of terror is similarly related to sexuality. The most celebrated proponent of the theory of terror was Alfred Hitchcock, who repeatedly stressed the difference between suspense and shock. Shock is a cheap commodity. An unexpected and violent event provides an adrenalin spurt in the audience. There is no anticipation, no build-up – merely the cinematic equivalent of a violent assault.

Suspense is an altogether different matter. The audience is placed in a position of anticipation, of knowing that something frightening or dreadful will happen, and being denied only the knowledge of precisely when that event will occur. In *Psycho*, as the private detective Arbogast (Martin Balsam) enters the Bates' house, it is obvious that he will be attacked. Hitchcock sustains the suspense by slowing down the time of his entering the house and of his ascent of the staircase on which he will be murdered.

The dynamics of this situation are twofold. First, the audience is put in the position of the aggressor. The audience knows, just as the aggressor knows, that a violent act will be committed but the victim is unaware of this. The audience thus becomes implicated as an accomplice to the act, and so when

Arbogast's murder does occur the gratification of its voyeuristic sadism is enhanced. At the same time, the audience watching Arbogast ascend the staircase is afforded an opportunity to disavow the murder in advance. Viewers can voice or imagine a warning shout, such as: 'Don't go up those stairs!' or they can shut their eyes as if to disclaim what is already known to be coming. This double manoeuvre of suspense achieves what all neurotic symptoms achieve: the audience is permitted both

The desire to see the forbidden, the unknown or the feared, attracts audiences to films of suspense

to indulge its violent fantasies and simultaneously to protest its innocence.

There can be no doubt that the sexualized expression of primitive desires is in operation here. The whole mechanism of suspense is that of the progressive build-up of a tension that demands release. Suspense is the voyeuristic equivalent of foreplay in genital sexuality. Just as the intensity of genital sexual desire is increased by foreplay, so is the intensity of the voyeuristic satisfaction of terror increased by suspense.

The consequence of this aspect of suspense is that the audience is entrapped in a state of everincreasing desire that will demand a resolution. As a stroke of promotional genius, Hitchcock refused to let anyone enter the cinema during the last reel of *Psycho*. But who in the audience could possibly leave, snared by the film's structure in undischarged sexual tension? DAVID WILL

Michael Klinger and Tony Tenser present
Roman Polanski's

Repulsion

starring
Catherine Deneuve, Ian Hendry, John Fraser, Patrick Wymark
guest star Yvonne Furneaux

screenplay by Roman Polanski and Gerard Brach   directed by Roman Polanski   produced by Gene Gutowski

Directed by Roman Polanski, 1965
Prod co: Compton/Tekli (Compton-Cameo). **prod:** Gene Gutowski. **assoc prod:** Robert Sterne, Sam Wayneberg. **sc:** Roman Polanski, Gerard Brach. **photo:** Gilbert Taylor. **ed:** Alistair McIntyre. **art dir:** Seamus Dalby. **ass dir:** Ted Sturgis. **r/t:** 104 minutes. London premiere, June 1965.
Cast: Catherine Deneuve (*Carol*), Yvonne Furneaux (*Helen*), John Fraser (*Colin*), Ian Hendry (*Michael*), Patrick Wymark (*landlord*), Valerie Taylor (*Mme Denise*), Helen Fraser (*Bridget*), Renee Houston (*Miss Balch*), James Villiers (*John*), Hugh Futcher (*Reggie*), Mike Pratt (*workman*), Monica Merlin (*Mrs Rendlesham*), Imogen Graham (*manicurist*).

Polanski opens *Repulsion* with one of the most memorable credit sequences in film history: an eye, fixed and sexless, stares out through the titles. Then the camera pulls back, slowly granting the context of a face. It is the near-magical face of absolute beauty, belonging to the young Catherine Deneuve as Carol. She lives in bedsitter-London with her sister, Helen. They are Belgian, not English, and though Helen is kind and motherly to Carol, she makes it clear without any hypocrisy that a man comes first. Her lover, Michael, is not exceptionally charming or rich, but, from the sounds Carol hears all too clearly through the wall, he is good in bed.

While Michael and Helen make love, Carol has nightmares of rape. When the couple go abroad for a holiday and no noises come through the wall, it is the wall itself which frightens Carol, first with cracks and protuberances, later by projecting hands that reach for her, and slime that pours down.

Unlike Hitchcock's films – particularly *Psycho* (1960) to which it is often compared – in *Repulsion* nothing is hidden. Polanski introduces no surprises or revelations. His technique consists of constructing, image by image and with skilful

sound effects, how Carol sees and hears the world around her, and how her vision and hearing are taken over by hallucinations. There is no plot, everything is static, except what is inside Carol's mind. Early in the film, small ordinary cracks in the pavement or the wall illustrate her exaggerated sensitivity. The fissures may in fact be there; she merely notices them more acutely than anyone else would.

Polanski does not offer Carol's 'reasons' for losing her mind or show the 'causes' of her illness; only critics saw her as frustrated, or as the victim of some unsatisfactory dialogue with the world. Polanski presents her as psychotic, and the process of her illness is shown with the rhythm of an avalanche: slow at first, then accelerating with the law of physics.

During her fits, she becomes totally irrational; she carries a putrefying rabbit-head in her handbag, and she cuts a client's finger in the beauty salon where she works. Her next, equally unexpected victim is Colin who is in love with her; she handles him with ease. Killing him has nothing to do with his breaking down the door, or intruding on her solitude; it is not a response to him – her lunacy has placed her outside

the dialogue which is action and reaction, the basis of rational life.

All horror films feed off some widespread, atavistic fear in people: in *Repulsion* it is the fear of madness. Moreover, by making his heroine so clean, so quiet, so prim in dress and manner Polanski also warns against trusting to appearances. The most saintly young woman is the most dangerous; just as the sweetest old woman in *Rosemary's Baby* (1968) is the most vicious and the gruffest; or the most respected old business-man in *Chinatown* (1974) the source of all evil. Polanski reverses and recycles accepted filmic stereotypes.

The cast hardly needs to act; besides, their lines are stilted – a sign of Polanski's working in a foreign language, without the benefit of a literary source such as Shakespeare, Ira Levin or Thomas Hardy provide for his later films. But the visual clues are enough: Carol is passive, Helen is sexy, Michael is dynamic, the neighbours are weirdos. Polanski seems to think that apartment buildings breed strange species – different from the rose-growers of the suburbs – and he came back to this later in both *Rosemary's Baby* and *Le Locataire* (1976, *The Tenant*).

There is no need to overcomplicate Polanski's symbolism. Pavements, walls, windows, buskers and road-menders are city scenery; they are ordinary, even pleasurable, and they become threatening only when something goes wrong. The beauty parlour is no more than a place where women go to be made young and beautiful. The convent which abuts on the flats houses happy nuns. But it is not Polanski who shows mistrust or hatred of these institutions: they

may well subvert and degrade femininity, but in the film everything simply spirals back to Carol's derangement.

The mad have always fascinated artists. Painters have tried to depict their mystery through their physiognomy, the greatest dramatists and novelists have been challenged by the subject, and film-makers have been attracted even more frequently to the picturesque visions and melodramatic actions of the insane. There have been films which handled the relationship of society and mental illness in greater depth, but very few images of madness stay as vibrant in the memory as *Repulsion*.

MARI KUTTNA

2

3

5

A Belgian girl, Carol, works as a manicurist in a London beauty salon (1). On her way home, a good-looking young man, Colin, catches her up and makes a date for another evening. After being teased by some road-menders (2), she eventually reaches the flat which she shares with her elder sister Helen (3). Her sister's married lover, Michael (4), brings out her dislike of men which she cannot explain to Colin (5).

When Michael takes Helen abroad for a holiday, Carol's moments of catalepsy and hallucination increase (6) and deepen into madness (7). She wounds a client in the salon; and when sent home to recuperate,

she locks herself in. When Michael's wife rings up to abuse Helen, Carol cuts the telephone cord.

Colin comes to see her and beats down the front door: Carol attacks him and kills him with a metal candlestick. She rushes to the kitchen (8) and tears out a shelf to nail up the door, but the landlord breaks in. Misunderstanding the slatternly state of both Carol and the flat, he propositions her; when he attempts to assault her sexually (9), she kills him with Michael's razor. She is unconscious when Helen and Michael return (10); Michael carries her downstairs to an ambulance.

8

9

10

Roman Polanski Life on a Knife Edge

For all his seeming success, Fate has occasionally dealt Roman Polanski some of her cruellest cards. It was, for instance, the purest chance that he was not among the party of rich and glamorous denizens of Hollywood slaughtered by Charles Manson and his 'Family' the night that his then wife, Sharon Tate, was brutally killed. Nor can he have been happy about the circumstances in which he became an exile from the United States after failing to turn up in court to answer charges of statutory rape lodged by a 13-year-old Pasadena Lolita and her mother. At moments like these it must have seemed that his private life – no longer anything like as private as he would wish – might swamp his professional life altogether.

And yet, each time, he has fought his way back to a more legitimate fame as one of the world's most skilled, if also most erratic, filmmakers. It is possible not to like any of his films very much; but impossible not to respect his achievement. His career has been astonishingly international – mirroring, no doubt, his own cosmopolitan background. Though of Polish parentage, he was born in Paris in 1933, and his French nationality proved useful when he ran into political difficulties in Poland or legal difficulties in the United States. He was brought up mostly in Poland, studied at the Polish film school, and began his career in films as an actor when he was 21, with a role in Andrzej Wajda's *Pokolenie* (1955, *A Generation*). He followed this with roles in two other Wajda films – *Lotna* (1959) and *Niewinni Czarodzieje* (1960, *Innocent Sorcerers*) – and by acting as assistant to various other Polish directors, including Andrzej Munk.

Meanwhile he had succeeded in making his own first film – a short called *Rozbijemy Zabawę* (1958, Let's Break Up the Dance). It was followed by another entitled *Dwaj Ludzie z Szafą* (also 1958, *Two Men and a Wardrobe*) which – for a short – had a remarkable international success, winning many prizes and being

Polanski has become cinema's poet of the sinister and disturbing. His eccentric vision has left his films imbued with the tension that accompanies man's fear of evil and fate . . . the pain of not knowing what comes next

Top left: Polanski with Nastassia Kinski, shooting Tess. *Above: chilling poster design for* Rosemary's Baby. *Below left: Polanski has a fascination with the surreal or absurd and the way the mind deals with it;* Two Men and a Wardrobe *poses a neatly enclosed cinematic enigma. Below right: Polanski makes a sharp start in* The Fat and the Lean

Right: with an eye for the extreme, the eccentric or the incongruous, Polanski's Mammals *contains this Godot-like image of blind slave with master. Below right: Zygmunt Malanowicz in* Knife in the Water. *Far right: starring Mia Farrow,* Rosemary's Baby *is conceived with the Devil's seed; terror is heightened by a humdrum setting*

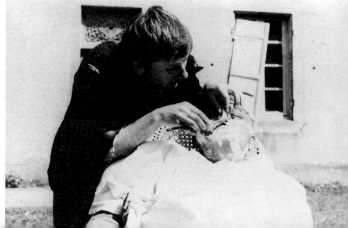

hown all over the world. It is a brief parable, obviously related to the then fashionable Theatre of the Absurd, about two strongly contrasted men who emerge from the sea carrying a large wardrobe at the beginning, and who, after various misunderstandings on a bare beach, return with the wardrobe whence they came. Polanski followed this with three other shorts along rather similar lines – *Gdy Spadaja Anioly* (1959, *When Angels Fall*), *Le Gros et le Maigre* (1961, *The Fat and the Lean*) and *Ssaki* (1962, *Mammals*). In the same year as the last of these he launched out on to a more ambitious career with his first feature.

The first cut

This was *Nóż w Wodzie* (1962, *Knife in the Water*) based on a script written by Polanski in collaboration with Jerzy Skolimowski (a contemporary graduate of the film school soon to make his own name as a director). In it Polanski moves a typical existential drama of jockeying for power to a superficially more realistic context than in the shorts. The basis of the construction is not so dissimilar from that of *Two Men and a Wardrobe* and *Mammals*, particularly the latter, which is entirely a choreographed ritual of aggression and entrapment staged on an icy sea. This time there is also a woman involved, largely as the object of the power-play between the two men (one young, one middle-aged). And again, the drama – involving some decidedly fiendish comedy as well – all takes place on and by water during a summer boating trip.

Knife in the Water had considerable success in the West, and confirmed Polanski as one of the most vital and original of the younger generation of Polish film-makers. Perhaps too vital to be kept easily in order; hence it was also, significantly, the last film he made in Poland. Not that Polanski became specifically a political exile – his relations with his native land have in fact remained quite cordial, if at a distance – but clearly, along with commercial

opportunities offered by film-making in Western Europe and America, came the possibility of working with greater freedom of expression than he could expect in Poland. When he came west he made three British-based films in three years, all of them from original screenplays and all of them exploring in one way or another the problem of evil and the darker side of human nature. First was *Repulsion* (1965), in which Catherine Deneuve played a pure and innocent-seeming girl apparently menaced by all sorts of outside dangers and persecutions, until it gradually transpires that she is in fact in an advanced state of schizophrenia.

Then followed *Cul-de-Sac* (1966), a very savage and horrific comedy, shot entirely in and around a house on Holy Island, off the north-east coast of Britain. Here, two gangsters take refuge with a neurotic married couple whom they begin by terrorizing and – in the kind of perverse power-play so dear to Polanski – end up being terrorized by. The third film of this group – *Dance of the Vampires* (1967) was slighter, and as the title implies, parodic in intent. Polanski himself played one of the leading roles, and it was his first colour feature and his first film made directly for a major American company. Otherwise it is interesting for its confirmation of Polanski as a strict, almost sadistic disciplinarian on set, and for his racking up a record number of takes on several of the simplest shots.

Fascinating riddles

All of that established him as a character – with perhaps the genius to go with it – by the time he arrived in America to make his first 'Hollywood' film, *Rosemary's Baby* (1968). It is based on Ira Levin's best-selling novel of witchcraft and demonic possession in modern New York, but has obvious parallels with Polanski's previous films in the ambiguous situation of the pregnant heroine (Mia Farrow) and the fascination with evil. It is brilliantly

staged, and had such an enormous success that it sparked off a whole series of films about diabolism throughout the next decade.

For Polanski himself it was followed, with bitter irony, by the murder of his wife and a period of great unhappiness and uncertainty from which eventually emerged his controversial film version of *Macbeth* (1971). Though it found relatively few defenders at the time, in retrospect it comes over as one of the most successful Shakespeare films ever, revitalizing the text without betraying it. However, it was disproportionately expensive, and could hardly be counted as a new triumph for Polanski. Even less could the riddling sex fantasy *Che?* (1972, *What?*), which indeed hardly got shown at all.

But before Polanski could be comfortably written off, he bounced unexpectedly back with his biggest commercial success to date – *Chinatown* (1974). This was the first film he actually made in Hollywood, and moreover was a distinctly Los Angeles film, with its loving re-creation of the pre-war world of Raymond Chandler and other West Coast writers of tough, convoluted mystery novels. The screenplay, an original, was by Robert Towne, but, turning as it does on a very intricate and mysterious power game and containing all sorts of perverse and secret motivations, it accorded very well with Polanski's own private world. He extracted brilliant performances from Jack Nicholson as the private eye, Faye Dunaway as the *femme fatale* who proves to be the key to the riddle, and John Huston as the evil and conniving millionaire behind it all. In fact, Polanski's great skill with actors – famous and unknown alike – has seldom been sufficiently noted among his many more sensational attributes.

Talent to let

Immediately after *Chinatown* Polanski undertook a much more modest, personal sort of production with *Le Locataire* (1976, *The*

Tenant). Made in Paris, the film starred himself in a subject which had many similarities with *Repulsion* – only this time the reclusive victim of delusions is a man instead of a girl. With the enormous success of *Chinatown* to make him 'bankable', he returned to Hollywood and his choice of major American projects. At which point came his tangle with the law over his own personal Lolita and his precipitate return to France, where his nationality protected him from subpoenas.

His next film, made there, turned out to be a highly ambitious English-language version of Thomas Hardy's novel *Tess of the D'Urbervilles*. Again, this ran into distribution difficulties, largely because of its lavishness, unmatched by familiar star names: Tess herself is played by a German actress – the actor Klaus Kinski's daughter, Nastassia, *Tess* (1979) is a work that risks the same kind of reception as *Macbeth* – offending purists on principle and putting off a general public with its aura of classic respectability before they have even given it a chance. However, it seems likely that in retrospect *Tess* will also be revalued and, at the very least, seen as far and away the most successful attempt yet to put one of Hardy's classic novels on screen.

Above: Polanski's naturalistic Macbeth *(left) is a masterly evocation of a royal house infused with evil, and stars Jon Finch (right). Below: J. J. Gittes, private detective (Jack Nicholson), faces up to an involuntary nose-job in* Chinatown. *Below right: Polanski as* The Tenant *with concierge Shelley Winters*

Meanwhile, Polanski remains a question mark in world cinema. He has proved proficient at making small-scale, art-house movies which gather around them a cult reputation. But he has also had major successes – artistic and commercial – with his two films nearest to conventional big-studio conditions in their making (*Rosemary's Baby* and *Chinatown*). They have shown him to be amazingly adept at carrying over his personal preoccupations with evil, power and corruption into a kind of popular cinema that mass audiences can understand and respond to. It is altogether possible that, if strict commercial disciplines are exerted on him, he may commit *folies de grandeur* which put his career in jeopardy, but at least there does seem to be in him a saving quality of basic horse-sense which will enable him to recover from his worst defeats and pull another commercial triumph out of the hat. And it may be one, moreover, which broadens and clarifies his dark, personal vision of the world without compromising it.

JOHN RUSSELL TAYLOR

Filmography
1953 Trzy Opowieści (actor only) (POL). **'55** Pokolenie (actor only) (POL) (USA/GB: A Generation); Zaczarowany Rower (actor only) (POL); Rower (short, unfinished) (POL). **'56** Koniec Wojny (actor only) (POL). **'57** Wraki (actor only) (POL). **'58** Morderstwo (short) (POL); Rozbijemy Zabawę (short) (+sc) (POL); Dwaj Ludzie z Szafa (short) (+sc;+act) (POL) (USA/GB: Two Men and a Wardrobe); Lampa (short) (+sc). **'59** Zadzwońcie Do Mojej Zony (actor only) (POL); Lotna (actor only) (POL); Gdy Spadają Anioły (short) (+sc;+act) (POL). **'60** Niewinni Czarodzieje (actor only) (POL) (USA/GB: Innocent Sorcerers); Do Widzenia Do Jutra (actor only) (POL) (GB: See You Tomorrow); Zezowate Szczęscie (ass. dir;+act) (POL) (GB: Bad Luck); Ostrożnie Yeti (actor only) (POL). **'61** Samson (actor only) (POL); Le Gros et le Maigre (short) (+co-sc;+ed;+act) (FR) (USA/GB: The Fat and the Lean). **'62** Ssaki (short) (+sc) (POL) (GB: Mammals); Nóż w Wodzie (+co-sc) (POL) (USA/GB: Knife in the Water). **'64** Les Plus Belles Escroqueries du Monde *ep* La Rivière de Diamants/Amsterdam (+co-sc) (FR-IT-JAP-HOLL) (USA: The Beautiful Swindlers); Aimez-Vous les Femmes? (co-sc. only) (FR-IT) (GB: Do You Like Women?). **'65** Repulsion (+co-sc) (GB). **'66** Cul-de-Sac (+co-sc) (GB). **'67** Dance of the Vampires (+co-sc;+act) (GB) (USA: The Fearless Vampire Killers, or Pardon Me, But Your Teeth are in My Neck). **'68** La Fille d'en Face (co-sc. only) (FR); Rosemary's Baby (+sc) (USA). **'69** The Magic Christian (actor only) (GB); A Day at the Beach (co-prod;+co-sc. only) (USA). **'71** Polanski Meets Shakespeare (short) (appearance as himself only) (GB) (shot as TV film but shown in cinemas) (USA: Polanski Meets Macbeth); Macbeth (+co-sc) (GB). **'72** Weekend of a Champion (doc) (prod;+appearance as himself only) (GB); Che? (+co-sc;+act) (IT-FR-GER) (USA: Diary of Forbidden Dreams; GB: What?). **'74** Andy Warhol's Dracula (actor only) (IT-FR) (GB: Blood for Dracula); Chinatown (+act) (USA). **'76** Le Locataire (+co-sc;+act) (FR) (USA/GB: The Tenant). **'79** Tess (+sc) (FR-GB).

Gripping Yarns

In March 1979, one year and a month before he died, they honoured him for the last time (as they had John Ford in *his* final months) with a glittering ceremonial dinner at which Hollywood's greatest stars paid tribute to the best-known film-maker in cinema history. Receiving the Life Achievement Award – a modest silver sculpture on a simple base – of the American Film Institute, Alfred Hitchcock listened with magisterial solemnity to a torrent of showbiz accolades. He nodded occasionally, out of courtesy, it seemed, rather than agreement. And when finally they were done, he looked calmly around his breathless congregation and with one quick scoop shoplifted the award out of sight under his dinner jacket.

The public Hitchcock was always a joker and, of course, the public loved him for it. If he had a serious side it emerged only when he described the technical virtuosity with which he had accomplished a favourite scene – the track across a dance-hall in *Young and Innocent* (1937), the light-bulb in a glass of milk in *Suspicion* (1941), the use of the zoom lens in *Vertigo* (1958). But he was not serious often, or for long. His whole image was mockingly avuncular, celebrating with an imperturbable relish the unfortunately criminal tendencies of the human race. His films, his crime-story anthologies, his television dramas with their Laurel and Hardy introductory music and unashamedly awful puns conspired with his audiences to observe man's weaknesses, persuaded them to share in every imaginable excess, and got them time and again to pay for that participation.

Just like a benevolent uncle, complete with a corrupting bag of sweets, he never had a straight answer to a straight question. At Cannes he was asked how he persuaded birds to attack humans. 'They were well paid', he said. The press had to get the story instead from Tippi Hedren, who described how her director (now watching complacently as if he had just invented her) put her in a cage and chucked feathered missiles at her for eight days. The result was the terrifying attic scene in *The Birds* (1963), when Melanie Daniels – who has previously escaped serious damage – is nearly torn to death by an explosion of beaks and talons. With its combined claustrophobia,

Above left: Hitchcock shooting Torn Curtain *with Paul Newman cast as an American scientist who escapes (below) from Leipzig with a secret formula, his girl (Julie Andrews) and the aid of a Polish countess (Lila Kedrova). Below left: John Vernon and Karin Dor as Cuban leader and murdered mistress in* Topaz

A final look at Hitchcock's tales of love, theft and murder most foul

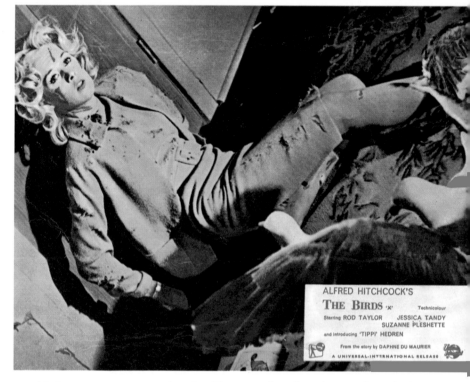

Above: blackmailed crook (Anthony Dawson) about to give heiress (Grace Kelly) reason to Dial M for Murder. *Above right: Scottie (James Stewart) prevents the suicide of Madeleine (Kim Novak) in* Vertigo. *Right: Melanie Daniels (Tippi Hedren), a victim of* The Birds

ALFRED HITCHCOCK'S

THE BIRDS ·X·   Technicolour

Starring ROD TAYLOR   JESSICA TANDY
            SUZANNE PLESHETTE
and introducing 'TIPPI' HEDREN

From the story by DAPHNE DU MAURIER

A UNIVERSAL-INTERNATIONAL RELEASE

helplessness, and sheer unreasoning savagery, the scene resembles, and indeed rivals, the classic shower murder in *Psycho* (1960).

Hitchcock's ladies always seemed to have received this kind of treatment, applied by their assailant in usually close proximity – a physical contact that carries a clearly sexual motivation. From the Ripper-style murders in *The Lodger* (1926) to the full-frontal strangulation 46 years later in *Frenzy* (the camera then retreating from the grotesque corpse as if in shameful detumescence), Hitchcock showed a special concern for female vulnerability. His blondes, whether arrogant like Miriam (Laura Elliot) in *Strangers on a Train* (1951) or simply unable to cope like Balestrero's wife (Vera Miles) in *The Wrong Man* (1957), habitually have their lives shattered by the unknown and the unforseeable. Margot Wendice (Grace Kelly) struggling against being throttled in *Dial M for Murder* (1954), the tattered death of Annie Hayworth (Suzanne Pleshette) in *The Birds*, Juanita de Cordoba (Karin Dor) sinking down from her lover's pistol-shot embrace in *Topaz* (1969) – the ghastly catalogue illustrates with urbane ferocity that murder is a sudden, very personal catastrophe. In *Torn Curtain* (1966), sexual motivation is replaced by political expediency, and killing becomes the more obscene and perverted as a result. Michael Armstrong (Paul Newman) embraces his victim in the desperate attempt to stifle him, while a knife is broken off in the man's chest. It takes a gas-oven to finish the business. 'I wanted to show,' said Hitchcock, 'just how difficult it is to kill someone.'

The maestro's bland insistence on discussing technicalities seemed calculated to discourage his general audiences from giving too much thought to his stories. His quirky advertizing campaigns, with their sly emphasis on gimmicks ('The Birds is coming', 'There's no body in the family plot', and so on) and their assurance of easy shocks and thrills, promised and delivered a macabre range of uncomplicated entertainment. But giving thought to Hitchcock grew more fashionable in the Seventies, when the countless imitations of *Psycho* demonstrated just how good his film – received in 1960 with a fair amount of critical disgust – really is. And if *Vertigo* has perhaps acquired a slightly unreliable glamour for being next-to-

invisible for over twenty years, the other films of the dazzling era between *Rear Window* (1954) and *Torn Curtain* seem to get better every time they are shown.

Why the change in our response to these elegantly violent portraits of instability? The secret is in their construction, and our more acute perception of it. When *Psycho*, for example, is seen a second or third time, it is evident that Hitchcock has placed jokes in scenes where they do not register at all the first time around but lie in wait for the viewer to understand *after* he has heard the full story. 'My mother isn't herself today', an apparently innocent remark by Norman Bates (Anthony Perkins), is one of the most quoted lines, but more subtly, the scene in which Marion Crane (Janet Leigh) decides to return the money she has stolen turns out to be full of allusions to her new predicament. Stuffed birds of prey stare down at her from the walls as her host, with bird-like movements such as the flicking of his hand like a wing, talks about his unpredictable parent. In hindsight, the viewer realizes that the room is full of danger signals, that Marion, if she had only read the signs, could there and then have saved herself from the ultimate rape by retreating back into the night. But Hitchcock's characters are no better at sign-

reading than the rest of us, which is why the problems are so easy to share.

Those problems revolve, simply and consistently, around love and money – too much of one, too little of the other, a perpetual imbalance. Marion Crane steals in *Psycho* for the purpose of 'buying' her marriage, and love – of an unexpected and horrifying kind – what she gets from Norman Bates. Melanie Daniels in *The Birds* is accustomed to buying whatever she wants, including men; pursuing her latest would-be conquest with a gift of lovebirds, she learns the hard way that cash makes poor life insurance. And in *Marnie* (1964), the case history of a kleptomaniac, the purchase of love is the heart of the whole matter, dissected by Hitchcock's finest and sharpest surgery.

Consider an example of the subtle interweaving of violence, theft and sexuality in Hitchcock's style. The opening shot of *Marnie* is of a yellow handbag held under the arm of a trim brunette walking away from the camera, stepping along a thin red line on a static platform, she heads purposefully into the distance until Hitchcock cuts abruptly to her recent employer. Only fifteen seconds of film, but they ring out with warnings – the lurid yellow bag, the red line leading nowhere, the

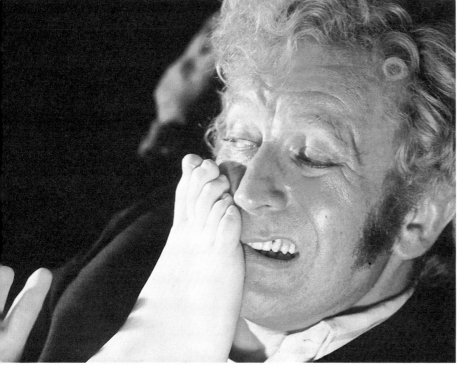

Above left: Marnie *(Tippi Hedren), Mark (Sean Connery) and the ill-fated Forio. Above: Jennifer (Shirley MacLaine) and young Tony (Jerry Mathers) discover* The Trouble With Harry *(1956). Left: Bob Rusk (Barry Foster) and another problematic stiff in* Frenzy

Marnie being led by the hand towards the possibilities of a new life. The process of rescue, while not necessarily successful – Brenda (Barbara Leigh-Hunt) gets strangled for her sympathy in *Frenzy* – prompts some of the best-remembered partnerships in Hitchcock's work: Richard Hannay (Robert Donat) and Pamela (Madeleine Carroll) handcuffed together in *The Thirty-Nine Steps* (1935); Roger Thornhill (Cary Grant) hauling Eve Kendall (Eva-Marie Saint) up Mount Rushmore and into bed in *North by Northwest* (1959); Armstrong and Sarah Sherman (Julie Andrews) hand-in-hand in *Torn Curtain*; and George Lumley (Bruce Dern) and Blanche Tyler (Barbara Harris) dodging a lethal car together in *Family Plot* (1976). The grip on the wrist, with its contrary implications of arrest and of security, guides his audiences through Hitchcock's psychological journeys more certainly than his often-quoted references to conventional law and order ('Oh look!' says the fugitive Hannay on encountering some sheep, 'It's a whole flock of policemen!'). For Hitchcock, the laws of nature are seldom in sympathy with the laws of the land.

It may seem excessive to wish upon the well-loved figure of the cinema's master of suspense ('the man who invented the modern thriller', as the *Daily Express* once called him) an encrustation of interpretations that risk taking the fun out of his characters. When he placed so much accessible ingenuity on the screen, why hunt for more? The answer, of course, is that the special agonies of *Psycho* and the other parables cry out loudly enough to be heard above Hitchcock's own modest protestations of simplicity. When Lina (Joan Fontaine), wrists gripped, hair disarranged, is seen on a traumatic hillock in *Suspicion*, and then finds her way back to the same hillock ten minutes later, a fugitive from loneliness calling for rescue, actually *inviting* the violence that previously terrified her, something more complex than mere entertainment is being revealed. And when that same trauma, in much the same bare setting, finds itself retold in *Torn Curtain*, we can be certain that Hitchcock's capacity for caring went further then he was ever prepared to admit. Maybe it's just that he liked to keep his rewards to himself, shoplifted under his jacket.

PHILIP STRICK

nnatural hair colour. The angry face that en confronts the viewer, so directly that the an (Martin Gabel) actually has to change his osition to continue speaking for the scene at follows, explains it all with a single word, urled out like an expletive: 'Robbed!' Not only es it explain the girl's retreating figure (the olen money under her arm), it explains why e committed the crime; she has robbed the an of a possible seduction. The bristling rkey-cock figure of Strutt (the name is a appy choice), all petty lechery and materia-sm, haunts Marnie (Tippi Hedren) through-t the film: the kind of tyrant she has always nown, whose imminent attacks she has ways fled from, for reasons she believes she nderstands only too well.

Only fifteen seconds, but all else follows from em. What Marnie gets from men is money nd the threat of sexual violence, because that what her mother always got from in-umerable father-substitutes, and Marnie has en brought up to be 'decent' like her mother. he is emotionally crippled, violent, bitter, just ke her mother, but 'decent'. And logically 1ough it is when one of her employers, Mark utland (Sean Connery), determines to claim ʰat (as a result of Marnie's theft) he has paid ɪr, that Marnie finds herself trapped into

marriage; her worst fears realized when her husband attempts her cure by forcing sex upon her. Only after a series of shocks, which include the destruction of the horse that was previously her sex substitute ('Oh, Forio, if you must bite someone, bite me', she whispers when she first mounts him), does she find that she needs her husband more than she needs his money. Marnie is then ready to understand her mother, and in turn to understand her own frigidity.

The climactic scene, with its thunderstorm and its appalling flood of red (as the sailor's head is split open with a poker) is perilously open to ridicule, but its saving grace is that it offers no easy cure. On the contrary, the tragic revelation of the film is that all the horrors have resulted from the best of intentions. 'You're the only thing I ever did love', confesses Marnie's mother, for whom money was once the means of keeping her daughter and is now the reason she has lost her . . .

It is a long way from the cosy vulgarity of Hitchcock's popular image, but if one symbol had to be selected to summarize the Hitchcock message in half a century of film-making, it should not, in fact, be one of mayhem, as the maestro would undoubtedly have recommen-ded. More accurately it would be the sight of

PSYCHO

Directed by Alfred Hitchcock, 1960
Prod co: Shamley (Paramount). **prod:** Alfred Hitchcock. **sc:** Joseph Stefano, from a novel by Robert Bloch. **titles:** Saul Bass. **photo:** John L. Russell. **sp eff photo:** Clarence Champagne. **ed:** George Tomasini. **art dir:** Joseph Hurley, Robert Clatworthy, George Milo. **mus:** Bernard Herrmann. **sd rec:** Walden O. Watson, William Russell. **r/t:** 108 minutes.
Cast: Anthony Perkins (*Norman Bates*), John Gavin (*Sam Loomis*), Janet Leigh (*Marion Crane*), Vera Miles (*Lila Crane*), John McIntyre (*Sheriff Chambers*), Martin Balsam (*Milton Arbogast*), Simon Oakland (*Dr Richmond*).

'For all the fake intimacy of the opening love scene and the manifest absurdity of the denouement, *Psycho* comes nearer to attaining an exhilarating balance between content and style than anything Hitchcock has done in years. Of course, it is a very minor work.'

This remarkable statement is taken from Peter John Dyer's review in *Sight and Sound* (Autumn 1960). Later in the same piece Dyer asserted that 'Hitchcock is not a serious director (except in his worst films)' and that *Psycho* has 'an unacceptable basic premise' but offers a high degree of 'craftsmanship'. In other words, it is a tasteless and cynical tale well told.

This review seems extraordinary today but it speaks volumes about critical priorities in 1960 when a film could be grudgingly and guiltily praised for technical excellence but haughtily dismissed on moral grounds. Serious directors were not allowed to dabble with genre material such as horror. The fact that *Psycho* is as complex and as challenging as Antonioni's *L'Avventura* (1960, *The Adventure*)

and Resnais' *L'Année Dernière à Marienbad* (1961, *Last Year in Marienbad*) – two notably Hitchcockian films of the same period – would not have occurred to most critics of the time for whom horror films (and Westerns and melodramas) represented the most blatant commercialism. Michael Powell's *Peeping Tom* (1960), a blood-brother of *Psycho*, was greeted with even more critical scorn.

Happily, the critical climate changed in the Sixties and many of the major battles were fought over Hitchcock's work in general and *Psycho* in particular – its box-office success had turned it into a social phenomenon. The film's importance is now acknowledged and it has influenced a wide range of filmmakers. Audiences, too, have been conditioned by *Psycho* to recognize the strategies at work in such films.

Psycho is a comparative rarity among horror films in that repeated viewings do not diminish its power; indeed, as the characters become more and more familiar each time the film is seen, so the viewer's unease and apprehension grow. **6**

Hitchcock himself has defined this as a response to 'pure film'. In the sense that 'pure film' implies more than 'craftsmanship', *Psycho* is perhaps the most detailed and rigorously constructed of Hitchcock's films. Its continuing fascination and power to involve (not to say enslave) its audience is also because *Psycho* is neither a whodunnit (Hitchcock was never interested in those) nor a conventional thriller (there is no hero); instead, it is an essay on the universality of evil in which the audience plays the most significant role. It is an appeal to and a criticism of the film audience's voyeuristic impulses and the cinematic apparatus.

Norman Bates' schizophrenia becomes the audience's, just as the audience is implicated in Marion Crane's submission to crime. At first the viewer identifies with Marion, sharing her panic when she encounters the traffic cop and understanding her irrational behaviour at the gas station. And after her decision to return the money,

her shower washes away her guilt – and that of everyone watching. Then comes the murder, and interest switches to Norman, culminating in the moment when Marion's car refuses to sink into the swamp. The sigh of relief, and then the grin that passes across Norman's face when the car finally does sink, again implicates 'the watcher' in his diabolism. Then Arbogast the detective, and then Sam and Lila become the focus for audience sympathy. The setting is equally schizoid – a Gothic gingerbread house and a banal modern motel.

The insistent mirror imagery emphasizes the theme and also alerts the audience to the characters and the actors playing them. Norman cares for his mother; Sam, apparently, is paying alimony and the debts of his dead father; Marion's office colleague has a prying mother; the rich businessman is a domineering father; the woman in Sam's hardware store is possibly buying insecticide to kill her husband; Marion's apartment is decorated with family photographs; and Lila has assumed the role of Marion's mother. Everyone talks incessantly about murder and family strife and Norman and Sam, and Marion and Lila, are even mirror images of each other.

This strategy creates an oppressive world from which escape is impossible (the audience is hooked). The suffocating bird imagery – Norman's stuffed birds, his mummified mother, Marion's surname, the city of Phoenix – suggests predestination, as does the license plate of Marion's last car, bearing the initials of Norman Bates, and Marion and Sam's early dialogue about the ignominy of hotel rooms.

For 108 minutes *Psycho* perforates the viewer's belief in the icons of the capitalist dream – money, family, sex – and analyses his demons instead. The film's abrasive wit prevents a total descent into the heart of darkness, while its effectiveness gains considerably from Bernard Herrmann's music and Anthony Perkins' performance which ranks with the finest the cinema has to offer. ADRIAN TURNER

After spending the lunch-hour in a hotel room with her lover Sam (1), Marion Crane returns to work. Her boss (2) entrusts her with $40,000 in cash but Marion goes home, packs a bag, and leaves town. She sleeps in her car and is woken by a cop who follows her to a garage where, using some of the stolen money, she changes cars. That night she stays at the Bates Motel and chats with the manager, Norman (3), who looks after his sick mother in the nearby house (4). Marion takes a shower and is stabbed to death (5). Norman, blaming his mother, cleans up the mess, puts the body into Marion's own car and drives it into a swamp (6).

Marion's sister Lila visits Sam and they are joined by Arbogast, a private detective. Arbogast checks hotels, interviews Norman (7) and is murdered when he returns to see Mrs Bates. Sam and Lila check into the motel and Sam keeps Norman talking while Lila (8) searches the house. Sensing trouble, Norman knocks Sam unconscious. Lila enters the cellar (9) and finds the clothed skeleton of Mrs Bates.

The ending? Hitchcock would turn in his grave if we told . . .

2

4

5

8

9

THIRD WORLD ON SCREEN

Conditions for film-making varied widely throughout the Third World; some countries had established industries while others had to start from scratch

Everywhere the Sixties were turbulent years. But the Third World, so-called because it comprised the areas outside the eastern and western power blocs, was making an unprecedented impact on the western capitalist world. Liberation struggles in Africa, Asia and Latin America had reached a decisive stage, gathering tremendous momentum, asserting a unity across three continents which was based on the ideal of self-determination and the ideology of anti-imperialism. The Cuban Revolution, the Algerian War of Independence, Africa and Vietnam – they were all exemplary situations, expressing the global scale of revolutionary consciousness within the oppressed Third World regions.

Third World cinema of the Sixties derived its impetus from these political developments. Its attitude towards cinema necessarily opposed the colonial film practices of the western countries, and was militantly political. Third World film-makers rejected the dominant values of escapist entertainment on the Hollywood model, and redefined the role of cinema as an integral part of the revolutionary process, a 'weapon' to be used against the dominant images of western cinema.

The antipathy towards the dominant Euro-American cinema was legitimate. The major film companies had monopolized film distribution and exhibition throughout the colonized regions, thereby preventing the emergence of any indigenous cinema industry that could effectively compete. Audiences in Third World countries were bombarded with third-rate films which invariably depicted non-European peoples in pernicious stereotypes. These negative associations, along with the films' idealized images of capitalist society, had a pervasive effect on the consciousness of the audience. Militantly political film-makers recognized the need to counteract these colonial pictures, and to construct alternative themes and images which would express a true identity and dignity. But different parts of the world had had different colonial experiences. Thus in Latin America the main target was American films; in North Africa it was the French and Egyptian film monopolies; and in black Africa the need was to destroy the Tarzan-type jungle mythology and the representation of Africans as 'savages'.

Of course nationalization was correctly seen by the newly formed Third World governments as the crucial factor in developing a national cinema, and therefore in evolving a new self-identity. But any moves in that direction were often met by opposition. When the Algerian government nationalized its film industry in 1964, for example, the major American companies, which controlled 40 per cent of the market, boycotted the country. Similar experiences occurred in other countries, as in Upper Volta in 1972.

Third World films vary widely, ranging from straightforward agit-prop newsreel and didactic documentaries to fictional narratives and films employing complex symbolism. These differences in

approach are to a large extent determined by the particular social, political, cultural and historical conditions in which individual film-makers work. But there are also stylistic differences based primarily on the film-maker's own aesthetic preoccupations.

The extent to which any of these differences

Above: El Tigre Saltó y Mató, Pero Morirá . . . Morirá *(1973, The Tiger Leaps and Kills, But It Will Die . . . Will Die) is a short Cuban documentary on the Chilean folksinger Victor Jara, killed by the ruling military junta*

152

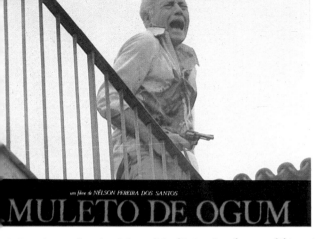

MULETO DE OGUM
um filme de NÉLSON PEREIRA DOS SANTOS

reinforced or undermined the political integrity of a political cinema was never very clear. Brazilian *Cinema Novo*, which included quite disparate film styles, got around the problem by emphasizing the importance of personal creative expression. Others, like the Chilean Miguel Littin, spoke in terms of adopting political 'strategies' in dealing with the question of politicized film practice, while the Chilean Aldo Francia insisted that: 'Films must also entertain.' The differences between varied postures did not pose a serious threat of disruption, since to be in some sense political was sufficient.

But at the same time there was a sense in which Latin American unity ran deeper than political alignments alone suggested. The majority of Latin American film-makers was uniformly concerned with theoretical questions, with notions of political engagement and with aesthetic methods. The terminology in which debates about political film were conducted was similar in the various countries. The films as well (in the way they manipulated imagery) reflected this sense of Latin American unity.

El Instituto Cubano del Arte e Industria Cinematográficos presenta

presents

The situation on the African continent was completely the opposite. The colonial impact on the region had produced four or five sharp demarcations which deeply affected how the African world perceived and expressed political and cultural activity. The sub-regions included Egypt and the Middle East; North Africa, including Algeria, Morocco and Tunisia; the black French-speaking area; the black English-speaking countries; and the white-dominated South. These historically-produced divisions help to explain why Africa had been unable to create a forceful cinema. As for black Africa in particular, only the French-speaking countries had produced any film-makers of note.

In looking at the emergence of progressive film-making in the Third World, a useful distinction can be made between those countries which already had an established film industry, such as Brazil, Argentina and Egypt, and those that lacked an indigenous cinematic tradition and so had to start from scratch, as in Cuba and black Africa.

Interestingly, Cuba emerged as the country most influential in developing progressive film-making, influencing the Third World as a whole. In 1959, the new revolutionary government led by Fidel Castro set up the Cuban Institute of Cinematographic Art and Industry (ICAIC), only three months after overthrowing the Batista regime. The swiftness

of this action shows the importance that was given to cinema in the rebuilding of Cuban society. ICAIC produced several feature films as well as documentaries and weekly newsreels throughout the Sixties. The profoundly political and international outlook of progressive Cuban cinema is particularly evident in the documentaries of Santiago Alvarez and in Julio Garcia Espinosa's *Tercer Mundo, Tercera Guerra Mundial* (1970, Third World, Third World War), a documentary shot in North Vietnam and aimed specifically at a politically militant audience.

Politicized film-makers of the Third World were particularly concerned with the role of cinema in relation to the audience; they wanted to counteract the consumer-oriented model of the passive spectator established in Euro-American cinema. Octavio Getino and Fernando Solanas' widely acclaimed monumental film-essay *La Hora de los Hornos* (1968, Hour of the Furnaces) presents a Marxist historical analysis of neo-colonialism and oppression in Argentina in the form of 'chapters' and 'notes' – captioned divisions in the film – which form the basis for political discussions with the audience.

Adopting a progressive political perspective entailed raising questions about history, as in *Hour of the Furnaces*. In a different vein, Humberto Solás' *Lucia* (1968) powerfully dramatized three historical moments in the Cuban struggle for liberation, and highlighted the participation of Cuban women in each period. But very few films set out, as *Hour of the Furnaces* did, to activate a critical engagement with the historical process. Most political films were of an agit-prop kind, more concerned with agitation and propaganda than with analysis.

A significant number of Third World films during this period dealt with rural themes, since the politicized film-makers identified with the peasantry, which was the most oppressed class in the society. But there were marked differences in tone between Latin American films and films from Africa and the Middle East. In the Latin American films – with the notable exception of the Bolivian Jorge Sanjines' *Yawar Mallku* (1969, Blood of the Condor) – the image of rural life did not evoke a sense of social and cultural cohesion, at any level. The films tended to emphasize the grim and hopeless position of the peasant, often depicted as an isolated outsider, with a dependent family. This image of bleakness, with its undertones of violence, was brilliantly conveyed in the Brazilian Nelson Pereira Dos Santos' *Vidas Secas* (1963, Barren Lives) and the Chilean Miguel Littin's *El Chacal de Nahueltoro* (1970, The Jackal of Nahueltoro).

In the African context, Ousmane Sembene of Senegal worked the themes of exploitation and human despair somewhat differently. His protagonists were similar to the Latin American peasants only to the extent that they both represented non-urban types struggling to survive within a repressive environment, moving through their daily lives

THE MONEY ORDER (Mandabi) (Senegal)
by Ousmane Sembene (colour)

Wolof with English subtitles
Special Jury Prize at Venice Film Festival

A hilarious and bitter picture
of bureaucracy, corruption
and daily life in Africa.

CANTATA DE CHILE
film cubano
dirección humberto solás
con: nelson villagra
eric heresmann
shenda roman

Top left: O Amuleto de Ogum *(1975, The Amulet of Ogum) is about a boy who is invulnerable to bullets.* Top: *the Brazilian bandit leader (Lorival Pariz) killed by* Antonio-das-Mortes *(1969, Antonio of the Dead).* Centre: The Money Order *shows how a poor man with two wives is ruined in Dakar by a money order sent from Paris.* Above: Cantata de Chile *(1976, Cantata of Chile) re-creates in a Cuban film the massacre of strikers by troops at Iquique in 1907*

153

Top: during the Battle of Algiers, *several Arab girls carry out bombs from the Casbah to plant in public places in the French quarter. Top right:* Lucia *(1968) shows the lives of three different Cuban girls called Lucia; in 1895 during the war of independence against Spain, in 1933 when the dictator Machado was overthrown, and in the Sixties during the literacy campaign. Above:* The Night of Counting the Years *culminates in the rescue of precious Egyptian mummies menaced by a tribe of tomb-robbers*

as isolated and vulnerable individuals. But the difference was that the Africans had a group identity or membership which they could ultimately fall back on. The peasants of the Latin American films did not have this; they occupied barren lands.

In Sembene's films, the main characters find themselves imprisoned in a deceptively attractive environment, the urban centre, and unable to return to their former lives in the village rural community. In *La Noire de . . .* (1966, *Black Girl*), the only film where he deals explicitly with colonial forms of relationships, the imprisonment is fatal. Sembene's preoccupation with the dichotomies between the rural and the urban, between tradition and change, was very much tied to the radical alterations which were occurring in African societies, and the effects these were having in the lives of ordinary people.

Egyptian films had been widely shown throughout the Arab world since the Thirties. These were mainly escapist comedies and cheap entertainment dramas. The revolution of 1952 led eventually to significant changes. In 1957, Nasser's government established the National Organization for the Cinema and, two years later, set up a film school. The Sixties saw the emergence of 'quality' films such as Youssef Chahine's *An-Nasr Salah Ad-Din* (1963, *Saladin*), which was Egypt's first epic film, and Hussein Kamal's *Al Mostahil* (1965, The Impossible) and *Al Boustagui* (1968, The Postman), while Shadi Abdelsalam's mysterious tale of mummy-robbers in the last century *El Mumia* (1970, *The Night of Counting the Years*) broke away completely from earlier conventions.

Another factor which contributed to the reorientation of Arab cinema was the Algerian Revolution. As in the Latin American experience, progressive cinema in Algeria was defined as an integral part of the Algerian cultural renaissance. The Provisional Government of the Algerian

Republic set up a film committee in 1961 which became the Cinema Service. It made four films, including Chanderli and Lakhdar Hamina's *Djazaïrouna* (1961), a history of Algeria. Between 1962 and 1971, Algerian 'Cinema Moudjahid' (Arabic for 'freedom fighter') was almost exclusively concerned with anti-colonial war films. There was also an emphasis on big-budget co-productions during this period. For example, Casbah Films, a private production company founded in 1961 by Yacef Saadi, a liberation leader and principal organizer of the battle of Algiers, partly financed major films by European directors, such as Gillo Pontecorvo's *La Battaglia di Algeri* (1966, *Battle of Algiers*).

But Algerian film-makers did not limit their scope to the Algerian experience alone. Like the Cubans, they maintained close relations with other Third World struggles: for instance, Ahmed Rachedi's documentary compilation *L'Aube des Damnés* (1965, The Dawn of the Damned) presented a sharp critique of the European powers' multiple intervention in the African continent and the Third World generally. The concentration on war films during this period was officially encouraged, but young film-makers and audiences alike began to criticize the trend, attacking the films for not dealing with such crucial questions as the status of women in Algerian society, or the abuse of power. But it was not until the agrarian revolution of 1971, which forced a rethinking of political and cultural organization, that a new Algerian cinema emerged.

After the military defeat it suffered in 1967, the Palestinian resistance movement began to contribute to the changes in Arab cinema; but the development of a unified Palestinian cinema was initially hampered by the fact that each political organization had its own cinema service, propagandizing for its own aims. One organization, El Fatah, produced a number of shorts and medium-length films, as well as helping several foreign film producers, including the Italian Communist Party, The American 'Newsreel' group, the Tricontinental group and Jean-Luc Godard. But Palestinian cinema was still at an embryonic stage, and depended on the support of other sympathetic Arab film-makers.

Neither was African cinema an emerging force during this period. It consisted of only a handful of film-makers from French-speaking countries such as Senegal, Niger, Guinea and Chad – whose films were made in French. Only Ousmane Sembene achieved international recognition, with *Mandabi* (1968, *The Money Order*), his third film, but the first in which he used his own language, Wolof. This use of an indigenous African language in a major film represented a radical shift from conventional practice; it amounted to a way of saying that the film was made by an African for Africans. A forceful African cinema would emerge in the Seventies.

JIM PINES

Last Tangos

During Hollywood's heyday, moviegoers were treated to a glossy montage of rumbas, tutti-frutti hats and funny accents. This was Latin America! In the Fifties and Sixties, however, Latin-American film-makers began to dispel the myth

Below left: the Quechua tribesmen declare independence in Blood of the Condor. *Left:* The Jackal of Nahueltoro *(Nelson Villagra) with new victims. Above: the films of directors such as Emilio Fernandez were in sharp contrast to the 'new breed'*

Since the arrival of the first projectors and films at the turn of the century, cinema in Latin America has been dominated from abroad. Screens soon filled with images from the United States, while the continent's own producers generally opted for competition by imitation. *Tango* musicals and *cangaçeiro* Westerns used elements of national cultures, but vulgarized them by adaptation to imposed genres. Some outstanding directors, like the Argentinian Leopoldo Torre Nilsson or the great Brazilian director Humberto Mauro, attempted to treat themes genuinely deriving from the surrounding societies, but in general such explorations were few.

However, in the Fifties and Sixties a different kind of cinema arose. An integral part of the nationalist and revolutionary political tide which was sweeping the continent, this 'new cinema' intended to express a truly Latin American vision of the world, affirming the continent's own cultural heritage and providing an ideological tool that would contribute directly to the struggle for social and political liberation. Its subjects were to be the continent's dispossessed majorities, while its language would only take that which was

155

useful to it from established cinematic traditions, while looking within the continent's own cultural traditions for new resources. The relationship with the audience – intended to be these same dispossessed majorities – would be didactic and interactive, breaking down the passive receptivity encouraged by 'industrial' cinema.

Capturing a culture

In Bolivia during the mid-Sixties a sustained attempt began to relate cinema to one of the continent's oldest cultures – that of the Quechua and Aymara Indian peoples. In a sequence of six films – including *Yawar Mallku* (1969, *Blood of the Condor*) and *El Coraje del Pueblo* (1972, *Courage of the People*) – the director Jorge Sanjines and the Ukamau Group production company made fewer and fewer concessions to orthodox structure as they attempted to build a film language from the patterns of Quechua/Aymara culture.

In the late Sixties and early Seventies, the Chilean new cinema movement declared itself with the appearance of four films made in 1969: Raúl Ruiz's portrait of urban petty bourgeoisie, *Tres Tristes Tigres* (1969, Three Sad Tigers); Miguel Littin's *El Chacal de Nahueltoro* (1970, *The Jackal of Nahueltoro*), about the capture, trial and execution of a notorious murderer; Aldo Francia's *Valparaiso, Mi Amor* (1970), Valparaiso, My Love), about the family of a poor worker who is imprisoned for stealing meat; and Charles Elsesser's *Los Testigos* (1971, The Witnesses), about a murder in a poor part of the capital. Between 1970 and 1973 such filmmaking flourished under the Popular Unity government of Salvador Allende.

During the military coup of September, 1973, documentarists such as Patricio Guzman – whose *La Batalla de Chile* (1975–79, *The Battle of Chile*) had to be edited in exile – immersed themselves in current events in order to capture history as it was made. By way of film it was then returned to the ordinary people who had made it for their reflection, discussion and deeper understanding. Directors such as Miguel Littin mobilized the resources of the feature film for a similar end. In his *La Tierra Prometida* (1973, The Promised Land), also edited in exile, past events are reconstructed by using the language and myths of popular memory so as to redeem them from 'official' interpretation and restore them to the people of whose living history they are a part.

Fernando Solanas' *La Hora de los Hornos* (1968, *Hour of the Furnaces*) is the best-known product of new cinema in Argentina. Clandestinely shot during the dictatorship of General Ongania, the film is a series of 'film-essays' exploring aspects of Argentine history and society, including Péronism, the political movement founded by Juan Péron. Strongly influenced by the Algerian writer Franz Fanon, the film calls for revolutionary violence as being both the only viable political option for liberation and a cathartic cultural necessity.

In all the above countries, right-wing military governments had suffocated the new cinema by the mid-Seventies, killing and imprisoning its practitioners, or driving them into exile. Only in Cuba, where it grew up after rather than before a social and political revolution, has it continued intact. There filmmakers such as Santiago Alvarez, Tomás Gutiérrez Alea, Humberto Solás and Manuel Octavio Gómez, to name but a very few, have

Above: Muerte de un Burocrata *(1966, Death of a Bureaucrat),* Tomás Gutiérrez Alea's *satirical dig at officialdom. Above right: powerful images from Fernando Solanas'* Hour of the Furnaces. *Above, far right: Humberto Solás' humorous and perceptive vision of women. Above, furthest right: Pastor Vega's stark picture of war,* De la Guerra Americana *(1969, On the American War)*

been able to make innovations and experiment with enormous success. In long films such as *De America Soy Hijo . . . y a Ella Me Debo* (1973, *Born of the Americas)* and *Y El Cielo Fue Tomado por Asalto* (1973, Heaven Was Taken by Assault), both recording foreign trips taken by Fidel Castro, and scores of shorts such as the tributes to Che Guevara, *Hasta la Victoria Siempre* (1967, *Forever Towards Victory*), and Ho Chi Minh, *79 Primaveras* (1969, *79 Springs*), Santiago Alvarez changed the language of documentary through a daring use of montage which brings the most disparate elements together in creative tension.

The critical re-discovery of history has also been a main preoccupation of Cuban filmmakers as exemplified by films such as Manuel Octavio Gómez's *La Primera Carga al Machete* (1969, *The First Charge of the Machetes*), about their War of Independence against Spain, or Humberto Solás' *Lucia* (1968), which examines the situation of woman at three different stages in the island's history.

The position of women has also been the subject of two recent films: *De Cierta Manera* (1974, One Way or Another), made by Sara Yera Gómez – Cuba's only woman director – who died tragically of asthma before it could be completed; and Pastor Vega's *Retrato de Teresa* (1979, *Portrait of Teresa*). Sara Gómez's film also examines the impact of revolutionary change in the ideology and habits of Havana's lumpenproletariat, as well as being an experiment in formal innovation, interweaving fiction and documentary, invented and real characters.   MALCOLM COAD

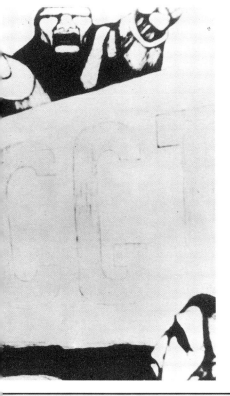

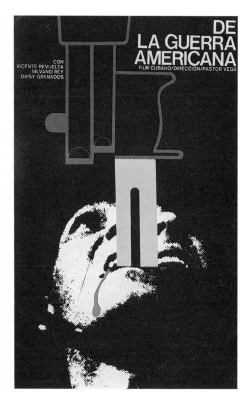

t: violence predominates in Ruy Guerra's e Guns. Above: bandits fearful of their rsuer in Black God, White Devil. *Above ht: glamorous images of Brazil are absent m Pereira dos Santos'* Barren Lives

nema Novo first emerged in the early Fifties, d was a result of the debates between young azilian critics and writers opposed to the npty cosmopolitanism' of Hollywood and e 'false populism' of national studios such as lantida and Vera Cruz.

A major impetus for early *Cinema Novo* was lian neo-realism which pointed the way wards a critical realist method based in few chnical resources. Although the movement s to flower fully in the early and mid-Sixties, groundwork was laid by films such as Alex ny's *Agulha no Palheiro* (1953, Needle in a ystack) and, Nelson Pereira dos Santos' cumentaries on the lives of ordinary people *Rio de Janeiro* – *Rio, 40 Graus* (1955, Rio, 40 grees) and *Rio, Zona Norte* (1956, Rio, North ne). These films in turn built on the legacy of brilliant director Humberto Mauro who

had, virtually alone and against all odds, taken his camera into Brazil's countryside and shanty-towns during the Thirties.

By the early Sixties *Cinema Novo* was drawing on a wide range of resources in its search for a renovated aesthetic appropriate to the real Brazil of starvation, violence and the gross concentration of wealth in the hands of the few. Styles ranged from the critical realism of Nelson Pereira dos Santos' *Vidas Secas* (1963, *Barren Lives*) to the 'baroque poetry' of Glauber Rocha's films, notably *Terra em Transe* (1967, *Earth in Revolt*). Popular history and myth were the major grounding for the movement. Films such as Rocha's *Barravento* (1962) and *Deus e o Diabo na Terra do Sol* (1963, *Black God, White Devil*) were based on the imagery and ritual of popular culture, proposing these as the essential source for a renewed and authentic Brazilian culture, but simultaneously defining them as insufficient to confront the realities of mid-twentieth-century exploitation and hunger. Carlos Diegues' *Ganga Zumba* (1964), about a seventeenth-century slave revolt, explored the past for its explanations of the

present, and Ruy Guerra's *Os Fuzis* (1964, *The Guns*) portrayed the yearning for a better life that this culture expressed, and its explosive violence.

In the later Sixties, *Cinema Novo's* themes moved away from the *sertão* (the harsh northeast) and the *favela* (shanty-town) to examine the culture of the urban middle-class. This reflected a desire not to fall into the trap of romantic primitivism, and to investigate the failures of Brazilian politics after the 1964 military coup. Films such as Paulo Cesar Saraceni's *O Desafio* (1965, The Challenge), Gustavo Dahl's *Os Bravos Guerreiros* (1967, The Brave Warriors) and Carlos Diegues' *Os Herdeiros* (1969, The Inheritors), examined this latter theme.

However, by the late Sixties, particularly after the intensification of government repression in 1968, *Cinema Novo* declared itself at an end. Film-makers such as Glauber Rocha and Ruy Guerra went into exile, while others found their films facing violent military censorship as well as the prejudices of commercial distributors. MALCOLM COAD

THE OTHER CINEMA

BLOOD OF THE CONDOR

A BOLIVIAN FILM BY JORGE SANJINES

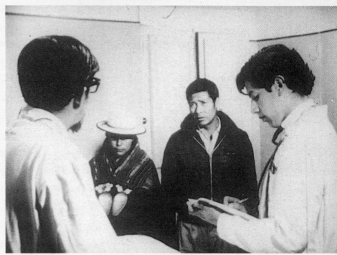
1

Yawar Mallku (*Blood of the Condor*) is a film of blinding anger. Made in 1969, it was inspired by a newspaper report of a sterilization programme carried out by a team of American doctors on Indian women in a Bolivian mountain region, without their knowledge or consent. With no time – or use – for subtleties or technical gloss, the director, Jorge Sanjines, pours out his fictionalized development of the story in a blaze of indignation and disgust.

Throughout the film, the events of the village are unfolded with urgent realism and striking visual imagery. They stand as a metaphor for the condition of the Indian people, 65 per cent of the population of Bolivia, who live in grinding poverty under the rule of whites and *mestizos* (mixed-race Bolivians) and their American backers. In an early flashback sequence, a US medical team is seen issuing the Quechua Indian villagers with a bizarre and wholly unsuitable assortment of American-style shoes and clothing, which the Indians quietly return to

the clinic during the night. The involuntary sterilization of the village women by the US Peace Corps is a more drastic and vicious variation of this meddlesome approach. In a country with an infant mortality rate of one in four, the Bolivian Indians have even less need for population control than they have for white canvas sneakers. Whatever the motives, such unwarranted interference could be interpreted as an extermination programme. There is symbolic justice in the husband's enraged retaliation by castrating the US doctors.

The flashback structure of the film enables Sanjines to frame this urgent and painful narrative inside another, more politically explicit, story – an account of the gradual change in the heart and mind of Sixto, brother of the village leader, who has left the village and is working for a pittance in a La Paz factory. As Sixto tramps the city streets in search of help to save his brother's life, he discovers that denial of his Indian origins is no protection against racial insult from

the wealthy. Shots of the dying brother are intercut with shots which highlight the grotesque contrast that Sixto observes between the Americanized life-styles of the prosperous whites and their *mestizos* underlings and that of the poverty-stricken Indians. He begins to understand that his future lies with his own people and their struggle for social justice.

Sanjines (b. 1936) spent ten years making shorts and documentaries before founding the Bolivian National Film Institute and becoming its director. He was dismissed from his post, however, after completion of his first feature film *Ukamau* (1966), also about the sufferings of the Indians, because the government thought it 'too negative'. *Blood of the Condor*, his second feature film, which was financed independently, was banned until a press campaign and massive street demonstrations forced a change of policy. In its first year of release, it was seen by more Bolivians than any previous film. Some of its audiences had never

seen a film before.

Sanjines and his colleagues wer out to remote country village where they set up specially pre pared presentations. A narrato would tell the story in the age-ol village tradition but with th modern aid of photographs. Th audience were encouraged to as questions and to discuss the impl cations of the events. Then the were shown the film.

This rapport between film makers and film audiences is vita to Sanjines' working methoc Within the general flowering of re volutionary cinema in Lati America, he has pioneered a ne way of creating and using film b involving whole communities in it preparation, financing, productio and presentation. *Blood of th Condor*, which features the popu lation of the Kaata rural area, wa partially financed by students, teac hers, technicians, workers an peasants. In his following film, *£ Coraje del Pueblo* (1972, *Courage the People*), a whole mining com munity, survivors of a massacre b

7

8

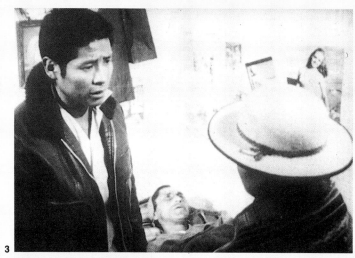

the Bolivian army in 1967, re-enacted their own story.

Like all Sanjines' films, *Blood of the Condor* makes no concessions to European tastes or perceptions. It was made for and with Bolivian Indians and it adopts a wholly Indian point of view, with a deep understanding of Indian ceremony and ritual.

'I believe', Sanjines has written, 'that the Latin American liberation struggle is not only a struggle to win freedom, but to define the reality of

the peoples, to return to ourselves and to renew ourselves. Yet the time for struggle is scarce if we want to survive as nations and human beings and prevent the destruction of our culture.'

His films not only seek, through what they reveal, to shake Bolivia free from American domination and to raise pride in its own cultural traditions; they are also in themselves a forceful contribution to the shaping of contemporary Bolivian culture. NINA HIBBIN

Directed by Jorge Sanjines, 1969

Prod co: Ukamau Limitado. **prod:** Ricardo Rada. **sc:** Oscar Soria, Jorges Sanjines. **photo:** Antonio Eguino. **mus:** Alberto Villalpando, Alfredo Dominguez, Gregorio Yana, Ignacio Quispe. **r/t:** 74 minutes. Bolivian title: *Yawar Mallku*.
Cast: Marcelino Yanahuava (*Ignacio*), Benedicta Mendoza Huanca (*Pauline*), Vincente Salinas (*Sixto*), the population of the Kaata rural community.

In a remote Bolivian mountainside village, a group of Quechua Indian men are rounded up by the police (1), told to run and then shot (2). Ignacio survives and his wife, Pauline, manages to get him to La Paz where she seeks out his brother, Sixto (3) who has denied his Indian origin. They take Ignacio to the hospital (4).

Pauline tells Sixto what happened. Their three children died of the 'plague' and Ignacio was elected head of the village (5). Pauline visited a fortune-teller (6) who told her that she could no longer have children. Other women in the village found they could not conceive and the families were in despair. Fertility rites were performed, but to no avail.

Back in the present, Pauline is told that Ignacio will die (7)

unless she can raise money for a blood transfusion. Sixto tramps the city streets but is unable to find anyone willing to help save Ignacio's life. Wherever he goes he meets with indifference and contempt.

Pauline's story continues. When Ignacio visited the American clinic, he learnt by chance that the US doctors had been sterilizing the women without their knowledge under the guise of general maternity treatment. Later Ignacio and other men from the village (8) marched on the clinic (9), burst in and castrated the doctors (10).

In the present again, Ignacio dies. Sixto puts on traditional Quechua clothing and returns to the village with Pauline. He now realizes that his only future is standing firm with the Quechua Indians.

'If a famous old film with the same title had not already existed, I should have liked to call *La Battaglia di Algeri* The Birth of a Nation. This, in fact, is the sense of the story . . . because it tells of the pains and the lacerations which the birth of the Algerian nation brought to all its people.'

In his own words, Gillo Pontecorvo thus described his film of the rise of the nationalist movement in Algeria and its crushing defeat by the French five years before independence. It is both an overtly political film, following the struggle of the Algerian Liberation Front (FLN), as well as a profoundly human one in its account of the politicization of the rebel leader Ali La Pointe, as he moves from being a petty criminal to leader of the underground resistance and ultimately a martyr. The confusions, doubts and fears of the Algerians in their struggle for independence are believably conveyed, as is the violence and terrorism that accompanied the struggle.

Production of *Battle of Algiers* was an exciting political event in itself, since it used the Algerian people to recreate their own history. Four years after independence, with the full cooperation of the Algerian government, Pontecorvo returned to the site of the strongest FLN resistance – the Casbah – to use the actual locations for his film. He and his assistants spent two years collecting information from the accounts of over 10,000 eye-witnesses. The result is a highly atmospheric work, which captures the flavour of the Arab quarters of Algiers.

Its style is a documentary one, yet the film uses no newsreel footage to construct its events. It has been estimated that in making the film all 80,000 inhabitants of the Casbah took part in one form or another. Only a few professional actors were used; most of the players were people recruited from the streets and cafés because their faces fitted the character. One old man cried when his part was over – he was a thief and had to return to jail for 15 days. Indeed, Yacef Saadi, organizer of the Casbah resistance, who by 1966 had become the president of the Casbah Film company, and was one of the producers of *Battle of Algiers*, played himself in the film: 'I have substituted the camera for the

machine-gun.'

Likewise, the production team was recruited on the spot. Pontecorvo only took a crew of nine with him from Italy. The rest was made up of local people with no previous experience of filming; this was the first feature film from independent Algeria. Marcello Gatti the cameraman virtually ran a training-school after each day's shooting, so that by the end of the film Algeria had a number of highly trained film technicians.

This central involvement of the Algerians in the production brings a vital authenticity to the historical events. The opposing forces are the French army, disciplined, trained and compact; and the FLN, disorganized and amateur in its fighting. The FLN argue that a terrorist campaign is needed to defeat the French, and thus organize themselves in a pyramidic structure. Each person knows only the contact that recruited him and the two or three people he has recruited. For them, the test of heroism is not the ability to inflict violence on others, but to

THE REVOLT THAT STIRRED THE WORLD!

Directed by Gillo Pontecorvo, 1966
Prod co: Casbah Films (Algiers)/Igor Films (Rome). **prod:** Antonio Musu Yacef Saadi. **prod man:** Sergio Merolle, Noureddine Branimi. **2nd unit dir** Giuliano Montaldo. **sc:** Franco Solinas, from a story by Franco Solinas and Gillo Pontecorvo. **photo:** Marcello Gatti. **ed:** Mario Serandrei, Mario Morra **art dir:** Sergio Canevari. **mus:** Ennio Morricone, Gillo Pontecorvo. **ass dir** Fernando Morandi. **r/t:** 135 minutes. Italian title: *La Battaglia di Algeri*. **Cast:** Jean Martin (*Colonel Mathieu*), Yacef Saadi (*Saari Kader*), Brahim Haggiag (*Ali La Pointe*), Tommaso Neri (*Captain Dubois*), Fawzia El Kade (*Hahmal*), Michèle Kerbash (*Fathia*), Mohamed Ben Kassen (*Little Omar*)

withstand torture for as long as possible to save other lives and protect the network. Torture becomes the central strategy in the French campaign, since their prime need is to obtain information quickly to trace the network before it can be disbanded. The ambivalent attitude of the French forces is examined sympathetically in this film. Colonel Mathieu reluctantly recognizes that his only choice is to condone torture or accept defeat: 'Why are the Sartres always on the other side?' he wistfully asks.

Pontecorvo makes no moral judgment in the film, he portrays only the

necessary violence of the struggle while showing his wholehearted support for independence for the Algerian people. Violence, after all, was integral to both sides in the bloody struggle. The outcome is so powerful an indictment of the French occupation that it had to be withdrawn from Paris cinemas following threats of violence from right-wing organizations. Pontecorvo's declared aim was to make a film that came as close to the truth as possible, and in this with the help of the Algerian people – he has undoubtedly succeeded.

SALLY HIBBIN

4

5

October 7, 1957. Ali La Pointe, a leader of the Algerian Liberation Army (FLN), is trapped in his house with three of his followers by Colonel Mathieu and his French paratroopers (1). He reminisces over the past three years.

1954. Ali La Pointe, a petty street criminal (2), is released from prison. After passing a test of loyalty to the FLN – shooting a policeman with a gun that he later discovers was not loaded – he is co-opted into the leadership.

November 1, 1954. The FLN begin to clear the town-centre's fortress-like Casbah of vice and crime. La Pointe kills a brothel-keeper; others methodically rid the area of prostitutes, drug-addicts, smugglers, spies and international outlaws. The Casbah becomes the fortified centre of resistance to the French.

November 2, 1954. European extremists, including prominent police officers, counter-attack by blowing-up sections of the Casbah (3). The FLN retaliate with a terrorist campaign of bombings in public places (4). Three Algerian women – disguised as French – smuggle bombs out of the Casbah in their baskets (5).

January 10, 1957. The French government sends in paratroopers, who receive a huge welcome from the European population (6). Colonel Mathieu swoops to make arrests and uses torture to extract confessions and information. A week's general strike is declared by the FLN to draw international attention to their struggle. Mathieu moves his men into the Casbah and escalates the assault. As the trap closes, the key leaders of the resistance are captured and die (7). Only La Pointe is left. Hunted at every turn (8), he tries to rebuild the now broken organization. One of his men is captured, and, under torture, discloses his whereabouts.

October 7, 1957. La Pointe's house, with him inside refusing to surrender (9), is blown-up in front of the crowded inhabitants of the Casbah. The movement has apparently been smashed.

December 1960. The entire Algerian population demonstrate with improvised FLN flags (10). The struggle continues.

July 5, 1962. Algeria achieves independence.

6

7

8

9

10

Pizza (or Pasta) Westerns

A new title for a famous movie menu. And the main ingredients? Clint Eastwood, a phantom of the plains swathed in the folds of his poncho; Lee Van Cleef, a grimacing black hawk – Zorro unmasked; a host of grubby villains with bandoliers over their shoulders; and the vision of director Sergio Leone, his cameras focused relentlessly on an echoing wasteland of blood and sand

The 'spaghetti' Western was never an accurate label. Spaghetti is all very well, a wholesome base for sauces, meats, clams, garlic and butter. But spaghetti is bland and monotonous to the eye, and the movies that bore the name were always startling visual events. The 'pizza' Western would have been closer, if you can imagine the lurid sunrise of bubbling cheese, the terracotta menace of pepperoni and the inevitable blood-bath of tomato paste. Pizzas are a sight to behold – if only they made them in CinemaScope shapes, they would be the perfect culinary equivalent for Sergio Leone's hallucinatory films. Except that most of them were actually shot in Spain. Perhaps the example really needed is paella – a desert background of saffron with the violent splashes of pimento, shrimp and chorizo.

These *are* edible films; they have so much ham in them. They are filled with stylized violence and cruelty; they are as serpentine with intrigue as they are loyal to the idea of destiny as the far, flat horizon. They know no other human impulses than greed, treachery, silent honour and the unswerving imperative of revenge, but they cannot be taken seriously. The Westerns made by Sergio Leone and Clint Eastwood are deliberate parodies, or fakes. They mark the end of the trustworthiness of the genre and the onset of a new riot of campness. It is as if the Western, and the American history it seems to represent, had been handed over to a director of television commercials for cheroots, serapes and hard liquor. The significance of the 'spaghetti' West-

ern is not just that non-Americans took over the genre, but that American audiences could no longer believe in their own greatest legend.

Early appetizers

There were uncompromising Westerns made in America in the Fifties, pictures that believed in the frontier, in the sheriff's essential role and in the epic dimension of heroism and landscape. *High Noon* (1952), *Shane* (1953) and the films of Anthony Mann are filled with genuine respect for physical space, small communities and a man's moral decision. But by the end of the decade, the Western was less convinced and far less solemn. Howard Hawks' *Rio Bravo* (1959) is a self-conscious reappraisal of the situation in *High Noon*, but it is also a game in which actors in cowboy hats and Western settings exchange the lines of a modern comedy. For Hawks, both *Red River* (1948) and *The Big Sky* (1952) had believed in the nineteenth century, in real space and problems to be overcome. *Rio Bravo* is a largely interior film in which the archetypal figures of John Wayne and Walter Brennan meet the unmistakably up-to-date Dean Martin, Ricky Nelson and Angie Dickinson. There are moments when the old situations are played straight, but *Rio Bravo*'s inner elegance and wit come from the sense of a stale ritual being jazzed up for 1959. Around the same time, old-timers like George Marshall and Raoul Walsh directed deflating comic Westerns, *The Sheepman* and *The Sheriff of Fractured Jaw* (both 1958). Newcomer Arthur Penn took the Billy the Kid saga, in *The*

Left-Handed Gun (1958), and gave it levels of psychological insight that would have terrified Robert Taylor, who played the outlaw in the 1941 version of *Billy the Kid*.

This is all relevant to the 'spaghetti' Western, for the parody could not occur before the myth of the West had been questioned. By 1960, with John F. Kennedy's manner suggesting the ultimate sheriff could be more like Cary Grant than John Wayne, America was suspicious of its own reliance on Western ethics as a basis for foreign policy. The new, ashamed awareness of Native Americans – so recently 'redskins' or 'hostiles' – was prompting a fresh study of frontier history. With *The Man Who Shot Liberty Valance* (1962) and *Cheyenne Autumn* (1964), even John Ford offered a sketchy apology for the wholesale dishonesty with which Hollywood had gilded the West. But on television, night after night, the same

Left: Rod Steiger (as the peasant bandit Juan), Sergio Leone and the crew of A Fistful of Dynamite. *Below: German poster of* For a Few Dollars More, *in which the two bounty hunters run down a drug-addicted killer*

lies were still being perpetrated in series like *Gunsmoke, Wells Fargo, Wagon Train* and *Rawhide*. Perhaps that was the final excess that made the Western seem sour and laid it open for satire.

Clint in the sun

Clint Eastwood was a veteran of *Rawhide*, but less than a star, when he went to Europe in 1964 to make *Per un Pugno di Dollari* (*A Fistful of Dollars*), a German-Spanish-Italian co-production, directed by Sergio Leone and shot in southern Spain. The headquarters of the Italian film industry, Cinecittà, had already tried to copy several American genres. But nothing matched the success of *A Fistful of Dollars*, a

162

Above, from left to right: icons of the 'spaghetti' Western – the good (Clint Eastwood), the bad (Lee Van Cleef), the ugly (Eli Wallach). Left: Claudia Cardinale as chief mourner Jill McBain in Once Upon a Time in the West; *she has arrived in Flagstone to join her husband and family at their ranch, only to find them all brutally slaughtered by a vicious outlaw gang trying to force the sale of their land to the railroad*

rewrite the bad scripts and, since he and Leone had no language in common, Eastwood cut out a lot of his dialogue to avoid directing problems. His character, the Man With No Name, became a beautiful but nearly absurd icon of taciturnity. He was an angel of death, squinting into the sun, given weird grace by the serape, the cheroot and the wide-brimmed hat, and always glorified in Leone's audacious but equally mannered use of TechniScope.

Second and third courses

A Fistful of Dollars was so successful that it launched a trilogy. But whereas the first picture had been 96 minutes long, the others, *Per Qualche Dollari in Più* (1966, *For a Few Dollars More*) and *Il Buono, il Brutto, il Cattivo* (1967, *The Good, the Bad and the Ugly*), were 130 and 161 minutes. Leone slowed the pace, turning tension into a mocking treacle. The music of Ennio Morricone – like a rattlesnake in a drum-kit – added to the tongue-in-cheek menace. There was always a strong supporting cast: Gian Maria Volonté, in the first two; Lee Van Cleef in the last two. Van Cleef had been one of the gunmen in *High Noon*; Eli Wallach, who is in *The Good, the Bad and the Ugly*, had been the bandit chief in *The Magnificent Seven*.

Eastwood was established, and he would become one of the most commercially reliable stars of the Seventies as well as an adventurous director-producer. *Hang 'Em High* (1968), in which he starred soon after his return to America, is a spaghetti dish in the Hollywood style. Indeed it could be argued that the laconic, vengeful and supreme Harry Callahan, the cop Eastwood plays in *Dirty Harry* (1971) and its sequels, is cousin to the Man With No Name. In 1973 Eastwood directed and starred in *High Plains Drifter*, an absurdist Western that must have made Leone proud.

Leone himself made two more notable pictures. *C'Era una Volta il West* (1968, *Once Upon a Time in the West*) is his best film – his most extreme, formal and ridiculous arrangement of Western imagery, a feast of colour, space and Jacobean ritual. There is no Eastwood in it, but the film has Henry Fonda as a deliciously

phenomenon that seems to spring from the sardonic visual imagination of Leone and the hitherto unappreciated smouldering glamour in Eastwood's screen presence.

The film was a rip-off from the Akira Kurosawa film, *Yojimbo* (1961). But that was reasonable, for Kurosawa had often owned up to the way his seemingly authentic samurai films had been inspired by Westerns. Truly, the Western had become a kind of Esperanto; no wonder no-one trusted it. In 1960 John Sturges had made *The Magnificent Seven* as a tribute to Kurosawa's *Shichinin No Samurai* (1954, *Seven Samurai*). The spectacular violence of that 'remake' and its Mexican settings influenced the films of Sam Peckinpah as well as the Italian Westerns. The seven, though, had been noblemen ready to die for their cause; Leone's invention was to make sleaziness and dishonesty the new norms. His pictures are full of unwashed, unshaved bandidos, the refugees from horror pictures. You know that they can't be trusted because their lip movements never fit what they are saying.

There was reason enough for Eastwood to say nothing. The actor was encouraged to

Above, left to right: 'vicious' Gian Maria Volonte, 'demonic' Henry Fonda – and the bounty. Right: the fathomless Man With No Name who cleans up a Mexican town in A Fistful of Dollars. *Eastwood – 'Italian actors come from the* Hellzapoppin' *school of drama. To get my effect I stayed impassive, and I guess they thought I wasn't acting. All except Leone, who knew what I was doing.' Below: Colonel Mortimer (Van Cleef) lights a match on the hunchback (Klaus Kinski) in* For a Few Dollars More; *he wants to find out whether the gang is concocting a plot more important to them than avenging insults*

wicked lead, along with Jason Robards Jr, Charles Bronson, Jack Elam, Woody Strode, Keenan Wynn and Claudia Cardinale, who has to take the leering abuse that is obligatory for voluptuous women in these films. *Giú la Testa* (1972, *A Fistful of Dynamite*) is remarkable for two ham-size performances: Rod Steiger as a Mexican outlaw; James Coburn as an IRA revolutionary.

The 'spaghetti' Western is not common now. Leone's films are few and far between, and Eastwood has moved further towards comedy. But its influence is total. There are so few Westerns made today because the genre has been revealed as not a true fable of rock, lead and dust, but a fabrication of pasta.

DAVID THOMSON

THE VIOLENT YEARS

Pain, fear, blood, violence, death – entertainment for the Sixties on
screens that reflected the real world but added to it a dash of style

From *Psycho* and *Spartacus* (both 1960) to *The Wild Bunch* and *Easy Rider* (both 1969), the Sixties might be regarded as the period when screen violence gained a new aesthetic self-consciousness and something approaching academic respectability, at least in the public mind. To put it somewhat differently, the contemporary spectator of 1960, shocked by the brutal shower murder of Marion Crane (Janet Leigh) in *Psycho* as an event – without observing that it was a composite film effect created by several dozen rapidly cut shots – would have been much likelier to notice, in 1969, the use of slow motion in the depiction of several dozen violent deaths in *The Wild Bunch*.

The key film document of the decade, endlessly scrutinized and discussed, was not an entertainment feature at all, but the record of an amateur film-maker named Abe Zapruder of the assassination of John F. Kennedy in Dallas on November 22, 1963; the close analysis to which this short length of film was subjected was characteristic of a changing attitude towards the medium as a whole.

In the Sixties many established cultural, social and political values were radically thrown into question, at the same time that the media – including television and pop music as well as cinema – were becoming closely examined in their own right. (The late Marshall McLuhan's book *Understanding Media*, published in 1964, was widely regarded as a seminal text.) These two phenomena converged to create a different conception of what violence was, both as a method and as a subject.

Alfred Hitchcock, who always kept a close eye on fashion, might be considered as one barometer of that change. In *Psycho* and *The Birds* (1963) he approached the intricate problem of how to create the impression of violence in the spectator through technique and technology, from fast editing to detailed special effects. Yet by the time he made *Torn Curtain* (1966), a spy thriller, he was implicitly criticizing the technological fantasy engendered by such James Bond films as *Dr No* (1962), *From Russia With Love* (1963) and *Goldfinger* (1964), whereby a villain could be despatched virtually with the cool flick of a switch or push of a button. Hitchcock made his point by depicting the killing of a heavy as protracted, messy and extremely difficult – not the sort of thing that suave 007 normally had to contend with.

The unusually long-drawn-out deaths in *The Wild Bunch*, on the other hand, were defended by the director Sam Peckinpah as a cathartic strategy: to make violence so repulsive as to turn people against it,' was the way he expressed it in a trade journal. Other film-makers argued, quite simply, that a liberal display of violence was merely what their stories and their subject-matter demanded – most notably, in war films such as Samuel Fuller's *Merrill's Marauders* (1962), Robert Aldrich's *The Dirty Dozen* (1967) and John Wayne's *The Green Berets* (1968), and in such critiques of the genre as Jean-Luc Godard's *Les Carabiniers* (1963, *The Soldiers*) and Peter Watkins' television film *Culloden*

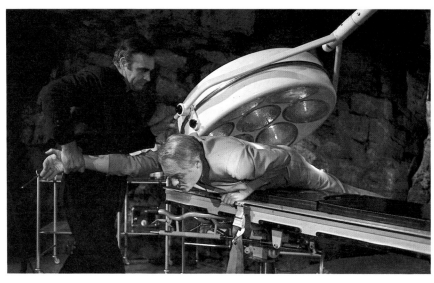

(shown by the BBC in 1964).

'Get up, you scum-sucking pig.' So the gunslinger played by Marlon Brando savagely challenged another tough character in *One Eyed Jacks* (1961). In the same year, gangs of juvenile delinquents fought each other in pitched battles ('rumbles') to the music of Leonard Bernstein in *West Side Story*, and a pool-hall hustler (Paul Newman) had his thumbs deliberately broken by rivals in *The Hustler*. But it would obviously be wrong to assign the Sixties any sort of monopoly in making violence look particularly glamorous, photogenic or graphic.

Yet the Sixties saw the introduction of the 'spaghetti' Western as well as the James Bond thriller; this suggests that the overall sense of violence possessing an aesthetic of its own was an increasingly international phenomenon, in which cultural cross-influences played a decisive part. This was no less true of the comic mishaps of Peter Sellers as Inspector Jacques Clouseau in *The Pink Panther* (1963) and *A Shot in the Dark* (1964) – both Hollywood comedies set on the Continent – and the violent, hallucinatory nightmares of European art

Above: James Bond (Sean Connery) getting the better of master criminal Blofeld (Charles Gray) in Diamonds Are Forever *(1971), Connery's last performance (until he returned as Bond in 1983) in the role that he had made his own in the Sixties. Below: a few of the lads have a friendly scrap in* Performance, *a complex British film combining the gangster genre with a way-out study of a reclusive pop star who has identity problems*

films as diverse as *Le Procès* (1962, *The Trial*), *Repulsion* (1965), *Blow-Up* (1966), *Weekend* (1967) and *Performance* (1970).

All these films highlighted the cross-breeding of American and European elements in a number of ways. 'Spaghetti' Westerns, for instance – spearheaded by a succession of hits starring Americans Clint Eastwood or Charles Bronson and directed by the Italian Sergio Leone, with music by the no less Italian Ennio Morricone – revitalized familiar American myths with Catholic symbolism, operatic intensity and a heavy emphasis on ritual, in films such as *Per un Pugno di Dollari* (1964, *A Fistful of Dollars*), *Per Qualche Dollaro in Più* (1966, *For a Few Dollars More*) and *C'Era una Volta il West* (1968, *Once Upon a Time in the West*). Later, this became intertwined with still other strains to produce even stranger mixtures: for instance, *El Topo* (1971, The Mole) was a gory Mexican surrealist variant of the 'spaghetti' Western with mystical, drug-culture overtones, and an early favourite in the midnight cult circuits.

Any thorough survey of international trends in stylizing violence would have to acknowledge the crucial role played by Japanese cinema – more specifically, by the team of director Akira Kurosawa and actor Toshiro Mifune, mainly in an inspired series of action films ranging from *Shichinin No Samurai* (1954, *Seven Samurai*) and *Kumonosu-Jo* (1957, *Throne Of Blood*) to *Yojimbo* (1961) and *Tsubaki Sanjuro* (1961, *Sanjuro*).

Violence was more sophisticated in some American films, but still remained harsh and controversial

Indeed, several commentators have claimed that the 'spaghetti' Western and all its derivatives can be seen growing directly out of *Yojimbo* – a film with plenty of American antecedents of its own. One American critic, Manny Farber, called it:

'. . . a bowdlerized version of Dashiell Hammett's novel *Red Harvest*, with a bossless vagabond who depopulates a town of rival leaders, outlaws and fake heroes.'

Another critic, Donald Richie, compared the town in the film to:

'. . . those God-forsaken places in the middle of nowhere remembered from the films of Ford, of Sturges, from *Bad Day at Black Rock* or *High Noon*.'

No less striking was the cross-fertilization in *Bonnie and Clyde* (1967) between *nouvelle vague* impulses (such as the mixture of moods and genres), Hollywood showmanship (in Arthur Penn's direction of Warren Beatty and Faye Dunaway) and perhaps just a dash of Kurosawa (in the slow-motion, balletic deaths, two years before *The Wild Bunch*). A grittier, black-and-white version of gangster lovers on the run followed in *The Honeymoon Killers* (1969) – interestingly enough, a favourite film of François Truffaut's – where the poetry had a more romantic tinge. Just prior to this, Truffaut had been paying his own homages to American-style violence in *Fahrenheit 451* (1966), his futuristic study of book-burning, and *La Mariée Etait en Noir* (1968, *The Bride Wore Black*), the tale of a widow's revenge on her husband's killers. And if the latter film smacked of Hitchcock even down to its emotive Bernard Herrmann score, English director John Boorman's exciting American thriller *Point Blank* (1967) drew upon the time-fragmented structures of *nouvelle vague* directors, particularly Alain Resnais. Here could also be detected a satirical offshoot of the equation of people with objects already noted in the Bond films; a violent gangster, played by Lee Marvin, in three separate scenes destructively attacks a car, a telephone and an empty bed.

A few real-life robberies of the period seemed to have been modelled closely after those in *Bonnie and Clyde*, once again raising the question of how seriously screen violence could affect public behaviour. To what degree should it be considered merely a reflection of already existing violence, as opposed to offering the spectator fresh inspirations and incentives? Recent studies of mass responses to violence, most of which have concentrated on television, have suggested that a great deal depends

TOO HOT...TOO BIG...FOR TV!

THE MANHUNT THEY HAD TO PUT ON
THE GIANT-SIZED MOVIE THEATRE SCREEN!

THE LINEUP

starring **ELI WALLACH**

(the sensation of "Baby Doll" as the killer!)

First full-length,
life-dimensioned
adventure of
"THE LINEUP"

ROBERT KEITH · WARNER ANDERSON as LT. GUTHRIE

*bove far left: Ray Fernandez
(Tony Lo Bianco), an ageing
gigolo, and Martha Beck (Shirley
Stoler), a murderous nurse, in
The Honeymoon Killers, based
on a real-life couple executed in
1951. Above: Tony Curtis as The
Boston Strangler and one of his
victims. Above right: Eli Wallach
plays a ruthless psychopathic
killer in The Lineup, a spin-off
from a TV police series set in San
Francisco; the story concerns drug
smuggling. Right: Walker (Lee
Marvin) is aided by his sister-in-
law Chris (Angie Dickinson) in
recovering some money owed to
him in Point Blank. Below:
Charlie (Lee Marvin) and Lee (Clu
Gulager) are The Killers on a
mission of death in an institution
for the blind; but their curiosity
about their victim leads in turn to
their own deaths. Far left: Perry
Smith (Robert Blake) killed a
family of four In Cold Blood and
was hanged five years later. Left:
George Segal in a production shot
from The St Valentine's Day
Massacre (1967)*

on how the audience's identification is solicited, and what sort of characters have been established as role models. In the Sixties, the general use of the gangster as identification figure gave way to a similar use of the law enforcer. The critic Robert Warshow had said in 1954:

'The two most successful creations of American movies are the gangster and the Westerner: men with guns.'

From this standpoint, there may be relatively little difference between film-maker and novelist Norman Mailer's playing successively a gangster in *Wild 90* and a policeman in *Beyond the Law* (both 1968), his first two independent features.

In fact, a closer look at the cinema's overall shift of attention away from the criminal's viewpoint may reveal a subtle subterranean continuity. The wolf in sheep's clothing can be no less bloodthirsty than the wolf without disguise, but his new social role and costume might be enough to exonerate him in part from guilt and society's censure. Thus, in 1963, Underground film-maker Kenneth Anger could explore the homo-erotic potential of Hell's Angels bikers putting on their gear in *Scorpio Rising* – a sort of striptease in reverse involving chain and leather fetishes. And precisely ten years later, a fledgling director, James William Guercio, could create a comparably worshipful context while presenting the detailed dressing-up of his own hero, a likeable highway cop (Robert Blake), in *Electra Glide in Blue* (1973).

In a recent study of crime movies, film historian Carlos Clarens has noted that action director Don Siegel shifted his own focus in mid-career from the mad criminal in *Baby Face Nelson* (1957), *The Lineup* (1958) and *The Killers* (1964) to the policeman in *Madigan, Coogan's Bluff* (both 1968) and *Dirty Harry* (1971). Hollywood's reluctance (with a very few exceptions, such as *The Green Berets*) to deal directly with the war in Vietnam during this period created its own forms of displacement, whereby the emotional weight of the Vietnam experience became transferred to domestic law-and-order thrillers like *Madigan* or *Bullitt* (1968), which 'brought home' the war only in the most oblique terms.

Meanwhile, as the political mood of the Sixties became increasingly polarized, violence often came to represent either society's aggression against the young or youth's own reprisals, in such hits as *Wild in the Streets, If. . . .* (both 1968), *Easy Rider* (1969) and *Joe* (1970). At the same time, the legacy of an equally violent past was being unearthed in certain period films – the marathon dances in *They Shoot Horses, Don't They?*, the oppression of the Paiute Indians in *Tell Them Willie Boy Is Here* (both 1969).

Confronted by a more recent past of senseless mass murders, *In Cold Blood, Targets* (both 1967) and *The Boston Strangler* (1968) all tried to deal with the missing motivations. *In Cold Blood*, adapted by Richard Brooks from Truman Capote's non-fiction account of the arbitrary murder of a family in Kansas by two disaffected loners, added heavy doses of Freudian flashback to the original material, while *The Boston Strangler* focused in a quasi-documentary manner on police procedure, using a striking multi-image technique. *Targets* depicted a character based on the real-life University of Texas sniper and counterpointed his case with the story of an ageing horror-film star (Boris Karloff), making little attempt to explain the sniper's motives beyond implied criticism of the gun laws and of the boredom of American family life. Dryly pursuing this two-part invention about contemporary horror, the director Peter Bogdanovich followed the lead of Truffaut by turning to Hitchcock for much of his inspiration, as would other disciples in the violent Seventies.   JONATHAN ROSENBAUM

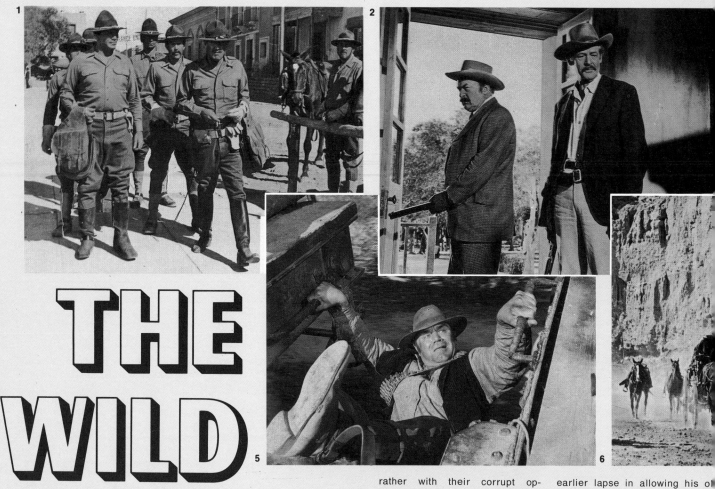

THE WILD BUNCH

The Wild Bunch is bracketed by two extraordinary set-pieces of chaotically lethal action. The film begins with the frantic shoot-up – slaughtering sundry innocent bystanders – that ensues from the Bishop gang's aborted raid on the Starbuck bank; and ends with the orgiastic ritual of destruction in which – hugely outnumbered – the gang's ultimate survivors go down fighting as they manage to take a horde of Mapache's troops to perdition with them. Never before had carnage been so graphically or operatically wrought upon the screen.

It is probably these that are the sequences which pin down the film in the popular memory. For all that its protagonists – ageing gunfighters stranded by the rising tide of modern life – are men out of their time, Peckinpah's movie coincided spectacularly (in all senses) with a given moment in film history. Although Arthur Penn's Bonnie and Clyde (1967) two years earlier had pointed the way to a treatment of death and injury both franker and more elaborate than had previously been deemed acceptable, it was

The Wild Bunch that fully embraced this development. 'I wanted to show,' said Peckinpah, 'what the hell it feels like to get shot.'

In some of Peckinpah's subsequent films his preoccupation with savagery may become sterile or even absurd, and the slow-motion effects which – following Penn's example – he put to such striking use in The Wild Bunch would later, in his own and other hands, become a cliché. But here the explicitness of the scenes of carnage completely unites with the implications of the material: the members of the Wild Bunch can only achieve a kind of meaning for themselves in obliteration by violent death.

At one level, of course, the movie offers a repudiation of the chivalric trappings of the Western genre: Peckinpah extends the conventions of the anti-Westerns of a decade earlier, such as Delmer Daves' Cowboy (1958). Unlike the hired guns of The Magnificent Seven (1960), Bishop and his followers do not sign up on the side of the oppressed Mexican peasantry, but

rather with their corrupt oppressors. Indeed, the desperadoes who comprise the Bunch, ready to shoot down perfunctorily one of their own wounded when he is unable to keep up with them, would surely in an earlier vintage have been treated as antagonists rather than the 'heroes'.

Finally, though, and not simply through the force of Lucien Ballard's magisterial wide-screen images of horsemen traversing daunting landscapes and engaging in exploits of derring-do (such as the dynamite nonchalantly touched-off with a lighted cigar in the train robbery), the vision which the film asserts is a romantic one. The plot crucially turns on the mutual dependence of Bishop and Thornton (played with marvellously haggard strength by Robert Ryan), and the former clearly accepts that Thornton's dilemma in becoming the 'Judas goat' of the railroad bosses stems from Bishop's own

earlier lapse in allowing his o[l] comrade to be captured.

There is, too, an almost luxuria[nt] romanticism about the Mexican vi[l] lagers' ceremonial farewell [to] Bishop and his men, a sequenc[e] which is repeated by Peckinpah a[t] the film's very end. And eventual[ly] – though too late – the Bunch them[-] selves set aside their façade o[f] cynical pragmatism in abandonin[g] Angel to his fate, and commit them[-] selves to an heroically suicidal ges[-] ture on his behalf: 'This time,['] declares Pike Bishop, 'let's d[o] it right'.

The Wild Bunch is not withou[t] flaws: there is too apparent a re[-] course to literary metaphor in th[e] deployment of children for ironi[c] effect, and in such details as th[e] vultures which symbolize the de[-] generate bounty hunters. But th[e] defects fade to unimportance withi[n] the grandeur of the overall design[.] This is a movie of true size.

TIM PULLEIN[E]

Directed by Sam Peckinpah, 1969
Prod co: Warner Brothers/Seven Arts. **prod:** Phil Feldman. **assoc. prod**[:] Roy N. Sickner. **prod man:** William Faralla. **2nd unit dir:** Buzz Henry. **sc**[:] Walon Green, Sam Peckinpah, from a story by Walon Green, Roy N[.] Sickner. **photo** (Technicolor, Panavision 70): Lucien Ballard. **ed:** Loui[s] Lombardo. **art dir:** Edward Carrere. **mus:** Jerry Fielding. **sd:** Robert J. Mille[r.] **ass dir:** Cliff Coleman, Fred Gamon. **r/t:** 145 minutes.
Cast: William Holden (Pike Bishop), Ernest Borgnine (Dutch), Robert Rya[n] (Deke Thornton), Edmond O'Brien (Sykes), Warren Oates (Lyle Gorch[),] Jaime Sanchez (Angel), Ben Johnson (Hector Gorch), Emilio Fernande[z] (Mapache), Strother Martin (Coffer), L. Q. Jones (T. C.), Albert Dekke[r] (Harrigan), Bo Hopkins (Crazy Lee), Bud Taylor (Wainscoat), Jorge Russe[k] (Zamorra), Alfonso Arau (Herrera), Chano Urueta (Don José), Soni[a] Amelio (Teresa), Aurora Clavel (Aurora), Elsa Cardenas (Elsa).

The place is Texas, the year 1914. Disguised as soldiers, the Wild Bunch – an outlaw gang led by Pike Bishop and his sidekick Dutch – ride into Starbuck to rob the bank of a railroad payroll (1). But an ambush has been prepared by the rail bosses, who have had Pike's former comrade Deke Thornton released from a prison sentence to lead a band of bounty hunters against the Bunch (2).

The ambush goes wrong, and in a hail of crossfire many of the townspeople are killed. Most of the gang escape, and after picking up their veteran comrade Sykes, deemed too old for action, they head into Mexico. There they encounter the villainous warlord 'General' Mapache (3), who hires them to steal guns from an American army munitions train. When Angel, a patriotic Mexican who rides with the Bunch, finds his girl is living with Mapache, a bloodbath is narrowly averted (4). After resting-up at Angel's home village, the gang goes ahead with the train robbery (5).

Bishop realizes that Thornton will be onto the scheme, but succeeds in outwitting him. Once the train has been held up, Mapache attempts to double-cross the Bunch in a canyon (6), but he is forestalled and has to pay up. However, Mapache finds out that Angel has given some of the stolen guns to Mexican revolutionaries, and takes him prisoner (7).

Initially, the Bunch abandon Angel to his fate, but after seeing him tortured by Mapache, Pike, Dutch and the Gorch brothers (Sykes is left behind as look-out) enter Mapache's camp and demand Angel's release. In reply Mapache slits Angel's throat (8); Pike shoots Mapache dead (9), precipitating a bloody pitched battle between the Bunch and Mapache's troops, ending with no survivors (10). Later, Sykes appears on the scene with a group of revolutionaries; Thornton also arrives and decides to join them.

Clyde was the leader, Bonnie wrote poetry.

C.W. was a Myrna Loy fan who had a bluebird tattooed on his chest. Buck told corny jokes and carried a Kodak. Blanche was a preacher's daughter who kept her fingers in her ears during the gunfights. They played checkers and photographed each other incessantly. On Sunday nights they listened to Eddie Cantor on the radio. All in all, they killed 18 people.

They were the strangest damned gang you ever heard of.

WARREN BEATTY
FAYE DUNAWAY
BONNIE
and CLYDE

MICHAEL J. POLLARD · GENE HACKMAN · ESTELLE PARSONS   DAVID NEWMAN and ROBERT BENTON · Charles Strouse · WARREN BEATTY · ARTHUR PENN   TECHNICOLOR® A WARNER BROS.–SEVEN ARTS RELEASE

4

The original script of *Bonnie and Clyde* passed through divers hands before the finished film opened in America to critical indignation and audience acclaim. David Newman and Robert Benton first submitted their script to Jean-Luc Godard and then François Truffaut, both of whom suggested improvements before turning it down. Then Warren Beatty bought the property and persuaded Warner Brothers (the studio responsible for the great gangster movies of the Thirties) to finance it with Beatty as star and producer and Arthur Penn as director. Robert Towne, who later wrote *Chinatown* (1974) and Beatty's *Shampoo* (1975), polished the final draft without taking screen credit. The result was one of the most popular and influential films ever made in America.

It is intriguing to speculate what Godard and Truffaut might have made of such an essentially American subject. There are echoes of *Bande à Part* (1964, *The Outsiders*) and *Pierrot le Fou* (1965, Pierrot the Fool) in Penn's approach to genre and his abrupt changes of mood but the connection with the French *nouvelle vague* is more general than specific: like the early films of the *nouvelle vague*, *Bonnie and Clyde* liberated a national cinema from aesthetic stagnation and, in so doing, captured the imagination of American youth who regarded the values of Hollywood as anachronistic and its genres as moribund. Not since Nicholas Ray's *Rebel Without a Cause* (1955) had young Americans seen their frustrations articulated quite so forcefully on the screen.

The film's vivid account of social banditry paralleled the growing counter-culture and Vietnam protest movement and was developed in many subsequent films – *Alice's Restaurant*, *Easy Rider*, *Butch Cassidy and the Sundance Kid* (all 1969), *Bad Company* (1971), *Badlands* (1973). The commercial success of *Bonnie and Clyde* was merchandized in the form of nostalgia for Thirties music and fashion and inevitably led to a rash of gangster movies. The film's graphic violence ricocheted into the Seventies and Eighties.

If the film's style was refreshingly contemporary, the subject was far from new. *Persons in Hiding* (1939) and *The Bonnie Parker Story* (1958) attempted to portray the squalid facts of the case whilst *You Only Live Once* (1937), *They Live By Night* (1948) and *Gun Crazy* (1949) were adapted from the same source material. In fact, Bonnie Parker and Clyde Barrow scarcely rated more than a footnote in the history books and their robberies, punctuated by a dozen murders, were little more than petty thefts. Clyde was thought to have been homosexual and Bonnie's husband was a gang member but their legend grew as romantic fugitives from their instinct for publicity. Bonnie's doggerel verse and their snapshots were published in newspapers and earned them the status of folk-heroes to the destitute farmers of the southern states.

The real Bonnie and Clyde would have loved Penn's film because it is their pathetic image of themselves that is evoked so arrestingly. It is essentially a film about those most fundamental American impulses – celebrity and material and sexual success. The film's heroes are located within the mythology of cinema: Bonnie sees Ginger Rogers sing 'We're in the Money' from *Gold-Diggers of 1933* (1933); Clyde consciously models himself on Al Capone; the farmers they meet on the road resemble the Joads in *The Grapes of Wrath* (1940). Indeed, the Barrow gang move across the derelict landscape like movie stars, travelling players in a script which contrives for them a vanglorious death and posthumous fame.

Snapshots of the real gang – grainy and unglamorous – are behind the credits which fade to blood red. From here Penn cuts to the glamorous features of Beatty and Faye Dunaway. The other gang members are photographed throughout in unflattering light (and Buck and Blanche are later facially disfigured) but Bonnie and Clyde are always beautiful. This romantic idealism of them is ambiguous – the film remains sufficiently detached for the audience to identify with them and the visceral pleasure derived from their exploits. Their naivety and conceit is disarming and the film's jauntiness is both amusing and seductive. But gradually the viewer's pleasure is undercut by sudden irruptions of appalling violence – a Keystone Cops getaway turns sour when a bank clerk has his face blown off. The film becomes preoccupied with death, foretold by Bonnie's poem which releases Clyde's sexuality and hastens his end. The slow-motion massacre turns the heroes into frenzied corpses. The ugly and humourless Texas Ranger, Hamer, lowers his smoking carbine and stares directly into camera, in silent admonishment of our own impulses.

ADRIAN TURNER

7

Bonnie Parker is easily attracted by Clyde Barrow's reckless charm and when he nonchalantly robs a store she joins him (1) for a life of crime. After one of their hold-ups they invite C. W. Moss, a car mechanic, to join them (2). The gang is completed by Buck, Clyde's ex-con brother, and his excitable wife, Blanche (3): they continue to rob banks.

The gang's exploits endear them to victims of the Depression but they narrowly avoid capture when the police surround their rented house (4, 5). Now wanted for murder, they are chased from state to state, notably by Sheriff Hamer who is humiliated when the trap he sets for them rebounds on himself.

2

3

6

5

8

9

10

Bonnie, though, senses the end is near and she visits her mother at a desolate rendezvous (6). Later the gang is ambushed (7), Buck is killed and Blanche, blinded, is taken prisoner. The others escape (8). C. W. takes Bonnie and Clyde to his father's house where they nurse their wounds (9). During this brief period of peace Bonnie has a poem published in a newspaper, and Clyde overcomes his impotence with Bonnie in a corn field.

Concerned for his son's safety, Mr Moss makes a deal with Hamer, and while driving in a quiet country lane (10 – production shot) Bonnie and Clyde die in a hail of bullets.

Directed by Arthur Penn, 1967
Prod co: Tatira/Hiller/Warner Bros. **prod:** Warren Beatty. **sc:** David Newman, Robert Benton. **photo** (Technicolor): Burnett Guffey. **ed:** Dede Allen. **art dir:** Dean Tavoularis, Raymond Paul. **mus:** Charles Strouse. **cost:** Theadora Van Runkle. **sd:** Francis E. Stahl. **r/t:** 111 minutes.
Cast: Warren Beatty (*Clyde Barrow*), Faye Dunaway (*Bonnie Parker*), Michael J. Pollard (*C. W. Moss*), Gene Hackman (*Buck Barrow*), Estelle Parsons (*Blanche*), Denver Pyle (*Frank Hamer*), Dub Taylor (*Ivan Moss*), Evans Evans (*Velma Davis*), Gene Wilder (*Eugene Grizzard*).

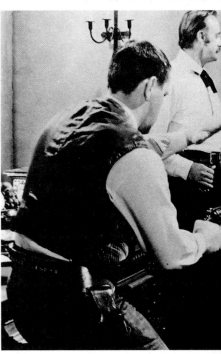

Penn Moves

The climax of Arthur Penn's *Bonnie and Clyde* is exactly that – a blood-wet explosion in which the bodies of the hero and heroine bounce and shudder in a blitz of police bullets. In the cinema, death and orgasm – perhaps the ultimate means of escape – had never before been so powerfully equated. Penn's films convulse and compel with such scenes, beautifully but never gratuitously violent, quick, alive and tactile. Their physical immediacy has made the director one of the most important and influential of modern film-makers

The same violence that played such an important part in the commercial success of *Bonnie and Clyde* (1967) is a central feature of the work of Arthur Penn, just as it is for a fellow director, Sam Peckinpah. But whereas Peckinpah – inspired by lost causes – adopts an ironic and nihilistic stance close to that of John Huston, Penn is ostensibly interested in the psychological roots of violence and in its repercussions on society. He radically polarizes *two* kinds of violence, maintaining a constant distinction between 'individual' violence – linked to the total development of a personality – and 'institutional' violence, the outcome of repressive social forces. In this way his films compare an overt violence, liberating and related to some sort of game, with a coercive, bottled-up violence whose object is merely the upholding of established law and order.

Billy the mixed-up Kid
This opposition was established by Penn at the very beginning of his career as a director with *The Left-Handed Gun* (1958), in which he re-examined the Billy the Kid myth but without seeking to justify, embellish or romanticize the character as had often been done in the past. Billy (Paul Newman) became a basically *modern* hero, close to those disturbed heroes embodied by James Dean, an impulsive man in search of an identity, who has not yet been defined on either a social or sexual level. He is a 'plastic' character, rich in potential but unmoulded, who makes his own random way through life. At first he seems perfectly innocent, despite his dangerous reputation. But he very quickly familiarizes himself with high-handedness, hypocrisy and murderous violence, and when his chosen father is killed he swears to exact revenge. Billy's own recourse is to play out the criminal role assigned to him by society, and acts of violence follow relentlessly, one after another.

Like all of Penn's early heroes, Billy remains a sort of a child. He disregards the subtleties of the law, only acknowledges his own pleasure and only feels comfortable with his two accomplices, retarded kids with whom he

Above left: Arthur Penn directing a sequence for the Olympic documentary Visions of Eight *(1973). He was born in Philadelphia in 1922. He seemed set to become a watch-maker, but during military service pursued his interest in the stage with Joshua Logan's theatre group and later attended the Universities of Perugia and Florence. In the Fifties he directed TV and on Broadway, and he has often returned to the stage between film projects*

indulges his taste for rowdy pranks. Driven on by a boundless energy, he expands it all in playing at murder as though it were just another game, no more reprehensible than hide-and-seek.

Through this character, Penn extols a way of life entirely determined by instinct and impulse. Billy is driven by a force that is out of his grasp; he tries to absorb it completely, instantaneously and without restraint. But this momentum runs head-on into a society committed to the denial and the taming of vital forces, a society that ultimately dominates.

ove: Billy the Kid (Paul Newman) doing
at he does best in The Left-Handed Gun;
t Garrett (John Dehner) watches anxiously.
p: the violent business of teaching the blind
see – Patty Duke as Helen Keller and Anne
ncroft as her teacher in The Miracle
orker. Top right: the fugitive as folk-hero –
irren Beatty in Bonnie and Clyde. *Above*
ht: Jack Crabb (Dustin Hoffman) embarks on
· gunfighter period in Little Big Man

aming the flashpoints

his films Penn makes every effort to capture
e strongest moments in the development of a
rsonality. He is more interested in the flashes
physical truths evident in a gesture than in
amatic continuity. He explores beyond his
aracters' actions to reconstitute their un-
nscious selves, to freeze the depth of their
ng that is manifest in some impulsive reflex.
is a cinema built on fragments, discon-
uity, tensions and climaxes in which every
gle move betrays an imprecise, effusive
perience. The characters are set in motion by

secret impulses that sentence them to a life of
fighting against an opaque society with all their
strength. These conflicts are brought to an end
more often than not when the hero meets his
death: Billy forces his sidekick Pat Garrett (John
Dehner) to shoot him down; Bonnie and Clyde
(Warren Beatty and Faye Dunaway) die in an
orgy of blood; the hunt for Bubber Reeves
(Robert Redford) in *The Chase* (1966) ends in an
enormous carnival where the whole town
releases its frustrations.

Violence is the key experience for Penn's
characters, and not only in genres like the
detective story or the Western. *The Miracle
Worker* (1962) provides a particularly en-
lightening example. The young heroine Helen
Keller (Patty Duke) – deaf, dumb and blind – is,
like all Penn's characters, confronted by a
world beyond her grasp. Her meeting with the
teacher Annie Sullivan (Anne Bancroft) is the
starting point for a difficult education, scattered with physical obstacles. Gradually,
through an alternately harsh and tender process of touch, Helen learns to harness her

instincts and to use her body to communicate
with the rest of the world and to understand
that 'everything has a name'. This film – Penn's
most lyrical and emotional – shows how
violence can be positive, allowing someone to
bring life to their existence and to reach full
maturity.

Running parallel to these experiences which
bring into play all their strengths, Penn's
characters also aspire to a form of harmony.
Helen finds it by the end of her education,
when she learns how to pronounce her first
word and rediscovers her childhood memories.
Most of his other heroes, more integrated in
society, find harmony by turning away from
their problems in the company of other exiles
like the gypsies who help Billy in *The Left-
Handed Gun*, or Bonnie's family in *Bonnie and
Clyde*, or the Indians – 'the Human Beings' – in
Little Big Man (1970), who symbolize for Jack
Crabb (Dustin Hoffman) a motherly and pro-
tective culture. With these various outsiders
Penn's protagonists can live out, briefly, the
illusion of a life suspended in the heart of an

173

**Maybe
he would
find the girl...
maybe he would
find himself.**

NiGHT moves x

AN "ARTHUR PENN FILM
A ROBERT M. SHERMAN PRODUCTION
GENE HACKMAN IN "NIGHT MOVES"
AND SUSAN CLARK
PRODUCED BY ROBERT M. SHERMAN WRITTEN BY ALAN SHARP
DIRECTED BY ARTHUR PENN ASSOCIATE PRODUCER GENE LASKO
TECHNICOLOR®
FROM WARNER BROS A WARNER COMMUNICATIONS COMPANY.
RELEASED BY COLUMBIA WARNER DISTRIBUTORS

Above: Night Moves *stars Gene Hackman as a careworn detective searching for a missing teenager. Top: the car-dump climax of* The Chase – *with Jane Fonda as the anguished wife*

enclosed society. The hippies of *Alice's Restaurant* (1969) – taking their inspiration from a pastoral ideal – manage in this way to achieve a new type of community. But the history they thought to escape catches up with them, just as it does Jack Crabb who sees each attempt to escape from the cruelty of the white man's world doomed to failure.

Apocalypse then and now

In an America shaken by the tragedy of Vietnam, Penn sees history as the sum total of a series of blind and bloody acts. Jack Crabb's life is one constant oscillation, more burlesque than tragic, between two cultures, a vain attempt to come to terms with uncontrollable forces. His Indian friends are eventually destroyed in a massacre by the cavalry; similarly, in *Alice's Restaurant*, the blissful Utopia found by Arlo Guthrie and his buddies ends in shreds with their group splitting up. The ideals of the counter-culture have faded away by the end of

the Sixties – only the principle of surviva remains intact. The private detective Harr Moseby (Gene Hackman) in *Night Move* (1975) lives his life inside his own thought: careful not to let himself be trapped or exploitec And in *The Missouri Breaks* (1976) Tom Logar (Jack Nicholson) learns to become a loner afte temporarily sharing the life of a gang of cattl thieves.

In the Seventies, vigilance has become necessity. The characters have bid goodbye t their adolescence for good; as adults the constantly evade the paralyzing structures of society they see to be more than ever founde on power, the worship of profit and the denia of pleasure. Some, like Logan, side with crime others, like 'the regulator' Robert Lee Clayto (Marlon Brando) – a monstrous personality seemingly the last incarnation of Billy the Kid with law and order. In either event the remain exiles. But Clayton must die an Logan's future is left uncertain. It was thus, o a note of doubt, that Penn's itinerary from *Th Left-Handed Gun* to the end of the Seventie came to a halt. The alternative lifestyle of th outlaws dies out; collective living is either prison or a Utopia – but the reckless, ur controllable excess of individual forces rep resented by Clayton ends in death. What wi Penn's heroes do in the Eighties?

The art of Pennmanship

Very receptive to the spirit of his age an sensitive to all the major 'nostalgias' that hav obsessed the century, Arthur Penn and h movies have mapped out an accurate chro nology of modern America: the Depression i *Bonnie and Clyde*; the parental crises of th Fifties in *The Left-Handed Gun*; the urban an; uish and paranoia of the Sixties in *Mickey O* (1965) and *The Chase*; the search for a tolerar and pacifist lifestyle in *Alice's Restaurant*. Th work is a saga of bruised innocence and th illustration of a ceaseless struggle again repressive forces. It relates a nostalgic passio for nomadism and the constant thirst fc freedom, combined with a lucid vision of th obstacles that people face when they try break away.

Through its mix of irony and lyricism, utopianism and anguish, Penn's work is ul mately a remarkable reflection of the moo and contradictions of the Sixties. By a violet and disrespectful return to the classic genre and by a simultaneous overthrowing of the o clichés, Penn reaffirms the essentially d mystificatory nature of his cinema. In the wa he expands the classic, physical representatic of the human body, emphasizes the breaks i mood, burlesques the most dramatic scen and seeks to affirm a certain beauty during convulsion (transforming a massacre into ballet and an ordeal into a love scenaric Arthur Penn can undoubtedly be regarded one of the most disturbingly relevant ar modern contributors to world cinema since th late Fifties.   OLIVIER EYQUE

Filmography
1958 The Left-Handed Gun. '62 The Miracl Worker. '64 The Train (some scenes only) (FR IT-USA). '65 Mickey One (+prod). '66 Th Chase. '67 Bonnie and Clyde. '69 Alice's Restaur ant (+co-sc). '70 Little Big Man. '73 Visions o Eight *ep* The Highest. '75 Night Moves. '76 Th Missouri Breaks. '81 Four Friends (GB: Georgia Friends.

CINEMA AND COUNTER-CINEMA

The counter-cinema is less a movement than an impulse, a rejection of Hollywood conventions concerning story, identification and entertainment as essential elements of film

What happens to the audience in the dark of the cinema? Consider these possible answers:

(a) They pay to be entertained.

(b) They permit themselves to be deluded by escapism.

(c) They absorb the capitalistic ideologies embodied in every entertainment movie.

(d) They follow a story with pleasure.

(e) They imagine that they are the figures in the story.

(f) They are capable of enjoying the illusion without being deceived by it: in other words, they respond both to the magic and to the process of trickery.

For over sixty years, the great bulk of film-going experience was apparently covered by categories (a), (d) and (e). Movies were warm, beguiling baths for the audience to lie and dream in – with this rare privilege: the water did not chill. Then, in the Sixties, the experience was gradually invested with far greater complexity. The reasons for this change were various, but they all had to do with the new realization that a great age of popular film was over. Pictures had a smaller audience, and thus the films made were often more challenging and more self-analytical. Once society emerged from unthinking allegiance to the movies – no matter that it had picked up instead the more pervasive climate of television – so it became more tempting to recognize the structures of film as a language and as an intrinsically persuasive medium. Categories (b), (c) and (f) were talked about. Movies were made, and film students were prompted, to question the constitution of the bath water and the mechanism that ensured its warmth. Suddenly the water went cold; the counter-cinema had begun.

It was always the assumption of the mainstream film industry that (a) was caused by (d), that people went to the movies for the stories. The very description of some of those stories as, say, 'Joan Crawford pictures' suggests the possible importance of (e). It also raises the question as to whether audiences went to see Joan Crawford, the parts she played or the strange interaction between them. Stardom seemed to imply that the significance of individual roles was transcended by the endlessly renewed image of the star. King Lear or Saint Joan are parts that many actors could fill. But even a movie role attempted by several actors – for example the private eye Philip Marlowe – is only a name waiting for a star. Dick Powell's Marlowe in *Murder, My Sweet* (1944), Humphrey Bogart's in *The Big Sleep* (1946) and Elliott Gould's in *The Long Goodbye* (1973) are three distinct parts because of the crucial ingredient of presence. The nature of a film alters according to the appearance in it of particular actors. How different, for instance, *Casablanca* (1942) would have been if George Raft had taken the Humphrey Bogart role of the bar-owner Rick, saying exactly the same lines, making the identical moves.

In other words, story may not be so vital to enjoyment; the atmosphere of appearance and presence is at least as important. *The Big Sleep* seems to be a 'thriller' and a 'mystery', terms that presuppose narrative suspense. But very few viewers could give an accurate and complete synopsis of the story after having seen it. There is an amusing legend about how the film's makers – Bogart, the director Howard Hawks and even Raymond Chandler, who wrote the original novel – could never untangle all the details of the story. Suppose instead that the picture succeeds for some or all of these reasons:

(I) Cinematic grace – elegant composition, tidy cuts, suggestive lighting.

(II) Humour and action – the amount of appealing incident (which is not the same as the progress

Above left: a moment of decision for Vivian (Lauren Bacall) in The Big Sleep – *should she release the captured Philip Marlowe (Humphrey Bogart) and so declare her trust and affection? She helps him. Above: a moment of decision for Patricia (Jean Seberg) in* Breathless – *should she go along with Michel (Jean-Paul Belmondo) on his planned escape to Italy? She betrays him. Perhaps the mirror shot visually implies her future duplicity*

Top: in Godard's Le Petit Soldat *(1960, The Little Soldier), Bruno Forestier (Michel Subor) is blackmailed into an assassination attempt by the right-wing organization to which he half-heartedly belongs. The juxtapositions in the image make a political comment. Top right: in Godard's more recent* Sauve Qui Peut (La Vie) *(1980, Slow Motion), Paul Godard (Jacques Dutronc) attempts to give a lecture on the media to an evening class when the promised speaker, novelist and film-maker Marguerite Duras, has failed to arrive. Above: Anna Karina plays a Humphrey Bogart-like investigator trying to make sense of a totally impenetrable plot in Godard's poetic, political film* Made in USA *(1966)*

of the plot).

(III) The opportunity to identify in the poker-faced romance of the Humphrey Bogart-Lauren Bacall partnership.

(IV) The creation of an atmosphere, including the use of effective incidental music in the darkness – a dark that merges the movie's night-time Los Angeles and any cinema's lack of light.

Critics sympathetic to the counter-cinema catalogued all of those responses – and sometimes confronted the undimmed allure and freshness of *The Big Sleep* as if it were an archaeological discovery from a remote past. To this day, there are many more people ready to be 'entertained' by *The Big Sleep* than there are those intent on its structural analysis. Still, in the Sixties enough critics and scholars of form did emerge, and some of them were film-makers.

Other narrative and representational arts had dispensed with giving the illusion of directly recording the real world early in the twentieth century. Was it coincidence, or did the coming of movies, with their nearly automatic rendering of the real thing, stimulate the emphasis on form and the use of subconscious elements in the work of the painter Pablo Picasso, the Surrealists, the novelists James Joyce and Virginia Woolf, and many more? The development of 'New Waves' in several countries in the early Sixties gave cinema a chance at formal innovation that had occurred previously only in the USSR in the Twenties.

The director Jean-Luc Godard began as someone in love with American movies; he was so knowledgeable about them, so intrigued by their formal properties and so constrained by lack of money that his *A Bout de Souffle* (1960, *Breathless*) was like a home-movie equivalent of a Bogart picture, as well as being a critical analysis of how such films functioned. Godard had been a critic himself, and the new mood depended upon a generation of film students and professors who could not justify their degrees and their jobs with mere 'entertainment'. The counter-cinema has all the strengths and weaknesses of an academic pursuit. Movies had at last come of age, even if film reviewer Pauline Kael estimated that the one thing certain to kill the medium was an academic approach.

There was another major influence: an increasing suspicion of the debilitating but concealed effects of the mass media; and in the Sixties, a scepticism towards America developed that began to wonder if a steady diet of John Wayne and suchlike might not have contributed to the involvement in Vietnam. Thus the entertainment movie was attacked as a lie leading to a loss of contact with reality. It was treated as a breeding ground for racism, sexism, imperialism and that larger life of fantasy which bourgeois capitalism depended on – according to its radical opponents. It followed that some film-makers tried to rid themselves of story-line, stars, glamour and illusion as an act of political faith. Structural analysis revived the interest in film montage as a clash of opposites, as originally perceived by Sergei Eisenstein and Dziga Vertov during the Twenties in the USSR.

Godard went from being the apostle of Hollywood to becoming its scourge. *Pierrot le Fou* (1965, Pierrot the Fool) is his last gesture towards convincing narrative cinema. But it is also a mournful farewell to it, itemizing its clichés and treating one sequence – the escape from the apartment of Marianne (Anna Karina) – as if it were only roughly cut together, still subject to different editing possibilities. *Une Femme Mariée* (1964, *A Married Woman*) had not been a story, but an essay on marriage that used fictional extracts, along with reportage, interviews with the actors and an overall collage-like amalgam of approaches. The audience does not identify with the characters but sees things in terms of the way they are filmed, cut and presented. The viewers become critics, just as Godard confesses to being neither a storyteller nor even a film-maker but someone engaged in making 'an attempt at film'. The focus of this attempt is not fiction or diversion,

Becoming more militantly left-wing, Godard turned against the Hollywood cinema he once loved

but the philosophical notion that: 'Cinema is something that comes between art and life'. It is a way of seeing, and so in the counter-cinema the possible link between seeing and understanding becomes a preoccupation.

It was a cultural revolution, even if it was not always as doctrinaire as Godard after about 1968. His and Jean-Pierre Gorin's *A Letter to Jane, or Investigation About a Still* (1973), a lengthy comment on a single still of Jane Fonda in North Vietnam, is a dismantling of the film actress's naive politics and of the treacherous role of photography. Chris Marker's *La Jetée* (1962, The Pier) – a film of still photographs and, in one shot only, a tremor of moving life – was far cooler; but its narrative point, depending on a moment vividly remembered, cannot be separated from the analysis of imagery. Michelangelo Antonioni's *Blow-Up*, Ingmar Bergman's *Persona* (both 1966) and Luis Buñuel's *Belle de Jour* (1967) are art-house classics, each quite

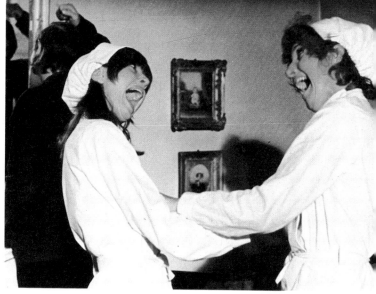

typical of its maker. But they all show an almost Godardian concern with the nature of illusion. Moreover, *Persona* was the subject of one of the novelist and critic Susan Sontag's best articles and surely helped develop the thinking that would later formulate her book *On Photography* – a study of the language and culture of appearance, not overtly political but still very disquieting.

The willingness to challenge old movie conventions was very creative – yet it could please only small audiences. There was now far less gap between the art-house film and experimental or Underground cinema. Andy Warhol, for one, made pictures that played upon the camp attitudes in Hollywood pictures, which replaced stars with derelicts and eccentrics, which used the minimum of style and exaggerated length. Without story, film might go on forever, mimicking time itself. Warhol made eight-hour films about buildings or people asleep. Paul Morrissey's *Trash* (1970) and *Heat* (1972) lampooned Hollywood story situations with Warhol's company of friends, static set-ups and the serene dissolution of pace or tension.

In Germany, Rainer Werner Fassbinder made melodramas – sometimes in honour of Douglas Sirk pictures – that put lurid incident in a deadpan framework. His *Warnung vor einer Heiligen Nutte* (1971, *Beware of a Holy Whore*) – which concerns the making of a film – is like a demented soap opera, frigid in feeling. In Japan, Nagisa Oshima employed a fierce, fragmented structure in *Shinjuku Dorobo Nikki* (1969, *Diary of a Shinjuku Thief*), which concerns a book-stealing student in the Shinjuku district of Tokyo. From Yugoslavia, Dušan Makaveyev produced *WR – Misterije Organizma* (1971,

WR – Mysteries of the Organism), a stunning collection of approaches to the relationship between sexual inhibition and totalitarianism. And in France, Jacques Rivette pursued the subjects of duration and coincidence, all leading to his masterpieces *Out One: Spectre* (1972) and *Céline et Julie Vont en Bateau* (1974, *Céline and Julie Go Boating*), which discover life as an infinite but essentially fictional arrangement.

In the lively mood of the late Sixties and early Seventies, many of these films had great popular success – albeit a fraction of the audience loyal to *The Sound of Music* (1965), *Jaws* (1975) and *Star Wars* (1977). Just as America endured Vietnam and Richard Nixon only to find after all an old-fashioned leader in Ronald Reagan, so Hollywood weathered the counter-cinema and continued to produce conventional, warm-bath movies.

There is one notable exception: Robert Altman – a fitful genius – has sensed another way of seeing, and he has done more than offer a cute mockery of old genres – of the kind that makes George Roy Hill's *Butch Cassidy and the Sundance Kid* (1969) so slick. *McCabe and Mrs Miller* (1971) takes the Western apart, and *The Long Goodbye* despairs of the old Philip Marlowe authority, rendering the hero relatively ineffectual. But the finest piece of American counter-cinema is *Nashville* (1975). Of course, Altman had to compromise: that film ends with the climax of assassination. But for over two hours it is a film about the flow of people and their lives, not the shape of story. *Nashville* reminds the audience of what may be the greatest lesson of the counter-cinema – that viewers like to watch time pass by.

DAVID THOMSON

Above left: Antonio-das-Mortes *(1969,* Antonio of the Dead*) combines melodramatic violence with lyrical interludes; here Colonel Horacio (Joffre Soares) skulks in the shadows while his treacherously promiscuous mistress Laura (Odete Lara) is restrained by his hired gunslingers. Above: in* Céline and Julie Go Boating, *Céline (Juliet Berto) and Julie (Dominique Labourier) enjoy a series of dream-like adventures suggesting the limitless possibilities of the cinema; the punning French title alludes to 'suspending disbelief'. Below: Barbara Jean (Ronee Blakley) is a country-music singer greeted at* Nashville *airport by enthusiastic fans, who include fellow-singer Haven Hamilton (Henry Gibson) and Lady Pearl (Barbara Baxley). Below left: Joe Dallesandro and Jane Forth in* Trash, *a series of apparently random encounters and conversations revolving mainly around drugs and sex, and the possible incompatibility between the two*

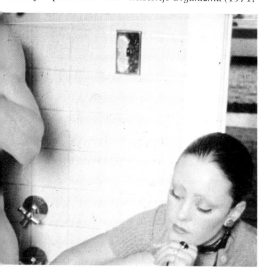

Jean-Luc Godard

Whatever is thought of his films, it cannot be denied that Jean-Luc Godard is the most important director of the last twenty years. This is shown by the enormous influence his films have had on other film-makers all over the world, and although the films of Alain Resnais, François Truffaut, Eric Rohmer or Jacques Rivette may be preferred, no-one has revolutionized cinematic ideas as much as Godard.

He burst onto the international film scene in 1960 with his first feature *A Bout de Souffle*. Unfortunately the English title – *Breathless* – is a mistranslation, for 'a bout de souffle' means 'out of breath', whereas 'breathless' has a more romantic, less despairing tone. But in another sense his film career had begun almost ten years earlier with his film criticism which first appeared in the short-lived *La Gazette du Cinéma*, and later in *Cahiers du Cinéma*. Born in

Is Godard brilliant or are his films impenetrably obscure and boring? Have audiences yet to catch up with his vision as they had to do with the work of cinema's other great innovators Eisenstein and Welles? One thing is certain – no other post-war director has inspired such confusion of admiration and scorn or has had such effect on the making, viewing and understanding of movies

Paris in 1930, Godard was first educated in Switzerland and went on to the Sorbonne to study ethnology. It was during his university days that he discovered his passion for cinema and, like Louis Delluc, his Twenties predecessor, he began his film career by writing about it.

Once upon a time

From the very beginning he considered himself a storyteller rather than an essayist, 'I write essays in the form of novels or novels in the form of essays. Instead of writing criticism, I now film it' he wrote, and it is true that conventional narrative – the backbone of most cinema – has never been the most important element in his films. Godard believes that the distinguishing feature of modern art is that it 'never tells a story'. Of course in his earlier films he felt the need for some sort of fictional support:

'I don't really like telling a story . . . I prefer to use a kind of tapestry, a background on which I can embroider my own ideas. But I do

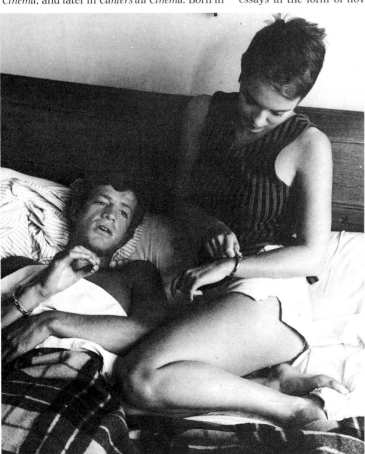

Two or three things we know about him

generally need a story. A conventional one serves as well, perhaps even best.'

As a story, *Breathless* is not much different from any of the American thriller novels he was later to adapt – D. Hitchen's *Fools Gold* for *Bande à Part* (1964, *The Outsiders*), and Lionel White's *Obsession* for *Pierrot le Fou* (1965, *Pierrot the Fool*). Even when he adapted literary works of a higher level – Moravia's *A Ghost at Noon* in *Le Mépris* (1963, *Contempt*) – he always transformed the original material with a massive injection of documentary material.

'You can either start with fiction or with documentary. But whichever you start with, you will inevitably find the other'. Eventually documentary was to gain the upper hand.

It is often said that Godard's career can be split into two – his films before and after 1968. With the advantage of hindsight, however, it

Above: Godard at London's National Film Theatre in 1980. Far left: a car-thief turned killer (Jean-Paul Belmondo) is finally given away to the police by his girlfriend (Jean Seberg) in Breathless. *Left: a young scriptwriter's marriage breaks up when his wife is attracted to the producer. Below: Raoul (Sady Rebbot) with Nana (Anna Karina), the prostitute in* Vivre Sa Vie. *Below right: Karina showing her emotional range as a woman desperate for a baby in* Une Femme Est une Femme *(1961,* A Woman Is a Woman*).*

seems as if the break was less violent than had been thought. His films before *La Chinoise, ou Plutot à la Chinoise* (1967, The Chinese Girl), in which a group of students sets up a Marxist cell during their holidays, were less overtly political than those which followed, and yet *Vivre Sa Vie* (1962, *It's My Life*) was in fact already as much a study of prostitution as the story of its heroine Nana; *Le Petit Soldat* (1960, The Little Soldier) was the first French film to attempt to deal with the Algerian war – and it was banned by the French government until 1963 as a result. Even the more intimate films – *Une Femme Mariée* (1964, *A Married Woman*), or *Contempt* – could be called studies in micro-politics, the politics of the couple, the politics of sex. And a film like *Deux ou Trois Choses Que Je Sais d'Elle* (1967, *Two or Three Things I Know About Her*) was in many ways a sociological essay.

The main difference between Godard and most of his contemporaries was that he was not only interested in the social content of his films, he was even more concerned by the way in which they were made. The nub of Godard's pre-occupation as a film-maker was that he didn't merely put forward political or social ideas, he was after the destruction of those forms that accept the *status quo*. The only way to attack the dominant ideology, according to Godard, was to attack the forms in art that, perhaps unknowingly, proceed from it. It was not sufficient merely to make a political

film, it was even more important to make a film politically.

The art of life

All Godard's films – even *Masculin-Féminin* (1966) which on the surface looks as casually put together as a TV film – reveal a very complex formal substructure under scrutiny. At the same time as being insistent on 'realism' – direct sound, filming on location – Godard was equally concerned in taking these pieces of direct reality and abstracting them. He takes a moment of real life, a moment in time, and transforms it into art through his editing. Most of his films are broken up into sections, tableaux, or chapters, just as individual sequences are often like mosaics, with each shot contributing a tiny tessera that goes to make up the complete picture. Godard is fascinated with the possibility of capturing reality on film, and then (and only then) doing something with it.

But if there was not such a total break between his films of the Sixties and those of the Seventies, it is true that in the Seventies – or even as early as *Un Film Comme les Autres* (1969, A Film Like the Others) – Godard gave up both stories and stars. He deliberately attempted to make unpopular films, and succeeded. As he explained at the time, 'The only way to be an intellectual revolutionary was to give up being an intellectual.' He did not want his films to be liked, he did not want them to be consumer objects, he did not want them to be

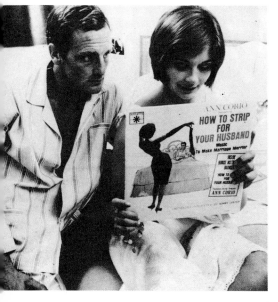

Above: a lesson in lust – Bernard Noël and Macha Méril in Une Femme Mariée. *Above right: despite a basic plot,* Masculin-Féminin *is a study of 'the younger generation'. Above, far right: inspired by a newspaper report, this film charts the day of a housewife whoring for pocket-money. Below: the apartment of the Marxist students in* La Chinoise. *Below right: a couple (Jean Yanne and Mireille Darc) have difficulty removing 'Romeo' (Jean-Pierre Léaud) from the phone-booth in* Weekend

accepted by the middle-classes. He set out to disturb, to frustrate, even to test the patience of his audience. But in so doing he successfully suppressed most of his talents as a film-maker. Although he was not a storyteller, his earlier films allowed his talent for the lyrical full rein; and although he often cast his stars against the grain – eking out extraordinary performances, such as Mireille Darc's in *Weekend* (1967) – they did contribute a great deal to his films.

In his post-1968 period of total ascetism, he

masochistically would not allow himself to do what he could do best. The critic Vincent Canby wrote of *Vladimir et Rosa* (1971) that it looked weak and under-nourished, like someone who has given his salary to The Cause, and must subsist on fish and chips. This is, metaphorically, exactly what Godard had done. If proof be needed, compare *Tout Va Bien* (1972, All Goes Well) with others of the period: there, the presence of Jane Fonda and Yves Montand again allowed him to display his talent for

Filmography

1950 Quadrille (short) (prod; +act. only). **'51** Présentation, ou Charlotte et son Steack (short) (actor only). **'54** Opération Béton (short) (+prod; +sc; +ed) (SWITZ). **'55** Une Femme Coquette (short) (+prod; +sc; +photo; +ed; +act) (SWITZ). **'56** Le Coup du Berger (short) (actor only). **'57** Tous les Garçons s'Appelent Patrick/ Charlotte et Veronique (short) (GB: All Boys Are Called Patrick); Le Sonate à Kreuzer (short) (prod. only). **'58** Charlotte et son Jules (short) (+sc; +ed; +voice); Une Histoire d'Eau (co-dir; +co-sc; +narr). **'59** Le Signe du Lion (actor only) (GB: The Sign of Leo). **'60** Le Petit Soldat (+sc; +act) (released in 1963); A Bout de Souffle (+sc; +act) (USA/GB: Breathless); Paris Nous Appartient (actor only) (USA/GB: Paris Belongs To Us). **'61** Une Femme Est une Femme (+sc; +lyr) (USA/GB: A Woman Is a Woman); Cléo de 5 à 7 (actor only) (FR-IT) (GB: Cleo From 5 to 7); Les Fiancés du Pont Macdonald (short) (actor only). **'62** Les Sept Péchés Capitaux ep La Paresse (+sc) (FR-IT) (USA: The Seven Capital

Sins *ep* Sloth); Le Soleil dans l'Oeil (actor only); Vivre Sa Vie (+sc; +voice) (USA: My Life To Live; GB: It's My Life). **'63** RoGoPaG/Laviamoci Il Cervello *ep* Le Nouveau Monde (+sc; +act) (IT-FR); Les Carabiniers (+co-sc) (FR-IT) (GB: The Soldiers); Shéhérazade (actor only); Le Mépris (+sc; +act) (FR-IT) (USA/GB: Contempt); The Directors (doc. short) (appearance as himself only) (USA); Petit Jour (doc. short) (appearance as himself only). **'64** Bande à Part (+sc; +narr) (USA: Band of Outsiders; GB: The Outsiders); Statues (doc. short) (co-comm; +voice only); Paparazzi (doc. short) (appearance as himself only); Témoinage sur Bardot-Godard (doc. short) (appearance as himself only); Begegnung Mit Fritz Lang (doc. short) (appearance as himself only); Les Plus Belles Escroqueries du Monde *ep* Le Grand Escroc (+sc; +narr; +act) (subsequently cut from film) (FR-IT-JAP-NETH); Une Femme Mariée (+sc) (USA: The Married Woman; GB: A Married Woman); Reportage sur Orly (short). **'65** Paris Vu Par . . . *ep* Montparnasse-Levallois (+sc); Alphaville, une Étrange

Aventure de Lemmy Caution (+sc) (FR-IT); Pierrot le Fou (+sc) (FR-IT). **'66** Masculin-Féminin (+sc) (FR-SWED); L'Espion (actor only) (FR-GER) (GB: The Defector); Made in USA (+sc; +voice). **'67** Deux ou Trois Choses Que Je Sais d'Elle (+sc; +narr) (USA/GB: Two Or Three Things I Know About Her); Le Plus Vieux Métier du Monde *ep* L'An 2000 (+sc) (subsequently shown separately); La Chinoise, ou Plutot à la Chinoise (+sc); Loin du Vietnam (co-dir; +co-sc; +co-narr; +appearance as himself) (USA/GB: Far From Vietnam); *ep* L'Amore/Andata e Ritorno dei Figli Prodighi (+sc) (IT-FR) (USA/GB: Love and Anger) (shown separately; part of complete film: Amore e Rabbia/Vangelo 70, 1968); Weekend (+sc) (FR-IT). **'68** Cinétracts (anonymous co-dir); One Plus One/Sympathy for the Devil (+sc; +voice) (GB). **'69** Le Gai Savoir (+sc) (FR-GER); Un Film Comme les Autres (+sc; +voice); British Sounds (GB) (USA: See You at Mao)*; Voices (doc) (appearance as himself only) (GB). **'70** Pravda (FR-CZ); Le Vent d'Est (FR-IT-GER); Lotte in Italia (IT). **'71** 1

directing actors. Although the film was austerely made, his genius for the staggering image, and his unique sense of sound and editing were very much in evidence. And he went back to fiction – although only as a support – with a large injection of documentary material. It was precisely the dialectics between reality and fiction that made *Tout Va Bien* a more successful film than his other films at that time.

Paris belongs to 'them'

Tout Va Bien was not the commercial success Godard had hoped for and he abandoned Paris and the world of commercial film-making, retiring to Grenoble to set up his own company Sonimage, making films for cassette and television. The films made in Grenoble were interesting in many ways, particularly *Ici et Ailleurs* (1976, Here and Elsewhere), in which he tries to explain why he could never finish his 1971 pro-Palestinian film *Jusqu'à la Victoire*. However, the Grenoble films were not seen by many people and Godard concentrated on television. He had made two films for television in 1969 – *British Sounds* for Britain's London Weekend Television, and *Le Gai Savoir* for the French radio and television company ORTF – but neither was ever shown on the small screen. This time he was more successful, for *Sur et Sous la Communication (Six Fois Deux)* (1978, On and Under Communication, Six Times Two) did get shown on French television – but only late at night and at the height of summer when most people were on vacation.

After one more attempt, Godard returned to feature-film making with *Sauve Qui Peut (La Vie)* (1980, *Slow Motion*) and the film achieved a greater success and wider audiences than any of his films since *Weekend*.

However, *Slow Motion* is not a masterpiece in the sense of being a perfectly balanced work of art. On the one hand it is an encapsulation of all his previous work, both of his Sixties' feature films and his Seventies' documentary essays, and on the other it is like all Godard's best films, an attempt to deal differently with familiar themes. If it is less perfect than *Two or Three Things I Know About Her*, that is because it is striking out on radically new lines and because Godard's sensibility matches the confusion of the world as it enters the Eighties. The hero of the film is actually called Paul Godard; he is a man at the end of his tether, and the film is a pessimistic and fragmentary reflection of the chaotic late Seventies, a collision course with catastrophe.

Many elements from Godard's earlier films reappear in *Slow Motion*. There is a parody of the end of *Vivre Sa Vie* in the scene where the prostitute (Isabelle Huppert) is not killed, but spanked by her pimp. The fragmentation of a film like *Made in USA* (1966) is surpassed in this new film, for Godard uses stop-motion technique to fragment even the simplest of movements. Probably inspired by the Instant Replay of television sportscasts, as well as by the early pre-cinema experiments of the Frenchman Étienne-Jules Marey, and the Anglo-American Eadweard Muybridge, he breaks down movement into its constituent steps, just as in earlier films he had broken sequences into brief shots.

Bewitched, bothered and bewildered

The main thematic difference between *Slow Motion* and its predecessors of the Sixties is that it is the story of three women and one man, whereas the earlier films usually dealt with one woman and two men (*Vivre Sa Vie*, *Contempt*, *Une Femme Mariée*). This change is particularly significant in *Slow Motion*: Godard is able to split the 'eternal feminine' into three because in a sense *all* the characters are

Left: this news photograph of Jane Fonda in Vietnam received stiff critical analysis in Godard's A Letter to Jane *(1973). Below: the young prostitute (Isabelle Huppert) and a client discuss her life in* Slow Motion

Godard himself. The fact that he calls his hero Paul Godard should not fool the audience, for there is as much of Godard in the three women as in the man. The prostitute represents that side of Godard which feels as if he has often had to 'sell' himself to make the films he wants to; Isabella Rimbaud, the girl who decides to leave town for the simple life in the country, is an image of Godard's flight first from Paris to Grenoble, and then to the Swiss countryside where he now lives; and Paul's ex-wife and their daughter Cecile would seem to represent all the women who have left Godard – Anna Karina, Anne Wiazemsky. They were not only his wives or mistresses, they were his stars.

Anne-Marie Mieville, Godard's present companion, is not an actress but she has contributed to his films over the past seven years. On the soundtrack of *Ici et Ailleurs* she intervenes to criticize things Godard says, and she is credited as co-scriptwriter on *Slow Motion*. Perhaps the fact that she is not an actress, or that Godard has not tried to put her in front of the camera, has obliged him to deal with several women in this film.

In spite of the fact that *Slow Motion* is an accurately chaotic reflection of the times in which it was made, it is also a highly accomplished work of art. A first viewing is perplexing or disorientating, but a second look reveals that for all its portrayal of chaos, it is a beautifully organized film. It is no accident that the credits read *composed* by Godard rather than *directed* by Godard. Music may be the title of only one of the four sections of the film (the others are The Imaginary, Fear, and Commerce), but the whole film is a musical composition with each section bearing a tempo marking (largo, allegro, etc) and all the themes coming together at the end.

Moving on in slow motion

It is doubtful whether *Slow Motion* will have as direct an influence on other film-makers as Godard's Sixties' films did, but in the long run it may prove to be even more influential in the sense that he has shown the world that a film can be as complex as any work of art – and still reach an audience. The old Hollywood adage, 'You're only as good as your last movie' seems especially fitting, for after several years' absense from the 'commercial' film scene Godard has re-affirmed his predominant place in world cinema.
RICHARD ROUD

.M./One Parallel Movie (+sc) (USA) (incorporating footage from unfinished film: 1 A.M./One American Movie); Vladimir et Rosa (+act) (GER-USA) (USA/GB: Vladimir and Rosa); Two American Audiences (doc. short) (appearance as himself only) (USA). '72 Tout Va Bien (co-dir;+co-c); La Longue Marche de Jean-Luc Godard (doc) appearance as himself only) (BELG). '73 A Letter o Jane, or Investigation About a Still (co-dir;+co-prod;+co-sc;+narr). '75 Numéro Deux +co-prod;+co-sc;+appearance as himself). '76 ci et Ailleurs (co-dir;+co-sc) (incorporating footage from unfinished film: Jusqu'à la Victoire, 971). '78 Comment ça Va (co-dir; +co-sc); Sur t Sous la Communication (Six Fois Deux) (co-ir;+co-sc)*; Der Kleine Godard (appearance as imself only) (GER) (GB: Junior Godard). '80 rance/Tour/Détour/Deux/Enfants (co-dir;+co-c)*; Sauve Qui Peut (La Vie) (co-dir;+co-sc) (FR-WITZ) (USA: Every Man for Himself; GB: Slow Motion).

Originally shot for television.

Weekend is an endless traffic jam amid a symphony of klaxons; *Weekend* is Emily Brontë as a human torch; *Weekend* is Mozart in a farmyard, an encounter with a band of cannibalistic hippies, an interminable pile-up on the autoroute with blazing cars and blood-stained corpses; *Weekend* is any middle-class outing to visit the mother-in-law.

What really links the above-mentioned sequences and set-pieces has nothing to do with the familiar logic of conventional mainstream cinema. Even before the viewer of *Weekend* has time to articulate any disorientation, Godard anticipates this response with two opening titles: 'A film adrift in the cosmos' and 'A film found on a scrap-heap'. In other words, if it does not seem to make sense or if it appears fragmented and disintegrated, that is how it is – and how

western culture looks through the critical viewfinder of Godard in the late Sixties.

The tendency of modern art-forms to expose the falsehoods and fissures in twentieth-century culture was powerfully in evidence even in Godard's earlier films. From 1967, the year of *La Chinoise, ou Plutot à la Chinoise* (The Chinese Girl) and also *Weekend*, the sense of fragmentation – of different, interlocking and overlapping discourses, of complex and contradictory images – acquired a sharp, political edge that in many ways foretold the temporary breakdown of the established order in France during May 1968.

Weekend stands as a watershed in Godard's career. It finally estranged those reviewers who tripped up on his odd mixture of brutal realism and exaggeration in the alienating style of the dramatist

Bertolt Brecht; yet it excited in a new generation of critics the belief that if cinema could be explosive, amusing, colourful and revolutionary all at once, this movie was the best example – it was the first real hit of the counter-cinema.

For all its radical admixture of fictional and famous historical characters, politics and plot, *Weekend* has a structure which is in essence no different from that of, say, *The Wizard of Oz* (1939) – familiar characters making a journey along a colourful road. The difference here is that Godard's typical middle-class couple witness

on the way, and become implicate in, nothing less than the collapse their own civilization. Though th dialogue is potent – ranging fro the grotesquely abusive scen where the girl harangues the peas ant who has killed her boyfriend in crash to the rhetorical speeche exchanged by the Algerian and th black African garbage collectors it is the images that speak mos powerfully: flaming automobile provide a horrific parody of con sumerism; a skinned rabbit rep resents the savage murder c Corinne's mother; and a pig slaugh tered on screen substitutes for th

Directed by Jean-Luc Godard, 1967
Prod co: Comacico/Les Films Copernic/Lira Films (Paris)/Ascot Cineraïd (Rome). **sc:** Jean-Luc Godard. **photo** (Eastman Colour): Raoul Coutard. **ed:** Agnès Guillemot. **mus:** Antoine Duhamel; Mozart's piano sonata K 576. **song:** 'Allô, Tu M'Entends' by Guy Béart. **sd:** René Levert. **ass dir:** Claude Miller. **prod man:** Ralph Baum, Philippe Senné. **r/t:** 95 minutes.
Cast: Mireille Darc (*Corinne*), Jean Yanne (*Roland*), Jean-Pierre Kalfon (*leader of the FLSO*), Valérie Lagrange (*his moll*), Jean-Pierre Léaud (*Saint-Just/man in phone booth*), Yves Beneyton (*member of the FLSO*), Paul Gégauff (*pianist*), Daniel Pommereulle (*Joseph Balsamo*), Yves Alfonso (*Tom Thumb*), Blandine Jeanson (*Emily Brontë/girl in farmyard*), Ernest Menzer (*cook*), Georges Staquet (*tractor driver*), Juliet Berto (*girl in car crash/member of the FLSO*), Anne Wiazemsky (*girl in farmyard/member of the FLSO*), Virginie Vignon (*Marie-Madeleine*), Isabelle Pons (*member of the FLSO*).

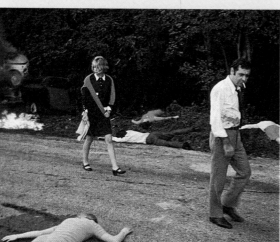

MIREILLE DARC
JEAN YANNE
DANS UN FILM DE
JEAN-LUC GODARD
Week-end
AVEC
VALERIE LAGRANGE
ET
JEAN-PIERRE KALFON

carcasses of humans who are cooked and eaten in the hippie encampment at the end.

At times the images may be merely glimpsed in brief flashes, sometimes to be returned to later; other shots are held for an unusually long time to focus the viewer's attention on what a particular scene is expressing, verbally or visually. The central example of the long-held shot occurs during the piano recital in the farmyard: in one unbroken take, the camera circles the farmyard three times, twice in one direction, once in reverse, thus paralleling closely the symmetry in

form of classical music. On one level, the whole sequence operates as a joke at the expense of government moves to bring culture to the people; but, on another level, this strangely compelling scene of a Mozart sonata performed to an audience of impassive peasant women and farm labourers can be taken as Godard's own farewell to bourgeois art forms, given the apparent gulf between artefacts and consumers. It is an ironic nod in the direction of culture that testifies to Godard's sense of humour even in the face of *Weekend*'s nihilistic narrative line.

Elsewhere in the film, conflicts and outrages are rendered as half-comic rows between motorists or as grotesque concoctions of the cannibal-hippies' chef. In publisher Ian Cameron's compilation *The Films of Jean-Luc Godard*, the critic Robin Wood argues that it is this unique sense of humour that enables Godard to pursue his analysis of western social and economic decadence beyond the point of despair, and still to remain 'horrifyingly optimistic'. The cue for this interpretation must be taken from the interlocking speeches of the Arab and the black African whose

address is direct to camera and who have consigned the stereotyped bourgeois couple among their garbage. The Arab says:

'I maintain that neither you nor I will ever win our freedom by non-violence, patience and love . . . we will never obtain our freedom until we can make the world realize that it is our right, yours and mine, to follow the example of all those who have sacrificed their own lives and taken the lives of other men in order to be free.'

Could there be a clearer call to arms than this most revolutionary of films?   MARTYN AUTY

3

4

7

8

Roland and Corinne, a married couple, are planning a weekend visit to her mother. They argue with a neighbour after bumping her parked Renault (1). Once on the road, they find themselves in a traffic jam that goes on for miles (2).

In a small town, a tractor has just hit a sports car and they witness an argument between the dead driver's girlfriend and the tractor driver (3). Roland and Corinne continue their journey into another mammoth traffic jam which turns into a horrific pile-up (4). When their own car is wrecked, they have to walk. (5).

The couple encounter Tom Thumb and Emily Brontë, who talk in riddles; annoyed, they set fire to Emily Brontë, who burns vividly (6). Continuing their

journey to Oinville by hitch-hiking, they arrive at a farmyard where scriptwriter Paul Gégauff is playing a Mozart sonata on a grand piano (7). People watch unmoved.

Eventually the couple hitch a ride with a garbage truck (8). The garbage collectors, an Arab and a black African, speak of the liberation of their countries. Roland and Corinne reach her mother's house but fail to secure the money they were hoping for, whereupon they kill the mother.

On their way back, they are taken prisoner by cannibalistic hippie-guerillas, the Seine et Oise Liberation Front (FLSO), in a forest (9). Roland is killed and Corinne capitulates, joining the hippies in their meal and eating the flesh of her husband (10).

183

File on Fonda

'I want to be responsible, positive, constructive. And I want to be the best actress I can be. I am a political animal, I am a woman who is personally engaged, and I am an actress. It has taken me some time to reconcile the two positions.'

Jane Fonda

It is hardly a new phenomenon for the children of famous show-business personalities to follow them into careers in the entertainment world. However, as Liza Minnelli once commented:

'Of course your parents' names open doors, but at 8.30 when the curtain goes up, it's you out there, not them. Without something of your own, those same doors can shut fast.'

The truth of that can be seen in the fact that Henry Fonda's name opened doors for both of his children, but while daughter Jane became an important international star with a reputation as a serious actress, her brother Peter's career, after an auspicious beginning, simply petered out.

Born in 1937 (her mother was Frances Brokaw), Jane went with her father to the East Coast when, in 1948, he went to New York to star in the Broadway production of *Mister Roberts*. She lived with her grandmother in nearby Connecticut, and then studied at Vassar, where she did a little acting in University productions. In the early Fifties her father cast her in his summer stock productions of the plays *The Country Girl* and *The Male Animal*. She was so dissatisfied with her own performances that she gave up acting to study

painting (in Paris) and piano (in New York). Feeling she was even less gifted at those two disciplines, she returned to enrol at Lee Strasberg's Actors Studio, supporting herself by modelling. Then the Fonda name began to open doors.

Joshua Logan – an old friend of her father – cast her in the college comedy *Tall Story* (1960) as a newly married cheer-leader, and in the ill-fated Broadway show *There Was a Little Girl*.

The reviews of both were negative, and personal notices were, at best, mixed. A another Broadway failure – *The Fun Coupl* she returned to movies. Critical opinion mained unsure as she moved through a mos mediocre series of films, playing a prostitute *Walk on the Wild Side*, a frigid wife in *Chapman Report*, a naive bride in *Period Adjustment* (all 1962), and an adultress in *In Cool of the Day* (1963). While the satiri magazine *Harvard Lampoon* named her 't year's worst actress', both critics and audie ces were beginning to notice that she h

Top: the two faces of baby Jane – as space-ag seductress Barbarella *with David Hemmings (left), and with husband-to-be Tom Hayden (right) on a troublesome visit to Britain in 1972 to promote their anti-Vietnam War campaign. Below:* In the Cool of the Day *Murray Logan (Peter Finch) has an affair wi a colleague's wife (Fonda)*

something; that magnetic quality which makes an actress watchable, no matter how awful the vehicle. She was also obviously sincere, intelligent, and attempting to make something worthwhile out of even the trashiest dialogue and situations. The fact that she was sexy and oddly beautiful kept her career going in spite of the less than magnificent box-office results.

It is impossible to guess what might have happened to that career – and her life – had she then not been called to France to appear in René Clément's *Les Félins* (1964, *The Love Cage*), in which (not surprisingly) her cool sexuality failed to strike sparks from Alain Delon's own glacial eroticism. But her temporary role as an international sex symbol – 'the American Bardot' – had begun. Immediately after the Clément film, she went to work in Roger Vadim's *La Ronde* (1964, *Circle of Love*). When asked later why she married her lover – the director who 'created' Bardot and was known for his elegant sex films – she said it was because he was charming, dashing, romantic and represented a kind of world that was very foreign to her.

Over the next five years, she returned to the United States to work but she lived in France. Vadim and Fonda had a daughter (Vanessa) and made four films together, in all of which she moved through titillating situations in various stages of undress. The most commercially successful of them was *Barbarella* (1968), based on a comic strip, and emphasizing even more than usual Vadim's cinematic conception of woman as sexual object and plaything. That particular image was, in reality, one which Fonda herself was less and less comfortable with.

Although she has since turned her back on the work done before *They Shoot Horses, Don't They?* (1969) – referring to that part of her output as 'when I wasn't very good' – she has never said even the least negative thing about ex-husband Vadim, with whom she has remained friendly. She now sees her experience in France as valuable: in 1968 France exploded politically, and more than a few people were politicized for the first time in their lives. Jane Fonda was one of them.

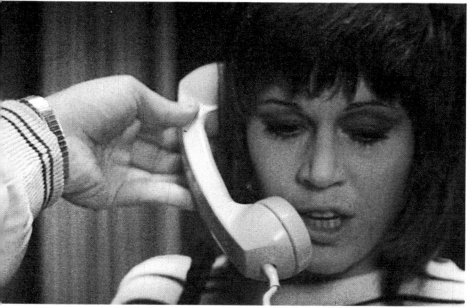

Above: Dove Linkhorn (Laurence Harvey) meets lost love Kitty Twist (Fonda) working in a brothel in Walk on the Wild Side. *Left: as a prostitute again in* Klute. *Below left: Jane at home with father Henry, husband Vadim and daughter Vanessa. Below: They Shoot Horses, Don't They? is a painful portrayal of the dance marathons of the Depression; Gloria (Fonda) and Robert (Michael Sarrazin) battle on*

By 1970 she was often called Hanoi Jane and was as well known for her political activities as for her screen performances. She explained that she came from a bourgeois liberal background – her father was a Roosevelt and Stevenson Democrat – and she, like her family, had donated money to various liberal causes and had signed petitions without actually engaging in politics on a personal level. It was the atrocities and misleading reports concerning Vietnam that led her to become interested – and active – in various causes, including the rights of American Indians and blacks and, most importantly, ending the war in Vietnam.

Whereas she won well-deserved awards for her performance as the threatened prostitute in *Klute* (1971), it was about the same time that the press and government crucified her as a 'traitor' and worse. She became active in the Free The Army movement, touring American Army bases with a revue in an attempt to get soldiers to refuse to fight in Vietnam. Neither of the two films which resulted from those tours – *F.T.A.* (1972) and *Steelyard Blues* (1973) – received wide distribution. She also returned to France briefly to appear in Jean-Luc Godard's *Tout Va Bien* (1972, All Goes Well), a forthrightly political film concerning, among other things, a strike in a factory. Fonda was not entirely pleased with either the film or with Godard as a director – a compliment he returned in the short *A Letter to Jane, an Investigation About a Still* (1973), which features a still photograph of her. This was an analysis of what he saw as Fonda's superficial

Left: Fonda continued her anti-war protest on film with Donald Sutherland in Steelyard Blues. *Below left: in* Coming Home, *Jon Voight plays a crippled veteran. Below: with James Caan in* Comes a Horseman *(1978).*

understand how to say things and still have a large number of people listen. In the new film we wanted to say something about the condition of secretaries, but *9 to 5* is first of all a very funny comedy.'

At a time when she has won all the acting awards available, when she is often called the most interesting actress of her generation (and not just by her father), she still claims to be frightened with each new role:

'I always think another actress would be better in the role. When I played Bree in *Klute*, I went to bars where prostitutes hung out to prepare the role. Nobody made even a single proposition to me and I went back terrified to Alan Pakula and told him I was obviously wrong for the role. Still, that's getting better and better, because I am beginning to know what I am capable of.'   DAVID OVERBEY

Quotations are taken from an interview by Henri Béhar, part of which was published in the May 1979 issue of Premiere.

nd 'radical chic' approach to the war and volution.

Since then, Fonda admits that her one error during the period of her first politicization and ie anti-war movement was that she was shrill preaching rather than talking to audiences – id that there was the chance that she ienated many who then refused to listen to er. She has noted that people now tell her she as become more human, although she has ot become any less political. She works tively with her politician husband, Tom ayden, for the political organization they unded – the California Campaign for Econic Democracy. At least half of her films now ave something of a political message: the war ıd returning Vietnam veterans in *Coming ome* (1978), the dangers of nuclear power ants in *The China Syndrome* (1979), the lives 'repression' lived by office secretaries in *9 to* (1980). Yet, there is, now, a difference: 'I chose to do *Fun With Dick and Jane* (1977)

No longer the sexy nymphet, Jane Fonda's screen image is now one of social and political concern – TV reporter in The China Syndrome *(top) or militant secretary with Dolly Parton and Lily Tomlin in* 9 to 5 *(above)*

because I thought the time had come to do a comedy, a film which would be commercial, a film in which I was pretty. It showed I was a good actress and that I was commercial. I think that *The China Syndrome* had a social and commercial impact that was very strong. It is an example of a fusion of two kinds of film. We wanted to have a film which said something we wanted to say, but we wanted to attract the widest possible audience to say it to. It functions as a suspense film, but it is also about something important in the daily lives of those who see it. Let's not exaggerate, of course. No film can support a mass movement. Films can have a certain effect, but they represent only a small step in a certain direction. I think I now

Filmography
1960 Tall Story. '62 Walk on the Wild Side; The Chapman Report; Period of Adjustment. '63 In the Cool of the Day; Jane (doc) (appearance as herself only); Sunday in New York. '64 Les Félins (FR) (USA: The Joy House; GB: The Love Cage); La Ronde (FR-IT) (USA: Circle of Love). '65 Cat Ballou. '66 The Chase; La Curée (FR-IT) (USA/GB: The Game Is Over); Any Wednesday (GB: Bachelor Girl Apartment). '67 Hurry Sundown; Barefoot in the Park. '68 Histoires Extraordinaires *ep* Metzengerstein only (FR-IT) (USA: Spirits of the Dead; GB: Tales of Mystery); Barbarella (FR-IT). '69 They Shoot Horses, Don't They? '71 Klute. '72 Tout Va Bien; F.T.A. (+co-prod; +co-sc). '73 Steelyard Blues (re-released in USA as: Final Crash); A Doll's House (GB-FR). '74 Jane Fonda on Vietnam (doc. short) (NOR) (appearance as herself only); Vietnam Journey; Introduction to the Enemy (doc) (+co-dir; +appearance as herself). '76 The Blue Bird (USA-USSR). '77 Fun With Dick and Jane; Julia. '78 Coming Home; Comes a Horseman; California Suite. '79 The China Syndrome; The Electric Horseman. '80 9 to 5; No Nukes (appearance as self only). '81 On Golden Pond. '82 Rollover.

Although massive media coverage could show the tragedy and suffering of war, and thus make its existence more real and believable, it also inured people to the level of bloodshed and killing that was taking place. News reporters only had access to American troops and actions, and could not venture behind enemy lines. Hence, it fell to film-makers to show the less obvious aspects and especially the Vietnamese view of the war. As early as 1965, the documentary film-maker Joris Ivens visited Vietnam to make *Le Ciel, La Terre* (*The Threatening Sky*), a film which showed the effects of the war on ordinary people and their lives. Reporter and broadcaster James Cameron made another early documentary – *Western Eye-Witness in the North of Vietnam* (1966) – a beautifully filmed humanitarian commentary on the energy and resourcefulness of the North Vietnamese in maintaining the bare necessities of life.

Then, in 1967, writer and film-maker Felix Greene obtained commissions for a series of articles for the *San Francisco Chronicle* and for a CBS Television News film. The result was *Inside North Vietnam* (1967). One difficulty faced by Greene was how to bring home to the American public the tragic transformation that they had wrought on Vietnam, given that the nightly news coverage had already shown every bloody aspect of battle. He chose to show people at work – peasants in their villages, work-crews repairing bomb damage, nurses and teachers – and film them as they responded to the everyday occurence of bombing raids. One particularly haunting image is that of young girls planting rice in paddy fields with rifles on their backs, then running to fire machine-guns when planes appear overhead.

A much-publicized visitor to the North in 1972 was Jane Fonda. She had already demonstrated her opposition to the war with Donald Sutherland in their touring anti-army review – the FTA Show. Next, she broadcast on Hanoi radio to United States servicemen in Indo-China: 'I implore you, I beg you to consider what you are doing . . . Are these people your enemy?' Newspapers in the West carried pictures of her at an anti-aircraft gun wearing a tin helmet. Fonda received criticism from all sides. Senators demanded she be tried for treason, and Jean-Luc Godard produced the film *A Letter to Jane, or Investigation About a Still* (1973) – an intellectual polemic which accused her of displaying clichéd, liberal responses to the war. Undeterred, once back in the United States, she co-directed the documentary *Vietnam Journey: Introduction to the Enemy* (1974) with Haskell Wexler and Tom Hayden, and several years later she made the fictional film *Coming Home* (1978), about a crippled veteran's agonizing return from the front line of battle.

Film was used for very different purposes by the Vietnamese themselves; they had no need to alert their population to the reality of war. Yet, despite the near-impossible conditions of filming – using crews of two or three people, protecting cameramen under fire, building cinemas underground to avoid bombings, transporting film to jungle laboratories on foot or bicycle – film was seen as so important to the morale of the Vietnamese that documentary production increased rapidly during the years of the war.

In America, although a great many training and propaganda films were made for the army,

Journeys Through Vietnam

The Vietnam War was closely watched by millions of civilians all over the world. By the late Sixties, in the United States, daily satellite transmissions brought the horrors and reality of war into everyone's living room. But it was a long time before the whole story emerged

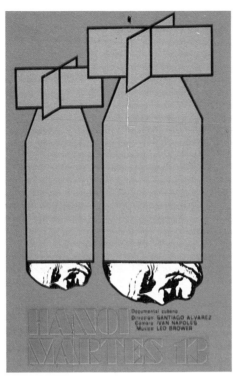

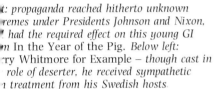

Left: propaganda reached hitherto unknown [ext]remes under Presidents Johnson and Nixon, [it] had the required effect on this young GI [i]n In the Year of the Pig. *Below left: [Ter]ry Whitmore for Example – though cast in [the] role of deserter, he received sympathetic [...]n treatment from his Swedish hosts*

Above left: Inside North Vietnam – *a peasant girl doubles as soldier. Above:* Hanoi, Tuesday 13th, *a powerful statement of Cuba's anti-American feelings. Below: Jane Fonda's own* Vietnam Journey: Introduction to the Enemy. *Bottom:* Far From Vietnam – *newsreel footage of an anti-war demonstration*

few films were made for the general public. John Ford was commissioned to produce a film along the lines of the *Why We Fight* series during World War II, but *Vietnam! Vietnam!* (1971) was put on the shelf and banned from public showing. At the same time, numerous protest films were being shot. They largely concentrated on the effect of the war on America rather than the effect of American intervention on Vietnam, as several fictional features would do a decade later. *Carry It On* (1970), for example, was a gentle documentary about the arrest of David Harris for non-co-operation with the draft, and the anti-war work of his wife, folk-singer Joan Baez, in concert and counselling non-violent resist-ance. *Interviews With My Lai Veterans* (1970) directed by Joseph Strick, traces (through discussions) the lives of five members of the US Army's Charlie Company who were involved in the My Lai massacre of March 1968. Other works recorded every aspect of the war as it affected the United States: veterans, student protest, government policy, etc.

With the exception of Eastern Europe (which produced a host of films designed to expose American imperialism) films from other countries highlighted the way the war affected them. Swedish films, not unnaturally in view of the number of GIs who took advantage of its traditional neutrality, looked at the problems of deserters. *Terry Whitmore for Example* (1969) and the dramatized documentary *Deserter USA* (1969) both showed how former American GIs in Sweden coped with their lives.

France produced *Loin de Vietnam* (1967, *Far From Vietnam*) – a sort of petition against the war signed by its six directors, Jean-Luc Godard, Joris Ivens, Alain Resnais, Agnès Varda, William Klein and Claude Lelouch, under the editorial supervision of the docum-entary film-maker Chris Marker. It was a varied film with episodes ranging from news-reel footage of America, Vietnam and France to Godard explaining from his house in Paris why it was difficult to make a film about Vietnam (he had earlier been refused permission to enter North Vietnam).

One of the most powerful condemnations of the war came from Cuba – *Hanoi, Martes 13* (1967, *Hanoi, Tuesday 13th*) directed by San-tiago Alvarez. With its caricatures of Lyndon B. Johnson as a monster, its newsreel footage of the vicious treatment of American protesters and shots of captured GIs, it says as much about Cuba's fear of American invasion as it does about Vietnam.

Emile de Antonio's *In the Year of the Pig* (1969) was one of the few films that depicted events as the people and politicians of Hanoi might see them. Consequently, by contrasting the determination of the Vietnamese to fight to the end with the ineptness of the American forces, it articulated the deep-rooted American fears of what the war did to them as a nation.

These films helped establish and support the international protest movement against the war. But the most consistent coverage was still on television, and even in Britain the evening news betrayed bias towards American 'facts'. The day the BBC News reversed its foreign-coverage policy and announced that the Viet-namese *had* shot down a number of planes whereas the Americans only *claimed* their figures, the world at large knew the conflict in South-East Asia was nearly over.

SALLY HIBBIN

189

LEFT TURN!

History – even film history – is a flux in which eruptions or sudden changes are rare. When they occur, they acquire an exaggerated importance from serving as the beginnings and ends of chapters or chronicles. 1968 has become such a peg for historians

Even though everything in 1968 was either a continuation or a culmination of the post-war partition of the world into countries that were capitalist, communist, undecided or under-developed, the year has assumed a kind of mythical potency. By the mid-Sixties it had become increasingly clear that 'left' or 'right' were no longer the proper words to describe the polarization of attitudes. Young intellectuals were equally discontented with capitalist exploitation on one side and stultified Leninism on the other. Criticism of either of the systems tended to be stifled by force in some places, but found free expression in the bourgeois democracies, where the New Left proved to be a fruitful influence on the arts, and especially on film.

It was mainly in France that particular importance was assigned to film in the cultural reorientation of a younger generation. A magazine was founded in Paris in 1951 by André Bazin and Jacques Doniol-Valcroze, called the *Cahiers du Cinéma*. As a theorist, Bazin favoured documentary realism, but as an editor, he did not enforce his views on the young critics who rallied to the *Cahiers*. The only doctrine which emerged by consensus from their group was the '*auteur* theory', insisting that a director must be as responsible for the subject and the style of a film as a writer is for a novel's. Documentary techniques were supposed to aim at the greatest possible honesty, as for instance in the work of the anthropologist-turned-film-maker Jean Rouch. Another cult grew up in praise of the cinematic essays, non-linear narratives and other experimental devices so skilfully deployed

by Chris Marker. Both directors, however, were more honoured than followed.

The young critics who wrote for the *Cahiers* were either making films already, like Louis Malle, or were soon to do so, like Chabrol, Truffaut, Rohmer and Godard, and are reputed to have coined the slogan 'Le cinéma de papa est mort' (Papa's films are dead). By the mid-Sixties their influence, singly or together, affected film-makers across four continents.

Even as far as South America – though political instability prevented the *nouvelle vague* from taking hold in the poorer countries – there was an ambitious movement; in Brazil the *Cinema Novo* was attempting to create a populist, revolutionary cinema. A National Institute of Cinema was also set up, but its slender resources were deployed in too many areas – education, archive storage, libraries and special seasons – to leave money for production. Although the *Cinema Novo*'s film-makers were soon out-manoeuvred by commercial interests, several of them made their mark: Glauber Rocha's *Deus e o Diabo na Terra do Sol* (1964, *Black God, White Devil*) and *Antonio-das-Mortes* (1969, Antonio of the Dead) achieved international festival and art-house success.

The outstanding director of the period remains Miguel Littin of Chile, who combines an aesthetic flair with the urgency of a strong political commitment. *El Chacal de Nahueltoro* (1970, *The Jackal of Nahueltoro*), about the social evils that turn a spirited man into a criminal, first drew attention to his talent. Since the defeat of President Allende, Littin has been in Mexico, following the example of

Above left: only in an ideal world could a revolution unite such disparate groups as workers, students and intellectuals; Paris Left Bank demonstrations made some attempt. Above: new German cinema – Artistes at the Top of the Big Top: Disorientated (1968)

another famous exile, Luis Buñuel, in gaining festival prizes and foreign currency for t Mexican film industry.

In Europe, the *nouvelle vague* had an almo immediate impact on West Germany; a gro of about twenty young film-makers in Muni began to look for the means to break t stranglehold of cheap sex films and hef yodelling musicals. Some of them had ma shorts which won prizes abroad, and at t 1962 Oberhausen Short Film Festival, 26 them signed a manifesto announcing th determination to produce their own films, a demanding government help in the name German prestige and culture. They also us small green stickers saying 'Papa's Kino tot'.

Among the leading lights of this group we Alexander Kluge, a lawyer turned film-mak Edgar Reitz and Ulrich and Peter Schamo (there are four Schamoni brothers, all worki in film or television). Soon after, Kluge a Reitz founded a film school in Ulm, and t director Wim Wenders was one of their earli graduates. By 1965 the government respond to the demand for a subsidy. It was issu through a committee called the Kuratoriu der Jungen Deutschen Film (Foundation Young German Film), and was meant to ta the form of loans rather than grants. Althou the first film under the scheme – Klug *Abschied von Gestern* (1966, *Yesterday Girl*) w a Silver Lion at Venice and did well at the bo office, it did not recoup its full costs. Li many other praiseworthy first films, such wo achieved critical acclaim without refilling t coffers of the Kuratorium, or even enabli directors to finance their next projects.

To ensure some continuity in their caree in 1971 a group of directors founded experimental production company: Filmverl der Autoren. Its production plans never ma the necessary money, but it still carries on a

Top: The Confrontation – *students force seminary pupils to burn their books in a pro-communist purge.* Above: *Bertolucci's* 1900 *chronicles the desperate peasant struggle to prevent the forces of repression from protecting landlords' interests.* Above right: *Alexandra Kluge as* Yesterday Girl. Right: *Eva Ras and Slobodan Aligrudić in* Switchboard Operator

distribution company. The early films of Werner Herzog, Volker Schlöndorff, Rainer Werner Fassbinder and Wenders all came through the Filmverlag. These films were all characterized by aesthetic originality rather than political messages, but there is a critical habit, particularly strong in Germany, of con-fusing a presentation of contemporary life with making political statements. It seems apparent that directors such as Herzog or Wenders are non-conformist rather than revolutionary.

In Italy, the post-war neo-realists had long since rebelled against papa's cinema. Films by Giuseppe De Santis, Vittorio De Sica or Luchino Visconti have become identified with a political

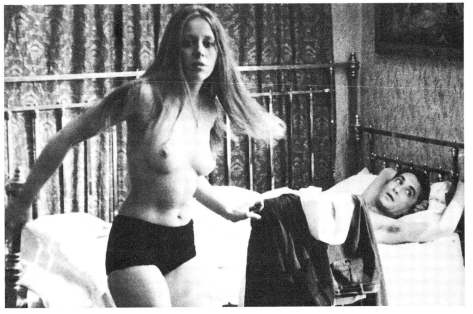

left mainly because of their intense compassion for the poor and exploited. However, it needed an outsider's eye to sum up the Italian situation and foreshadow the approaching years of crisis, murders and kidnappings. The film *La Pacifista* (1971, The Pacifist) about student riots contained by an anti-leftist police force who turn a blind eye to a right-wing band of murderers, was made in Milan by the Hungarian Miklós Jancsó. Apart from Jancsó – somewhat on the sidelines in Italy – the only politicized directors of the Sixties were Gillo Pontecorvo and the Taviani brothers, even if some would argue that Bernardo Bertolucci used political polarization as an aesthetic device from the 1968 film *Partner* to *1900* (1976).

The student riots and factory sit-ins of May 1968 in France affected the entire contemporary intelligentsia. Superficially, the events marked the end of dreams about a student-worker solidarity, but the aspirations of most people were even more vague. All they had hoped was that the growing affluence of the west throughout the Sixties would lead to a freer and more just society. Police bullets across the torn-up Parisian cobblestones proved that the only difference between affluence and poverty was that, when rich, the establishment manipulated the people with more subtlety and less brute force – until it felt itself under attack.

It was a lesson also demonstrated in Eastern Europe; the Polish student riots which had preceded the Paris outbreak by some two months had even more depressing consequences. The purges which followed had an anti-Semitic bias. Of the leading directors, Aleksander Ford emigrated to Israel; Jerzy Bossak was removed as head of the documentary studio; Roman Polanski and Jerzy Skolimowski settled abroad.

History took an even tougher turn in Czechoslovakia, where a governmental move towards more democratic socialism ended in the armed Soviet invasion during August 1968. The artistic upsurge of the Sixties – which enabled Miloš Forman, Jiří Menzel, Ivan Passer, Věra Chytilová and others to create sharp and witty social satires – was replaced by a repressive regime, even in the studios. Miloš Forman, Ivan Passer and Vojtěch Jasný emigrated; Chytilová's film plans were aborted again and again, and those she has finished are hardly shown. Menzel has continued to work, but his films – still exquisitely crafted – are all in a minor key.

Only in Hungary could 1968 pass as a good year, with the release of Jancsó's *Csend és Kiáltás* (1968, *Silence and Cry*) and the shooting of *Fényes Szelek* (1969, *The Confrontation*), Pál Sándor's *Bohóc a Falon* (1968, Clown on the Wall) András Kovács' *Falak* (1968, Walls) and Sándor Sára's *Feldobott Kö* (1968, The Upthrown Stone).

Yugoslavia, however, had undergone an earlier crisis during the break with Soviet foreign and economic policy. After the new constitution of 1963, regional development was encouraged. Outstanding and thoroughly modern work came from the Zagreb Studios, and directors who had ideas beyond the Partisan epics which were the staple of the Yugoslav cinema – especially Aleksander Petrović and Dušan Makavejev – proceeded to international co-productions. In his best-known film *Skulpjači Perja* (1967, *Happy Gypsies . . !*) Petrović portrayed a community of gypsies whose failings and corruption could be taken as a more general metaphor.

From Dušan Makavejev came originality and a message which repeatedly shocks the puritan pretensions of the socialist countries. Makavejev has always taken his story as a text for preaching sexual freedom, from his early shorts until his first feature *Čovek Nije Tica* (1966, Man Is Not a Bird) and his *Ljubavni Slučaj ili Tragedija Službenice PTT* (1967, Switchboard Operator). He achieved world fame with *WR – Misterije Organizma* (1971, *WR – Mysteries of the Organism*) when the West, without being shocked, was delightedly titillated by this hilarious tragedy of repression.

Even in the sometimes detached world of cinema, it is useful to recall that 1968 does not stand merely for the Paris student riots, the defeat of the 'Prague Spring' and the tightening of Poland's circumstances. In the same year Martin Luther King was assassinated and Richard Milhous Nixon was elected President of the United States. A new wave had broken: a new age was dawning.
                                                    MARI KUTTNA

The Exploits of Roger Corman

the flowers that kill in the Spring TRA-LA

THE FUNNIEST PICTURE THIS YEAR!

The Little Shop of Horrors

Starring
JONATHAN HAZE / JACKIE JOSEPH
MEL WELLES

Roger Corman is one of the most important and exemplary figures in the modern American cinema. No other film-maker at work in the industry since the early Fifties has been so prolific – over 150 films as director, producer, executive producer or uncredited patron. And no other has had as much effect on the shape and character of contemporary Hollywood film production and distribution

Corman was born in Los Angeles in 1926. As a young man he graduated in engineering (later reading English for a term at Oxford) and then joined the navy. His movie career began, in the best tradition of Hollywood success stories, with a lowly job as a mail clerk at 20th Century-Fox. After selling a story to the Poverty Row company Allied Artists in 1953, he pulled together his own first production, *The Monster From the Ocean Floor* (1954), for $12,000 and the promise of free publicity for the inventor of the film's central showpiece, a miniature one-man submarine.

Such entrepreneurial ingenuity was necessary throughout the initial (and, indeed, all) phases of Corman's career. His early films for the fledgling American International Pictures (AIP) were financed in a most unorthodox fashion. Corman would fly around the USA showing his most recently completed movie to theatre operators as a means of persuading them to bankroll his next.

Roger – and out!
Fast and cheap were the watchwords of those early years. The facts of commercial life on the

Above left: Corman directs Susan Strasberg and Peter Fonda in The Trip. *Above: a Corman quickie shot in 'two days and a night'. Below left:* Swamp Women, *early exploitation fare. Below: Corman's debut as producer*

TERROR STRIKES!
...FROM BENEATH THE SEA!

MONSTER FROM THE OCEAN FLOOR

ANNE KIMBEL
STUART WADE
DICK PINNER

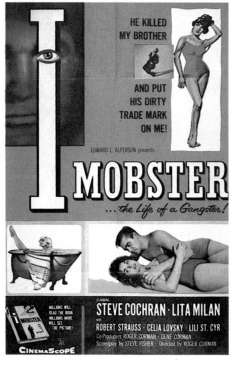

Top: cashing in on Fifties nuclear neuroses – a mutant and his victim in The Day the World Ended. *Top right: William Shatner (left) in the social drama* The Intruder. *Above: like most of Corman's films,* I, Mobster *(1958) – a torrid gangland thriller – was advertized with typical sensationalist panache*

exploitation circuit (the drive-ins and grind theatres where B movies played) were that a grabby title – *The Beast With 1,000,000 Eyes, Swamp Women, The Day the World Ended* (all 1955) – and feverish genre expectations were alone sufficient to compel the attendance of a sizeable audience, especially at weekends. If Corman and his collaborators could keep a story situation alive for 60 or 70 minutes (be it horror movie, racing drama, rock'n'roll romance, whatever), contrive to end each scene with the promise of new terrors or distractions, and get the whole thing on film for a ludicrously small amount of money in several days' shooting (he claims to have shot 78 camera set-ups in a single day for the 1958 film *Viking Women and the Sea Serpent*), their production enterprise would remain viable.

Corman's own work on the twenty or so films with which he is credited as director in the period 1955–60 was not motivated by the desire to serve a personal vision. Rather, by directing the films himself, Corman saved the salary that he would have had to pay another

director. But his most devout admirers cite his courageous social-protest film *The Intruder* (1962), in which William Shatner played a Southern bigot, as evidence that Corman could have made important, personal films. The movie attracted favourable attention from critics but failed at the box-office.

Streamlined strategies
Corman's work in the Sixties suggests a greater degree of seriousness overall. With AIP, he graduated to higher levels of budget and production with the series of Edgar Allan Poe adaptations dating from 1960; the great commercial success of these Gothic horror pictures, themselves politically innocuous, may well have encouraged Corman to balance the scales with more tendentious contemporary subjects. But it is probably truer to the mark to say that Corman realized a soupçon of social significance could both agreeably season and thematically sanctify the sorts of melodrama favoured by the exploitation-film audience.

What is undeniable is that those melodramas were being made more forcefully and more fluidly. *The Man With the X-Ray Eyes* (1963), starring Ray Milland as a scientist whose vision is finally able to probe the very core of the universe, achieves a hysterical bleakness. *The Wild Angels* (1966), harking back to the motorcycle-gang films of the mid-Fifties but excelling them in savagery and sheer physical power, was applauded on the international film-festival circuit as an allegorical indictment of contemporary American values (and denounced at home for the same reasons). Corman's sympathy – half genuine, half opportunistic – for counter-cultural values found further expression in *The Trip* (1967), about a weekend experimentation with LSD, and in two 'communal' films from different genres: *Bloody Mama* (1970), a period gangster film built around Depression outlaw Ma Barker (Shelley Winters) and her incestuous brood; and *Gas-s-s-s, or It Became Necessary to Destroy the World in Order to Save It* (1970), a barely futuristic item about a world in which everyone over 25 has been annihilated.

Throughout this period, Corman was being wooed by the major Hollywood studios – Columbia at one time hinting strongly that he could oversee their production schedule, and 20th Century-Fox providing the opportunity to make an expert slice of gangster-film history on an A budget, *The St Valentine's Day Massacre* (1967). That one notable film aside, none of Corman's flirtations with the majors went anywhere. But change was in the air. After a lively and profitable association lasting more than a decade, AIP was proving constricting to

Corman's personal ambitions. When the company recut *Gas-s-s-s* without his approval, he broke away to form his own corporation, New World Pictures.

Corman has not directed another film since starting New World (though he has occasionally stepped in to direct parts of ailing company projects). He has concentrated instead on perfecting his own production and exploitation apparatus on the old AIP model; becoming one of the key American distributors of important foreign films (handling the work of Ingmar Bergman, Federico Fellini, Akira Kurosawa, François Truffaut, Joseph Losey, and others); and, perhaps most crucial of all, continued a practice of his AIP days – the discovery and development of exciting new talent, offscreen and onscreen.

Student princes
A list of Roger Corman alumni reads like an honour role of present-day Hollywood. Performers like Jack Nicholson, Bruce Dern, Ellen Burstyn, Robert De Niro, Peter Fonda, Dennis Hopper and David Carradine owe Corman their starts, or at least significant career nudges. More remarkable is the roster of distinctive directing and writing talents who have emerged from what Jonathan Demme, director of *Citizens Band* (1977) and *Melvin and Howard* (1980), has affectionately called 'the Roger Corman Academy of Film Technique': Peter Bogdanovich, Monte Hellman, Francis Ford Coppola, Martin Scorsese, Robert Towne, John Sayles, Demme himself, Stephanie Rothman, Paul Bartel, Jonathan Kaplan, John A Alonzo . . .

It should not be inferred that either Corman or his protégés view him as an altruist. As a producer – and, in some cases, as a director in need of uncredited second-unit work – Corman could profitably exploit the services of young enthusiasts eager to break into films and willing to work for small wages.

Sometimes it has been possible for the protégés to work on personal, imaginative projects under Corman's patronage: Bogdanovich made *Targets* (1967); Monte Hellman created an extraordinary pair of absurdist Westerns, *The Shooting* and *Ride in the Whirlwind* (both 1966). Others completed assignments more consistent with Corman's needs in the exploitation line – Coppola's first directorial credit appeared on the silly, if nicely atmospheric, thriller *Dementia 13* (1963). But the lessons Corman taught in the name of keeping schlock films visually and narratively vital has served his apprentices well in their subsequent, more prestigious endeavours.

If none of Corman's own pictures approach greatness, it is also happily true that few

LE BEYOND THE STARS" Starring RICHARD THOMAS · ROBERT VAUGHN · JOHN SAXON
GEORGE PEPPARD as Cowboy Co-starring DARLANNE FLUEGEL · SYBIL DANNING
posed by JAMES HORNER Screenplay by JOHN SAYLES Story by JOHN SAYLES and ANNE DYER
N PICTURES Release TV: WARNER BROS. A WARNER COMMUNICATIONS COMPANY Executive Producer ROGER CORMAN Producer ED CARLIN Directed by JIMMY T. MURAKAMI

p: Ben Gazzara as the American owner of a
ngapore brothel in Saint Jack *(1979). Top*
ght: sultry scene from The Hot Box *(1972),*
bout American nurses who are kidnapped by a
ople's army. Above: Battle Beyond the Stars
1980) saw New World Pictures topping the
3 million budget mark

em are dull. His work is distinguished by a
olid movie sense, an ingenuous adaptability
o circumstance and opportunity, and an
ppealing lack of pretension. His career has
een an agreeably outrageous paradigm of
nlikely survival; and his movies stand as a
nonument to the sort of artless profession-
ism that once flourished in the American
nema, but is now little seen outside the
eighbourhood of Roger Corman and his
erennially new world of picture-making.
RICHARD T. JAMESON

Filmography

Films as director: **1955** Five Guns West (+prod);
Apache Woman (+prod); Swamp Women; The
Day the World Ended (+prod). **'56** The Oklahoma Woman/Bandit Queen (+prod); Gunslinger (+prod); It Conquered the World
(+prod); Not of This Earth (+prod); Attack of
the Crab Monsters (+prod). **'57** The Undead
(+prod); Naked Paradise (+prod); She-Gods of
Shark Reef (GB: Shark Reef); Carnival Rock
(+prod); Teenage Doll (+prod); Sorority Girl
(+prod) (GB: The Bad One). **'58** Viking Women
and the Sea Serpent (+prod) (GB: Viking
Women); War of the Satellites (+prod;+act);
Machine Gun Kelly (+prod); Teenage Caveman
(+prod) (GB: Out of the Darkness); I, Mobster
(+co-prod) (GB: The Mobster). **'59** The Wasp
Woman (+prod;+act); A Bucket of Blood
(+prod). **'60** Ski Troop Attack (+prod; +act);
Fall of the House of Usher/House of Usher
(+prod); The Last Woman on Earth (+prod;
+act); The Little Shop of Horrors (+prod;+act).
'61 Atlas (+prod;+act); Creature From the
Haunted Sea (+prod;+act); The Pit and the
Pendulum (+prod). **'62** The Premature Burial
(+prod); The Intruder /I Hate Your Guts (+prod)
(GB: The Stranger); Tales of Terror (+prod);
Tower of London. **'63** The Raven (+prod); The
Young Racers (+prod;+act); The Terror
(+prod); The Haunted Palace (+prod); The Man
With the X-Ray Eyes (+prod). **'64** The Masque of
the Red Death (+prod) (GB-USA); The Secret In-
vasion; The Tomb of Ligeia (+prod) (GB-USA).
'66 The Wild Angels. **'67** The St Valent-
ine's Day Massacre (+prod); The Trip (+prod); A
Time for Killing (some scenes only) (GB: The Long
Ride Home). **'69** How to Make It (+act) (shot as
TV movie but shown in cinemas; reissued as Tar-
get: Harry); De Sade (some scenes only) (USA-
GER). **'70** Bloody Mama (+prod); Gas-s-s-s, or it
Became Necessary to Destroy the World in Order
to Save It (+prod) (GB: Gas!, or It Became
Necessary to Destroy the World in Order to Save
It). **'71** Von Richtofen and Brown (GB: The Red
Baron). *Films as producer or uncredited supervisor,
and films produced by Corman's companies (screen
credits where appropriate):* **'54** Highway Dragnet
(co-prod;+co-sc); The Monster From the Ocean
Floor (prod); The Fast and the Furious
(prod;+co-sc). **'55** The Beast With 1,000,000
Eyes. **'58** Stakeout on Dope Street; Monster From
Galaxy 27; The Cry-Baby Killer (exec. prod); Hot
Car Girl (exec. prod); Night of the Blood Beast
(exec. prod); The Brain Eaters. **'59** Paratroop

Command; Tank Commando; Crime and Punishment USA; T-Bird Gang (GB: The Pay-Off); High
School Big Shot (GB: The Young Sinners); Attack
of the Giant Leeches (exec. prod) (GB: Demons of
the Swamp); Beast From Haunted Cave. **'60** The
Wild Ride; Battle of Blood Island. **'61** Master of
the World; Night Tide. **'62** The Mermaids of
Tiburon; The Magic Voyage of Sinbad (re-ed. and
dubbed version of USSR film: Sadko, 1952). **'63**
Battle Beyond the Sun (re-ed. and dubbed version
of USSR film: Nebo Zobyot, 1959); Dementia 13
(prod) (GB: The Haunted and the Hunted). **'65**
The Girls on the Beach; Ski Party; Beach Ball. **'66**
The Shooting; Ride in the Whirlwind; Blood Bath
(exec. prod); Queen of Blood. **'67** Devil's Angels
(prod); Targets. **'68** Wild Racers (exec. prod). **'69**
Naked Angels (exec. prod); Pit Stop (exec. prod).
'70 Angels Die Hard!; The Dunwich Horror (exec.
prod); Paddy; Bury Me an Angel; Student Nurses
(exec. prod). **'71** Angels Hard as They Come;
Women in Cages; The Big Doll House; The Velvet
Vampire. **'72** Private Duty Nurses; Boxcar Bertha
(prod); The Big Bird Cage (exec. prod); Night Call
Nurses; Fly Me; The Young Nurses; The Hot Box;
Sweet Kill/The Arousers; The Unholy Rollers;
Night of the Cobra Woman. **'73** Stacey!; Savage!;
I Escaped From Devil's Island (co-prod). **'74** The
Arena; The Student Teachers; Tender Loving
Care (GB: Naughty Nurses); Caged Heat; Big Bad
Mama (prod); The Godfather, Part II (act. only).
'75 TNT Jackson; Capone (prod); The Woman
Hunt; Death Race 2000 (prod); Cover Girl
Models; Tidal Wave (re-ed. and dubbed version of
Japanese film: Nippon Chinbotsu, 1973). **'76**
Summer School Teachers; Fighting Mad (prod);
Eat My Dust! (prod); Hollywood Boulevard; Jack-
son County Jail (exec. prod); Cannonball (+act)
(GB: Carquake); Moving Violation; Nashville
Girl/New Girl in Town; The Great Texas Dy-
namite Chase (GB: Dynamite Women); Blast. **'77**
Black Oak Conspiracy; I Never Promised You a
Rose Garden (co-exec. prod); Grand Theft Auto
(exec. prod); Thunder and Lightning (prod). **'78**
Deathsport (prod); Roger Corman – Hollywood's
Wild Angel (doc) (appearance as himself only);
Piranha (co-exec. prod); Fast Charlie – the
Moonbeam Rider (prod); Avalanche (prod); Out-
side Chance (prod). **'79** Saint Jack (prod); The
Lady in Red. **'80** Humanoids From the Deep (GB:
Monster); Battle Beyond the Stars (exec. prod);
Shogun Assassin (re-ed. and dubbed version of
Japanese film: Kozure Okami Sanzu No Kawa No
Ubaguruma, 1972).

Riding Easy

For a star, Jack Nicholson has some surprisingly un-starlike qualities. He will take a minor role as soon as a starring one, merely for the challenge; he won't ask the salary he is worth if he knows the picture is of limited appeal; he will take parts out of a desire to work with a specific director or as a favour to a friend; and he dislikes publicity. Yet, it is just this sort of non-conformity that has made each of his performances to date so appealing

Jack Nicholson

Today, no-one would dispute Jack Nicholson's right to stardom. He has an Oscar, the reputation for being hard to reach and is reluctant to give interviews – no matter that he might be bumped into at a neighbourhood restaurant or basketball game. As a box-office personality he has had several big hits that have pushed his salary very close to the top level.

Yet the casual, low-down mood of B pictures still hangs over him. He can be unshaven, shabby or downright unwholesome on screen – and he never comes near the monolithic glamour of Robert Redford or Clint Eastwood – but he is a most droll sexual rascal, as knowing as he is familiar and as likely to eat up a woman

Below: Jack Nicholson as the drifter in Rafelson's Five Easy Pieces, *seen here with two of the girls at the bowling-alley.*
Below right: with Bruce Dern as the brothers Staebler in The King of Marvin Gardens

as he could the camera. As a movie lover he goes all the way in terms of emotional commitment. He knows how absurd love is, but nothing deters him from its compulsion. Nicholson has never been tied down by the anxious self-esteem that limits Burt Reynolds. He is a very relaxed person and a truly romantic actor, always in search of extremes: death or ecstasy – the twin destinies of the B picture.

Other results of his low-budget background are that he believes in some pictures more than others; that he is rarely content to be a bankable star; and that the allegiances he formed in the Sixties still affect his choices of work. It is very difficult to think of a Nicholson film from the Seventies that is impersonal and unadventurous, and easy exploitation of his stardom doesn't move him much. He wants to shape his projects and be more deeply involved in things than is the case with most actors, and

the path he has taken is an example of how often the B-picture revival of the late Sixties was a breeding ground for people who were not just drug- or bike-crazy, but mad about movies too.

Born in New Jersey in 1937, Jack Nicholson had a difficult early life. His father was an alcoholic who left home before Jack was born, and his mother had to go into business to support the family. Never happy or occupied in high school, he drifted to Los Angeles in the late Fifties, one of the many who fancied being the next James Dean. He found a job in the cartoons department at MGM and took classes at the Jeff Corey acting school.

Sex and drugs and . . .
Over the next ten years Nicholson knocked around Hollywood, experimented with his life and did more hustling than most of his contemporaries. He married actress Sandra

Knight, had a daughter and divorced. He played around with motorbikes and drugs, and as far as work was concerned he was ready for whatever the low-budget director Roger Corman – or anyone else – could toss his way. His movies during this period included *The Cry-Baby Killer* (1958), *Too Soon to Love, The Little Shop of Horrors, Studs Lonigan* (all 1960), *The Trip, Hell's Angels on Wheels* (both 1967) and *Psych-Out* (1968).

The last two were directed by Richard Rush, who has finally received belated recognition for the stylish, camp existentialism of *The Stunt Man* (1980). Nicholson's work with Rush is a testament to his habit of working with odd, interesting people. Time and again he has found a special creative rapport with directors, and in the Sixties he managed this with both Monte Hellman and Bob Rafelson.

The ones that got away
Nicholson went to the Philippines with Hellman to make two back-to-back quickies – *Back Door to Hell* (1964) and *Flight to Fury* (1965). Those films are now only marginally harder to see than two intriguing, cryptic, sparse and beautiful Westerns they made together, *The Shooting* and *Ride in the Whirlwind* (both 1966).

Nicholson actually wrote the latter film, the clearest early sign of his ambition to be involved in the conception and creation of pictures. He has already directed twice – the excellent *Drive, He Said* (1971), about a college basketball star dodging military service, and *Goin' South* (1978), the story of a reforming outlaw – and while neither was a commercial success, it is probable that he will direct more as his looks match the raddled middle-age he tried out so thoroughly in *The Shining* (1980).

Raving with Rafelson
Bob Rafelson was a fellow-spirit, scornful of the old Hollywood. He and Nicholson have now worked together four times and are as close as, say, François Truffaut and Jean-Pierre Léaud. Rafelson was part inventor and owner of The Monkees, a pop group fashioned on the principle that any four kids with unkempt hair could be a rave for a year or so. With Nicholson as co-author, Rafelson made *Head* (1968), a surreal farce starring The Monkees, one of the best portraits of Sixties' lyrical anarchy. Thereafter, under Rafelson's direction, Nicholson did two diverse pieces of work that remain the best display of his acting versatility. In *Five Easy Pieces* (1970) he plays Bobby Dupea, a rough-

Nicholson as the lawyer who gives it all up for the life of a drifter in Easy Rider *(above, far left); as the boy who murders the men who beat him up in* The Cry-Baby Killer *(above left); and as the private eye hired by the mystery woman (Faye Dunaway) in* Chinatown *(above)*

neck oil-rigger who is actually a refugee from an earnest, musical family. The movie is a study of the thin line between liberty and irresponsibility, and it is a vital expression of Nicholson's equal interests in art and work and the life of outlaw sensuality.

Rafelson's *The King of Marvin Gardens* (1972) is a further exploration of the same theme. Nicholson and another old buddy, Bruce Dern, play the Staebler brothers. Nicholson depicts a lonely, introverted host on late-night radio: the artist as depressive, hoping to crystallize life's anguish, but despairing of his own happiness. Brother Dern is another kind of artist, a

Below left: Nicholson plays a sailor who decides to give a recruit a night to remember before being jailed for thieving in The Last Detail. *Below: looning around with the inmates in* One Flew Over the Cuckoo's Nest

and the movie is patently esoteric, with all its emphasis on space, colour and identity. Yet Nicholson adapted very well to the fresh idiom, grasping the fatalism of the reporter who has a brief reprieve from stagnation when he takes on the identity of a dead man. It took Marlon Brando in *The Missouri Breaks* (1976) to make Nicholson look overawed, despite his brave attempt to stand up to the aggressively brilliant and versatile star. However, he did contribute to this very underrated picaresque Western, and seemed to learn from it for his own *Goin' South*.

Twinkle, twinkle, little star

In 1980 he gave one of his most daring performances as Jack Torrance in Stanley Kubrick's *The Shining*. The film and his playing received a mixed reception, some accusing Nicholson of over-acting. Yet *The Shining* was a comedy, not a horror movie, and no-one understood its dainty command of fantasy better than the actor. It is, to date, the most bravura display of Nicholson's mastery of style and parody, turning intimacy into a grinding assault.

DAVID THOMSON

Above: a young woman (Mary Steenburgen) marries a 'bum' (Nicholson) to save him from hanging, then sets about his reform in Goin' South. *Below right: not a face to come home to – Nicholson as Jack Torrance in* The Shining

relentlessly extrovert huckster who has crazy plans for a gambling kingdom in Hawaii. The balance of manic and depressive leads to a sharper tragedy than *Five Easy Pieces* offered, and *The King of Marvin Gardens* was too harsh for a big audience. It remains a masterpiece and the most deeply felt and self-effacing performance Nicholson has yet given.

However, those films were made in the wake of *Easy Rider* (1969) in which he had really made his mark. When Rip Torn refused to do the movie after a row with producer/star Peter Fonda and director/star Dennis Hopper, they cast Nicholson as the disillusioned young lawyer who tags along on the trip. It is probable that the enormous popularity of the movie owed much to Nicholson. He plays the sort of character a middle-class audience could identify with if it were to go along with the motorized vagrancy of the road.

Nicholson's new status allowed him to pick his parts more carefully in the Seventies. *On a Clear Day You Can See Forever* (1970) is the only unaccountable choice: a result of his financial need and a studio's forlorn attempt to reach the young audience. *Carnal Knowledge* (1971) came from a wish to work with the director Mike Nichols, and it was a highly profitable movie that established the actor as a model for many American sexual drives and disorders.

Flying high

Also in the Seventies, Nicholson was the figurehead of two unerringly commercial movies. *Chinatown* (1974), in which a Los Angeles private eye sets out on a seemingly simple case, was not a great risk, but it showed how fully Nicholson was the heir to Humphrey Bogart and John Garfield – an actor flawed with the dismay of *film noir*, however robust he may seem. *Chinatown* also enabled him to stand as a helpless victim of love and paranoia: though set in the Thirties, the film is utterly modern in its politics. *One Flew Over the*

Cuckoo's Nest (1975) was a more daring project, and Nicholson was probably the most negotiable element in the film. His raffish charm as MacMurphy, imprisoned in an insane asylum for rape, made the madman appealing; his anger moved audiences all over the world. The film was a triumph, despite MacMurphy's death. Significantly, Nicholson dies or fails on screen more often than any other star.

Despite these commercial departures, Nicholson's urge to experiment was not exhausted. Henry Jaglom's *A Safe Place* (1971) is a very personal, poetic film that was only made because of Nicholson's wish to help an old friend. *The Last Detail* (1973), in which Nicholson plays a naval officer escorting a prisoner to jail, is more middle-of-the-road, but *Professione: Reporter* (1975, *The Passenger*) was proof of Nicholson's undiminished appetite for challenge. Its director, Michelangelo Antonioni, is notoriously aloof from his actors,

---

Filmography
1958 The Cry-Baby Killer. '60 Too Soon to Love; Studs Lonigan; The Little Shop of Horrors; The Wild Ride. '62 The Broken Land. '63 The Raven; The Terror (+ add. dir. uncredited); Thunder Island (co-sc. only). '64 Ensign Pulver; Back Door to Hell (USA-PHIL). '65 Flight to Fury (+sc) (USA-PHIL). '66 The Shooting (+ co-prod); Ride in the Whirlwind (+co-prod; +sc). '67 Hell's Angels on Wheels; The St. Valentine's Day Massacre; The Trip (sc. only). '68 Psych-Out; Head (+ co-prod + co-sc). '69 Easy Rider (+ add. ed, uncredited). '70 Rebel Rousers; On a Clear Day You Can See Forever; Five Easy Pieces. '71 Drive, He Said (dir; +co-prod; +co-sc. only); Carnal Knowledge; A Safe Place. '72 The King of Marvin Gardens. '73 The Last Detail. '74 Chinatown. '75 Tommy (GB); Professione: Reporter (USA/GB: The Passenger) (SP-IT-FR); The Fortune; One Flew Over the Cuckoo's Nest. '76 The Missouri Breaks; The Last Tycoon. '78 Goin' South (+dir). '80 The Shining (GB). '81 The Postman Always Rings Twice.

Z-MOVIE MADNESS

Drugs, beach parties, werewolves, Hell's Angels, zombies, pop music – a film menu to complement the hamburgers in the Sixties drive-ins

The simple workings of a sundial were once explained to Sam Goldwyn. 'Whatever will they think of next?' is reputed to have been his response, and that almost sums up Hollywood in the Sixties, desperate for ideas to cope with its problems. After the uncertainties of the Fifties, the battle lines between the cinema and its great competitor, television, were firmly established – and television was winning. Audience numbers had been steadily dropping; although audience figures would rise in the final part of the decade, by 1969 they were still less than a quarter of the 1946 figure. There were also fewer movies to see. The number of films released in 1959 was 187, little more than half of the 1950 figure. By the early Sixties, an estimated three-quarters of the Hollywood work force was engaged either directly or indirectly in television rather than cinema film production.

The history of Hollywood in the Sixties is dominated by board-room crises, take-over bids, asset sales and a general retraction by all the major studios. The movies they made seem of almost secondary importance and, with a handful of exceptions, they cannot compare with the flowering of European cinema in the same decade. Compensating achievements, and even perhaps the seeds of Hollywood's salvation, must be sought elsewhere.

There could be no greater contrast between the history of the Hollywood major studios during this time and that of AIP (American International Pictures). Throughout the decade it was run by Samuel Z. Arkoff and James H. Nicholson, as it had been since its inception in 1954. Their policy was also unchanging: cheaply produced double-feature bills (an average total of about twenty movies per year) made specifically for the ever-buoyant market of independent and drive-in cinemas that were unable to show major studio output, which went to the circuit cinemas in towns. They were also aimed squarely at the 16–25 age group which made up 80 per cent of the filmgoing population. AIP followed fashions, occasionally created them and exploited any subject that was even remotely filmable. The only difference from the Fifties was that, with eventual sales to television in mind, the movies were now all in colour.

The black-and-white teenage-delinquent dramas of the late Fifties were replaced by the plastic colourfulness of the Beach Party movies, inspired by the musical success on records of The Beach Boys and Jan and Dean. After the establishing formula of *Beach Party* (1963) itself, only the titles changed in the eight movies that followed. Whether they were called *Bikini Beach* (1964) or *Beach Blanket Bingo* (1965), the formula was the same: sun, sea, sand and surfing; no drinking, no smoking and no real love-making; antiseptic heroes and heroines (usually played by Frankie Avalon and Annette Funicello); adults such as Robert Cummings and Basil Rathbone always treated as figures of fun; and the depiction of a life-style that seemed to be totally dedicated to all-day surfing and all-night parties.

By the late Sixties, AIP was depicting a more realistic, although still fantasized, life-style. American involvement in Vietnam dominated the airwaves and newspapers, and it was once again a time when young people were disillusioned. But it was no longer just a question of broken families leading to juvenile delinquency. There was now a mood of open warfare against the whole of established society, and it was organized on a grand scale. AIP reflected the growth of this rebellion and

Top: in The Trip *Paul Groves (Peter Fonda), dissatisfied with work and marriage, tries the drug LSD; the results are pleasant at first but then turn sour. Above: youth goes* Wild in the Streets *when Max Frost (Christopher Jones) adds LSD to Washington's water with the help of Sally LeRoy (Diane Varsi)*

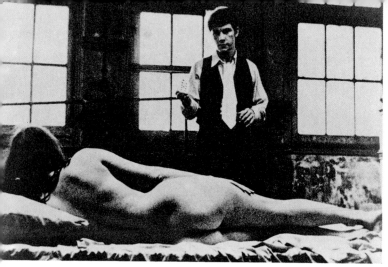

of what was to become known as the alternative society. *The Wild Angels* (1966) was the precursor of a seemingly endless series of motorbike-gang movies. The drug culture which became an accepted part of the alternative society was explored in *The Trip* (1967) and *Maryjane* (1968). The arrival of the hippies of Haight-Ashbury and the dawn of Flower Power in San Francisco was celebrated in *Psych-Out* (1968). In the ultimate youth fantasy *Wild in the Streets* (1968), a millionaire pop star and drug pusher actually becomes President of the United States after the voting age is lowered to 14. Yet, to their credit, AIP never over-exploited the violence and drug themes of these movies, although this was perhaps due as much to Samuel Z. Arkoff's business acumen as to any degree of social conscience. After the shootings at Kent State University, in which real students were killed by real national guardsmen, AIP withdrew from making youth-revolt pictures. Arkoff thought that the subject had become much too serious to be used simply as entertainment. This same acknowledgement of public outcry had earlier in the decade resulted in AIP's most enduring contributions to the list of outstanding independent productions of the Sixties, Roger Corman's Edgar Allan Poe cycle. The company had received criticism about the cheap exploitation of sex and violence in such films, now seemingly harmless, as *I Was a Teenage Werewolf* (1957), concerning an aggressive youth subjected to dangerous experiments, and *The Cool and the Crazy* (1958), which examined the drugs problem in high schools. Arkoff's answer was a series of intelligent, literate and almost-respectable movies based on classics of popular literature; they could feature in library displays even though they were showing at the local drive-in, where their basic horror-movie storylines anyway guaranteed them immense popularity. Although the series established Roger Corman as a major film-maker and comparisons were even drawn with the work of Ingmar Bergman, Arkoff knew the real reason why the young audiences went to see them: 'They go on the basis that they're campy – campy fun.'

Roger Corman was AIP's major director in the Sixties, but his importance in Hollywood history goes beyond his immense talents as a film-maker. Just as important as the 23 movies he directed in the Sixties and the many that he produced is what has become known as 'The Corman Connection'. This consists of a group of film-makers, later to make important contributions, whose earliest work is represented in the credits of undistinguished AIP productions. They were often film students who were anxious to work in the industry and therefore put in long hours of hard work, unrestricted by union membership; they were paid little but learned greatly from the valuable experience. Thomas

Colchart, for example, was listed as the director of *Battle Beyond the Sun* (1963). In fact, this was *Nebo Zobyot* (1959, The Sky Calls), a Russian space movie Americanized by dubbing and the shooting of additional scenes; and 'Thomas Colchart' was actually Francis Ford Coppola, a 24-year-old UCLA graduate who served his apprenticeship with Corman as sound man, dialogue coach, assistant director and second-unit director. His reward was *Dementia 13* (1963), a horror movie he made in Ireland using the resources and left-overs of Corman's own *The Young Racers* (1963). Others who learned their craft at AIP had their enthusiasm similarly rewarded.

A notable example, Monte Hellman, had already made his directorial debut in 1959 with the Corman-produced *Beast From Haunted Cave*; but by 1963 he was still helping Corman to shoot *The Terror* in three days by taking charge of second-unit filming. He was more than adequately rewarded three years later when Corman produced the two movies on which Hellman's high, although not widespread, reputation is largely based, *The Shooting* and *Ride in the Whirlwind* (both 1966), two rough, violent, mythic Westerns shot simultaneously in the Utah desert and featuring Jack

The motorbike displaced the horse as the favourite mount of a new breed of movie heroes who were taking the fast road to nowhere

Nicholson, until then an undistinguished Corman juvenile lead. They have been little seen, unlike *Targets* (1967); this was the first movie directed by the critic Peter Bogdanovich, who reputedly had fuelled the motorbikes on Corman's *The Wild Angels*.

If the combination of Roger Corman and AIP was the most successful of the Sixties, it was not without competitors. Joe Solomon's Fanfare Corporation, for example, was modelled on much the same lines as AIP; its huge success with *Hell's Angels on Wheels* (1967) not only furthered the career of the director Richard Rush, the star Jack Nicholson and the cameraman Laszlo Kovacs, but also pointed directly ahead to *Easy Rider* (1969).

There were stirrings, too, on a truly independent level. Brian De Palma was planning to become the American equivalent of Jean-Luc Godard with mixtures of political documentary, improvisation and irreverence such as the commercially successful *Greetings* (1968), a portrait of the young, aware and liberated Vietnam generation, and *The Wedding Party* (1967), which was co-directed with Cynthia

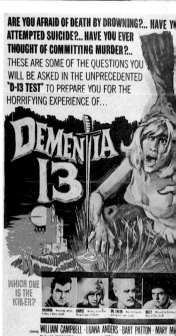

Top left: J. R. (Harvey Keitel) is prevented by his Catholic conscience from making love to his 'nice' girlfriend and has an erotic dream about an imaginary nude (Ann Collette) in Who's That Knocking at My Door? *Top: Jack Nicholson stars as a San Francisco hippie who tries to help a deaf teenage girl to find her brother in Richard Rush's* Psych-Out. *Above:* Dementia 13 *tells the story of an axe-murderer who kills several of his own family; the use of Irish locations and the creation of atmosphere are more outstanding than the plotline and give an early inkling of the director Francis Ford Coppola's talents*

right, but of greater importance in that of the first 32 of their shows, 29 were made by new directors, including Rafelson himself. This success was also the base on which Raybert launched into feature-film production, at first with the heavily satirical *Head* (1968), directed by Rafelson, written by Jack Nicholson and starring The Monkees in a series of film parodies in which they ridiculed themselves. Then came *Easy Rider*, and the floodgates opened.

Easy Rider cost $400,000 and earned $19 million in North America alone for Columbia, who bought it for distribution. Rafelson and Schneider form-ed BBS Productions with aid from Columbia to make feature films. As a result, such movies as Rafelson's *Five Easy Pieces* (1970) and Bogdano-vich's *The Last Picture Show* (1971) would soon be forming an intelligent and talent-filled base for the Seventies, and one that would eventually create a whole new audience for Hollywood movies.

Yet all this seemed very distant in 1970, when the major studios were simply reacting to the great success of *Easy Rider* in the traditional, and equally traditionally disastrous, way of emulating their independent teachers. Columbia was employing Richard Rush for a satirical look at campus unrest in *Getting Straight*, while MGM was treating the same subject seriously in *The Strawberry Statement*

Top: sex and revolution are readily combined in Stuart Hagmann's The Strawberry Statement *as students occupy a university administrative building. Above: in* Head *The Monkees rush out of a pop concert to escape their fans and find themselves involved in a war-movie parody; Peter Tork and Micky Dolenz try to keep a stiff upper lip, without much success. Above right: the logo of American International Pictures has introduced many popular films and quite a few critical successes*

Munroe and Wilford Leach and featured Jill Clayburgh and Robert De Niro in a story of a couple who marry after doubts and hesitations. At about the same time, Martin Scorsese was strugg-ling to complete his first feature *Who's That Knock-ing at My Door?* (1968), similarly influenced by *nouvelle vague* techniques and portraying a young man's growing up in New York's Little Italy. In deepest Pittsburgh, George A. Romero had com-pleted his tale of menacing resurrection *Night of the Living Dead* (1968), financed by a local advertising agency. Yet this most influential of modern horror movies was described by the trade paper *Variety* at the time as 'amateurism of the first order'. Never-theless, the so-called amateurs were poised to take over Hollywood itself, just as Romero's zombies took over in his memorably scary movie.

The clearest indication of that can be seen in the early history of Raybert Productions, set up by independent entrepreneur Bert Schneider and writer/producer Bob Rafelson in 1965 to produce a television series that was inspired by the example of The Beatles and the zany, almost surrealist style that Richard Lester had created in their first feature film *A Hard Day's Night* (1964). The totally manu-factured group featured in the series was The Monkees, who were a great success in their own

and trying to understand the failure of Michelangelo Antonioni's curious contribution to the rebellious-youth cycle *Zabriskie Point* (all three 1970). Dennis Hopper, the director of *Easy Rider*, was in Peru making *The Last Movie* (1971) for Universal, who never gave it a general release. On Hopper's avowed intent to save Hollywood, the verdict can be summed up in the words of *Easy Rider* itself: 'We blew it'. Francis Ford Coppola was setting up his first American Zoetrope studio in San Francisco with finance from Warner Brothers; but its first movie, George Lucas's *THX 1138* (1970), was a failure, being misunderstood and mispromoted by Warners. So the idea was abandoned and Coppola's dream of an independent film studio away from Hollywood was postponed until late in the decade.

Perhaps it would have been easier for Sam Goldwyn to comprehend the workings of that sundial than for Hollywood to enter the new age successfully. Only slowly would the major studios begin to understand that, as the independent producers of the Sixties had so clearly shown, the key to survival was new talent working in a new structure on original and not necessarily expensive projects that with intelligent marketing could create a new movie-going audience.

PETER HOWDEN

201

Easy Rider

'A man went looking for America and couldn't find it anywhere' announced the posters that advertised *Easy Rider*. It was a fitting summation of the low-budget film which defied Hollywood traditions and, at the same time, grossed more money than many of the lavish productions of the same year. Although this was the first film either of them had directed, Dennis Hopper and Peter Fonda sold their product to Columbia for $355,000: it went on to take more than $20 million at the box-office.

With its spontaneity and sincerity and its roots firmly in Sixties culture, *Easy Rider* established a new trend in movies: the 'road' film. Hollywood was quick to catch on to the idea of films whose characters had no history and travelled for no apparent reason; the journey becoming a metaphor for life, and the adventures on the road an allegory of man's search for himself. It also fostered a new taste in motorcycles – the Harley-Davidson 'Chopper'.

Wyatt and Billy set off across America on their own personal odyssey looking for a way to lead their lives. On the journey they encounter bigotry and hatred from small-town communities who despise and fear their non-conformism.

and it is these who finally kill off the dreams that they do not understand. Although Wyatt and Billy also discover people attempting 'alternative life-styles' who are resisting this narrow-mindedness, there is always a question-mark over the future survival of these drop-out groups. The gentle hippy community who thank God for 'a place to stand' are living their own unreal dream. The rancher and his Mexican wife are hard-pushed to make ends meet. Even LSD turns sour when the trip is a bad one. Death comes to seem the only freedom. It is significant that, in the final scene, the solitary burning bike remains: Wyatt's spirit lives on.

The film's essential philosophy is controversial, if unspoken. Nonetheless, it is eloquently articulated through the pulsating rock soundtrack, the emphasis on dope-smoking as a common aspect of life, the loving shots of the rolling scenery as they ride across America, and the equation of motorbikes with freedom rather than with the hooliganism of *The Wild One* (1953) and its successors. It was, perhaps, the only film to portray the new culture from within that culture itself.

Easy Rider also works on a

number of mythic and symbolic levels. Hopper had recently become engrossed in Thomism (a philosophical system based on the teachings of Thomas Aquinas) and indeed, it has been seen as the story of a modern prophet . . . from the difficulties of getting hotel rooms to the final violent 'crucifixion'. Another interpretation might suggest that Wyatt and Billy are the drop-out versions of their famous Western namesakes, reversing the traditional journey by travelling east on motorbikes rather than west on horses: a rejection of the old Hollywood and its myths and dreams. One further ironical aspect of this view is that Henry Fonda – Peter's father – once played Wyatt Earp in *My Darling Clementine* (1946). But there are no heroes in *Easy Rider*; identification is stimulated by the mood of the film rather than by characters who have no history and are therefore ideal subjects for mythical legend.

The filming process also rejected Hollywood traditions, as the crew themselves followed the same eastward journey, picking up their actors in the towns they passed through – often improvising action and dialogue. One dramatic scene in the diner, for instance, was done in this way: the locals were told that Hopper and Fonda were sexual

child-molesters, and the customers reacted appropriately vehemently. One actor not recruited *en route* was Jack Nicholson, who gained fame and an Oscar nomination for his portrayal of the liberal lawyer who drowns his uncertainties in alcohol.

In itself, *Easy Rider* is a work full of contradictions – including the fact that Hopper took time off from shooting to appear in *True Grit* (1969), a film with almost the opposite philosophy. Wyatt and Billy finance their journey from the proceeds of a cocaine sale, a hard drug which does not have the same idealistic connotations as marijuana. After their disappointment at the Mardi Gras, Wyatt acknowledges to Billy that 'we blew it'. There had to be another way to search for their freedom, one that was not betrayed from the start.

But despite its depressing message – that America has become so corrupt and bigoted that even those who try to find ways of escaping the system will be destroyed by it – the film is an exhilarating celebration of the alternatives that the Sixties offered. *Easy Rider* seems to say that if anyone blew it, it was America for not allowing a new and challenging, freer, more personal culture to exist.

SALLY HIBBIN

5

Directed by Dennis Hopper and Peter Fonda, 1969
Prod co: Pando Company/Raybert Productions. **exec prod:** Bert Schneider. **prod:** Peter Fonda. **assoc prod:** William Hayward. **sc:** Peter Fonda, Dennis Hopper, Terry Southern. **photo** (Technicolor): Laszlo Kovacs. **sp eff:** Steve Karkus. **ed:** Donn Cambren. **art dir:** Jerry Kay. **songs:** 'The Pusher', 'Born to Be Wild' by Steppenwolf, 'I Wasn't Born to Follow' by The Byrds, 'The Weight' by The Band, 'If You Want to Be a Bird' by The Holy Modal Rounders, 'Don't Bogart Me' by Fraternity of Man, 'If Six Was Nine' by The Jimi Hendrix Experience, 'Let's Turkey Trot' by Little Eva, 'Kyrie Eleison' by The Electric Prunes, 'Flash, Bam, Pow' by The Electric Flag, 'It's Alright Ma (I'm Only Bleeding)', 'Ballad of Easy Rider' by Roger McGuinn. **sd:** Ryder Sound Service. **prod man/ass dir:** Paul Lewis. **r/t:** 95 minutes.
Cast: Peter Fonda (*Wyatt*), Dennis Hopper (*Billy*), Antonio Mendoza (*Jesus*), Phil Spector (*connection*), Mac Mashourian (*bodyguard*), Warren Finnerty (*rancher*), Tita Colorado (*rancher's wife*), Luke Askew (*stranger*), Luana Anders (*Lisa*), Sabrina Scharf (*Sarah*), Sandy Wyeth (*Joanne*), Robert Walker (*Jack*), Robert Ball, Carman Phillips, Ellie Walker, Michael Pataki (*mimes*), Jack Nicholson (*George Hanson*), George Fowler Jr (*prison guard*), Keith Green (*sheriff*), Hayward Robillard (*cat man*), Arnold Hess Jr (*deputy sheriff*), Buddy Causey Jr, Duffy LaFont, Blase M. Dawson, Paul Guedry Jr, Suzie Ramagos, Elida Ann Hebert, Rose LeBlance, Mary Kaye Hebert, Cynthia Grezaffi, Collette Purpera (*customers in café*) Toni Basil (*Mary*), Karen Marmer (*Karen*), Cathi Cozzi (*dancing girl*), Thea Salerno, Ann McLain, Beatriz Monteil, Marcia Bowman (*hookers*), David C. Billodeau, Johnny David (*men in pick-up truck*).

After the successful completion of a cocaine sale in California (1), Wyatt (known as Captain America) and Billy stash their money in Wyatt's fuel-tank and set off on their motorbikes across America (2) in order to reach New Orleans in time for Mardi Gras. Unable to get a hotel room because of their

long hair and general unkempt appearance, they sleep out in the open. A couple who are trying to make a living from their small ranch give them a meal. Continuing on the road, they pick up a hitch-hiker who takes them to a hippy community that he is heading for (3). The life-style

8

seems idyllic, but after a brief stay Wyatt and Billy move on.

When they arrive at a diner in a small town, they are insulted by the local rednecks as weirdo degenerates (4). They are arrested on some minor pretext by the local sheriff and thrown into jail where they meet George

Hanson, a liberal alcoholic lawyer (5). He gets them out and decides to join them on their trip to New Orleans. The next night, when the three of them are sharing a joint (6), their camp is attacked and George is clubbed to death by the sheriff he had antagonized.

Wyatt and Billy ride on (7). They

pick up two girls from the House of Blue Lights, the brothel that George dreamed of visiting, and go to the Mardi Gras, which seems plastic and dull. In a cemetery they all take LSD and share a bad trip (8).

Wyatt and Billy decide to carry on riding to Florida. On the road,

a jeep driver thinks he'll have a little fun with the two of them (9) and takes a pot shot at Billy, whom he accidentally shoots in the stomach (10). Wyatt rides off for help, but the driver returns and deliberately shoots him. In the closing image his bike lies burning on the tarmac.

NEW MARTS FOR ART

Personal themes, motifs, obsessions, viewpoints became valuable assets for European directors as they made their mark with the world's expanding art-house audiences

Europe has traditionally been the centre for those sudden leaps forward in creative expression in the cinema that crystallize into movements. America generally absorbed the more obviously adaptable influences rather than allowing such movements to flower in its own ranks, as would happen in the Seventies. Hollywood has habitually tended to wait, watch the box-office success or otherwise of new styled European imports, and has then tried to enlist to its own ends the new stars and directors who have made a considerable mark.

But the Sixties was to see a new kind of development in the European cinema, something which would permeate production tendencies more gradually and become permanently rooted. The Sixties trend of personalized expression in the cinema was to infiltrate the upper levels of American production at least. It would also lead to the fuller acceptance of the European cinema in its own right and in its own languages during the decade and more especially during the Seventies in the expanding business of the art-house (or specialized) theatres to be found in the greater urban centres of the United States.

The new development in the European cinema was the increased international reputation earned by the outstanding work of such established and new directors as Robert Bresson, Alain Resnais, François Truffaut, Claude Chabrol and Jean-Luc Godard in France, Federico Fellini, Michelangelo Antonioni and later Pier-Paolo Pasolini, Bernardo Bertolucci and Marco Bellocchio in Italy, Ingmar Bergman in Sweden and, more particularly with his work in Spain and France, the veteran Luis Buñuel. This highly personalized cinema was created by directors with the tenacity and integrity to stick to careers in film-making which were essentially self-made and which flourished on top of the mainstream, more purely commercial entertainment; its cumulative effect was to be the great contribution of the Sixties to modern cinema. But it could never have succeeded without the backing of an increasingly large, international public composed on the whole of the younger age-groups with the continuous, insistent support of a considerable number of informed critics and writers in the press and the specialized film journals.

What is meant by a personalized cinema? It must imply that a director feels himself to be in a sufficiently strong, or at least confident, position with his medium to allow his choice of subject to be determined by its relationship to his own private experience, observation and inspiration. Such choices stem from personal idiosyncrasies, personal instinctual needs, interacting with a complex, ancient and deeply rooted social structure. In much the same way as the serious novelist, the film-maker selects his subject-matter and style in accord with his own impulse to self-expression and his perception of the social world which he is portraying, pursuing his own themes and obsessions and working through his unresolved psychic tensions. This manner of working has generally been more

available to the European than to the American film-maker, because the cinema was accepted more whole-heartedly there as an art-form as well as a branch of the entertainment industry.

Europe is a continent comprising a variety of societies which, though distinctive, are all quite highly structured and rigid in their own national styles of living. The individual film-maker can take many rules and conventions for granted within the context of his own country.

Most European countries have either had a freer and more open system of production, distribution and exhibition (sometimes international) than in the United States or have been granted a measure of government subsidy – and sometimes both. This has allowed relatively low-budget experiment to take place, gradually building up a public for the new until it is adequate to cover costs and eventually become accepted. The many European film festivals also provide a market-place and forum in which new reputations can rapidly be made.

During the Sixties, European films on the higher levels of mainstream, international distribution established a wide public following. There was, for example, Bergman, most notably in demanding work that ranged from *Tystnaden* (1963, *The Silence*) to *Persona* (1966), each powerfully depicting a pair of contrasted women. Bergman's films were often, on his own admission, a form of personal therapy. He has rightly maintained that film is the art that, above all others, is responsive to portraying 'psychic states'. No film made up to its time was more complex in its demands on audiences than *Persona*, which entered into the ambivalent nature of a theatre actress's nervous breakdown occasioned by her deliberate withdrawal both from the tensions of private life and from her distress at the tortured

Top: Ingrid Thulin (left) as Ester in The Silence, *with Gunnel Lindblom as her younger sister Anna and Jörgen Lindström as Anna's ten-year-old son Johan; they are in a strange foreign city. Above: Balthazar the donkey is a childhood pet of Marie (Anne Wiazemsky) in* Au Hasard, Balthazar *and both are victimized by young thugs when Marie falls for their leader*

condition of the troubled world outside.

There was the very different case of Fellini, whose films became in the Sixties increasingly, and sometimes indulgently, an entertaining projection of some personal dilemma, as in *Otto e Mezzo* (1963, $8\frac{1}{2}$) – which is a study of a film director moving in and out of a condition of nervous exhaustion when the pressures become too great for him both in his career and in his private relationships. The following film *Giulietta degli Spiriti* (1965, *Juliet of the Spirits*), dedicated to Giulietta Masina, his wife and constant collaborator, reflected, at least in part, certain problems such as she might have faced in their marriage.

Godard, again to take a totally different personality of the Sixties, developed an entirely new, dialectical technique in film-making in order to make the screen a platform from which to debate or assert his personal position socially and politically; in the process, he became one of the most discussed and influential directors of the time. *A Bout de Souffle* (1960, *Breathless*) posited an existentialist

France and Italy dominated the field of personal cinema during the newly art-conscious Sixties

ethic of living for the moment; the hoodlum hero and his American girlfriend accept murder, theft and betrayal as the natural consequences of their values. Godard's later films of the decade were essentially works that confronted audiences with challenging social and political concepts involving them just as much as himself and his players, thus creating a new director-actor-audience form of combined relationship.

Bresson's obsessive melancholy darkened such poignant films as *Au Hasard, Balthazar* (1966, *Balthazar*) and *Mouchette* (1967); in these studies of the suffering of young girls, the downtrodden were trod even further down. The Sixties was the great decade of Antonioni's unique achievements, from *L'Avventura* (1960, *The Adventure*) to his American *Zabriskie Point* (1970). *L'Avventura* examined minutely the sudden and uncertain blossoming of a love affair in a couple searching for a missing girl, the man's fiancée. Avoiding any kind of conventional, dynamic theatricality, Antonioni's camera scrutinized the behaviour of people at the natural speed it would take them to resolve their personal dilemmas – the viewer was compelled to watch the nature of human indecision.

Eric Rohmer began in the Sixties a series of *Six Contes Moraux* (Six Moral Tales) which included *Ma Nuit Chez Maud* (1969, *My Night With Maud*) and *Le Genou de Claire*, (1970, *Claire's Knee*); these studies in conscience and repressed sexuality encouraged audiences to discover the details of the characters' reasoning rather than to observe their actions. Such extended, intimate contemplation was new to cinema, yet in time it came to command the respect of those audiences. Resnais' films revealed his deep interest in the way that responses to present experience are coloured by the traumas of the past, whether recollected or subconscious. He established himself in the Sixties as one of the more profound of modern film-makers, especially with *Hiroshima, Mon Amour* (1959, Hiroshima, My Love), *Muriel, ou le Temps d'un Retour* (1963, *Muriel*) and *La Guerre Est Finie* (1966, *The War Is Over*). Truffaut made personal, at times partially autobiographical films in the series about Antoine Doinel's growing up, including *Les Quatre Cents Coups* (1959, *The 400 Blows*), *Baisers Volés* (1968, *Stolen Kisses*) and *Domicile Conjugal* (1970, *Bed and Board*).

Buñuel was always the close observer of suffering rather than projecting any suffering he might himself have experienced during his difficult career; sardonic but never inhumane, he melted the icecap of bourgeois religious and sexual pretensions, daring to make a bold, personal challenge to his native country under Franco (or settle a personal vendetta) with *Viridiana* (1961), a critique of Spanish religious and moral values; and, in one of his

most startling films, to strip the archetypal sexual masks from a conventional, well-brought-up woman of the upper-middle class in *Belle de Jour* (1967). The socio-political, Marxist-influenced cinema represented by Pasolini's *Accattone* (1961) and *Il Vangelo Secondo Matteo* (1964, *The Gospel According to St Matthew*), Bellocchio's study of an inbred family *Pugni in Tasca* (1965, *Fists in the Pocket*) and Bertolucci's examination of the rise of Fascism *Il Conformista* (1970, *The Conformist*), established its roots during the Sixties. The period also saw the production in France of the highly personalized films of Louis Malle, Alain Jessua, Jacques Rivette and Agnès Varda.

In Britain, less inhibited, more openly proletarian subjects reached the screen with Karel Reisz's *Saturday Night and Sunday Morning* (1960), based on Alan Sillitoe's novel, and *Morgan, a Suitable Case for Treatment* (1966), from David Mercer's play; with Lindsay Anderson's *This Sporting Life* (1963), adapted from David Storey's novel; and with Tony Richardson's *Look Back in Anger* (1959), from John Osborne's play, and *A Taste of Honey* (1961), based on Shelagh Delaney's play. But these films were personalized cinema at one remove, since the subjects were more personal to the writers than to the directors themselves, as was so often the case in the British cinema of the Sixties.

In response to all this individualized work, critics began to adopt the word 'auteur', in the sense of 'author of films', and apply it rather indiscriminately in order to discover personal veins, thematic predilections or technical quirks or twists in the work of directors in the more widely popular American genres of film-making. The European film had proved, however, that the personalized cinema was gradually moving into the forefront of critical attention. This trend was backed by the film festivals, the writings of the leading critics and commentators, the growing library of books about films, the increasing popularity of film studies in the universities – particularly in North America – and the growth of the influence of the specialized cinemas and film societies. The more mature among the younger audiences turned their back on the banalities of television and made the highbrow cinema into a cult; the more markedly individual directors with artistic or socio-political interest, and those prepared to deal in depth with psychological and sexual subjects were particularly favoured. As the general film theatres and their audiences declined rapidly in numbers, the proportion of audiences remaining faithful to the art-house cinema, or newly discovering it as a lively, contemporary artform, rose – again bringing increased recognition to the work of the directors already discussed.

The effect in America of this maturation of the European cinema was to be only gradual. The strict bar against allowing financial backing for anything that seemed to suggest minority interests relaxed very rarely. American film-makers with a strongly individual flair – such as Stanley Kubrick, John Huston, Joseph Losey or John Cassavetes – worked in some instances abroad, notably in Britain. The rise of the independent producer and producer-director as the determining factor in superior American films led to a much greater variety of subject. Few American films of the period could be regarded as strictly personalized cinema in the sense that they fulfilled the inner needs of their makers, or projected their personal problems or exceptional personal experiences. Elia Kazan certainly made attempts at this when filming his own novels in *America, America* (1963) and *The Arrangement* (1969). But the more personalized cinema was to emerge in America during the Seventies, notably in the work of Woody Allen, whose first tentative comedy as writer, director and star was *Take the Money and Run* (1969), or in the post-Sixties work of such directors as Hal Ashby, Robert Altman, Paul Mazursky, Francis Ford Coppola and Martin Scorsese.   ROGER MANVELL

Top left: the murder of Professor Quadri (Enzo Taroscio), a political activist, by Italian Fascist hirelings in France shortly before World War II – a climactic scene from The Conformist. *Top:* Viridiana *(Silvia Pinal), a few hours out of the convent where she is a novice, tries on her symbolic crown of thorns with a misplaced touch of innocent vanity. Above: Christine Doinel (Claude Jade) in* Bed and Board *makes herself up to resemble her husband's boring Japanese mistress Kyoko; the erring Antoine is eventually relieved to return to his wife*

Maestro

Charming, cool and sophisticated, or withdrawn, shy and very private? Every woman's idea of the ultimate Italian Romeo, or a reluctant Casanova? Which is the true Marcello Mastroianni?

Mastroianni

Marcello Mastroianni shot into the orbit of world fame in 1959. The rocket to launch him was director Federico Fellini's *La Dolce Vita* (The Sweet Life), even though by then Mastroianni was 35 and had appeared in over forty films. The man he plays in *La Dolce Vita* is immature rather than young; attractive to women without knowing how to make them happy; living in high society, without being rich.

Clearly it was this ability to project inadequacies that helped him to embody the disenchantment of the post-war generation so successfully. Casually elegant and suave, a snob-symbol rather than a sex-symbol, it was largely the publicity campaigns which built him up as the great Latin lover. In fact he has always been as popular with men as with women: men could identify with him. There are very few stars of this kind, but they shine longest: Humphrey Bogart, Steve McQueen or Clint Eastwood in the USA; Jean Gabin, Yves Montand and Jean-Louis Trintignant in France. But they are all tough action-men. Only Mastroianni has ever reached the top by appearing soft and passive, with the manners and bearing of an old-fashioned gentleman.

It is of course as misleading an image as only a consummate actor could project. The son of a small tradesman, Mastroianni has always been ambitious, as well as talented, and extremely hard-working, making three or four films a year; and in complete control of the considerable achievements of his career.

He was born in 1924 in Fontana Liri, near Frosinone, roughly halfway between Rome and Naples; but his family moved north to Turin during his childhood, and soon after to Rome, where he began training as a draughtsman. During World War II he was captured and sent to a German prison camp, from which he escaped, hiding in Venice until 1945, when he returned to Rome and found a job in the

accounts department of Eagle Lion Films, a Rank subsidiary. He spent most evenings at a drama club and was eventually noticed by the director Luchino Visconti who recruited him for his professional theatre company, and helped him to his first small part in the film, based on the novel by Victor Hugo, *I Miserabili* (1948, Les Misérables), directed by Riccardo Freda.

After a few more minor roles, he attracted attention in *Vita da Cani* (1950, *It's a Dog's Life*) and he was given increasingly important parts in a long series of unmemorable films, which established his popularity in Italy. He finally reached the festival circuit when Visconti cast him in *Le Notti Bianche* (1957, *White Nights*)

with Maria Schell and Jean Marais.

In 1959 Federico Fellini began to shoot *La Dolce Vita*, casting Mastroianni as the journalist Marcello, who hangs around with Rome's high society; more than an observer, but less than a catalyst. His boyish charm and obvious availability draw the attentions of beautiful women. But when the friend he admires as a clear-headed intellectual, kills himself and his two children, Marcello abandons journalism for the pursuit of pleasure but thereby only

The more mature Mastroianni (above), and as seen in an early film (below), I Soliti Ignoti (1958, Persons Unknown), with Vittorio Gassman (left) and Renato Rascel

burdens himself with a sense of futility as well as guilt.

Mastroianni then went on to appear in *Divorzio all'Italiana* (1961, *Divorce – Italian Style*), directed by Pietro Germi, which afforded him his first really good role, as the effete Sicilian nobleman who, in love with his teenage cousin, wants to rid himself of his wife. Most Italian comedies fail to travel but Germi's film contrived to caricature Italian stereotypes to everyone's liking.

A sharp contrast was called for from Mastroianni by the director Michelangelo Antonioni in *La Notte* (1961, *The Night*), in which Mastroianni plays a fashionable novelist, surrounded by lovely women, who fails to give, or even to understand, what they want of him. Unlike Fellini, Antonioni does not treat lack of emotion as a colourful neurosis which makes its victim more interesting; his images are bleak and distanced, showing his figures as cut off from each other and their own humanity. However, even in this negative role Mastroianni holds the balance against any other actor or actress.

Meanwhile, *Divorce – Italian Style* continued to win him acclaim, including the British Film Academy's Best Foreign Actor Award. Mastroianni became one of the most sought-after actors in Europe; in Italy, he ranked second only to Alberto Sordi. In 1962, he played in director Louis Malle's *Vie Privée* (*A Very Private Affair*) with Brigitte Bardot, and also in *Cronaca Familiare* (*Family Diary*) directed by Valerio Zurlini, before returning to Fellini for his second most famous role as the director-hero Luigi in *Otto e Mezzo* (1963, $8\frac{1}{2}$). As in so many of Fellini's films, dreams and memories come together with a present which is less real than either. Luigi is at a point of crisis: he has withdrawn to an out-of-season resort to re-write his script, but the people who claim his attention all turn up. The film's ending is a dream sequence which is also a resolution of his conflicts: he assumes the powers of a circus-master and brings everyone together in the ring for a grand finale. Throughout, Mastroianni hardly needs to act: he is there, while the others cavort around him.

The next major collaboration between Fellini and Mastroianni came twenty years after their first, in *La Città delle Donne* (1980, *City of Women*), which Mastroianni claims to be his hundredth film. Fellini's subject is the inability

of his generation to cope with even the first steps of female emancipation. Professor Snaporaz, played by Mastroianni, wants to have an affair with a beautiful woman he meets on a train: she leads him to a women's lib conference, which, like a nightmare, expands into a world run by women where he is totally bewildered by all that happens.

Mastroianni has repeatedly said that filming with other directors is work, but with Fellini it is a game. They are close friends: they share their attitudes and their sense of humour. But just as Fellini denies that his films are directly autobiographical, Mastroianni rejects the suggestion that he models any character he plays on Fellini. They both aim at creating the typical, sophisticated Italian of their generation. Their joint creation reflects centuries of male egotism which prevents such a man from formulating a dialogue with women, or even noticing that they are autonomous beings. In this way they have brought forth the anti-heroes of four shrill, flamboyant films, *La Dolce Vita*, $8\frac{1}{2}$, *Fellini's Roma* (1972) and *La Città delle Donne*, in which Mastroianni gives deliberately low-key performances, just being himself. But an actor's self is seldom as interesting as a complex part scripted by a good writer. To judge Mastroianni as an actor his work with other directors should also be looked at.

For example, in *Leo the Last* (1970), written and directed by John Boorman and made in London, Mastroianni uses his aristocratic manner and kindliness as an exiled prince who tries to found something like the Kingdom of Heaven in Bayswater. Boorman's film is as eccentric and unclassifiable as any of director Marco Ferreri's, and, while it failed at the box-office, it still contributes more to Mastroianni's standing than any number of routine comedies.

By this time Mastroianni's talents were divided equally between pot-boilers and serious acting in such masterpieces as Ferreri's *La Grande Bouffe* (1973, *Blow-Out*) in which he

plays the light-hearted playboy who joins his friends in eating themselves to death. In *Allonsanfán* (1974) under the joint direction of Paulo and Vittorio Taviani, he had to retain his patrician mannerisms and still lead a revolution; to become a traitor, and still hold the audience's sympathy. Many critics thought that he should have won the acting award at Cannes for playing the gentle, homosexual radio announcer in director-screenwriter Ettore Scola's *Una Giornata Particolare* (1977, *A Special Day*). Waiting for the police to arrest and deport him, he offers a tired, exploited but fervently fascist housewife, played well by Sophia Loren, her one and only genuine human contact.

The following year he turned in another heart-rending performance in Ferreri's *Ciao Maschio* (1978, *Bye Bye Monkey*) as an asthmatic, seedy professor in the desolate New York of the future. He was back in Cannes in 1980 in Scola's *La Terrazza* (1979, *The Terrace*) in which he plays a journalist whose ex-wife is more interested in her work than in his romantic attempts to woo her again. Like all the other fiftyish men in the film, he is

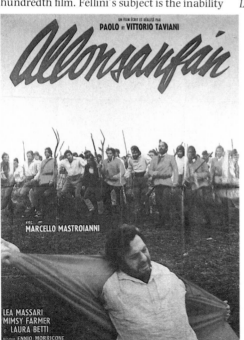

nonplussed by the change in women, by their wanting more from life than loving and being loved. Mastroianni manages to convey both nostalgia, and an intellectual capacity to respect, while regretting, the equal rights of women.

On quite different levels, Scola and Ferreri are directors concerned with tensions between society and individuals, giving Mastroianni scope to act, while Fellini is a director of grand spectacles and in his films, Mastroianni merely triggers off each new tableau. But as long as the world loves a carnival, Mastroianni's fame will depend on Fellini's mastery of his circus. With other directors, he works; with Fellini, he plays; and in over a hundred films, he has proved his excellence either way.

MARI KUTTNA

Below far left: the poster for Allonsanfán. *Below left: Mastroianni, Vittorio Gassman and Ombretta Colli as members of a group of people who meet on* La Terrazza *during one hot Roman summer. Below: Mastroianni trapped in his nightmare world of female domination in* La Città delle Donne

Filmography

1948: I Miserabili (IT). '50 Vent'Anni (IT); Domenica d'Agosto (IT) (GB: A Sunday in August); Vita da Cani (IT) (GB: It's a Dog's Life); Cuori sul Mare (IT-FR). '51 Atto d'Accusa (IT) (GB: The Charge Is Murder); A Tale of Five Cities ep Passaporto per l'Oriente (GB); Contro la Legge (IT); Parigi è Sempre Parigi (IT-FR). '52 Le Ragazze di Piazza di Spagna (IT) (USA: Three Girls From Rome; GB: The Girls of the Spanish Steps); L'Eterna Catena (IT); Sensualità (IT) (GB: Enticement). '53 Gli Eroi della Domenica (IT); Febbre di Vivere (IT); Viale della Speranza (IT); Lulù (IT); Penne Nere (IT); Non è Mai Troppo Tardi (IT). '54 Tempi Nostri ep Il Pupo (IT-FR) (USA: The Anatomy of Love; GB: Slice of Life); Cronache di Poveri Amanti (IT); Tragico Ritorno (IT); La Valigia dei Sogni (IT); La Schiava del Peccato (IT); La Muta di Portici (IT); Casa Ricordi (IT-FR) (USA: House of Ricordi). '55 Giorni d'Amore (IT); Peccato che Sia una Canaglia (IT) (GB: Too Bad She's Bad); Tam Tam Mayumbe (IT-FR); La Bella Mugnaia (IT) (USA: The Miller's Beautiful Wife; GB: The Miller's Wife). '56 La Fortuna di Essere Donna (IT-FR) (GB: Lucky to be a Woman); Il Bigamo (IT) (USA: A Plea for Passion; GB: The Bigamist); La Principessa della Canarie (IT). '57 Padri e Figli (IT-FR) (USA: A Tailor's Maid; GB: Like Father, Like Son); La Ragazza della Salina (IT-GER-YUG); Il Momento più Bello (IT-FR) (USA/GB: The Most Wonderful Moment); Le Notti Bianche (IT-FR) (USA/GB: White Nights); Il Medico e lo Stregone (IT-FR). '58 Un Ettaro di Cielo (IT) (GB: An Acre of Paradise); Racconti d'Estate (IT-FR) (USA: Love on the Riviera; GB: Girls for the Summer); I Soliti Ignoti (IT) (USA: Big Deal on Madonna Street; GB: Persons Unknown). '59 La Loi (FR-IT) (USA/GB: Where the Hot Wind Blows); Il Nemico di Mia Moglie (IT); Tutti Innamorati (IT); Amore e Guai (IT); La Dolce Vita (IT-FR). '60 Fernando I Re di Napoli (IT); Il Bell'Antonio (IT-FR); Adua e le Compagne (IT) (USA: Love à la Carte; GB: Hungry for Love). '61 La Notte (IT-FR) (GB: The Night); L'Assassino (IT-FR) (USA: Lady-Killer of Rome; GB: The Assassin); Fantasmi a Roma (IT) (GB: Phantom Lovers); Divorzio all'Italiana (IT) (USA/GB: Divorce – Italian Style). '62 Vie Privée (FR-IT) (USA/GB: A Very Private Affair); Cronaca Familiare (IT) (USA/GB: Family Diary). '63 Otto e Mezzo (IT-FR) (USA/GB: 8½); I Compagni (IT-FR) (USA/GB: The Organizer). '64 Ieri, Oggi e Domani (IT-FR) (USA/GB): Yesterday, Today and Tomorrow); Matrimonio all'Italiana (IT-FR) (USA/GB: Marriage Italian Style). '65 Casanova 70 (IT-FR); Oggi, Domani, Dopodomani (IT-FR); La Decima Vittima (IT-FR) (USA/GB: The Tenth Victim). '66 Io, Io, Io . . . e gli Altri (IT) (GB: Me, Me, Me . . . and the Others); Danger Grows Wild/The Poppy Is also a Flower (United Nations); Spara Forte, Più Forte, Non Capisco (IT) (USA: Shout Loud, Louder . . . I Don't Understand). '67 Lo Straniero (IT-FR) (USA: The Stranger; GB: The Outsider). '68 Questi Fantasmi (IT-FR) (USA: Ghosts, Italian Style); L'Uomo dai Palloncini (IT-FR) (USA: Break Up); La Moglie Bionda (IT-FR) (USA: Kiss the Other Sheik); Diamonds for Breakfast (GB); Amanti (IT-FR) (USA/GB: A Place for Lovers). '70 I Girasoli (IT-USSR) (USA/GB: Sunflower); Leo the Last (GB); Dramma della Gelosia, Tutti i Particolari in Cronaca (IT-SP) (USA: The Pizza Triangle; GB: Jealousy, Italian Style); La Moglie del Prete (IT-FR) (USA/GB: The Priest's Wife); Giuochi Particolari (IT-FR). '71 Scipione detto Anche l'Africano (IT); Ça N'Arrive Qu'aux Autres (FR-IT) (USA: It Only Happens to Others); Permette? Rocco Papaleo (IT). '72 Fellini's Roma (IT-FR); Correva l'Anno di Grazia 1870 . . . (IT); Liza/La Cagna (FR-IT); Che? (IT-FR-GER) (USA: Diary of Forbidden Dreams; GB: What?). '73 Mordì e Fuggì (IT); La Grande Bouffe (FR-IT) (USA/GB: Blow-Out); Rappresaglia (IT-FR) (USA/GB: Massacre in Rome); L'Evénement le Plus Important Depuis que l'Homme a Marché sur la Lune (FR-IT) (USA/GB: The Slightly Pregnant Man); Salut l'Artiste (FR-IT) (USA: The Bit Player). '74 Touche Pas la Femme Blanche (FR-IT); Allonsanfán (IT); La Pupa del Gangster (IT-FR); C'Eravamo Tanti Amati (IT) (USA: We All Loved Each Other So Much). '75 Per le Antiche Scale (IT-FR) (USA/GB: Down the Ancient Staircase); Divina Creatura (IT) (USA: Divine Nymph). '76 La Donna della Domenica (IT-FR); Culastrisce, Nobile Veneziano (IT); Todo Modo (IT). '77 Signore e Signori, Buonanotte (IT); Una Giornata Particolare (IT-CAN) (USA/GB: A Special Day); Mogliamante (IT) (USA: Wifemistress). '78 Doppio Delitto (IT-FR); Bye Bye Monkey/Ciao Maschio/Ciao, Male (IT-FR); Così Come Sei (IT) (USA: Stay as You Are). '79 Fatto di Sangue Fra Due Uomini (IT) (USA/GB: Blood Feud); L'Ingorgo (IT-FR-SP-GER); Giallo Napoletano (IT); La Terrazza (IT-FR). '80 La Città delle Donne (IT-FR). '81 La Pelle; Fantasma d'Amore.

1

2

5

Films about people making films, films about their makers' personal problems and films full of intellectual references are three of the most irritating genres there are. 8½ appears to be all three. Its exuberant tempo and striking imagery may carry one along, but it is just as likely to seem needlessly difficult and self-indulgent. Still, to treat it as a purely personal and intellectual film may be misleading.

8½ certainly does invite a personal reading. Its title refers to the number of films Fellini had directed up to then; Guido is, like Fellini, a film director of international repute; his marital difficulties seem obviously to refer to Fellini's own widely publicized problems. Moreover, the film is full of characteristic Fellini touches: clowns and tatty showbiz performers, big-breasted women and sexual grotesques, Marcello Mastroianni as hero, and a sweetly melancholic Nino Rota score.

Yet 8½ can be taken as a metaphor of much wider significance. It recreates, with all the frustrations and vicissitudes, the experience of trying to come to terms with the world. Fellini's 'private' material stands for any person's individual experience as she or he confronts the world, trying to make sense of it.

If 8½ is about making sense, it is also itself rather hard to make sense of. It seems to cry out for intellectual interpretation. Its complex structure, weaving between memories, dreams and waking life,

is made even more confusing by the welter of references to religion, ideas, the arts, the occult and so on. This allusive richness seems to be begging for a set of footnotes explaining each reference. Yet it is perfectly possible simply to treat each one as examples of different ways of making sense as they confront Guido.

Besides, in many ways 8½ is a profoundly *un*intellectual film. There is, as elsewhere in Fellini, explicit anti-intellectualism in the figure of the critic Daumier. Played by the critic Jean Rougeul, he is cast, as is characteristic of Fellini, for his looks – a sharp-nosed, very unfleshy appearance, representing the carping anti-life stance that Fellini identifies as typical of intellectuals.

The ending of 8½ too is a rejection of all kinds of intellectual or systematic attempts at making sense, and also of scouring one's past (as Guido has been doing) for clues to the present. When Guido meets Claudia, the screen goddess who is to play the ideal woman (here played by screen goddess Claudia Cardinale), he meets a pleasant, ordinary woman . . . not an ideal. It kills off an aspect of the film – how is he ever to find a woman to embody the ideal woman? – but he also learns from this that the real problem with his character (the character in the film, Guido himself) is that he does not know how to love. This is the clue to the final scene of the film where Guido, sitting in a car

listening to critic Daumier droning on, imagines gathering together everyone he has known and dancing round a circus ring with them. That will be the conclusion to the film, and it is also the conclusion to 8½ – a simple celebration of the dance of life, a warm acceptance of other people.

However, the very last image is not this, but a small boy playing a melancholy tune on a flute. The boy is Guido as a child seen through Guido's memories. It was only in his imagination that he embraced

life simply; behind that he is still a confused small boy playing a sad little melody.

It is a difficult conclusion to come to terms with. Rhythmically it is hypnotic. Nowhere has Fellini more ravishingly combined music, the tempo of editing and the pace of both movement within the frame and movement of the camera, all orchestrated into a crescendo of affirmation with a coda of melancholy. For all this, 8½ has set off a multitude of intellectual hares, and does offer itself as some kind of

Directed by Federico Fellini, 1963
Prod co: Cineriz. **prod:** Angelo Rizzoli. **sc:** Federico Fellini, Ennio Flaiano, Tullio Pinelli, Brunello Rondi. **photo:** Gianni Di Venanzo. **ed:** Leo Catozzo. **art dir:** Piero Gherardi. **mus:** Nino Rota. **prod man:** Nello Meniconi. **ass dir:** Guidarino Guidi. **r/t:** 138 minutes.
Cast: Marcello Mastroianni (*Guido Anselmi*), Claudia Cardinale (*Claudia*), Anouk Aimée (*Luisa Anselmi*), Sandra Milo (*Carla*), Rossella Falk (*Rossella*), Barbara Steele (*Gloria Morin*), Guido Alberti (*Pace, the producer*), Madeleine Lebeau (*actress*), Jean Rougeul (*Fabrizio Carini*), Caterina Boratto (*vision*), Annibale Ninchi (*Anselmi's father*), Giuditta Rissone (*Anselmi's mother*), Mario Pisu (*Mozzabotta*), Jacqueline Bonbon (*dancer*), Alberto Conochia (*production manager*), Ian Dallas (*mind-reader*), Edra Gale (*La Saraghina*), Tito Masini (*cardinal*), Cesarino Miceli Pardi (*production inspector*), Neil Robinson (*agent*), Mino Doro (*Claudia's agent*), Mario Tarchetti (*Claudia's press representative*), Eugene Walter (*American journalist*), Gilda Dahlberg (*his wife*), Annie Gorassini (*Pace's girlfriend*), Mary Indovino (*mind-reader's partner*), Mario Conocchia (*director*), Bruno Agostini (*production secretary*), John Stacy (*accountant*), Mark Herron (*Luisa's admirer*), Elisabetta Catalano (*Luisa's sister*), Alfredo De Lafeld (*cardinal's secretary*), Frazier Rippy (*lay secretary*), Maria Tedeschi (*college president*), Georgia Simmons (*nun*), Yvonne Casadei (*ageing soubrette*), Nadine Sanders (*air hostess*), Hazel Rogers (*negress*), Hedy Vessel (*dresser*), Rosella Como, Francesco Rigamonti, Matilde Calnam (*Luisa's friends*), Roberto Nicolosi (*doctor*), Riccardo Guglielmi, Marco Gemini (*Anselmi as a boy*).

3

4

7

testament to both film-making and Fellini himself. In the face of this, there is something too ingratiating about the fantasy affirmation of life, something too maudlin about the little-boy-lost image. What Guido has supposedly learned from Claudia is the need to love, and the final images are supposedly an enactment of a new-found love. Nonetheless, as so often with the male-artist-in-crisis, familiar from mid-century art, it is not so much a declaration of love as a demand for it, and a demand for that most unconditional form of love that the small boy supposedly elicits from his mother. Musically, the ending feels like an affirmation; imagistically it looks like a plea. Ultimately, if $8\frac{1}{2}$ is to stand as a testament to creativity, it will depend on how the audience decides where its sympathies lie.   RICHARD DYER

Guido, an internationally successful Italian film director, is trying to make his latest film (1). He already has some expensive sets and the rudiments of a story about a man who chases an ideal woman who rejects him. But he cannot get started.

He is overwhelmed by the clamour of his professional colleagues (2) and entangled in personal problems of his own making. These are exacerbated when his feather-brained mistress, Carla (3), and disconsolate wife, Luisa (4), both turn up where the film is being made.

Memories of childhood (5) and sexual fantasies assail him: a visit to a Cardinal; a vision of a harem (6); meeting his ideal – Claudia (7). Perhaps these ought to be the material for the film?

At a press conference he hides from reporters and his producer who want to know what film he is making, when he is saved by a band of clowns (8) and finally the whole cast of the film (9). He has various options – to commit suicide, to give up filming altogether, to make his peace with the world. . . .

9

There can be no accurately objective synopsis of *Persona*, since its events occur at varying levels of 'reality' that cannot be decisively defined. It was Bergman's conscious intention to blur the distinctions between the real and the imaginary. He wanted to produce a piece of fiction which has as its main theme the subjectivity of perception, and in its style is so subjective as to be open to a multitude of interpretations.

Why is *Persona* such a deliberately 'difficult' film and at the same time such an intensely personal work? To find useful answers, it is important to consider Bergman's predicament in the mid-Sixties. Having left behind the medieval symbolism of *Det Sjunde Inseglet* (1957, *The Seventh Seal*), he continued using allegory to probe spiritual problems in *Såsom i en Spegel* (1961, *Through a Glass, Darkly*) and *Nattvardsgästerna* (1962, *Winter Light*); but he appeared to be acquiring the gloomy reputation of a brooding, ascetic moralist of the movies. *Persona* changed all that. Bergman, emerging from a period of severe ill-health, experimented with a fresh, direct and uncluttered style which allowed him scope to broach profound psychological problems. *Persona* also inaugurated what many take to be the most fertile period of his career – the decade leading up to *Ansikte mot Ansikte* (1975, *Face to Face*).

In 1966 Bergman ended a three-year spell as head director of the Royal Dramatic Theatre in Stockholm. Towards the end of this time, in 1965, he wrote the script for *Persona*, which was mostly shot in the summer of 1965, with some additional scenes early in 1966. In terms of his career, it was a key moment for him to reconsider his relationship to the medium of film, in which he was to work almost exlusively thereafter.

Thus *Persona* is not only the story of two women or a psychological exploration, but also a confrontation with cinema, examining the nature of film and its capacity to manufacture images of reality and illusion. When Bergman reveals, within the film, the action of the movie projector and interrupts the narrative in mid-flow with a false breakdown (torn sprocket holes and burnt frames), he forcibly reminds the audience that they are watching a film, breaking their involvement with the story. He obliges them to reconsider how they are experiencing this film fiction. Within the narrative itself, the responses and memories of the characters are shown to be highly subjective – there are hints that some sequences are more imaginary than others, but no clear markers that differentiate actual events from individual perceptions of them

or fantasies departing from them. The only 'objective' character, not involved in the complex relationship of the other two women, is the doctor. She is allowed to address the camera directly when speaking to Alma or Elisabeth, thus having a privileged position with the audience. This gives her comments added authority but does not necessarily make her diagnosis entirely correct or complete.

Alma can never be sure if Elisabeth visited her room at night during their stay in the summer house. Nor does she know for certain whether Elisabeth actually did speak, as she twice seemed to do, very briefly – once in response to Alma's threat of scalding her during a fight and once in repeating the word 'nothing'. The appearance of Elisabeth's husband towards the end of the film is manifestly imaginary yet it would be entirely inappropriate for Bergman to signal this as a 'dream sequence'. This film is not a drama of fully-rounded characters caught up in an action but an exploration of the inconsistency of identity.

A 'persona' was originally an actor's mask, and by extension a character, in classical Roman drama. The same term is used in psychology to mean an aspect of personality as shown to other people. Bergman draws on both notions to suggest that Alma and Elisabeth are perhaps, as the critic Roy Armes has suggested, complementary halves of a single personality. Or it may be that Elisabeth behaves as a sort of vampire, drawing on Alma's personality to sustain her own – in which case Elisabeth may well represent the self-doubt that often afflicts inveterate role-players, for whom the metaphor of an actress is ideal.

In interviews, Bergman has recounted his first meeting with Liv Ullmann who was introduced to him by Bibi Andersson; he was struck by a curious likeness between the two women. From this encounter and from his own period in hospital came the early ideas for *Persona*, which crystallized around certain key images, such as the snapping of the film in the projector. Bergman has likened these motifs to poetic images insofar as both are personal in origin and yet susceptible to much broader interpretation than merely as personal fantasies or obsessions of their creator.

In its stark simplicity of style, *Persona* marked a turning point for Bergman. It may be possible to identify him, in some measure, with the actress/artist in the film, since

Directed by Ingmar Bergman, 1966
Prod co: Svensk Filmindustri. **sc:** Ingmar Bergman. **photo:** Sven Nykvist. **ed:** Ulla Ryghe. **art dir:** Bibi Lindström. **cost:** Mago. **mus:** Lars-Johan Werle. **sd:** P. O. Petersson, Lennart Engholm. **ass dir:** Lenn Hjortzberg. **prod man:** Lars-Owe Carlberg. **r/t:** 81 minutes. Stockholm premiere, 18 October 1966. **Cast:** Liv Ullmann (*Elisabeth Vogler*), Bibi Andersson (*Nurse Alma*), Margaretha Krook (*the woman doctor*), Gunnar Björnstrand (*Mr Vogler*), Jörgen Lindström (*the boy*).

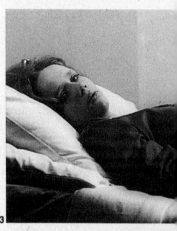

3

6

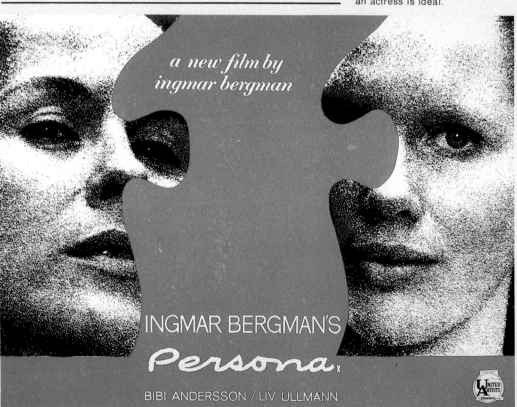

Elisabeth, a celebrated stage actress, is in hospital after loss of speech during a performance of *Electra* (1). After tests by a woman doctor, she is pronounced healthy (2); but she remains silent and stays in the ward (3). Alma, the nurse assigned to look after her (4), builds up a tentative relationship in which she does all the talking.

The patient and the nurse move to the doctor's summer house by the sea (5) and Elisabeth improves in health but remains mute. Alma confides her intimate feelings and memories, describing how she and another girl seduced two teenage boys on a beach. She also remarks to her patient how alike they look. Elisabeth appears to come to Alma's room at night (6) but, with a shake of the head, denies she presumably returns to work after leaving the summer house, recovered from her illness. (In Bergman's original script, the doctor tells the audience that Elisabeth returned to the theatre; but the film's shot of her on the stage near the end is more ambiguous in time and tone.) Certainly Bergman found a new clarity of vision in making this film.

It should be added that the extraordinarily sensitive performances of Liv Ullmann and Bibi Andersson and the pellucid black-and-white photography of Sven Nykvist add enormously to the film's synthesis of form and feeling, of analysis and imagination. *Persona* is Bergman's most mature and enduring work as well as a key movie of the Sixties.   MARTYN AUTY

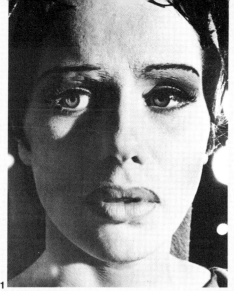

1

2

4

5

7

8

having done so.

Their relationship is shattered when Alma chances to read a condescending letter written by Elisabeth about her. (The film itself seems to break and then resumes). The atmosphere becomes increasingly tense and antagonistic (7).

Elisabeth's husband arrives and, mistaking Alma for Elisabeth, makes love to her (8). Alone again, the two women almost exchange roles. Alma expresses Elisabeth's thoughts about her traumatic pregnancy and childbirth, which may have contributed to her breakdown (9). Alma then abandons her task of nursing Elisabeth, who possibly returns to her work in the theatre.

The film studio and the projector are shown; the film breaks off . . .

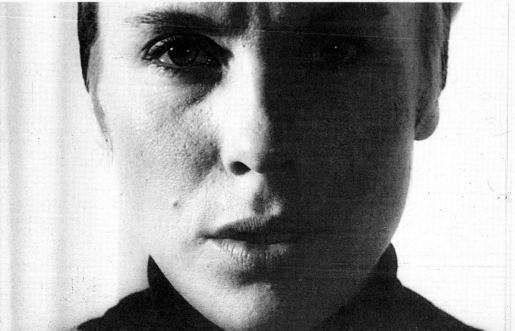

9

Portrait of an anarchist: LUIS BUÑUEL

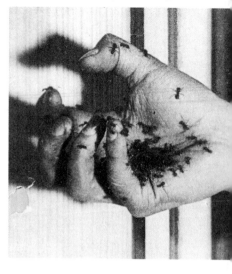

Left: an atheist and a cross – Buñuel helps out during the filming of The Milky Way. *Above: one of the images that caused public outcry in* Un Chien Andalou *– a film of free association with no preconceived ideas*

'They call Buñuel everything: traitor, anarchist, pervert, defamer, iconoclast. But lunatic they do not call him. It is true, it is lunacy. This stinking chaos which for a brief hour or so amalgamates under his wand, this is the lunacy of civilization, the record of man's achievement after ten thousand years of refinement'

Henry Miller, Paris 1932

Luis Buñuel's own famous paradox is still as accurate a summing up as any of his complex and contradictory personality: 'Thank God I am still an atheist!' Only a believer could generate a disbelief, scepticism and anti-religiosity as vehement as his, just as no-one but a true-born bourgeois could sustain so scabrous and fierce an attack on the bourgeoisie as he has done for more than half a century.

Buñuel was born in 1900 in Calanda, Spain, and the drums of the famous Calandan Holy Week procession provide a recurrent motif in his films. His family were well-off and his childhood seems to have been happy. He was

educated at a Jesuit College which fuelled his anti-clericalism, even though he was rated a clever and well-behaved pupil. From the College he went on to the University of Madrid where he read philosophy and letters. While there, he made the acquaintance of a whole lively generation – special friends included the poet Federico Garcia Lorca and the writer and painter Salvador Dali – enthusiastically caught up in all the '-isms' of the time.

In 1925 Buñuel arrived in Paris. Handsome and athletic (he was a boxing champion) he quickly made his way in artistic circles, and took a job as assistant to the film director Jean Epstein. However, this relationship ended

due to the energy with which Buñuel insulted Epstein's fellow director Abel Gance when offered a job as assistant on Gance's epic *Napoléon* (1927). During this period he was also occupied with sending back highly perceptive and intelligent – not to say malicious – film articles to the Spanish press.

Dali-ing in Paris

However, he found his true spiritual home with the Parisian Surrealist group in which he and Dali – who had also gone to Paris in 1925 – rapidly became key figures. Together they made the first truly surrealist film (it was declared to be so by Louis Aragon, the high priest of Surrealism himself) with $2,500 given by Buñuel's devoted mother. *Un Chien Andalou* (1928, An Andalusian Dog) was a genuine attempt to create out of the subconscious by proper surrealist rules: Buñuel and Dali said that they told each other their dreams every morning and created the scenario out of them.

The insolent and horrifying opening shot of a razor slicing through an eye was in itself sufficient to guarantee the film a major *succès de scandale*, and to attract enthusiasm and execration in equal degrees. Buñuel and Dali were then given a sum of money by the Vicomte de Noailles, a distinguished patron of the arts, to make a feature-length film; the result was *L'Age d'Or* (1930, The Golden Age). In the outcome, it was made by Buñuel alone, and marked the beginning of a life-long rift between himself and Dali.

L'Age d'Or is like no other film before or since. With its extraordinary images revealing the bizarre and horrific in the everyday, its anti-clericalism, anti-authoritarianism, anti-bourgeoisism, sadism, blasphemy, celebration of *l'amour fou*, above all its humour and irony, it is the definitive declaration of Buñuel's credo (or anti-credo) and was to provide a continuous source of reference for his subsequent films.

Perhaps the most durable of all the great film

classics, *L'Age d'Or*'s first showings in Paris were the occasion for right-wing demonstrations (bombs were thrown in the cinema) and police activities which reflected the growing political reaction in France in the pre-war decade.

Lean years

Returning to Spain, Buñuel made an extraordinary documentary, *Las Hurdes-Tierra Sin Pan* (1932, *Land Without Bread*), which applied an angry and essentially surrealist vision to the plight of a wretchedly poor, ignorant and oppressed Spanish rural community. After this, having firmly established himself as a major figure in the international cinema, Buñuel virtually disappeared for twenty years. During this time he worked obscurely in Hollywood making foreign language versions, supervising a short-lived production venture in Spain, and collaborating on some documentaries about the Spanish Civil War. By 1939 he was glad to take a job with the Museum of Modern Art in New York; but lost it again when the Cardinal Archbishop threatened dire reprisals if the Museum did not instantly expel this anti-Christ.

Buñuel did not resume feature-film direction until 1947 when he began a series of lightweight, low-budget, popular films in Mexico, which culminated in *Los Olvidados* (1950, *The*

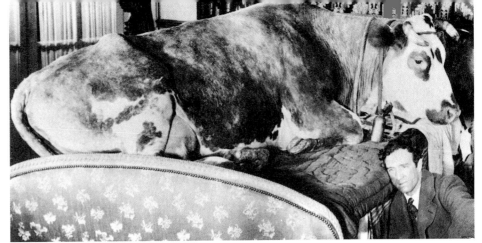

Top right: an eccentric scene from the long-banned L'Age d'Or. *Right: Simon (Claudio Brook) meditates before 'a night out' in* Simon of the Desert. *Below: a discomfited Célestine (Jeanne Moreau) and the foot-fetishist (Jean Ozenne) in* The Diary of a Chambermaid

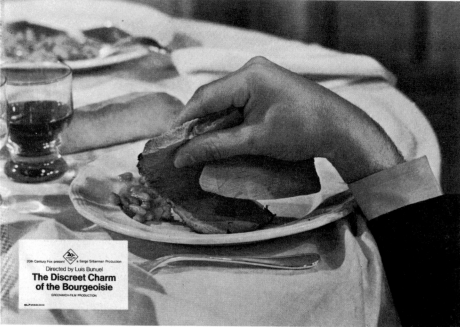

Below left: the hand's owner is killed as greed gets the better of him during a military raid in The Discreet Charm of the Bourgeoisie. *Left: an exhumation of a heretic during a pilgrimage in* The Milky Way. *Above:* Belle de Jour *(Cathérine Deneuve) indulges in fantasy*

Young and the Damned), a melodrama about delinquent boys in Mexico City – distinguished by Buñuel's characteristic blend of the cool documentary and hallucinated surrealist vision. When the film won the Official Jury Prize for direction at Cannes in 1951, Buñuel was definitely restored to the ranks of the great international film artists.

El maestro

An impeccable craftsman who liked to work fast and efficiently, Buñuel never spurned purely commercial chores and he poured his own personality and preoccupations into them. He succeeded in making films that appealed to a popular audience, without in any respect compromising his own distinctive and essentially austere view of the world. From the Mexican period came such masterworks as *Él* (1953, *This Strange Passion*), a marvellous study of pathological jealousy; his intelligent, heretical *Robinsón Crusoe* (1954); and the great black comedy *Ensayo de un Crimen: La Vida Criminal de Archibaldo de la Cruz* (1955, *The Criminal Life of Archibaldo de la Cruz*). The climax of the Mexican period was *Nazarín* (1958), an ironic and yet touching fable on the impossibility of leading a truly Christian life in an imperfect world.

This theme was developed further in *Viridiana* (1961), made in Spain after he had been invited back as a distinguished and honoured son. Buñuel – always convinced that you should eat the hand that feeds you – set the Spanish establishment by the ears with his joyous blasphemy and indecency in a film which, having had its first showing at the Cannes Festival where it won the Palme d'Or, defied subsequent attempts to suppress it. He returned briefly to Mexico to make two last films, *El Angel Exterminador* (1962, *The Exterminating Angel*) which returned to purely surrealist themes with the utmost gaiety and humour in a story of a group of bourgeois trapped by some inexplicable force in a *salon*; and the mischievous little moral tale *Simón del Desierto* (1965, *Simon of the Desert*), about a saint dedicated to such abstract works of devotion as sitting atop pillars in the desert.

Never changing or compromising, Buñuel has always shown an infinite capacity for renewal. Since 1960 he has announced each new picture as his definitive farewell to the screen. Yet, in 1964, well past sixty, he embarked on a new and triumphant phase in his career. That year he completed his adaptation of a subject Renoir had made in Hollywood some seventeen years before, Octave Mirbeau's *Le Journal d'une Femme de Chambre (The Diary of a Chambermaid)*. In Buñuel's hands the novel – almost romantic in Renoir's version – became a ferocious assault on the manners and political morals of the bourgeoisie. The film was the start of a long and happy collaboration with the producer Serge Silberman and the writer Jean-Claude Carrière that was to continue to provide Buñuel with ideal conditions in which to make films as and when he felt the inspiration. Silberman even provided special

Right: Fernando Rey dressed for a confusing world in which people socialize while 'on the throne' and eat in private in The Phantom of Liberty. *Below: Rey again in a bizarre situation in this film concerning a man constantly humiliated by the love of his life*

video equipment to minimize the strains of directing – Buñuel was already 77 when he came to make his youthful and vigorous *Cet Obscur Objet du Désir* (1977, *That Obscure Object of Desire*).

Indiscreet charms

The only film made by Buñuel in this period – and not produced by Silberman although Carrière remained his co-writer – was the brilliant comedy of a woman's sexual fantasies, *Belle de Jour* (1967), which established the director – at 67 – as a major box-office attraction. It is the sort of irony he enjoys; his subsequent films continued to maintain this reputation even when, as in *La Voie Lactée* (1969, *The Milky Way*) – a curious comic essay on the heresies of the Catholic Church – the subject matter was not obviously popular. *Le*

Charme Discret de la Bourgeoisie (1972, *The Discreet Charm of the Bourgeoisie*) and *Le Fantôme de la Liberté* (1974, *The Phantom of Liberty*) were beautiful, absurdist comedies that, without altering the direction or the intensity of Buñuel's hatreds against his life-long targets, seemed to gain in gaiety and dexterity. *That Obscure Object of Desire* returned to a subject he had wanted to make more than twenty years before (when, instead, it went to Julien Duvivier), an adaptation of Pierre Louÿ's 'decadent' novel of the late nineteenth century, *La Femme et le Pantin*, in which the opposing aspects of a man's ideal woman are personified by two different actresses.

Buñuel must figure among the few undisputed giants of the cinema. In his intellectual austerity, moral intransigence, total integrity, unweakening anger, rich humour, and underlying humanism, he has never faltered or compromised. In the use of the medium he has always displayed the simplicity, directness, confidence and correctness of an impeccable craftsman. Buñuel's complex vision is expressed through means and images that are clean, classical, limpid; and it is the apparent transparency of the means through which his intense concerns and surreal vision find their outlet that gives his films their irresistible appeal.
DAVID ROBINSON

Filmography
1926 Mauprat (ass. dir; +act. only) (FR). **'27** La Sirène des Tropiques (ass. dir) (FR). **'28** La Chute de la Maison Usher (ass. dir) (FR) (GB: The Fall of the House of Usher); Un Chien Andalou (co-dir; +co-prod; +co-sc; +ed; +act) (FR). **'30** L'Age d'Or (+co-sc; +ed) (FR). **'32** Las Hurdes – Tierra Sin Pan (doc) (+ed) (SP) (USA/GB: Land Without Bread). **'35** Don Quintín el Amargao (co-dir. uncredited; +prod. sup; +exec. prod) (SP); La Hija de Juan Simón (co-dir. uncredited; +prod. sup; +exec. prod) (SP). **'36** Quién Me Quiere a Mí? (prod. sup; +exec. prod; +ed) (SP); Centinela Alerta! (co-dir. uncredited; +prod. sup; +exec. prod; +act) (SP). **'39** Triumph of the Will (sup. ed; +narr. only) (montage of German films: Triumph des Willens and Feuertaufe) (USA). **'47** Gran Casino/En el Viejo Tampico (MEX). **'49** El Gran Calavera (MEX). **'50** Los Olvidados (+co-sc) (MEX) (USA/GB: The Young and the Damned). **'51** Si Usted no Puede, yo sí (co-sc. only) (MEX); Susana/Demonio y Carne (MEX); La Hija del Engaño/Don Quintín el Amargao (MEX). **'52** Una Mujer Sin Amor/Cuando los Hijos Nos Juzgan (MEX); Subida Al Cielo (+co-sc) (MEX). **'53** El Bruto (+co-sc) (MEX); Él (+co-sc) (MEX) (USA: This Strange Passion). **'54** Robinsón Crusoe/Adventures of Robinson Crusoe (+co-sc) (MEX-USA); Abismos de Pasión/Cumbres Borrascosas (MEX) (+sc); La Illusión Viaja en Tranvía (+co-sc) (MEX) (USA: Illusion Travels by Streetcar). **'55** El Río y la Muerte (+co-sc) (MEX) (USA: The River and Death); Ensayo de un Crimen: La Vida Criminal de Archibaldo de la Cruz (+co-sc) (MEX) (USA/GB: The Criminal Life of Archibaldo de la Cruz). **'56** Cela S'Appelle l'Aurore (+co-sc) (FR-IT); La Mort en ce Jardin/La Muerte en este Jardin (+co-sc) (FR-MEX) (USA: Gina; GB: Evil Eden). **'58** Nazarín (+co-sc) (MEX). **'60** La Fièvre Monte à El Pao/Los Ambiciosos (+co-sc) (FR-MEX) (GB: Republic of Sin); The Young One/La Joven (+co-sc) (USA-MEX) (GB: Island of Shame). **'61** Viridiana (+co-sc) (SP-MEX) **'62** El Angel Exterminador (+co-sc) (MEX) (USA/GB: The Exterminating Angel). **'64** Le Journal d'une Femme de Chambre (+co-sc) (FR-IT) (USA/GB: The Diary of a Chambermaid); Llanto por un Bandido (actor only) (SP-IT-FR). **'65** Simón del Desierto (+co-sc) (MEX) (USA/GB: Simon of the Desert); En Este Pueblo no Hay Ladrones (actor only) (MEX). **'67** Belle de Jour (+co-sc; +act) (FR-IT). **'69** La Voie Lactée (+co-sc) (FR-IT) (USA/GB: The Milky Way). **'70** Tristana (+co-sc) (FR-IT-SP). **'72** Le Charme Discret de la Bourgeoisie (+co-sc) (FR-SP-IT) (USA/GB: The Discreet Charm of the Bourgeoisie). **'73** Le Moine (co-sc. only) (FR-IT-GER) (GB: The Monk); La Chute d'un Corps (actor only) (FR). **'74** Le Fantôme de la Liberté (+co-sc) (FR) (USA/GB: The Phantom of Liberty). **'77** Cet Obscur Objet du Désir (+co-sc) (FR-SP) (USA/GB: That Obscure Object of Desire).

The last thing to trust in a Buñuel film is the story outline. The synopsis of *Belle de Jour* could be told in half-a-dozen ways, for the events that materialize on screen are always subject to the enigma of whether they are real or fantastic.

Early in the film, as Séverine and Pierre are riding in the landau, their good mood gives way to his frustration with her. He stops the landau and orders the coachmen to deal with her. They drag her through the undergrowth, hang her by the wrists from a tree and strip her to the waist. Pierre orders them to whip her, and then tells them to have their way with her. At this point Séverine wakes up in their bedroom and tells Pierre she was thinking of their life together.

It might be that the entire film is a dream – for surely it is the hope of all Surrealists that the whole of life might achieve the pregnant suspension of revery? The ending of *Belle de Jour* (the incapacitated husband and the passing of the empty landau) could be read as the passing fantasy in an ordinary, happy marriage – it would only be necessary to believe in such an alliance. Buñuel has never considered the possibility of total emotional happiness, and he sees sexuality as a form of pathology. He does not seek or believe in cure, and the sentimentality of the 'hospital' genre, where everyone is cured and made 'whole', is always replaced by an astringent humour and a reverence for fantasy.

Séverine is not a bitch or a victim. She is an obscure object of desire – supremely personified by the numbing beauty of Cathérine Deneuve in one of the outstanding examples of screen presence – and as such, Séverine's brimming sexual readiness is the perfect masquerade while Deneuve's impassivity is a touching rendering of inhibition.

Séverine cannot accept her sexuality in terms of love and marriage. She seeks abuse and humiliation, until the grotesque swagger of Marcel enters her life. She needs a way to tame the threat of marriage, and the eventual blankness of her husband is the one thing that can allow her security. Pierre becomes as still and obliging as all the antique furniture in her apartment and Séverine is left as a presiding nullity: like the meal that can never be eaten in *Le Charme Discret de la Bourgeoisie* (1972, *The Discreet Charm of the Bourgeoisie*).

Luis Buñuel was 67 when *Belle de Jour* was made. He said it would be his last film; he was weary, bored and unwell. With Jean-Claude Carrière, he adapted the Joseph Kessel novel for the Hakim Brothers' production company – it is their office in which Marcel pulls off a hold-up. By casting Catherine Deneuve, and showing her in various deliriously erotic situations – naked and in underwear – Buñuel effortlessly complied with and parodied the 'sexy art film'. *Belle de Jour* was the greatest commercial hit Buñuel had ever had: a perfect movie for wealthy women with free afternoons.

In all Buñuel's great work there is no distinction between humour, sexuality and terror, and he is unawed by the cruelty and loneliness of people. Buñuel denies tragedy or salvation; but he is devoted to the exquisite discrepancy between event and imagination. His shooting style is insolently effortless. Buñuel has the barest beauty in cinema: his sense of the single image is so intense that he can be contemptuous of expressiveness. The same attitude awaits the actors – everyone is cast in the way a director might cast television commercials. And yet, a tenderness prevails, so that no-one is ever patronized or exploited.

Above all, *Belle de Jour* is a warning against complacency. After seeing it, the potential in any staircase, any back-street, any refined woman is exposed. Buñuel enables the audience to see that photography cannot record the world because the world has no meaning. Film can only convey feeling and inwardness, and leaves no need for camera angles and expressive devices. It is a peephole into the soul – for anyone with the strength to look without dismay or hysteria. *Belle de Jour* hovers between the deadness of life and the ecstasy of imagination.

DAVID THOMSON

Directed by Luis Buñuel, 1967
Prod co: Paris Film/Five Films (A Robert and Raymond Hakim production).
prod: Henri Baum. **sc:** Luis Buñuel, Jean-Claude Carrière from the novel by Joseph Kessel. **photo:** Sacha Vierney. **ed:** Louisette Hautecoeur. **art dir:** Robert Clavel. **cost:** Hélène Nourry. **sd:** René Longuet. **ass dir:** Pierre Lary, Jacques Fraenkel. **r/t:** 100 minutes. Paris premiere, 24 May 1967
Cast: Catherine Deneuve (*Séverine Sevigny*), Jean Sorel (*Pierre Sevigny*), Geneviève Page (*Mme. Anaïs*), Michel Piccoli (*Henri Husson*), Francisco Rabal (*Hyppolite*), Macha Méril (*Renée*), Pierre Clementi (*Marcel*), Georges Marchal (*the duke*), Françoise Fabian (*Charlotte*), Maria Latour (*Mathilde*), Francis Blanche (*M. Adolphe*), François Maistre (*the teacher*), Bernard Fresson (*pock-marked man*), Muni (*Pallas*), Dominique Dandrieux (*Catherine*), Brigitte Parmentier (*Séverine as a child*), Iska Charvey (*Japanese client*).

Séverine is the young wife of Pierre, a successful surgeon. She is frigid in bed (1) but lusty in her dreams (2) and after Husson, an acquaintance, tells her that some other bourgeois wives are part-time prostitutes (3), Séverine makes her nervous way to a brothel (4) and begins to work for three hours every afternoon.

Her cool, blonde classiness is a great attraction, and Anaïs, the madam, prizes and schools her (5). Séverine yields to the humiliation and revels in it; she joins in the necrophiliac rites of a duke; enjoys the mysterious ways of a Japanese client (6); and finds satisfaction and love with Marcel, a young gangster (7). He is so enamoured of her that he follows her to her home and shoots Pierre down in the street, crippling him for life (8).

Séverine's afternoon activities remain a secret until Husson decides to tell Pierre what she has been doing. Pierre is crushed by the news and retreats into himself. Séverine is left watching over his helplessness (9), no longer troubled by her own sexual problems. The previously occupied landau – the perpetual dream image of her sexuality – passes the house, empty (10).

2

5

6

9

10

INDEX

221

223